British Gove
and Politics

SECOND EDITION

British Government and Politics

SECOND EDITION

R. M. PUNNETT
*Lecturer in Politics in the
University of Strathclyde*

W · W · NORTON & COMPANY · INC
New York

JN
234
1971
.P82

Library of Congress Catalog Card No. 71-172525

ISBN   0   393   09384   0

PRINTED IN THE UNITED STATES OF AMERICA

3 4 5 6 7 8 9 0

Preface to Second Edition

The production of a second edition of this book has allowed me to pay attention to the many important political developments of the three years since it was first published. Apart from updating facts and figures throughout the book, I have replaced the study of the 1966 general election with one of the election of June 1970. I have completely revised Chapter 3 on the Social Structure of the Parties; and I have been able to describe the various reforms in the machinery of government which have been made in these years. Finally I have extended the bibliography to include many recent books and articles on British government and politics.

Glasgow, 1971

Preface to First Edition

This book is designed to give a more detailed and all-embracing account of government and politics in Britain than is to be found in the various general works that already exist. It is presented in the hope that it will help to fill the gap that exists at present between the brief introductory guides to British government and politics, and the larger works on specific aspects of the system. My approach to the subject has been largely, but not exclusively, empirical, and I have endeavoured to include all material (sociological, institutional, constitutional or historical) that helps towards an understanding of the British political system as it operates today. In this I have tried to provide detailed information about the various aspects of the system, but at the same time I have sought to balance description with analysis. In this reprint of the first edition I have made a number of minor corrections and updated the text and bibliography.

I would like to acknowledge the considerable help that I have received from numerous sources in the preparation of the book. In particular, Professor Richard Rose of the University of Strathclyde, Mr W. Thornhill of the University of Sheffield, J. P. Mackintosh, M.P., and Professor W. A. Robson and Mr John Barnes of the London School of Economics, have commented upon large sections of the book. In addition, Dr J. A. Brand, Mr J. B. Sanderson, Mr A. L. M. Smith, Mr D. W. Urwin (all of the University of Strathclyde), Mr J. G. Bulpitt, Mr N. Johnson (both of the University of Warwick), Dr Robert J. Jackson (of Carleton University), and Dr M. Margolis (of the University of Pittsburgh) have looked at particular chapters. I am also greatly indebted to the University of Strathclyde for providing me with funds, and to both the University of Strathclyde and Carleton University, Ottawa, for giving me considerable clerical assistance. Finally, I would like to thank my wife, Marjory, for her encouragement and patience, especially during the arduous stages of revision and re-writing.

Any errors of fact or judgement remain, however, my sole responsibility.

Glasgow, 1969   R. M. PUNNETT

Contents

List of Tables

To my mother and father

Acknowledgements

I am grateful to the following for permission to quote from material published by them: Princeton University Press—G. A. Almond and S. Verba, *The Civic Culture*, Princeton 1963; Macmillan & Co. Ltd and Macmillan Company of Canada—D. E. Butler and J. Freeman, *British Political Facts*, London 1963, D. E. Butler, *The British General Election of 1951*, London 1951, D. E. Butler, *The British General Election of 1955*, London 1955, D. E. Butler and R. Rose, *The British General Election of 1959*, London 1960, D. E. Butler and A. King, *The British General Election of 1964*, London 1965, D. E. Butler and A. King, *The British General Election of 1966*, London 1966, *The Statesman's Year Book 1966–67*, London 1967; The Clarendon Press, Oxford—J. D. Stewart, *British Pressure Groups*, London 1958; Sir Isaac Pitman & Sons Ltd—J. A. G. Griffith and H. Street, *Principles of Administrative Law*, London 1967; Cambridge University Press—Sir Ivor Jennings, *The British Constitution*, London 1966, Sir Ivor Jennings, *Cabinet Government*, London 1959; Stevens & Sons Ltd— J. P. Mackintosh, *The British Cabinet*, London 1962; Oxford University Press—Lord Morrison, *Government and Parliament*, London 1964; Pall Mall Press Ltd—S. E. Finer, *Anonymous Empire*, London 1965; Fontana Books—Walter Bagehot, *The English Constitution*, London 1963; Benn Brothers Ltd—*Newspaper Press Directory*, London 1966; Hutchinson Publishing Group Ltd—D. E. Butler, *The Study of Political Behaviour*, London 1959; Victor Gollancz Ltd—Lord Attlee, *The Labour Party in Perspective—and Twelve Years After*, London 1949; J. Whitaker & Sons Ltd—*Whitaker's Almanack*, London 1967. I would also like to thank National Opinion Polls Ltd, Social Surveys (Gallup Poll) Ltd and The Observer Ltd for permission to quote from public opinion poll findings.

part one

Introduction

1

The Social Context
of British Politics

HOMOGENEITY, consensus and deference are often cited as
outstanding features of British society.[1] Britain is widely seen
as being fundamentally homogeneous in its ethnic, religious
and socio-economic composition, while the British people are
often said to exhibit a considerable degree of consensus on basic
political issues, and show a marked degree of deference towards
political leaders. How valid are these generalizations about the
British political culture, and how do they affect the workings
of the political system?[2]

Geography and Insularity

From a political standpoint the most significant features of
the geography of Britain are its size and insular position, and
the density and distribution of the population. Consisting of a
large island and numerous smaller islands, the United Kingdom of Great Britain and Northern Ireland comprises a total
area of some 94,500 square miles. It is thus physically small in
comparison with most major European and world powers, but
more significant than the actual size of the islands of Britain

[1] See the first chapters of W. Harrison, *The Government of Britain*, London
1966; G. C. Moodie, *The Government of Great Britain*, London 1964; R. Rose,
Politics in England, London 1965; J. Blondel, *Voters, Parties and Leaders*,
London, 1963; E. A. Rowe, *Modern Politics*, London 1969.

[2] See COI, *Britain: An Official Handbook*, published annually; D. C. Marsh,
The Changing Social Structure of England and Wales, London 1965; A. M.
Carr Saunders (*et al.*), *Social Conditions in England and Wales*, London 1958.

are their position close to the north-west coast of Europe. Largely because of her insular position, combined with the maintenance of a powerful navy, Britain has been able to resist successfully all attempts at foreign invasion since 1066, apart from the relatively peaceful 'invasion' by William of Orange in 1688. Nevertheless, despite periods (as for much of the nineteenth century) when a policy was adopted of 'splendid isolation' from European alliances, proximity to Europe has meant that British history inevitably has been closely bound up with that of Europe. At the same time, Britain's economic dependence on international trade has meant that British foreign policy has tended to seek peace and stability in Europe, and further afield, so that Britain could more effectively pursue her colonial and trading activities on a world-wide scale.

In the past, British political involvement in European affairs was designed primarily to prevent one power dominating the continent and thereby forming a threat to Britain. This brought

TABLE I

Population Density

	Area (sq. miles)	Population	Density
United Kingdom*	94,499	52,676,000	557
England	50,331	43,460,000	863
Scotland	30,405	5,178,000	170
Wales	8,016	2,644,000	328
Northern Ireland	5,461	1,425,000	260
USA	3,554,000	193,473,000	54
Germany	96,000	60,788,000	633
France	213,000	48,699,000	229
Italy	131,000	50,003,000	382
Netherlands	13,500	12,091,000	896
Belgium	11,800	9,428,000	791
Spain	197,000	31,604,000	160

* 1961 Census Figures

Source: *Whitaker's Almanack*, 1970, and Census Report 1961

England, and later the United Kingdom, into conflict with Spain in the sixteenth century, France in the eighteenth century, and Germany twice in the first half of this century. Britain's traditional insularity, however, has become less and less appropriate in modern conditions. The defensive advantage that Britain gained from her insular position has no longer applied since 1945, with the emergence of 'super' powers like the USA and the USSR, and with the development of modern forms of warfare. At the same time, in recent years Britain has been subject to a peaceful economic invasion from Europe and the USA (and it is perhaps significant that two of the biggest firms in Britain, Unilever and Shell, are at least partly foreign-owned), while the widened scope of international trade has led Britain to develop her interest in European trading communities.

With a total population of some 54,000,000, Britain is one of the most densely populated countries in the world, and as is shown in Table I, population density is particularly high in England. There has been a remarkable rise in the population of the United Kingdom over the past century, again particularly in England (see Table II). The population of the United

TABLE II

Population Growth (in millions)

	1801	1841	1881	1901	1921	1951	1961
England and Wales	8·9	15·9	25·9	32·5	37·9	43·7	46·1
Scotland	1·6	2·6	3·7	4·5	4·9	5·1	5·2
Northern Ireland*	1·4	1·6	1·3	1·2	1·2	1·4	1·4
United Kingdom†	11·9	20·2	31·0	38·2	44·0	50·2	52·7

* Figures for Northern Ireland refer to the area which is now Northern Ireland
† Excluding the Isle of Man and the Channel Isles

Source: Census Report 1961

Kingdom more than trebled between 1801 and 1901, and in this century it has increased by almost a half, largely as a result of a fall in the death rate. Today 11% of the population is aged

65 or over, while women outnumber men by about two million.[1] The greatest increase in population in the nineteenth century was in the new industrial areas of northern England. In the nineteen-sixties, however, it was the movement of population from the north of England and Scotland to the midlands and south-east of England that attracted most attention. Some 80% of the population of the United Kingdom live in England, and about 35% of the population of England and Wales live in the seven main industrial conurbations. London alone accounts for 15% of the total population of the United Kingdom, and it is often argued that this, combined with the capital's vital role in the economic, social, cultural and political life of the country, enables London and the south-east of England to impose its character to a considerable extent on the whole of Britain. It is questionable, however, whether London 'dominates' Britain to the extent that France is dominated by Paris. Physical communications between London and the rest of Britain are not aided by the elongated shape of the country, and by the location of the capital in the extreme south-east corner of England. In Wales and Scotland mountains form a barrier to communications, while the Irish Sea, separating Northern Ireland from the rest of the United Kingdom, represents a barrier to communications that is physically as formidable as the channel that separates Britain from Europe. In England, however, the chief mountain range runs from north to south, and thus does not hamper road or rail links between London and the north.

The Economy

Britain is essentially an industrial and trading nation, and most of the working population are engaged in manufacturing and commerce. As is shown in Table III, only about 2% of the population are engaged in agriculture or fishing, and Britain depends heavily on imported foodstuffs. At the same time, natural resources are limited, so that a large proportion of the raw materials needed by British industry have to be imported, making the British economy doubly dependent on

[1] These and other population statistics are based on the 1961 Census Report.

international trade. The numbers employed in agriculture are decreasing, while the numbers employed in manufacturing and engineering industries have increased over the past twenty years. Significant increases have also taken place in the various 'white collar' employments, including the distributive trades, the professions, and local government administration. Although Britain is primarily an industrialized and urbanized society, there is not the distinction between urban wealth and rural poverty that is sometimes to be found in heavily industrialized countries. This is partly because a big proportion of those engaged in agriculture are large-scale farmers who own their own land.[1]

In recent years the aspects of the economy that have attracted

TABLE III

Distribution of Civil Employment (in thousands)

	1940	1950	1960	1969
Agriculture and fishing	925	1,161	983	413†
Mining and quarrying	886	852	761	447
Manufacturing industries	7,128	8,510	8,811	8,646
Building and contracting	1,064	1,434	1,567	1,443
Gas, electricity, water	213	353	370	395
Transport and communications	1,146	1,781	1,662	1,584†
Distributive trades	2,639	2,571	3,284	2,773†
Financial, professional, miscellaneous	*	3,969	4,847	5,454†
Public administration:				
National	} 1,793	619	502	584†
Local		743	741	818†

* Figures not available
† 1968 figures
Figures for different years are not completely comparable owing to changes in methods of classification.

Source: D. E. Butler and J. Freeman, *British Political Facts*, London 1963, p. 233, and *Whitaker's Almanack*, 1970

[1] See Blondel, *Voters, Parties and Leaders*, p. 24, for a fuller discussion of this factor.

most attention have been the rate of economic expansion and
the trade 'balance' between imports and exports. The technological advances of the eighteenth and nineteenth centuries,
which produced an industrial revolution earlier in Britain than
in other countries, enabled the economy to expand rapidly,
and led Britain to be described as the 'workshop of the world'.
The economy has continued to expand during the twentieth
century, despite the recession between the wars, and over the
past fifteen years Britain, along with most other western industrial nations, has enjoyed an increase in the general level of
prosperity that has been based partly on technological advances
in industrial methods. Perhaps inevitably, however, Britain's
economic growth rate in the twentieth century has been unable
to match the expansion that came in the early years of the
industrial revolution. At the same time, Britain's international
trading position has declined relative to that of the countries
whose initial economic expansion came later than that of
Britain. Britain's dependence on imports for foodstuffs *and* raw
materials for industry has meant that successive Governments
have been faced with the problem of trying to ensure that
exports were of sufficient quantity to balance imports. The loss
of many overseas markets and the using up of foreign investments and reserves during the second world war, combined
with the emergence of powerful competitors in recent years,
have meant that balance of payments difficulties have been
particularly acute since 1945.

The link between the economy and modern British politics
is thus fundamental, economic difficulties inevitably limiting
the ability of Governments to pursue adventurous social policies.
In recent general election campaigns, economic issues have
been particularly prominent, and undoubtedly one of the factors that led to the defeat of the Conservative Government in
1964, and of the Labour Government in 1970, was the feeling
that neither had succeeded in dealing with Britain's basic
economic problems. In 1964 the Labour Party criticized the
Conservative Government's inability to break out of the recurrent 'stop-go' cycle of economic deflation and re-flation, and
Labour claimed to have an alternative economic policy which,
given time and careful long-term planning, would give economic expansion without uncontrollable inflation. In 1970 the

Conservatives argued that Labour's strategy had failed, and had merely produced inflation without an adequate growth rate. The ability of the Heath Government, and future Governments, to deal with inflation, achieve steady economic growth, and maintain the strength of sterling, will be of vital importance at the next and subsequent general elections.

At the same time, many basic industries are publicly owned, largely as a result of the nationalization measures of the 1945–51 Labour Government. Because of the Labour Party's traditional commitment to the 'common ownership of the means of production, distribution and exchange',[1] the question of whether the policy of public ownership should be extended to other sections of industry, or should be reversed, has been a major issue between the parties.[2] Industrial questions remain fundamental to British politics because of the links between the Labour Party and the trade unions, and the Conservative Party and the business world.

Mass Media

The press, radio, and TV are for the most part London-based and London-orientated. There are about 150 daily and Sunday newspapers in Britain, which is a smaller number than in most comparable western nations.[3] At the same time more copies of newspapers are sold in Britain than in any country in the western world. The *News of the World* has the largest circulation of any newspaper in the world, and the *Daily Mirror* has the largest circulation of any daily newspaper (see Table IV). These large circulations result from the fact that the major newspapers in Britain are national rather than local papers, although many of the big national dailies do have separate editions for the various regions of Britain. In addition to the national dailies, however, each region has its own local newspapers, many of which out-sell the national dailies in their particular locality. England's best-known regional newspaper, the *Manchester Guardian*, changed its name to *The Guardian* in 1962, and is now printed simultaneously in Manchester and London, but there remain more than two dozen English local

[1] *Labour Party Constitution*, clause 4 (IV).
[2] See below, Ch. 12.
[3] For details see the *Newspaper Press Directory*.

morning papers including the *Birmingham Post, Yorkshire Post,* and the *Sheffield Telegraph.* In Scotland, *The Scotsman* and *Glasgow Herald* are particularly long established and widely circulating morning papers. The *Western Echo* is read widely in south Wales, as is the *Liverpool Daily Post* in north Wales, while Northern Ireland has its own morning newspapers printed in Belfast.

The *Morning Star* is linked with the Communist Party, but none of the large-circulation national papers have any such direct ties with a political party. All the national papers and most of the local papers do exhibit some degree of political alignment, however, and the majority tend to be pro-Con-

TABLE IV

Newspaper Circulations 1965–9

Chief national dailies	Average daily circulation (in millions)		Proprietors
	1965	1969	
Daily Mirror	4·9	4·9	IPC Newspapers Ltd
Daily Express	3·9	3·7	Beaverbrook Newspapers Ltd
Daily Mail	2·4	2·0	Harmsworth Publications Ltd
Daily Telegraph	1·3	1·4	Daily Telegraph Ltd
Sun	1·2	1·2	News of the World Ltd
Daily Sketch	0·8	0·9	Harmsworth Publications Ltd
The Guardian	0·2	0·3	Guardian Newspapers Ltd
The Times	0·2	0·4	Times Newspapers Ltd
Chief Sunday papers			
News of the World	6·1	6·2	News of the World Ltd
The People	5·7	5·4	Odhams Press Ltd
Sunday Mirror	5·0	5·0	IPC Newspapers Ltd
Sunday Express	4·1	4·2	Sunday Express Ltd
The Sunday Times	1·2	1·5	Times Newspapers Ltd
The Observer	0·8	0·9	The Observer Ltd
The Sunday Telegraph	0·6	0·7	The Sunday Telegraph Ltd

Source: *Newspaper Press Directory,* 1966 and 1970

servative, or at least generally right wing in outlook.[1] The *Daily Herald*, which was owned partly by the TUC, was replaced in 1962 by the *Sun*, which has no direct links with the Labour Party or the Unions, although in general the *Sun* and *Daily Mirror* tend to be left wing in outlook. Ownership of the national press tends to be concentrated in comparatively few hands, and this has caused some criticism in recent years. The *Daily Express*, *Sunday Express*, *Evening Standard* (London), and *Evening Citizen* (Glasgow) are all associated, while the *Daily Mail*, *Daily Sketch*, and the *Evening News* (London) are all owned by Harmsworth Publications Ltd. The International Publishing Corporation owns the *Daily Mirror*, *The People* and *Sunday Mirror*, while Lord Thomson owns *The Times*, *The Sunday Times*, and a large number of provincial newspapers.

National sound broadcasting in Britain has been a legal monopoly of the BBC, but the introduction of commercial local radio services is being considered by the Conservative Government. The BBC was created a public corporation by Royal Charter in 1926, and revenue comes primarily from the sale of radio and TV licences rather than from any form of commercial advertising. The Governors of the BBC are appointed by the Prime Minister, but once appointed they are free from direct Government control. The BBC is required to be impartial in its presentation of political items, although the ideal of complete impartiality is difficult to attain.[2] Until 1954 the BBC had a television monopoly, but in 1954 the Independent Television Authority was created with overall control over several regional programme contracting companies, the largest now including Granada, Thames, and Yorkshire TV. The ITA and the programme contracting companies are financed from the sale of advertising time, although the programmes are not directly sponsored by the advertisers. Like the BBC, ITA is required to be politically impartial, and political advertising is not permitted. Since the introduction of the ITA, with its greater emphasis on regional programmes, the BBC's regional services have been extended, although national network programmes still predominate on BBC and Independent Television alike. The impact of television on British politics has been considerable over the past ten years. It has probably been most noticeable in the sphere of electioneering, and a study of the effect of television on the 1959 general election campaign suggested that of all the means of mass communication, television did most to increase the electorate's awareness of political issues and personalities.[1] In the 1966 and 1970 election campaigns all three main parties clearly attached considerable importance to the contact that could be achieved through television between the party leaders and the electorate.[2]

Nationalism, Regionalism and Religion

Within the broad framework of the United Kingdom there exist the separate national communities of England, Wales, Scotland, and Ulster, each with its own historical, cultural, and ethnic background, and each to some extent with its own economic and political characteristics. In the distant past Britain was subjected to invasion by numerous different ethnic groups. The inhabitants of Britain today are descended either from the British or Celtic tribes who were the original inhabitants of Britain, or from the Romans, north Europeans, and Norman French who invaded Britain between 100 BC and AD 1100, or from the numerous waves of immigrants, particularly from Europe and the Commonwealth, who have peacefully invaded Britain in more recent years. The nineteenth-century Irish influx into the big cities of Great Britain created problems for British society, as has coloured immigration more recently. In 1958 there were a series of racial disturbances in parts of London, and in the 1964 general election racial issues were of considerable importance in a small number of constituencies in the English midlands and in London. Racial conflict could perhaps become a major issue in British politics, particularly in industrial towns. Although the party leaders have sought to keep the colour question 'above party politics', the Conservative Party in general has adopted a tougher line

[1] J. Trenaman and D. McQuail, *Television and the Political Image*, London 1961.
[2] See J. G. Blumler and D. McQuail, *Television in Politics*, London 1968.

than the Labour and Liberal Parties on the question of coloured immigration, and on the racial issue in general.[1]

Despite this, however, it is probably true to say that Britain exhibits a greater degree of ethnic unity than most European or English-speaking countries. Similarly, regional factors do not play as important a part in British politics as they do for example in the politics of the USA, Canada, or Germany. Britain is a unitary, not a federal state, and the unification of Britain into one political unit is now of comparatively long standing. The principle of strong central administration was established in England early in the middle ages. Wales was conquered (militarily) by the English in the fourteenth century. The union of the thrones of England and Scotland dates from 1603, and the Anglo-Scottish union was completed in 1707. The union of Great Britain and Ireland was achieved in 1800, though Southern Ireland gained full independence in 1922. This is not to say, however, that regional issues have been absent from British politics in the past, or are completely absent today. The question of the succession to the throne led to Anglo-Scottish conflict in 1715 and 1745, culminating in the military occupation of much of Scotland by English armies. The question of Irish home rule in the last century and the early years of this century presented a major threat to the unity of the United Kingdom, while dissatisfaction in Eire over Northern Ireland's continued union with Great Britain means that the question of Irish nationalism has not been finally settled. Scottish and Welsh nationalist movements also exist today, but so far they have not had the impact on British politics that Irish nationalism had before 1922. Regionalism, however, as opposed to Scottish, Welsh, or Irish nationalism, has had a growing impact on national politics in recent years, and to some extent this is a result of the fact that the growth in material prosperity over the last fifteen years has not been enjoyed equally by all the regions of the country.

In the United Kingdom as a whole, religion is not a major divisive force, although this is not true of all parts of the country. The religious conflicts that divided British society in the sixteenth and seventeenth centuries were largely settled in 1688

[1] C. Hill, *Immigration and Integration*, London 1970; I. Macdonald, *Race Relations and Immigration Law*, London 1968.

TABLE V

Nominal Religious Affiliation

England and Wales	
Church of England	27,600,000
Roman Catholic	4,000,000
Methodist and Independent Methodist	765,946
Baptist	281,008
Methodist Church of Wales	113,468
Congregational Union	187,128

Scotland	
The Church of Scotland	1,201,833
Roman Catholic	809,680
Episcopal Church	93,332

Northern Ireland	
Roman Catholic	497,000
Presbyterian	413,113
Church of Ireland	344,800
Methodist	71,865

Source: *The Statesman's Year Book*, 1970–1

by the acknowledgement of the Protestant ascendancy, and by the gradual acceptance of the principle of religious toleration. Today, the vast majority of people in Britain are not church-goers, but of those who are, the majority attend Protestant churches, with the Established Church of England claiming the largest number of devotees (see Table V). The proportion of active members of the Church of England, however, is much smaller than even the 10,000,000 or so confirmed Anglicans, and the other Protestant Churches and the Roman Catholic Church claim that a much larger proportion of their members are regular church attenders.

In some areas of Britain there is a clear connection between religion and political affiliation. In Northern Ireland, religion and politics are almost inseparable, with the strength of the Ulster Unionists being based on Protestant opposition to the Catholic majority in Eire, and to the large and growing Catholic element in Ulster. In Glasgow and Liverpool the existence of large Catholic communities with Irish origins means that some of the attitudes of Ireland are apparent. In the nineteenth century in Great Britain as a whole, and particularly in Wales, there was a traditional alignment between the Conservative Party and the Established Churches of England, Scotland, Ireland (disestablished in 1869), and Wales (disestablished in 1920), and between the Liberal Party and the Nonconformist Churches. In some respects this alignment remains today, with the Labour Party inheriting some of the Liberal Party's non-conformist traditions, and this is reflected to some extent in voting patterns and in the religious affiliations of MPs. Some religious bodies, like the Lord's Day Observance Society, are active pressure groups, but in general the churches do not inter-fere directly in party politics, and apart from the exceptions noted above, religion does not play the part in British politics that it did in the past.

Homogeneity and Social Class

Britain is often said to be a homogeneous nation, a united and cohesive unit in geographical, ethnic, religious, economic, and social terms.[1] This is generally applied in a comparative sense, with the implication being that Britain is more homogeneous than most other countries. It is argued that such divisions as do exist in British society are of a minor nature, and that there is no equivalent in Britain to the racial divisions of the USA, the national or ethnic divisions of Canada and Belgium, the religious and regional divisions of France and Western Germany, or the extremes of wealth and poverty that are to be found in Italy and Spain. To place too great an emphasis on British homogeneity, however, is to over-simplify the nature of British society. As has been shown above, national, regional, religious, and ethnic variations *do* exist within the United Kingdom and are an essential part of some political questions. More important than any of these factors, however,

[1] See, for example, Blondel, *Voters, Parties and Leaders*, Ch. 2.

distinctions of social class represent a fundamental disunity in
British society, in many ways as significant as the regional,
ethnic, or religious factors that dominate society and politics in
other countries. Comparative surveys have revealed that Britain
is much more class-conscious than similar Anglo-Saxon communities like the USA, Australia, and Canada.[1] The significance of class factors in determining voting behaviour, and in
the social composition of the parties, is revealed below,[2] and
here it is sufficient to emphasize the general importance of class
as a divisive force within society.

It is sometimes argued that class stratification in Britain is a
national one, cutting across regional boundaries and thus help-
ing to break down any tendencies towards regionalism. In so
far as they do this, however, class factors merely replace one
form of national division for another, and thereby place an
essential limitation on any notion of British homogeneity. Thus
of all the factors involved in presenting a background to British
politics, considerations of social class are probably the most
significant of all. The various criteria that determine class
groupings are essentially vague, but family background, education, occupation, and wealth are probably the main factors.

Family Background and Education. Despite the fact that mobility
between the social classes from one generation to another has
increased since the principle of free and compulsory secondary
education was established, family background remains fundamentally important in determining social class.[3] Occupation
and wealth to a considerable extent are determined by education, which in its turn is determined to a large extent by family
background. The earliest school leavers, in the main, become
manual workers, those who stay on at school beyond the age
of 15 tend to move into white collar and managerial jobs,
while those with the most exclusive education generally enter
the professions or the business world. As well as any general
tendency there may be for middle-class parents to produce

[1] R. R. Alford, *Party and Society*, London 1964. See also D. E. G. Plowman,
W. E. Minchinton and M. Stacey, 'Local Social Status in England and
Wales', *SR* 1962, pp. 161–202.
[2] Ch. 3.
[3] R. Turner, 'Sponsored and Contest Mobility and the School System',
APSR 1960, pp. 855–67.

THE SOCIAL CONTEXT OF BRITISH POLITICS 17

children with a higher academic ability than children of working-class parents, the educational system contains certain inequalities which help to consolidate established class distinctions. In the first place, a clear distinction emerges between the state schools, which cater for the mass of the population, and the independent public schools which provide a boarding-school education for a very small and exclusive section of the population (some 3%). This is mirrored even among the public schools themselves, and there is a clear stratification ranging from the lesser public schools to the top nine 'Clarendon Schools',[1] with Eton, Harrow, and Winchester generally acknowledged as the top three. As well as seeking to produce an educational elite by providing excellent teaching facilities, the best public schools encourage the self-perpetuation of a social elite through their emphasis on the importance of 'character building', leadership training, and social education.[2]

Within the state educational system a stratification does not appear at a primary level, where all children attend comprehensive infant and junior schools up to the age of 11 (or 12 in Scotland, where a separate system exists). At a secondary level, however, in many local educational authorities in England and Wales, a clear distinction still emerges between the 25% or so of the children who are allocated to grammar schools on the basis of the 'eleven plus' examination and the bulk of the children who attend secondary modern or technical schools. Over the past ten years there has been a big increase in the number of comprehensive secondary schools, which provide all types of secondary education for all levels of ability, and in 1965 the Labour Government announced plans for a rapid extension of the principle of comprehensive secondary education. With the change of Government in 1970, however, this process is likely to be slowed down. One of the claims advanced for comprehensive secondary schools is that they will remove some of the divisions within society which are partly created by the segregation of children at the age of 11 into strict educational

---

[1] That is, Eton, Harrow, Winchester, Rugby, Westminster, Charterhouse, Merchant Taylors', St Paul's, Shrewsbury, all of which were subject to an enquiry by a Royal Commission headed by Lord Clarendon in 1864.

[2] R. Wilkinson, *The Prefects*, London 1964; R. Wilkinson, 'Political Leadership and the Late Victorian Public School', *BJS* 1960, pp. 320–30.

categories. Despite the development of comprehensive schools, however, only about 15% of children stay on at school beyond the age of 15, and of these the vast majority tend to be from middle-class homes.

To some extent these educational distinctions are continued at a University level, for although there are some forty Universities in Britain, Oxford and Cambridge Universities are accorded the greatest prestige and status, both in an academic and a social sense. They are theoretically open to any student with the necessary academic qualifications, but the close link that has long existed between Oxbridge and the public schools, and which is not based entirely on academic considerations, means that the upper and middle-class section of society predominates at the two senior Universities. To some extent the upper-middle-class and public school associations of Oxford and Cambridge tends to make the children of working-class parents look to the provincial Universities for the completion of their education, thereby emphasizing further the social divisions within the education system.

In an attempt to develop a more egalitarian and more modern University system a number of new Universities were created in the nineteen-sixties, and a number of existing technological institutions were expanded and given University status. This has done something to meet the educational needs of the increased population (particularly the immediate post-war population 'bulge'), and to deal with the needs of the technological age. The problem remains, however, of the loss by Britain of many good graduates through the 'brain-drain' to the USA and other English-speaking countries. This factor, particularly in the technological sphere, represents something of a threat to Britain's future educational and industrial development.

Occupation and Wealth. A simple division of the community into two broad groups of middle class and working class is perhaps adequate for broad generalization, but is too vague for a detailed examination of British society. In the 1961 Census seventeen socio-economic groups were distinguished, and, excluding the armed forces, these can be simplified into three main categories to distinguish the manual groups, the non-manual groups, and the professional, managerial, and proprietorial groups (see Table VI). Although recent years have seen a big increase in the number of non-manual workers at the expense of the manual workers, the numerical supremacy of the manual workers is pronounced, and undoubtedly will remain for many decades.

Britain no longer exhibits the sharp inequalities of wealth and poverty that were to be found in the nineteenth century, and which are to be found today in many western countries. Industrial expansion, and the development of the welfare state and of taxation policies designed to some extent to redistribute wealth, have combined to raise general living standards and eradicate the worst poverty. The general rise in prosperity, however, has not been shared equally by all sections of the community (or by all regions of the country), and to some extent this is reflected in the range of personal incomes shown in Table VII, with roughly a quarter of net incomes in 1968 being below £10 per week. Even this factor takes no account of

TABLE VI

Census 1961: Socio-Economic Groups (England and Wales)

Proprietorial, managerial, and professional			15·3
1 and 2	Employers and managers	9·5	
3 and 4	Professional	3·8	
13 and 14	Farmers	2·0	
Other non-manual			17·4
5	Intermediate non-manual	3·9	
6	Junior non-manual	12·6	
7	Personal service	0·9	
Manual			63·6
8	Foremen and supervisors	3·3	
9	Skilled manual	31·6	
10	Semi-skilled	14·7	
11	Unskilled	8·3	
12	Own-account workers	3·4	
15	Agricultural workers	2·3	
Others			3·7
16	Armed forces	2·0	
17	Indefinite	1·7	
			100·0

Source: 1961 Census Report

TABLE VII

Distribution of Personal Income 1968

Range of net income (after taxation)		Number of incomes (in thousands)
£	£	
50 to under	250	2,338
250 ,, ,,	500	5,906
500 ,, ,,	750	5,418
750 ,, ,,	1,000	4,822
1,000 ,, ,,	2,000	8,298
2,000 ,, ,,	5,000	954
5,000 ,, ,,	10,000	63
10,000 and over		1

Source: *Whitaker's Almanack*, 1970

accumulated wealth, and it has been estimated that as much as a quarter of the personal wealth in Britain is owned by 0·5% of the population.[1] In social terms, many of the harsh consequences of the industrial revolution are still apparent in the slums of the major British cities. These factors are essential limitations on any broad view of Britain as a generally prosperous and egalitarian community. While in economic terms the various sections of the community may be coming closer together, this is much less the case in social terms. A well-paid car worker in Coventry, for example, may in terms of income be in much the same category as a young doctor, but he remains in a very different social category. Thus with regard to occupations and wealth the main consideration in determining social class is not so much the amount of wealth, but rather how the wealth was acquired, just as with education it is the type of school and University that is significant as well as the level of academic attainment.

*   *   *

Writing in 1867, Walter Bagehot presented a picture of British society as one that was essentially deferential in its attitudes towards the Monarchy, the Peerage, and the trappings

[1] See S. Brittan, 'Tax Wealth, Not Gains', *The Observer*, 8.4.62.

of society. Indeed he argued that the secret of the constitution was that real power lay with the 'efficient' parts of the Constitution, chiefly the Prime Minister and his Cabinet colleagues, while the Monarchy and the other 'dignified' elements of the Constitution served to mesmerize the mass of the population into a respect for the system as a whole. Thus he claimed that:

> In fact, the mass of the English people yield a deference rather to something else rather than to their rulers. They defer to what we may call the theatrical show of society . . .[1]

In many respects Bagehot's interpretation of the British people as being essentially deferential remains valid today. Feelings of deference today, however, are directed not so much towards the Monarchy, the Peerage, or the dignified parts of the Constitution, as towards the vague concept of a social elite which is based on the public schools, but which in its broadest sense embraces Oxbridge, the 'officer class', and the top levels of the business and professional worlds.[2] In the party political context this deference has extended particularly towards the Conservative Party, because the composition of the leadership of the party is based to such a great extent on this social elite. The significance of this factor in voting behaviour is considered below,[3] but it may be noted here that to a considerable extent the electoral success of the Conservatives in this century can be attributed to the deferential attitude of a large section of the electorate towards the party.

Class-consciousness in social and political attitudes, a pre-occupation with pageantry and with past historical greatness, and the retention of many once powerful but now largely symbolic political and social institutions, are all undoubted features of modern Britain which help to strengthen the impression of a deferential, passive, and largely politically inactive community which is content to be led by a small, select, and self-perpetuating elite. This interpretation of the relationship between a social elite and the political system thus echoes the view that Bagehot presented, and applauded, of political power

---

[1] Walter Bagehot, *The English Constitution*, Fontana Library edition, London 1963, p. 248.
[2] See, for example, W. L. Guttsman, *The English Ruling Class*, London 1969.   [3] p. 70.

in Britain lying with an elite who exercise their authority behind the shield of the 'theatrical show of society'. Unlike Bagehot, however, the modern writers who present this picture generally deplore the situation that they describe.

Consensus and Cleavage

Linked very closely with the question of deference is that of consensus and cleavage in British politics. There exists in Britain a marked degree of agreement of opinion with regard to basic political questions, and the existence of this consensus has a vital effect on the working of the political system.[1] Undoubtedly the overwhelming majority of people in Britain agree on fundamental issues and accept the basis of the constitutional and political systems. This consensus is most marked in the general acceptance of the main features of the Constitution, with Parliament, the electoral system, the legal system, and the principles of Cabinet government being accepted by the overwhelming majority of the British people. In this respect Britain can be contrasted with the less constitutionally stable countries on the continent. As well as agreement and satisfaction with the system of government, however, a remarkably broad degree of agreement is also often said to exist with regard to other aspects of British society. It is argued that the vast majority of people in Britain are essentially moderate and conservative in their attitudes, and are basically satisfied with the existing social, economic, and political systems. There is thus a clear link between the notion of consensus in British political attitudes, and the deferential nature of British society, and Sir Ivor Jennings has claimed that:

> If the people of this country want to overthrow capitalism, the public school system, the House of Lords, or the Monarchy, they have the power in their hands. If they have not done so, the explanation is that they have not wanted to do so.[2]

[1] See J. P. Nettl, 'Consensus or Elite Domination: the Case of Business', *PS* 1965, pp. 22–44; W. G. Runciman, 'A Method for Cross-National Comparison of Political Consensus', *BJS* 1962, pp. 151–5. See also G. A. Almond and S. Verba, *The Civic Culture*, Princeton 1963, for a comparative study.

[2] Sir Ivor Jennings, *The British Constitution*, London 1966, p. 211.

TABLE VIII
Aspects of National Pride

Percent who say they are proud of	US	UK	Germany	Italy	Mexico
Governmental, political institutions	85	46	7	3	30
Social legislation	13	18	6	1	2
Position in international affairs	5	11	5	2	3
Economic system	23	10	33	3	24
Characteristics of people	7	18	36	11	15
Spiritual virtues and religion	3	1	3	6	8
Contributions to the arts	1	6	11	16	9
Contributions to science	3	7	12	3	1
Physical attributes of country	5	10	17	25	22
Nothing or don't know	4	10	15	27	16
Other	9	11	3	21	14
Total % of responses*	158	148	148	118	144
Total % of respondents	100	100	100	100	100
Total number of cases	970	963	955	995	1,007

* Percentages exceed 100 because of multiple responses

Source: G. A. Almond and S. Verba, *The Civic Culture*, Princeton 1963, p. 102. Reproduced by permission of Princeton University Press.

The argument is often extended, and it is asserted that the consensus that exists within the community is reflected in the political parties, and indeed a refinement of the consensus theory is provided by those who accept that the parties agree on fundamental constitutional and political issues, but deny that there is any pronounced consensus exhibited by the community as a whole—thereby arguing that the main political parties are not representative of the attitudes of the various sections of the community. Undoubtedly, both parties tend to be dominated by moderate or 'centre' elements, and while extreme elements undoubtedly exist in both the main political parties, in general they are minority groups. Partly because of this, there is agreement between the parties on fundamental constitutional issues, in that while each party may have its own views on what policies are most desirable, or what means should be used to achieve certain agreed ends, the parties are not prepared to go to unconstitutional lengths to gain power, to retain power, or to oppose the policies of their opponents. Also, both parties accept the 'politics of compromise', and of 'gradualism' as the means to achieve political ends, this perhaps being epitomized by the constitutional convention that a Government accepts in the main the achievements of the previous Government (a convention that is not based solely on the practical consideration that often it is administratively impractical to reverse some policies). Thus despite the denationalization of the steel industry and of road haulage, the Conservative Government elected in 1951 accepted the bulk of the Attlee Government's policies, while the Labour Government in 1964 made even fewer changes in the case of legislation passed by the previous Conservative Government. The broad agreement between the parties is also reflected in the fact that despite the Labour Party's attachment to the principle of public ownership, and the Conservative Party's devotion to private enterprise, both parties when in power have accepted the principles of the mixed economy, and of 'un-doctrinaire collectivism' as the basis of the relations between the state and industry.

The notion of a broad political consensus between the British parties seemed to be particularly valid in the nineteen-fifties and sixties. After the ideological debates that took place during the 1945–51 period of Labour rule, over the issues of public ownership, the welfare state, and the growth of state authority, the long period of Conservative rule between 1951 and 1964 and the 1964–70 period of Labour Government, produced merely conflict over details.[1] The acceptance by the Conservatives after 1951 of the bulk of the Labour Government's legislation, the eclipse of extreme left-wing elements from positions of authority within the Labour Party, the growth of material prosperity and of consequent feelings of security and well-being within the community, and the very length of the

[1] See S. H. Beer, 'The Future of British Politics', *PQ* 1955, pp. 33–43; G. Loewenburg, 'The Transformation of British Labor Party Policy since 1945', *J of P* 1959, pp. 234–57.

THE SOCIAL CONTEXT OF BRITISH POLITICS   25

Conservative period of office with its emphasis on stability, moderation, and preserving the *status quo*, all combined to produce political conflict over details rather than over basic political, economic, or social principles. Thus the phrase 'Butskellism' was coined to describe the essentially moderate policies common to the Conservative Government, in which R. A. Butler was prominent, and the Labour Opposition, led by Hugh Gaitskell. Writing originally in 1955, one authority on the British parties was able to argue forcibly that because of agreement on fundamental issues, there was no real difference between the parties, and that 'Two great monolithic structures now face each other and conduct furious arguments about the comparatively minor issues that separate them.'[1]

Many people saw the ideological conflict of the 1945–51 period as exceptional, and attributable to the fact that in 1945 the Labour Party came to power with an overall majority in the Commons for the first time in the party's history. The attainment of the bulk of the Labour Party's long-standing programme of reform by 1951, and the eventual acceptance of most of it by the Conservative Party, seemed to leave the political parties with disagreements over only minor aspects of policy. The Conservative Party is often credited with having a traditional desire to hold office for its own sake, and at almost any price, and to some extent this attitude was adopted by the Labour Party after its defeats in 1951, 1955, and 1959, when many party members argued that the defeats were attributable in large part to electoral distrust of its more adventurous policies. Certainly, tendencies towards the adoption of more extreme policies were deterred in this period by the parties' preoccupation with the uncommitted floating voters, and with Liberal voters, who might be antagonized by extreme policies and attitudes.

The picture that has been presented of a broad political consensus in Britain, and of a considerable degree of agreement between the parties on fundamental political issues, is undoubtedly valid in many respects. As with the question of homogeneity, however, too broad an interpretation of the extent of the agreement can under-estimate the very real differences

[1] R. T. McKenzie, *British Political Parties*, London 1955 (first edition), p. 586.

of attitude that still exist, and can lead to a distorted and over-generalized view of British politics. For example, Sir Ivor Jennings's statement, quoted above, probably greatly over-estimates the extent of public satisfaction with the institutions that he mentions. The continued existence of the Monarchy, the House of Lords, or the public schools indicates the absence of widespread revolutionary forces in Britain, but it does not necessarily indicate universal acceptance of the value of these institutions. Similarly, the extent of the agreement between the political parties is often over-stated. Compared with right wing fears of the Communists coming to power in Italy or France, Conservative fears of Labour Governments in Britain may be slight, but it is surely an over-simplification of the relationship between the parties in Britain to state (as does one distinguished American observer of British politics[1]) that because of their broad agreement on most issues the British party leaders are not greatly concerned at the prospect of their opponents being in office. This view is difficult to reconcile with the Labour Party's concern over the Conservative election victories of the nineteen-fifties, particularly that of 1959. It is also difficult to reconcile with the fact that for the 1964 election the Conservative Party and business and commercial interests spent almost £3,000,000 (about ten times the cost of the Labour campaign) in an effort to secure the return of a Conservative Government,[2] or with the fact that the major feature of the British political scene from early 1963 to March 1966 was the almost continuous process of electioneering in which the parties indulged. One aspect of the party system in Parliament is the rigidity of party loyalties, and the strength of internal party unity, and to some extent this is reflected at an electoral level by the tendency of the vast majority of the electorate to have fixed party loyalties. If, how-ever, there was little to choose between the political parties, it might be expected that there would be a greater transfer of loyalties from one party to another, both at Parliamentary and electoral level. Also, if the attitudes of the Labour and Con-servative Parties are basically much the same, it is difficult to

[1] H. Eckstein in S. H. Beer and A. B. Ulam, *Patterns of Government*, London 1962, p. 179.
[2] Based on figures quoted in D. E. Butler and A. King, *The British General Election of 1964*, London 1965, p. 378.

explain the continued existence of the Liberal Party, even as a minority party, and the absence of any lasting 'Lib-Lab' or 'Lib-Con' alliance.

In fact, it is possible to point to many fundamental differences between the parties, both in their structures and attitudes. As is revealed in detail below, the two parties have very different social structures, at electoral, membership, and Parliamentary levels.[1] These differences inevitably produce different policy *attitudes* within the two parties which are more fundamental and permanent than the day-to-day Parliamentary and electoral differences over particular policy items.[2] In general, fundamental Conservative philosophy is inclined towards a hierarchical view of society, and towards the 'Tory' interpretation of the Constitution. While the Labour Party, with its democratic ideals, tends to regard a Government's authority as stemming from the people, the 'Tory view of the Constitution' sees a Government's authority as stemming from the Crown, with the role of the people being to choose the leaders but not the policies. Thus the doctrine that a Government needs an electoral mandate for any major policy has tended to receive more support from Labour politicians than from the Conservatives. Further, Labour Party policies always have had an ideological basis, with the party originally being committed to Socialism, public ownership, and the transformation of society, and with any attempted revision of basic doctrines being in the form of a search for a new ideology rather than in any attempt to abandon ideology completely. In contrast, the Conservative Party has been primarily concerned (at least in the past) with the attainment of power rather than with the pursuit of ideological ends, and the party has been able to recover so quickly from its setbacks (particularly that of 1945) largely because of this. At the same time, because of its trade union connections the Labour 'Movement' regards action through Parliament as only one means of achieving its ends, whereas the Conservative Party can perhaps be said to be more exclusively Parliamentary in its outlook.

[1] Ch. 3.
[2] See S. H. Beer, *Modern British Politics*, London 1965; H. J. Steck, 'The Re-emergence of Ideological Politics in Great Britain', *WPQ* 1965, pp. 87–103; T. E. M. McKitterick, 'Radicalism After 1964', *PQ* 1965, pp. 52–8.

These differences in attitude, combined with the differences
that exist in party structure and organization, all represent
limitations to the argument that there is little difference between the parties in Britain. What has to be admitted, however,
is that when a party is in power, and is faced with the realities
of political office, it is often forced to abandon attitudes and
policies that it had advocated in Opposition. The various
practical limitations on a Government's power that are noted
elsewhere,[1] may prevent, or at least hinder, the fulfilment of
the more adventurous policies framed in Opposition, and may
force a Government to adopt policies very similar to those of
its opponents. The Labour Party found this to be the case when
they came to power in 1964, as did the Conservatives in 1951
(and perhaps again in 1970). All Governments are faced with
the inescapable fact that it is what is possible rather than what
is ideal that is important in Government. Thus what a party
wishes to do, and what it is able to do when it is in power, are
often very different, and in this sense there is a compulsory
agreement on many political issues that is forced on the parties
by the realities of political office.

[1] See below, pp. 184 and 419.

part two

Parties, Pressure Groups and the Electorate

2

Case Study of the British Electoral System: The 1970 General Election[1]

On May 13th 1970 a Gallup Poll published in the *Daily Telegraph* suggested that the Labour Government's standing with the electorate had improved quite dramatically in the preceding weeks. After three years of marked Government unpopularity, during which time Labour had suffered numerous setbacks in by-elections and local government elections, and had lagged behind the Conservatives in the opinion polls, the May 13th Gallup Poll seemed to indicate that the trend in public opinion was moving towards the Government. This was reinforced the next day by a National Opinion Poll survey, published in the *Daily Mail*, which also indicated a clear Labour advantage over the Conservatives. These polls came after local government elections in April and May had shown a recovery in Labour's position, and the combined effect of these factors was to intensify speculation as to whether the Prime Minister would take advantage of a favourable (and perhaps temporary) turn in public opinion in order to call a Spring general election. The Parliament elected on March 31st 1966[2] had less than a

[1] For a detailed coverage see 'The Times', *House of Commons 1970*, London 1970. See also B. Lapping, *The Labour Government 1964–70*, London 1970; R. Oakley and P. Rose, *The Political Year 1970*, London 1970; A. Watkins and A. Alexander, *The Making of the Prime Minister*, London 1970.

[2] For the 1966 election see D. E. Butler and A. King, *The British General Election of 1966*, London 1966. See also 'Daily Telegraph', *Election '66*, London 1966; 'The Times', *House of Commons 1966*, London 1966; P. Bromhead, 'The General Election of 1966', *Parl. Aff.* 1965–6, pp. 332–45.

year of its maximum legal life to run. Most political commentators expected a 1970 election, but October seemed to be the most likely month. The Prime Minister, however, decided to face the country in June, no doubt encouraged by the indications of the recovery in Labour's position. Thus on May 18th the Prime Minister had an audience with the Queen, and she granted his request for a dissolution. Accordingly, Parliament was dissolved on May 29th, and the nineteenth general election of the century was held on June 18th. With the dramatic Conservative victory at the polls, Britain experienced a change of Government for the second time in six years, and Edward Heath took office as the new Prime Minister on June 19th. The new Parliament met ten days later, so that the whole process was completed in just six weeks.

The Dissolution

That the Prime Minister was able to make use of a period of comparative Government popularity in order to hold an election, stems from the fact that Parliament can be dissolved at the discretion of the Prime Minister. In the United States, Presidential and Congressional elections are held at fixed intervals, which can be altered only by constitutional amendment, while in most foreign systems where the power of dissolution does exist, as in the German Federal Republic and the French Fifth Republic, it is rarely or never used. Britain is one of the few examples of a political system where the possible use of the power of dissolution plays a vital part in the balance of power between Government and Opposition. Historically the power to dissolve Parliament was based on the principle that each Parliament was the Monarch's Parliament, and could therefore be dissolved at his discretion. Until the law was altered in 1867, the death of a Monarch was followed automatically by the dissolution of 'his' Parliament and the election of a new one for the new Monarch. The last occasion when this happened was in 1837, on the death of William IV, but ceremonial lip service is still paid to this principle in that the Monarch, in person or through Royal Commissioners, still opens, prorogues, and dissolves Parliament.

In modern constitutional terms the dissolution principle is

TABLE IX

Gallup Poll, 1966-70

Response to Question: If there were a general election tomorrow, which party would you support?*

Year (in quarters)		Con.	Lab.	Lib.	Con. lead over Lab.
1966	2	39	52	8	−13
	3	43	47	9	− 4
	4	44	43	11	1
1967	1	41	46	11	− 5
	2	48	40	10	8
	3	45	42	11	3
	4	48	37	11	11
1968	1	51	34	11	17
	2	57	28	11	29
	3	51	33	11	18
	4	52	34	10	18
1969	1	55	33	10	22
	2	53	32	12	21
	3	51	35	11	16
	4	49	42	7	7
1970	1	48	41	8	7
	2	45	46	7	− 1

* In percentages (after excluding 'Don't Knows'): each figure represents the quarterly average

Source: *Gallup Political Index*, Nos. 71 to 120, Social Surveys (Gallup Poll) Ltd.

based on the responsibility of the Monarch's Ministers to Parliament, but with the improbability of a major defeat for the Government in the House of Commons today, and with the recognition of the principle that the Monarch must accept the Prime Minister's advice, the power to request a dissolution has become a practical political weapon in the hands of the Prime Minister. In 1966, for example, Harold Wilson sought a dissolution of Parliament only eighteen months after the previous election, at a time of Government popularity as reflected in by-elections and opinion polls. In 1966 the Government had not lost the confidence of the House of Commons, and the Government's majority, though small, was intact. A dissolution was sought merely in order that the Government's Parliamentary majority might be increased. Salisbury in 1900, MacDonald in 1931, and Eden in 1955, also successfully used this tactic, while early dissolutions were apparently considered but rejected by Disraeli in 1878, after the Congress of Berlin, by Baldwin in 1926, after the general strike, and by Chamberlain in 1938, after his return from Munich.[1] In the 1959–64 Parliament an extended period of Government unpopularity, as reflected in the public opinion polls and by-election results, meant that an early dissolution was not practical, but Sir Alec Douglas-Home was able to delay the request for dissolution until the last possible moment in the hope that there would be a rallying of Government fortunes.[2] In 1970 Harold Wilson could have waited until the Spring of 1971 before seeking a dissolution, but he followed the more normal practice of seeking a dissolution while the Parliament still had the best part of a year to run.

The right to advise the Monarch on the dissolution lies with the Prime Minister, but it is not clear precisely how much influence his Cabinet colleagues may have on the matter. Evidence is scanty about dissolutions in the past, but at least the precise timing of the controversial requests for dissolution by Baldwin in 1923[3] and Attlee in 1951,[4] seem to have been personal decisions. Lord Morrison has declared that the presence of members of the Secretariat at Cabinet meetings precludes the discussion of such matters as the political factors involved in a dissolution,[5] but in 1970 and on other past occasions, informal discussions presumably took place between the Prime Minister and some of his colleagues.

Theoretically, Wilson could have held an election at any time after March 1966, but practical considerations limited his choice. A number of months, particularly July and August

[1] For details see C. S. Emden, *The People and the Constitution*, London 1962, p. 269.

[2] Butler and King, 1964, p. 73, for comments on the 1964 dissolution.

[3] K. Feiling, *The Life of Neville Chamberlain*, London 1946, p. 108; C. L. Mowat, *Britain Between the Wars*, London 1956, pp. 165–8. Also see below, p. 416.

[4] J. P. Mackintosh, *The British Cabinet*, London 1962, p. 387.

[5] Lord Morrison, *Government and Parliament*, London 1964, p. 24.

(summer holiday months) and April (the Budget month), are not generally regarded as being suitable for election purposes. The winter months of November to February are also regarded as unsuitable for election campaigning, though in fact eight of the eighteen elections of this century have been held in this winter period. May and October are usually quoted as the best months, and because June breaks into the holiday period it is not usually considered a particularly suitable time. Six elections of this century have been held in October,[1] and at one time it seemed possible that Wilson would wait until October 1970. Wilson's choice, however, was also conditioned by the possibility of a foreign or economic crisis developing during the summer of 1970.

An international crisis over the Middle East, a clash with the unions and employers over wages and prices, the beginning of negotiations over the Common Market, were all factors which in the spring seemed to be possible sources of trouble for the Government later in the year. Thus the temptation for Wilson was to hold an early election while the going was good, but he had to avoid making it appear as though he was seeking to make political capital out of constitutional machinery, as 'sharp practice' could be electorally disadvantageous. In the nineteenth century this mattered less, and Sir Robert Peel argued that as an unsuccessful dissolution was harmful to the Crown, a Prime Minister should only seek a dissolution if he could secure a majority for 'the King's Government'.[2] In 1970, the Opposition parties made some attempt to denounce the Government for seeking an election against a background of 'a few weeks of sunshine' (literal and economic), but in this respect Opposition parties suffer from the necessity of having to appear eager for an election at any time, regardless of how they may secretly feel about the prospects.

With the exception of the 1945 election, all general election voting has been on the same day since 1918, and since 1935 this has been a Thursday. Notice of a dissolution is not legally necessary, but by giving ten days' notice of the dissolution (which must come seventeen days before polling day, excluding Sundays and bank-holidays) Wilson in 1970 (as in 1966) was

[1] See Table X.
[2] Emden, *The People and the Constitution*, p. 205.

following the same timetable as Macmillan in 1959 and Douglas-Home in 1964.

Because the Government's unpopularity was so pronounced during much of the 1966–70 Parliament, by-elections produced a number of dramatic wins for the Opposition parties. In all, there were thirty-eight by-elections during the 1966–70 Parliament, and Labour lost fifteen of the twenty-six it was defending (some of the Labour defeats being in normally 'safe' seats).[1] It is often argued that by-elections can be a good mid-term mirror of a Government's popularity, but it should be remembered that different criteria apply at by-elections than at general elections, and the electors can consider different factors when deciding how (or whether) to vote.[2] The protest vote, whether against the Government or against traditional party loyalties, is more likely to manifest itself in by-elections, and the personal qualities of the candidates probably count for more than they do in general elections. Thus at the 1970 general election, Labour re-gained nine of the fifteen seats that it had lost in by-elections in the 1966–70 Parliament. In particular, the results at West Walthamstow in 1966 and 1970 (Labour majorities of 7,000 and 4,000) suggest that Labour's by-election defeat there in 1967 was a freak result. Because by-election results can be unpredictable, and as the party that held the seat determines when the writs for a by-election will be issued, there is often a time lag between a seat becoming vacant and the by-election being held, and in 1970 there were two seats vacant at the time of the dissolution.

*　　*　　*

The 1966–70 Parliament, lasting just over four years, was about average length for the Parliaments of the century (as is shown in Table X). Since the Parliament Act 1911, Parliaments have had a maximum life of five years from the date of the issuing of the writs to summon the Parliament, but the average length of Parliaments since 1910 is just four years—even with

[1] For details of these results see 'The Times', *House of Commons 1970*, London 1970.
[2] See R. M. Scammon, 'British By-elections 1951–5', *J of P* 1956, pp. 83–94.

the exceptionally long wartime Parliaments of 1910–18 and
1935–45, which were extended beyond the five-year limit by
emergency legislation. Five years is a purely arbitrary limit on
a Parliament's life. The Chartists sought annual Parliaments,
while in the United States members of the House of Representatives serve for two years, the President for four years, and Sena-
tors for six years. The French President is elected for seven
years, while the French Assembly serves for five years, and the
German Bundestag for four years. In Britain three distinct time
limits have applied over the past three centuries. The Triennial
Act 1694 placed a three-year limit upon the life of a Parliament,
and in 1716 it was extended to seven years by the Septennial
Act. The Parliament Act 1911 amended the Septennial
Act to make five years the maximum length of a Parliament,[1]
and this is the limit that has applied ever since. Parliaments
rarely last this full legal limit however. Between 1715 and 1966
there were fifty-seven full Parliaments, but apart from the two
exceptionally long wartime Parliaments of this century, the
only Parliaments to extend to the full limit were those of 1715–
1722 and 1959–64. Some Parliaments were dissolved early because
the Government could not continue in office, as in 1924 and
(some would argue) in 1951.[2] On other occasions, as in 1955
or 1966, the Government could have continued, but an early
election was sought in an effort to improve the Government's
position. On yet other occasions, as in January and December
1910, a dissolution was sought in order that the Government
could secure an electoral 'mandate' on a specific issue, though
the whole feasibility and desirability of the mandate concept is
one that is open to question.[3] In 1970 the Prime Minister could
have delayed the dissolution until the spring of 1971. A Prime
Minister will generally try to avoid doing this, however, and
will seek a dissolution some months before he is forced to do so,
partly in order to keep the Opposition guessing as to the date
of the dissolution, and also in order to have some time in which
to manœuvre towards the end of the Parliament. In 1964 Sir
Alec Douglas-Home presumably delayed the election until

[1] See below, p. 269, for more details.
[2] See, however, Mackintosh, *The British Cabinet*, p. 478, and J. D.
Hoffman, *The Conservative Party in Opposition, 1945–51*, London 1964, Ch. 7.
[3] See below, p. 416.

TABLE X

General Elections 1900–1970

Parliament	Length of Parliament		Election month at the end of the Parliament	Party in power and Prime Minister at the dissolution		
	Years	Months				
1895–1900	5	1	Oct.	Unionist	Salisbury	@
1900–6	5	1	Jan.	Lib.	Campbell-Bannerman	×*
1906–10	3	9	Jan.	Lib.	Asquith	@
1910		9	Dec.	Lib.	Asquith	@
1910–18	7	9	Dec.	Coalit.	Lloyd George	@
1919–22	3	8	Nov.	Con.	Bonar Law	@†
1922–23		11	Dec.	Con.	Baldwin	×‡
1924		9	Oct.	Lab.	MacDonald	×
1924–9	4	5	May	Con.	Baldwin	×
1929–31	2	3	Oct.	National	MacDonald	@
1931–5	3	11	Nov.	National	Baldwin	@
1935–45	9	6	July	Con.	Churchill	×
1945–50	4	6	Feb.	Lab.	Attlee	@
1950–1	1	7	Oct.	Lab.	Attlee	×
1951–5	3	6	May	Con.	Eden	@
1955–9	4	3	Oct.	Con.	Macmillan	@
1959–64	5	0	Oct.	Con.	Home	×
1964–6	1	5	March	Lab.	Wilson	@
1966–70	4	2	June	Lab.	Wilson	×

@ Indicates that the Government was returned to power at the election.
× Indicates that the Government was *not* returned to power.
* The Unionists were in power until December 1905 when Balfour resigned. A Liberal Government was formed, Parliament was dissolved at once, and the Liberals won the election.
† In 1922 the Conservative-dominated Coalition broke up. Bonar Law formed a Conservative Government, Parliament was dissolved, and the Conservatives won the election.
‡ The Conservatives remained the largest single party in the Commons, but lost their overall majority.

the last possible moment only as the lesser of two evils: as was shown in the 1959–64 Parliament, to delay the dissolution for too long inevitably leaves the Government open to accusations of clinging to power.

The Voters

Those eligible for registration as electors in 1970 were British citizens (or Irish or Commonwealth citizens resident in Britain) who were aged over 18, provided they were not Peers or Peeresses in their own right, felons, or lunatics, and provided that over the previous five years they had not been convicted of electoral malpractice.[1] For the 1970 election the total electorate was 39·3 million. This was an increase of almost 3·5 million compared with 1966, due largely to the lowering of the voting age from 21 to 18. It seems, however, that many of those eligible to register as electors failed to do so, either out of apathy or of ignorance of their new rights. October 10th 1969 was the qualifying date for the register on which the election was fought and the register came into operation on February 15th 1970. The election was thus fought on a relatively new register, though the 'Y voters' (the special category made up of those who become 18 between the qualifying date and the following June 15th) would have been eligible to vote only if the election had been postponed until after October 2nd 1970. The Representation of the People Act 1948 originally demanded a half-yearly renewal of the register, but in 1949 this was dropped as being impractical. An alternative to the present system would be to have a permanent register based on a card index which could be kept permanently up to date.

Before 1832 only about 5% of the adult population was eligible to vote, but the Reform Acts of 1832, 1867, and 1884 raised the figure to 28% of the adult population, all voters being male. The Representation of the People Act 1918 changed the voting qualification from the payment of local rates to adulthood (deemed as 21), and also enfranchised women over the age of 30, provided they or their husband owned or occupied property valued at least £5 a year. The 1918 Act thereby rewarded the activities of the Suffragettes, and acknowledged the social changes brought about by the 1914–18 war.[2] In 1928 the voting age for women was lowered to 21, equalizing the male and female qualifications and raising the number of

[1] For the details of electoral law see A. N. Schofield, *Parliamentary Elections*, London 1959. See also M. Rees, 'Defects in the System as Electoral Registration', *PQ* 1970, pp. 220–3.

[2] See R. Fulford, *Votes For Women*, London 1957.

TABLE XI

Stages in the Extension of the Franchise, 1832–1969

1832	Change from corporate to individual basis of representation
1867	Working class enfranchisement
1884	Change from a minority to a majority electorate
1918	Universal Manhood Suffrage
1928	Universal Adult Suffrage (qualifying age 18)
1948	End of Plural Voting
1969	Qualifying age lowered to 18

eligible voters to 96% of the adult population. The 1918 Act allowed the holders of a business premises qualification to vote in their business constituency as well as their residential constituency (provided they were not the same), and the 1928 Act allowed their wives to vote on this basis also. University graduates also had two votes, one in their University seat and one in their residential constituency.[1] The University representation dates back to the Parliament of 1301, and after 1918 there were twelve University representatives in the Commons. There were unsuccessful legislative attempts to abolish plural voting in 1913 and 1931, and even though the 1944 Speaker's Conference on Electoral Reform advocated its retention,[2] the Representation of the People Act 1948 finally abolished the University and business franchise and established the principle of 'one adult one vote'. Had plural voting not been abolished, the Conservatives would possibly have won the 1950 and 1964 general elections, and at the very least the University members would have held the balance between the parties.

In 1970 the qualifying age for the vote was 18. For the 1918 'Khaki' election the voting age was temporarily lowered to 19, and the 1944 Speaker's Conference considered but rejected the idea of lowering of the age to 18.[3] In 1969, however, the Representation of the People Act introduced the principle of votes at 18. In favour of this it can be argued that young people

[1] See T. Lloyd Humberstone, *University Representation*, London 1951.
[2] Report of the Speaker's Conference on Electoral Reform, Cmd. 6534 and 6543 (1944).
[3] Cmd. 6534 (1944).

are today better educated, mature earlier, are wealthier, and pay more in taxes than at any time in the past, and that in a number of legal and social respects adulthood and maturity are taken to date from the eighteenth rather than the twenty-first birthday. Whatever the qualifying age may be, there is an inevitable time-lag between qualifying for the vote and having a chance to use it in a general election. Someone who just missed the qualifying date for the 1970 general election may be 25 or 26 before the next general election is held. Because of this, any qualifying age in a sense must be arbitrary, and the new limit of 18 is perhaps as logical as any other. The lowering of the qualifying age to 18 will add some two million to the electoral register. It has been estimated that if the 18 to 21 age group showed the same voting tendencies as the 21 to 29 age group, the Labour Party would have benefited from a lowering of the qualifying age at every post-war election, with the possible exception of 1959.[1] On this basis Labour would also have benefited most from the Y voters in 1970, had the election come after October 2nd instead of in June.

The Constituencies

The United Kingdom is divided into 630 single-member constituencies. In 1970 there were considerable variations in the sizes of the constituencies, the boundaries of which had not been revised since 1954. The biggest constituency (in terms of population) in Great Britain was Billericay, with an electorate of 123,000, while in Northern Ireland, South Antrim had 143,000 voters and North Down 120,000. At the other extreme, Birmingham Ladywood had only 18,000 voters, Glasgow Kelvingrove 19,000, and Manchester Exchange 21,000. Thus Labour won Ladywood with 5,000 votes, but lost Billericay with 43,000.

The drawing of constituency boundaries is a difficult task, and is more difficult with single-member than with multi-member constituencies, as the greater the number of boundaries the greater the chances of discrepancies. The franchise extensions of 1832, 1867, 1884, and 1918 were accompanied or followed by a redistribution of seats, reducing the ratio between the

[1] R. Rose, *The Times*, 26.11.65. See also P. Abrams and A. Little, 'The Young Voter in British Politics', *BJS* 1965, pp. 95–109.

biggest and the smallest seat from 1 : 60 after the 1832 Act, to
1 : 3 in 1918.[1] More recently, boundary revisions were made in
1944, 1948, and 1954. Following the recommendations of the
Speaker's Conference in 1944,[2] four permanent Boundary Commissions were created, one each for England, Scotland, Wales,
and Northern Ireland. The Speaker of the House of Commons is
chairman of each Commission, and appeal from the Commissions is to Parliament, even though electoral malpractice
is now tried by the Courts rather than by Parliament.[3] The
task of the Boundary Commissions is not to try to create constituencies of precisely equal size, as this is virtually impossible
to achieve. Every year there are inevitable population movements, particularly from the centres of large cities to the sub-
urbs. Thus between 1954 and 1970 the electorate of the Billericay constituency grew from 58,000 to 123,200, while Birmingham Ladywood fell from 47,000 to 18,000 (despite the extension
of the franchise in 1969). Boundary revisions cannot be made
too often as this can cause administrative problems, and hinders
the development of party organizations in the constituencies.
The Redistribution of Seats Act 1944 stipulated that boundary
revisions be made every three to seven years (that is, once per
Parliament on average), but in 1958 the period was extended
to every ten to fifteen years.

The 1970 election, however, was fought in the constituencies
drawn up in 1954. During the course of the 1966–70 Parliament
the Boundary Commissions produced plans for new boundaries
for 410 constituencies, increasing the total number to 635. As
demanded by law, the proposals were laid before Parliament
in 1969. The Government, however, asked Parliament to postpone the implementation of the revisions until new local
government boundaries had been agreed upon in 1974 or 1975,
and accordingly the Boundary Commission proposals were
shelved. The Opposition criticized the Government's attitude,
claiming that the Government was postponing the implementa-

[1] W. J. M. Mackenzie, *Free Elections*, London 1958, p. 108.
[2] Cmd. 6534 (1944).
[3] See D. E. Butler, 'The Redistribution of Seats', *Pub. Admin.* 1955,
pp. 125–47; J. T. Craig, 'Parliament and the Boundary Commissions', *PL*
1959, pp. 23–45; V. Vale, 'The Computer as Boundary Commissioner',
Parl. Aff. 1968–9, pp. 240–9.

tion of the Boundary Commission proposals only because the old boundaries were more favourable to Labour than were the new ones. After the election, the new Conservative Government announced that the new boundaries would be implemented in time for the next general election (although during the Parliament, by-elections would be fought on the old boundaries).

Even with new constituencies, however, equal electoral districts will not be achieved, as this is never fully sought. In the 1918 redistribution, precise equality in constituency size was aimed at (though unsuccessfully), but in the redistributions since then regional variations have been recognized as inevitable, and indeed desirable. Certainly, the view that MPs represent not only their own constituents but the whole nation, implies that it is not necessary to have strictly equal districts, as each elector is 'virtually' (or 'communally') represented by all MPs. The Redistribution of Seats Act 1944 recommended that all constituencies be within 25% of the average national size, but in 1948 this recommendation was rejected as impractical. Today, the task of the Boundary Commissions is to prevent the discrepancies in the sizes of the various constituencies from becoming too big, while at the same time considering administrative convenience and respecting the boundaries of local government, geographical, and natural regions.

The 1948 redistribution reduced the number of seats in the House of Commons from 640 to 625, and in 1954 the figure was adjusted to 630, England having 511 of them, Scotland 71, Wales 36, and Northern Ireland 12. On a strictly population basis, Scotland and Wales are over-represented, and England and Northern Ireland are under-represented, the latter because it is partly self-governing.[1] On a 1954 population basis, England was entitled to eight more seats, and these would probably have gone to London and Lancashire.[2] Similarly, on a population basis, the boroughs are under-represented as compared with the counties, an average difference of 2,000 voters between borough and county constituencies in 1948 being widened to 4,000 in 1954.[3] In Britain the conscious over-representation of some areas is defended as a safeguard for minority interests, be they national or economic, and as a concession to geographical

[1] See below, p. 162.
[2] Butler, 'Redistribution of Seats', p. 133.   [3] ibid., p. 138.

factors of remoteness and population sparsity. Whatever policy is adopted, however, population ratios inevitably fluctuate markedly between one redistribution and another.

The Candidates[1]

The 1970 election was contested by 1,837 candidates, Conservatives and their supporters accounting for 628, Labour (and Northern Ireland Labour) for 624, Liberals 332, Communists 58, Plaid Cymru 36 (contesting all the seats in Wales), and SNP 65 (contesting all but 6 of the Scottish seats). Other parties and Independents accounted for 94. All the seats were contested. The only seats that the Conservatives did not contest were the Speaker's seat of Southampton Itchen (although he was opposed by Independent and National Democratic Party candidates), and Greenock, where Labour only narrowly won against Liberal and Communist candidates. Labour did not contest the seats in Ulster, although some were fought by the Northern Ireland Labour Party. The Liberals fought twenty-one more seats than in 1966, but thirty-three less than in 1964. Before 1945, uncontested seats were more numerous than they are today, and between the wars there were normally 30–50 unopposed candidates at each general election.[2] Since 1951 there have been no uncontested seats in general elections, despite the fact that at least two-thirds of the seats are regarded as safe for one of the parties. In 1970, only 87 seats changed hands, (or 88 if S. O. Davies' seat is counted as having 'changed hands'),[3] and even in the Labour landslide of 1945 only 227 out of 640 seats changed hands.[4] It seems, however, that while contesting all seats, the parties are concentrating their campaigning efforts more and more into the marginal constituencies.

All that is required in order to be a candidate at an election is eligibility for the vote, and the support of ten electors.[5] A

[1] For comments on the social background of the candidates see below, p. 85.

[2] J. F. S. Ross, *Elections and Electors*, London 1955, pp. 218, 236.

[3] See below, p. 252.

[4] For comments see J. Rasmussen, 'The Implications of Safe Seats for British Democracy', *WPQ* 1966, pp. 517–29.

[5] See A. Barker, 'Disqualification from the House—the "Reverse System" ', *Parl. Aff.* 1958–9, pp. 69–74.

deposit of £150 has to be paid, but this is returned if the candidate receives one-eighth of the total poll. In 1970, 406 candidates lost their deposits, only 17 of them Labour or Conservative candidates. There are a number of factors, however, that disqualify from membership of the House of Commons. Those who do not qualify for the franchise are excluded, as are members of the armed forces,[1] the clergy, and holders of 'offices of profit under the Crown' (as defined by the House of Commons Disqualification Act 1957). These disqualifications apply to membership of the Commons, but not to candidature, and the validity of such disqualifications is determined by an Electoral Court after the election. Thus Anthony Wedgwood Benn was held to be no longer eligible for membership of the Commons when he inherited his father's Peerage in 1960, but he was able to contest and win the by-election caused by his own disqualification, only for a second time to be deemed ineligible to sit in the Commons.[2] When, as in Wedgwood Benn's case, the candidate's ineligibility was known to the electorate at the time of his election, the seat is awarded to the runner-up, but when his ineligibility was not generally known, a further election is held.

In order to have any real chance of being elected, however, it is generally necessary to be an official candidate of one of the main parties (and in most cases of one of the two main parties). In 1970 six Liberals and six other candidates were successful (the six 'others' being Protestant Unionist, Independent Labour, Republican Labour, SNP, Irish Unity, and the Speaker). In the main, however, the two main parties dominated the 1970 election as they have dominated all postwar elections. To have any hope of election, however, a party candidate must be contesting a seat that is either safe for his party or is a marginal.[3] Thus while most adults who can raise the £150 deposit are eligible to contest a Parliamentary election,

[1] For the peculiar position of servicemen as Parliamentary candidates see A. A. Barrett, 'Service Candidates at Parliamentary Elections 1962–3', *Table*, 1963, pp. 39–43; N. Johnson, 'Servicemen and Parliamentary Elections', *Parl. Aff.* 1962–3, pp. 207–12, and 440–4.

[2] For details of the Wedgwood Benn case see C. O'Leary, 'The Wedgwood Benn Case and the Doctrine of Wilful Perversity', *PS* 1965, pp. 65–79; G. Borrie, 'The Wedgwood Benn Case', *PL* 1961, pp. 349–61.

[3] See above, p. 36, however, for comments on the situation in by-elections.

there is clearly a vast difference between being a Parliamentary candidate and being an officially adopted Parliamentary candidate of one of the main parties in one of their winnable seats. The proportion of vacancies that occur in winnable seats is quite low, as the vast majority of encumbent MPs (592 in 1966 and 551 in 1970) normally seek re-election. Nevertheless the selection of party candidates is of great significance.[1] The choice of candidates eventually determines the make-up of the Parliamentary Party, with all the consequences that this has for party policies, choice of leaders, and general party image. Also, the ability to refuse to readopt an MP as official party candidate can be a weapon for discipline within the party, though it has been estimated that between 1950 and 1964 there were only 18 attempts (12 of them successful) to force Conservative MPs to retire, and only 16 attempts (again, 12 of them being successful) to force Labour MPs to retire.[2] However, the ultimate power to withold readoption from an MP undoubtedly to some extent acts as a deterrent to rebellion within the Parliamentary Parties.[3]

The selection of party candidates is very much an internal party affair, with the general public taking very little notice. All three main parties apply the same principle of the choice being made by the local constituency party, but with the central party machine supervising the process and retaining the ultimate power to intervene. Within the local parties, real power in the selection process lies with the small group of local activists who hold office and serve on the management committee (the Executive Committee in the case of the Conservative and Liberal Parties and the General Management Committee in the case of the Labour Party[4]), and their role in the selection process is possibly the most significant contribution that they make to the affairs of their party. None of the parties uses a system of primary elections to choose candidates, though

---

[1] For detailed studies see A. Ranney, *Pathways to Parliament*, London 1965 and M. Rush, The Selection of Parliamentary Candidates, London 1969, See also A. Ranney, 'Inter-Constituency Movement in British Parliamentary Candidates 1951–9', *APSR* 1964, pp. 36–45; P. W. Buck, 'First-Time Winners in the British House of Commons Since 1915', *APSR* 1964, pp. 622–7.

[2] Ranney, *Pathways to Parliament*, pp. 74 *and* 182.

[3] See below, p. 171.   [4] See below, pp. 122 and 127.

in very rare and exceptional circumstances a ballot of the members of the local association has been used to select Conservative candidates. In the Conservative Party the process of adopting a new candidate begins with the submission of names to the local party association concerned. Any individual party member can propose himself or suggest someone else, though there is an Approved List of candidates drawn up by the National Union's Standing Advisory Committee on Candidates. Real influence with this Committee, however, lies with the Vice-Chairman of the party, and he generally suggests names from the list to the local associations in an attempt to secure seats for particular candidates or particular types of candidate. The SACC is also responsible (again under the influence of the Vice-Chairman) for the rules and procedures to be followed in the selection process, and for the granting of final approval to the selected candidate. From the names that are submitted to the local association a short list is drawn up by a sub-committee of the local association's Executive Committee, and the power of this body is considerable in that the list can be weighted in favour of one candidate. Those on the short list appear before the Executive Committee at a selection meeting (attended also by the Central Office Area Agent), and a choice is made after each contender has addressed the meeting. The Executive Committee's decision is presented to the full Association for approval, which is nearly always forthcoming, and though Central Office can veto the decision, it almost never does (there being only one instance of a direct veto since 1945.)[1] At this stage the candidate is merely 'prospective', however, and in order to avoid incurring official election expenses, he does not become the official candidate until the election date is named.

Thus the choice of candidate is made locally, with Central Office being able to influence the process, but in practice doing so only to a very limited extent. The same general principle applies with the selection of Labour candidates, though the local activists perhaps are subject to rather more influence from the central party machine than is the case in the Conservative Party. The Constituency Labour Party cannot begin to look for a candidate until the Labour Party's National Executive Committee consents, though this consent has not been withheld

[1] Ranney, *Pathways to Parliament*, p. 43.

since 1945. The rules governing the selection procedure are laid down in the party's 'model rules', and the NEC has the power to suspend the normal procedure in an emergency. The NEC also lays down certain very general qualifications for candidates, including acceptance of the policy, principles, and constitution of the party. Unlike the Conservative Party, nominations cannot be made by individual party members, but must come from organizations affiliated to the CLP. A clear distinction emerges between what are referred to as unsponsored candidates, nominated by a ward committee or socialist society, and sponsored candidates nominated by a trade union which agrees to contribute towards the election expenses of the candidate and to make payments to the CLP's funds.

In 1933, in an attempt to reduce the practice of the wealthy unions 'buying' the best seats for their members, limits were placed on the contributions that a union could make to the election expenses and funds of a CLP. Today a union can contribute up to 80% of the candidate's election expenses, plus £350 a year to the funds of the CLP in the case of borough constituencies, and £420 in the case of county constituencies. These are maximum sums, however, and generally the contributions fall short of these figures. On the other hand, in some cases the maximum sums are exceeded in order to 'buy' a seat, but the extent of this practice is often exaggerated.[1]

Of the Labour MPs elected in 1970, 114 were sponsored by Trade Unions (20 of them by the National Union of Mineworkers). Since 1945 some 80% of union-sponsored candidates have won their seats, with the largest unions generally being most active in sponsoring candidates, and most successful in getting them elected. The National Union of Mineworkers alone has accounted for a quarter of all union-sponsored candidates since 1945, and it has had over 90% of them elected.[2] On the other hand, the Amalgamated Engineering Union, Electrical Trades Union, and Agricultural Workers Union have frequently sponsored candidates in hopeless seats in a 'missionary' cause.

From the various names that are submitted to the CLP, a short list is drawn up by the CLP Executive Committee, and as

[1] See Ranney, *Pathways to Parliament*, p. 225, for comments.
[2] ibid., p. 226.

with the Conservative selection process, this is the vital stage when certain candidates (or types of candidate) can be excluded. The short list has to be approved by the NEC, and then by the CLP's General Management Committee, and though there is no clear evidence of the NEC attempting to alter the short list (though unofficial pressure may be exerted at an earlier stage), the GMC sometimes does seek to remove or add names. Those on the short list then appear before a GMC selection meeting, and the candidate is chosen. The choice has to be endorsed by the NEC. Inclusion on the NEC's lists of approved candidates does not guarantee endorsement, nor does exclusion from the lists necessarily prevent endorsement, and since 1945 there have been only five instances of this being refused. An alternative means that the NEC has of vetoing a candidate is to expel him from the party, and this happened to a group of rebel MPs in 1949.

In the selection of Liberal candidates, the national party machine exercises even less control over the local parties than is the case with the Labour and Conservative Parties. In general, the Liberal Party is so short of candidates that the local activists are given virtually unlimited freedom to choose whoever they wish. There is an officially approved list of candidates drawn up by the party secretary and a sub-committee of the Liberal Party Organization, but constituencies are by no means limited to this list in their search for a candidate. The national party machine has no power to veto a constituency party's choice, and has no power to prevent a seat being contested. Also, there are no limits placed on the financial contributions that a candidate can make towards the cost of his campaign.

In all three parties, and particularly with the Labour Party, the central machine tends to play a bigger role in the selection of candidates for by-elections, partly because the candidate counts for more in by-elections, partly because more national interest is centred on individual constituencies in by-elections, and partly because the central machine is able to devote more time to by-election selections. Whether for by-elections or for general elections, however, the very significance of candidate selection would seem to make inevitable some degree of conflict between national and local leaders. In fact, however, such conflict has been slight, and central interference in the selection process has not been great, no doubt largely because of the desire of the national party leaders not to offend the activists who manage the local electoral machinery. Also, in some respects central interference in candidate selection has been unnecessary, in that Labour and Conservative local activists alike have generally tended to support the national party leaders in questions of internal party discipline.

The Campaign

To a remarkable extent the 1970 general election campaign was dominated by the public opinion polls.[1] There were more polls published during the 1970 campaign than in any previous British general election, and National Opinion Polls (in the

TABLE XII

Main Opinion Polls Published During the 1970 General Election Campaign: Size of Labour Lead*

Week Published	Gallup	NOP	Harris	ORC	Marplan
May 17–23	7	—	2	1	2
24–30	5	3	—	2	—
31–June 7	5	5	5	4	8
June 8–14	2	12	7	7	3
15–18	7	4	2	—1	—

*In percentages, fractions of a per cent excluded.

Source: *Daily Telegraph, Daily Mail, Daily Express, Evening Standard, The Times.*

Daily Mail), Gallup (*Daily Telegraph*), Harris (*Daily Express*), Marplan (*The Times*), and Opinion Research Centre (*Evening Standard*) all published the results of national surveys regularly

[1] For the general influence of the opinion polls on the political process see R. Hodder-Williams, *Public Opinion Polls and British Politics*, London 1970. See also M. Abrams, 'Public Opinion Polls and Political Parties', *POQ* 1963, pp. 9–18; M. Abrams, 'Opinion Polls and Party Propaganda', *POQ* 1964, pp. 13–19; R. Rose, 'Political Decision Making and the Polls', *Parl. Aff.* 1962, pp. 188–202; D. E. G. Plowman, 'Public Opinion and the Polls', *BJS* 1962, pp. 331–49.

during the campaign. A number of other national and local polls were conducted for other newspapers, and the political parties commissioned their own private surveys. The findings of the various polls also gave rise to more comment than in previous elections, for while most polls indicated a clear Labour lead throughout the campaign, the extent of Labour's advantage varied considerably from one poll to another, and from one week to another. Further, at no British general election in recent years had the final findings of the major polls been so much at variance with the actual result as they were in 1970. One explanation offered by the polls to account for the discrepancy between their final surveys and the actual result, is that while opinion poll samples are drawn from the electorate as a whole, Labour was much less successful than in recent elections in persuading its supporters to cast their vote. Labour voters are generally seen as being much more likely to abstain than are Conservative voters, and it may be that in 1970 Labour suffered even more than usual from abstentions among potential Labour voters. Another suggestion is that there were major shifts of opinion in the last few days of the campaign, after the opinion pollsters had completed their surveys. Gallup found evidence of this in re-interviews that they conducted after the election.[1] If there were major shifts of opinion in the final day or so before polling, it destroys one of the assumptions of general election campaigning, that all but a small minority of voters make the final decision on how they will vote well before polling day. Either or both of these factors (low turnout and last minute changes) may explain the discrepancy between the final opinion polls and the actual voting pattern, but there is little hard evidence either way.

In the campaign both parties emphasized personalities and general themes rather than specific policies. Labour caricatured the Conservative leaders as 'Yesterday's Men', while the Conservatives attacked 'Labour's Broken Promises'. Throughout the 1966–70 Parliament the opinion polls had suggested that Edward Heath lagged behind his party in terms of public esteem, whereas Wilson generally had a higher opinion poll rating than did his party. This situation seemed to persist

[1] See *Gallup Political Index* No. 122 (Sept. 1970) Social Surveys (Gallup Poll) Ltd.

during the campaign, and much of Labour's strategy was thus centred on Harold Wilson's personal appeal. The main theme of Labour's campaign was that the Wilson Government had succeeded in solving the balance of payments problem that had plagued Britain during the nineteen-sixties, and that consequently there was opportunity in the 'seventies for a rise in the general level of prosperity, and for an extension of the public services.[1] Thus the title of Labour's election manifesto was 'Now Britain's strong, let's make her great to live in.' The Conservatives were accused of being irresponsible and unfit for office because they promised an 'impossible' combination of reduced taxation and increased public expenditure, notably on defence. Harold Wilson also argued that Labour was now the 'natural ruling party', and that the Conservatives were demonstrably a party of privilege, lacking a social conscience.

The Conservative campaign emphasized the rapidly rising cost of living (clearly looking for 'the housewives' vote'), the levels to which direct taxation had risen under Labour, and the problem of strikes and industrial unrest. The Conservatives also claimed that the country's seeming economic recovery had very fragile foundations, and that a further period of Labour rule would mean renewed economic restraint, with perhaps another devaluation and a wages 'freeze'. Labour's failure to deal with the problem of strikes was also highlighted, and in their manifesto ('A Better Tomorrow') the Conservatives undertook to tackle the problem of industrial relations as a priority. A bad set of trade figures published only four days before polling day added weight to Conservative claims, and although the Government argued that they were freak figures, which would not be repeated in later months, they probably did much to undermine public confidence in Labour's talk of economic recovery.

In their manifesto 'What A Life!', the Liberals stressed the need for a 'third force' at Westminster, in view of the failures of thirteen years of Conservative rule and twelve years of Labour rule since 1945. The national campaign of the Liberal Party, however, was hindered by the fact that the party's leading figures had to devote most of their time to the campaign in

[1] See C. A. E. Goodhart and R. J. Bhansali, 'Political Economy', *PS* 1970, pp. 43–106.

their own marginal constituencies. The Scottish National Party and Plaid Cymru also emphasized the desirability of breaking down the dominance of the two main parties, and in this context they complained that they did not receive adequate coverage in the press or on radio or TV.

As the campaign began, the Government asked the MCC to call off the South African cricket tour during the summer because of the possibly violent demonstrations that it might provoke among anti-apartheid groups in Britain. In general, however, the issue of law and order did not figure prominently in the election campaign (despite numerous eggs being thrown at party leaders). Also, unlike the elections of the nineteen-fifties and 'sixties, nationalization and defence did not figure prominently in the campaign, despite some controversy before the campaign over Conservative plans to maintain military forces 'east of Suez'. The problems associated with Commonwealth immigration received some attention when Enoch Powell spoke out on the subject.[1] The general publicity given to Powell during the campaign was widely seen as representing a challenge to Edward Heath's position as party leader, and Labour sought to capitalize on the situation through the theme of 'who is the *real* leader of the Conservative Party?' In the end, however, the Conservatives may well have gained more votes than they lost through Powell's controversial speeches during the campaign.

In 1970, as in all general elections since 1959, the main contact between the parties and the electorate was through TV and the press.[2] The weekly 'Panorama' (BBC) and 'This Week' (ITV) current affairs programmes examined specific election issues in some depth, while the BBC and ITV evening news programmes examined the progress of the campaign day by day. The parties were allocated time at peak viewing hours on the national networks for party political programmes, in which

[1] N. Deakin and J. Bourne, 'Powell, the Minorities and the 1970 Election', *PQ* 1970, pp. 399–415. See also Institute of Race Relations, *Colour and the British Electorate*, London 1965.

[2] For the place of television in election campaigning see Blumler and McQuail, *Television in Politics*; Trenaman and McQuail, *Television and the Political Image*; Lord Windlesham, 'Television as an Influence on Public Opinion', *PQ* 1964, pp. 475–85; W. Pickles, 'Political Attitudes in the Television Age', *PQ* 1959, pp. 54–66.

a variety of techniques were used to 'sell' the parties and their leaders. There was no direct TV confrontation between the leaders, however. The various TV arrangements were mirrored for sound broadcasting, but, as in the elections of the 'sixties, the parties devoted much less effort to radio than to TV campaigning. Although all the parties to some extent based their campaign issues on the impact that they would have in the press and on TV, there is little clear evidence that either medium dictated the issues that were to be raised during the campaign.[1] Of the national daily newspapers the *Sun*, *Guardian* and *Daily Mirror* were broadly pro-Labour in their attitude, while the *Daily Sketch*, *Daily Telegraph*, *Daily Mail* and *Daily Express* were pro-Conservative. *The Times*, while nominally uncommitted, had clear Conservative sympathies. For four days at the height of the campaign (June 10th to 13th) a strike prevented the publication of the national newspapers, although some local newspapers continued to be published.

All three major parties held daily press conferences, conducted by one or more of the leading party figures, while other party notables addressed outdoor meetings on strenuous speaking tours which were designed primarily to raise morale in the constituencies. A major verbal battleground was also provided by evening meetings which were addressed by the party leaders, and which were covered in some detail by TV and radio news. Also, Harold Wilson (and to a lesser extent Edward Heath and Jeremy Thorpe) indulged in 'meet the people' tours, paying flying visits to key constituencies and mixing with party workers and electors in general, with only a minimum of formal speech making. This proved to be a major point of news interest in the campaign, and although it did not bring electoral success for Harold Wilson in 1970, it is an aspect of American style campaigning that may grow in popularity in Britain.

The campaign in the constituencies was directed mainly towards familiarizing the electors with the party candidate by means of public meetings, posters, election addresses, and door-

[1] For the political influence of the press see J. B. Christoph, 'The Press and Politics in Britain and America', *PQ* 1963, pp. 137–50; D. McLachlan, 'The Press and Public Opinion, *BJS* 1955, pp. 159–68; A. H. Birch, P. Campbell and P. G. Lucas, 'The Popular Press in the British General Election of 1955', *PS* 1956, pp. 297–306.

to-door canvassing, so as to achieve on polling day a maximum turnout of party workers and voters.[1] Local publicity was aided by the increased coverage of local constituencies by regional TV programmes, although despite this, public attention in the campaign remained centred on the national leaders and national issues. As in all British general elections, the campaign in the constituencies was limited by the fact that there is a legal restriction on the amount of money that can be spent by each candidate. The candidate has to nominate an agent (though he can be his own agent), and all expenditure has to be made through him. On the basis of a formula laid down in 1948, and revised in 1969, a candidate in an average sized county constituency can spend a maximum of about £1,250, and a candidate in a borough constituency about £1,125.[2] It is generally accepted, however, that in a number of ways these limits can be evaded, and the situation is somewhat anomalous in that there is no limit on the amount of money that can be spent up to nomination day. Also, while expenditure within each constituency is limited, there is no such limit on the amount of money that can be spent by the central party machine on the *national* campaign, as opposed to the individual *constituency* campaigns. Both parties spent vast sums on their national campaigns, although one consequence of the election coming in June rather than the Autumn was that neither party was able to mount the expensive advertising campaigns they had planned for the summer months. Theoretically the purposes of an election is to choose between individual candidates rather than parties (and thus until 1970 party affiliations were not recorded on the ballot papers). A consequence of this myth is that limits on spending apply only to expenditure by each candidate, and not to party spending on a national scale.

The significance of any election campaign does not lie solely in the immediate results, in that during a campaign the parties are also concerned with long term education of the electorate,

[1] J. C. Brown, 'Local Party Efficiency as a Factor in the Outcome of British Elections', *PS* 1958, pp. 174–8.
[2] See R. Rose, 'Money and the Election Law', *PS* 1961, pp. 1–15; J. F. S. Ross, 'The Incidence of Election Expenses', *PQ* 1952, pp. 175–81; F. C. Newman, 'Money and the Election Law in Britain—Guide for America', *WPQ* 1957, pp. 582–602.

with half an eye being kept on the next general election.[1] At the same time, the part played by individual politicians during an election campaign can be important in the balance of power within the parties. In 1970, for example, Edward Heath, as well as trying to secure a Conservative victory, was concerned with trying to strengthen his own position within the Conservative Party, as had the Conservatives been defeated, Heath's political future as a twice defeated Leader of the Opposition would have been extremely uncertain.

The Results

At the 1970 general election the turnout was 72% of a total electorate of some 39 million. This was the lowest turnout since before 1945, despite the fact that the 1970 election was fought on a fairly new register. It compares with 75% in 1966 and 84% in 1950, the highest percentage turnout since the 1918 franchise extension. The highest percentage turnout in any one constituency in 1970 was 92% in Fermanagh and South Tyrone, while Mid Ulster was 90%. The lowest turnout was 44% at Stepney, while half a dozen other London boroughs were below 50%. Unlike Australia, voting in Britain is not compulsory. In favour of compulsory voting it can be argued that voting is a duty as much as a right; that everyone in a democratic community should take part in choosing a Government; and that abstention condones bad government. On the other hand, compulsory voting is perhaps incompatible with the principle of free elections, while from a practical point of view, expense and administrative problems can be involved in imposing punishments and allowing for genuine excuses. Compulsion inevitably allows martyrs to emerge, and as deliberately spoilt papers cannot be penalized, it is perhaps illogical to punish non-attendance. At present, provision is made for postal votes or proxy votes for those who cannot vote in person, and postal votes generally account for 2% or so of the total electorate.

It is generally accepted, however, that the vast majority of postal votes are cast for the Conservatives, and in 1970 there were 19 seats won by Conservatives with majorities of less than

[1] See H. Pollins, 'The Significance of the Campaign in British Elections', *PS* 1953, pp. 207–15.

CASE STUDY OF THE BRITISH ELECTORAL SYSTEM 57

2%. It has been claimed that in 1966 the majority of those who did not vote were potential Labour supporters, particularly in safe Labour seats, and this is probably true of 1970 and of all post-war elections.[1] Thus compulsory voting would probably be to the advantage of the Labour Party rather than the Conservatives.

The votes and seats won by each party in 1970 are shown in Table XIII. Compared with 1966 the Conservatives made a

TABLE XIII

1970 General Election Result

	Votes		Seats	
Conservative	13,144,000	46·4%	330	52·4%
Labour	12,179,000	42·9%	287	45·6%
Liberal	2,117,000	7·5%	6	0·9%
Others	903,000	3·2%	7	1·1%

net gain of 77 seats, and Labour a net loss of 76. The Liberals won only 6 seats compared with 12 in 1966, but other parties and Independents secured 7 seats (only one of them in England) compared with just 2 in 1966. The Conservative vote rose by more than 1·5 million while Labour's fell by almost a million (despite the increase in the size of the electorate). The Liberal vote also fell, by some 200,000, which was enough to lose them 6 seats compared with 1966. The mean two party swing was 4·7% to the Conservatives (that is, the Conservative share of the vote rose by 4·5% while Labour's fell by 5·0%).[2] As in 1966, the swing was remarkably uniform throughout the country, and in England the swings in the various regions were nearly all within 1% of the national figure. At the same time, the Conservatives did not do as well in Scotland (swing 3·3%) or Wales (swing 2·8%) as in England, and had the Scottish or Welsh results been mirrored in England, Labour would have

[1] Butler and King, 1966, p. 274.
[2] For general comments on the swing concept see J. Rasmussen, 'The Disutility of the Swing Concept in British Psephology', *Parl. Aff.* 1964–5, pp. 443–54. See also G. N. Sanderson, 'The "Swing of the Pendulum" in British General Elections', *PS* 1966, pp. 349–60.

retained power. There were above-average swings in some constituencies, particularly in the English midlands. In Enoch Powell's seat of Wolverhampton South-West, the swing was 8·3% to the Conservatives, and in the other Wolverhampton seat it was 8·7%. Labour lost Cannock (Jenny Lee's seat) with a 10·7% swing, but at Rugby there was a 2·6% swing *to* Labour. In Scotland, the South Angus constituency swung 2·8% to Labour, just as in 1966 it had swung to the Conservatives, again against the national trend. In seats contested by the Liberals, the swing to the Conservatives (4·4%) was lower than in seats not contested by the Liberals (5·2%), suggesting that the Liberal 'intervention' helped the Conservatives. On the whole, however, the main feature of the swing in the 1970 election was the general uniformity of the movement towards the Conservatives.

TABLE XIV

1970 General Election Result by Region

| | Seats | | | | % Votes | | | |
	Con.	Lab.	Lib.	Other	Con.	Lab.	Lib.	Other
England	292	216	2	1	48·4	43·2	7·9	0·5
Scotland	23	44	3	1	38·0	44·5	5·5	12·0
Wales	7	27	1	1	27·7	51·6	6·8	13·9
Northern Ireland	8	—	—	4	54·2	12·6	1·5	31·7
United Kingdom	330	287	6	7	46·4	42·9	7·5	3·2

Although the Government secured an overall majority of 22 seats in the Commons, it did not win an absolute majority of the electoral votes. The only elections in this century when the Government did receive 50% of the votes cast were in 1900 and 1906, before the Labour Party emerged as a serious electoral force, and in 1931 and 1935, when the Government was a National Coalition of Conservatives and some Labour and Liberal elements (though in 1931 the Conservatives alone did receive more than half the total votes). The inability of the Labour or Conservative Parties to win 50% of the total poll at any election since 1951 has been due to the existence of a substantial following for the Liberal Party and other minor parties. The only way either of the two main parties could secure more than half of the national vote would be by a landslide win (even the Labour landslide of 1945 was based on only 48% of the votes), or by the elimination of the minor parties from the scene. This could result from a severe decline in the fortunes of the Liberals and other minor parties, or it could be achieved by limiting the electoral choice to two alternatives, Government and Opposition, either unofficially by means of electoral pacts between the parties, or officially by means of an electoral law. It can be argued that this would be logical, in that in Parliament issues and divisions resolve themselves into a straight choice between supporting or opposing the Government, and that this situation should be mirrored in the choice before the electorate. None of these possible developments seems to be imminent, however, despite the demands over the years for a Lib.–Lab. 'Radical Alliance'.

*   *   *

The anomaly of a Government with an absolute majority of seats in the House, based on a minority of votes in the country, is reflected in many individual constituencies, in that many MPs are elected without receiving a majority of the votes cast in their constituency. In Colne Valley, for example, the 1970 result was:

Clark	Lab.	18,896	39·9%
Wainwright	Lib.	18,040	38·1%
Davy	Con.	10,417	21·9%
Lab. majority		856	1.8%

At Wallasey the result was:

Marples	Con.	24,283	44·9%
Wells	Lab.	21,172	39·2%
Evans	Lib.	5,577	10·3%
Hill	Ind.	2,946	5·4%
Con. majority		3,111	5·7%

The election of a number of candidates on a minority vote results from the present electoral system, whereby the voter merely indicates his first preference on the ballot paper (the 'spot vote' method),[1] and to be elected a candidate merely has to get more votes than any other candidate (the simple majority, or relative majority, or 'first past the post' method). This system does not work entirely satisfactorily when there are more than two candidates in a constituency, as with three or more candidates the votes given to the defeated candidates can exceed the votes given to the winner.[2] In such cases the question is raised of what would have been the effect if the contest had been limited to the two main contestants. There need not necessarily have been any change in the constituency result, and in the example of Wallasey quoted above, most of the Liberals and Independents faced with a straight choice between Labour and Conservative candidates, might well have voted Conservative and thus have increased the majority. In this way a minority seat of this type can be much 'safer' than a marginal seat won in a straight fight. However, there is no guarantee that this would have happened, and most of the Liberal and Independent voters in Wallasey might well have preferred the Labour to the Conservative candidate, while in Colne Valley the vast majority of Conservative voters would almost certainly have preferred the Liberal to the Labour candidate.

In elections like 1970, which are quite closely fought, the result could be decided by the effect of the minor parties on the main parties' votes. An absolute majority for each winning candidate could be achieved by limiting the contest in each constituency to two candidates by one of the means suggested above, though the practicality of this can be questioned. Alternatively, the electoral system could be changed to introduce a second ballot if no absolute majority is achieved on the first ballot. At American Party Conventions to select Presidential candidates, an unlimited number of ballots are held until one candidate receives an absolute majority, and the leader of the Labour Party is elected by means of a limited number of

[1] See C. R. Bagley, 'Does Candidates' Position on the Ballot Paper Influence Voters' Choice?', *Parl. Aff.* 1965–6, pp. 162–74.

[2] See W. S. Livingston, 'Minor Parties and Minority MPs 1945–55', *WPQ* 1959, pp. 1017–38; W. S. Livingston, 'British General Elections and the Two Party System 1945–55', *MJPS* 1959, pp. 168–88.

ballots, one candidate withdrawing after each ballot, until an absolute majority is achieved. These systems are perhaps unsuitable for a general election, in that they can lead to a considerable number of ballots, but much the same effect as the second ballot can be achieved by means of the Alternative Vote, whereby the elector indicates his order of preference for the candidates by placing numbers opposite their names on the ballot papers. If no candidate receives 50% of the votes on the first count, the bottom candidate is eliminated and the votes that were given to him are re-allocated according to the second preferences among the remaining candidates. This process is continued until an absolute majority for one candidate is achieved. This is more practical for a general election than is the second ballot, in that it involves two or more counts, but only one poll, though of course it does not allow for second thoughts by the electorate after the initial count. A provision for the introduction of the Alternative Vote was included in the Representation of the People Bill 1918, only to be removed during the passage of the Bill through the Lords. It was discussed but rejected by the Speaker's Conference in 1930,[1] but it was nevertheless included in the Government Bill of that year. The House of Lords opposed the Bill, however, and it was lost with the fall of the Labour Government in 1931. After 1918, some of the University seats used the Alternative Vote, and recently the Liberal Party and the Electoral Reform Society have campaigned for its adoption.

The Alternative Vote could be grafted on to the present system without too much difficulty, and unlike many proposed electoral reforms, the voting and counting processes are easy for the electorate to understand and are easy to operate. In the present party situation the Alternative Vote would probably benefit the minor parties, and the Liberal Party in particular, in that the minor parties would have a better chance than at present of attracting the first preference votes of their potential supporters. A first preference vote for a minor party candidate could be accompanied by a second preference choice between the two major parties, so that no votes would be 'wasted' as is often said of Liberal votes at present. In those constituencies

[1] Report of the Speaker's Conference on Electoral Reform, Cmd. 3636 (1930).

where an absolute majority was not achieved on the first count, and where the Liberal (or SNP or Plaid Cymru candidate in Scotland or Wales) managed to come second to the Labour or Conservative candidate on the first count, the Liberal would probably win, in that the Liberal would normally take all or most of the second preferences of the eliminated Conservative or Labour candidate. Further, the Liberal cause would benefit in that the Labour and Conservative Parties would have to court potential Liberal voters for their second preferences. Thus the introduction of the Alternative Vote would probably accentuate tendencies towards moderation in the two main parties—for good or ill. However, while ensuring that in each constituency the winning candidate received at least 50% of the votes, the introduction of the Alternative Vote would do nothing to solve the problem of the *Government* elected on a minority vote, and indeed it would probably add to the problem by increasing the size of the Liberal vote.[1]

Proportional Representation

Though the Conservative Party did not receive an absolute majority of the total votes cast in 1970, it did win a clear majority of the seats in the House.[2] The number of seats won by the respective parties was out of all proportion to their share of the votes, and as can be seen from Table XIII, the Conservative Party was greatly over-represented in the Commons in proportion to its share of the vote, the Liberals were greatly under-represented, and Labour was slightly over-represented. One of the things that causes distortion between votes and seats is the fact that constituencies are not the same size (and are not meant to be the same size, as factors other than a strict population ratio are used to determine electoral boundaries). Even with precisely equal electoral districts, however, proportional representation in the House of Commons would still not result, as it is the 'first past the post' system, with its discrimination against the minor parties, that is the main factor producing the distortion.

[1] See P. M. Williams, 'Two Notes on the British Electoral System', *Parl. Aff.* 1966-7, pp. 13-30.

[2] See J. C. March, 'Party Legislative Representation as a Function of Election Results', *POQ 1958*, pp. 521-43.

In 1910, the Royal Commission on Electoral Systems[1] observed that there was a pattern in British election results, whereby in a contest between two parties, the proportion of seats that the winning party received would be the cube of the proportion of votes that it received: if it got twice as many votes as the other party, it would receive eight times as many seats as the other party. Academic interest in the 'Cube Law' revived in the nineteen-fifties, and in the general elections of 1950 and 1951 the Cube Law pattern emerged fairly clearly, providing that allowance is made for some complications caused by the presence of minor parties, and by seats won by very big majorities.[2] In more recent elections, however, the principle has been less clearly observable, and consequently it has received much less attention than it did in the nineteen-fifties. Nevertheless, the general principle remains of a distortion between votes and seats in favour of the winning party at a general election, with the discrimination against the smaller parties increasing as their voting strength diminishes.

In the elections of the nineteen-fifties, the distortion between votes and seats was increased by the existence of an anti-Labour 'bias' within the electoral system. Until 1948 there was a slight pro-Labour 'bias', in that the Conservatives had to poll more votes than Labour in order to win the same number of seats. As a result of the 1948 redistribution of seats, however, the situation was reversed, and there emerged an anti-Labour bias of about 2% (equivalent to some 25 seats). Thus at the 1951 election Labour received more votes than the Conservatives (13,911,000 to 13,708,000) but won 27 fewer seats, just as at the 1929 election the Conservatives received nearly 300,000 more votes than Labour, but won fewer seats. These distortions are not entirely explained by the return of some unopposed candidates. The anti-Labour bias after 1948 was partly caused by the fact that rural constituencies, which the Conservatives dominate, are smaller (and thus need fewer votes to win them) than the Labour-dominated urban constituencies, though population movements after 1948 did reduce the effect of this factor.

---

[1] Report of the Royal Commission on Electoral Systems, Cd. 5163 (1910).
[2] For details see D. E. Butler, *The British Electoral System Since 1918*, London 1963, pp. 194–204; M. G. Kendall and A. Stuart, 'The Law of the Cubic Proportion in Election Results', *BJS* 1950, pp. 183–96.

However, the anti-Labour bias was also a result of the fact that in the industrial areas, where there are a number of safe Labour seats, Labour builds up large and surplus majorities which add to the total Labour vote without contributing to the election of any more Labour candidates. This affects both main parties, but Labour and the industrial constituencies particularly, and it would remain even with electoral districts of precisely equal size. At the 1959 election the anti-Labour bias was reduced, and in the last three elections it was not evident at all, partly as a result of population movements in the nineteen-fifties and 'sixties, and partly because turnout of Labour voters in safe Labour seats was lower than elsewhere.[1] With the new constituencies, based to some extent on the over-representation of rural areas, it is possible that in the elections of the nineteen-seventies the Conservatives will enjoy, as in the nineteen-fifties, a 'bonus' of some 1% to 3%.

*   *   *

Because, in the electoral system as it operates at present, there is no straightforward and simple relationship between the votes received and the seats won by the parties, the question arises of whether the system should be altered to achieve a more proportional relationship between votes and seats. Proportional representation, which is a principle rather than a system (all systems having some degree of proportionality), seeks to establish an exact relationship between electoral opinion and its representation in the legislature by allocating seats to the parties in direct proportion to the votes they receive, a party with two-thirds of the total national vote receiving two-thirds of the seats.

Different degrees of proportional representation can be achieved by different voting and counting methods, and there is no one universally accepted system.[2] The ultimate and only precise means of achieving direct proportionality is to have only one constituency, composed of the whole country, with the

[1] See Butler and Rose, 1959, p. 240; Butler and King, 1964, p. 357; Butler and King, 1966, p. 272.

[2] For an analysis of the different systems see Mackenzie, *Free Elections*; Institute of Electoral Research, *Parliaments and Electoral Systems*, London 1962. For a more detailed analysis see E. Lakeman and J. D. Lambert, *Voting in Democracies*, London 1959, and Ross, *Elections and Electors*.

parties presenting lists of candidates and the electors voting not for individual candidates, but for the whole party list. Seats are then allocated to the parties in proportion to the votes received by each party list. This ultimate situation of having one national constituency applies nowhere in the world at present (though the Israeli electoral system comes closest to it), and advocates of the system usually seek constituencies of five to seven members in an attempt to reconcile the principle of proportional representation with the maintenance of ties between representatives and constituencies. With constituencies of this size, various mathematical formulae are used to determine precisely how many seats each party is entitled to. The party list system is popular on the continent of Europe, and Belgium, the Netherlands, Switzerland, and the Scandinavian countries are among those that operate variations of the system.

The Single Transferable Vote is an alternative to the party list. Here the electorate in multi-member constituencies vote in the same way as with the Alternative Vote, listing the individual candidates in order of preference. In the counting of the votes the principle that applies is that the candidate only needs a certain number, or 'quota', of votes to be elected, and any votes that he receives beyond this figure are surplus, and serve only to build up an unnecessary majority. Once the candidate has received the quota necessary to secure his election, the 'surplus' votes are redistributed among the other candidates according to second preferences. As with party list systems, there are several variations based on the procedures used to determine the quota, count the votes, and redistribute the surplus votes. One version of the system operates in Eire at present. The adoption of STV in Britain was advocated by the Speaker's Conference on Electoral Reform in 1917,[1] and unsuccessful attempts were made to incorporate it in the Representation of the People Bill 1917. STV was used, however, for some of the University seats between 1918 and 1948. It has been claimed that if STV did operate in Britain in five-member constituencies (as is most generally advocated), a precise ratio between votes and seats would still not be achieved, while the Liberal Party would need to get 16% of the national poll in

[1] Report of the Speaker's Conference on Electoral Reform, Cd. 8463 (1917).

order to benefit markedly[1]—a percentage that the Liberals have achieved at no election since the war. Nevertheless, the introduction into Britain of one of these systems would result in a greater degree of proportionality than is achieved at present.

There are, however, a number of things to be said in favour of the electoral system as it operates at present. It has the merit of simplicity, whereas the counting methods (if not the voting methods) of many of the alternatives are difficult to understand. It is perhaps not absolutely necessary for the voter to be able to understand the counting methods that are used, as he is concerned only with the voting process, but in order that justice may be seen to be done there is much to be said for a system that is simple to understand in all its processes. Also, by over-representing in the Commons the two main parties, and the winning party in particular, the present system helps to produce Governments secure in their control of the House. The elections of 1910 (January and December), 1923, and 1929 did not produce a clear majority in the House for one party, and those of 1950 and 1964 provided the Labour Party with only a small majority, but in the other thirteen elections of this century the winning party did secure a clear absolute majority in the House, even though it did not necessarily receive an absolute majority of electoral votes. If seats in the Commons had been distributed between the parties strictly in proportion to votes, only in 1900, 1906, 1931, and 1935 would the Government have had the security of tenure that goes with an overall party majority in the Commons.

The merits of 'strong' government can be over-stated, and much can be said in favour of Coalition Governments, or Governments based on the support of more than one party. It must be realized, however, that the general under-representation of the Opposition parties in the Commons helps to give to Governments the strength and stability that is often quoted as being one of the outstanding features of the British political system.[2] While the proportional representation in the Commons of the Liberal and minor parties may be ethically desirable, it

[1] Butler, p. 190.
[2] See, however, R. Rose, 'Parties, Factions and Tendencies in Britain' *PS* 1964, pp. 33–46.

would make it unlikely that one party would be able to achieve an overall majority in the Commons, and would give to the minor parties a bargaining power out of all proportion to their electoral strength. Also, one merit of single-member constituencies, whatever their drawbacks, is that each member represents a specific constituency, and does not share his constituency duties with any other member. Thus there is achieved in the British system a closer contact between an MP and his constituents than can be achieved with the multi-member constituencies that are necessary for party list or STV systems.

To change the present system in an attempt to remove its deficiencies and achieve a greater degree of proportional representation, would inevitably endanger some of the system's merits. Thus with the question of whether or not to alter the electoral system, the choice can only be between two imperfect solutions. One factor that militates against any change is that the present system benefits the two major parties, and the Government party particularly. It is unlikely that any party will alter a system that works to its advantage, unless it is prepared to sacrifice current advantage and look ahead to a time when, in opposition, its fortunes may be on the decline.

3

The Social Structure
of the Parties

AN EXAMINATION of the social structure of the political parties
in Britain must extend to all levels of party structure and
support, from those members of the community whose political
activity goes no further than voting at elections, to the party
members, activists, and local leaders, and to the party's candidates, MPs, and Parliamentary leaders.

The Electors

The considerations which cause an elector to vote for one
party rather than another are difficult to gauge with precision.
Definite information is limited, although it is increasing,[1] while
there seems to be general agreement among students of voting
behaviour that electoral opinions tend to be based on irrational
and often inconsistent considerations. Nevertheless, some general assessments can be made of the factors which influence
voting behaviour, and also of the way in which different
sections of the community distribute their support among the
parties. The personal qualities of a candidate would not seem
to be major factors in determining voting behaviour. In by-
elections, when a Government is not being elected, the qualities
of the candidates can be important, and in the 1964 general
election, and to a lesser extent in 1966 and 1970, there was
evidence to suggest that some of the leading figures of all parties

[1] The most recent major study is D. E. Butler and D. Stokes, *Political
Change in Britain*, London 1969. See also P. G. J. Pulzer, *Political Representation and Elections in Britain*, London 1968.

gained (or lost) votes through their personal appeal (or lack of it).[1] On the whole, however, it is probably true that the personal appeal of a candidate is worth less than 500 votes in an average constituency. The personal appeal of the party leader would seem to be of greater significance for a party's electoral success, however. This is perhaps epitomized in the personal appeal of Harold Macmillan in 1959, and of Harold Wilson in 1966.[2] On the other hand, it is probably fair to say that the Conservatives lost in 1945, and Labour in 1970, despite having more dynamic and personally popular leaders than the Opposition. Linked with this is the impression that the electorate has of the general competence of the Government and Opposition leaders as a whole, but specific policy issues are probably not of major significance in determining electoral support, whether the issues be long-established aspects of party policy, or merely transitory issues that emerge during an election campaign. It is unlikely that a voter will agree with every aspect of the policy of the party he supports, and surveys have revealed that a voter may support a party while disagreeing with some fundamental aspect of its policy. Often a voter will change his own view to conform with party policy, rather than change his party allegiance.

Of much greater significance in Britain is the question of party 'image'.[3] The general impression that an elector has of a party is based on the party's attitudes to an accumulation of issues. It may be felt for example that the Labour Party is 'soft' and the Conservative Party is 'tough' on foreign affairs or defence policy, or that the Labour Party is 'for the working man', while the Conservatives are 'for big business'. Nevertheless, no matter how vague or general the elector's impression of a party may be, this image is readily accepted today as being of much greater significance in determining electoral loyalties than any identification of the parties with individual policy issues.[4]

The forces that mould an elector's attitude to a party, and

[1] Butler and King, 1964, p. 147, and Butler and King, 1966, p. 179. See also Williams, *Parl. Aff.* 1966–7.

[2] See above, p. 50.

[3] P. Crane, 'What's in a Party Image?', *PQ* 1959, pp. 230–43.

[4] See above, p. 51.

which cause him to prefer the image of one party to that of another, arise from various social, economic, demographic, regional, and religious considerations. In Britain the chief determinants of voting behaviour would seem to be family and

TABLE XV

*Voting Intention, 1964 and 1966 General Elections: Social Class**

1964	All	Middle class AB (10%)	Lower middle C1 (20%)	Skilled working C2 (39%)	Unskilled 'very poor' DE (31%)
Con.	43	75	61	34	31
Lab.	45	9	25	54	59
Lib.	11	15	14	11	9
Other	1	1	1	1	1
1966		(12%)	(22%)	(37%)	(29%)
Con.	41	72	59	32	26
Lab.	49	15	30	58	65
Lib.	9	11	10	8	7
Other	1	1	1	1	2

* Social groupings used by the Registrar General in Census returns

Source: Based on tables in Butler and King, 1964, p. 296; Butler and King, 1966, p. 264

social factors, and it is generally accepted that the most significant division in electoral loyalties is that the well-to-do members of the community predominantly vote Conservative, while those of a lower social status and a lower income group tend to vote Labour.[1] For example, findings in some recent elections suggest that the Conservatives have the support of the vast majority of middle- and lower-class middle voters (who make

[1] See M. Abrams, 'Social Class and British Politics', *POQ* 1961, pp. 342–51; M. Abrams, 'Social Trends and Electoral Behaviour', *BJS* 1962, pp. 228–42; R. Rose, *Politics in England*, London 1965, Ch. 3 and 4.

up about a third of the electorate), while Labour has the support of most of the skilled and unskilled working class (who make up about two-thirds of the electorate). The Liberals tend to draw a bigger percentage of votes from the middle class than from the working class, although the fluctuation in their support between the various classes is not as great as for the two main parties.

Using general elections as case studies of voting behaviour can be dangerous, in that voting intentions can fluctuate to some extent from one general election to another.[1] At the same time, comparisons between one general election and another are complicated by the changes that inevitably occur over the years in the social structure of the community. Nevertheless, Table XV shows that compared with 1964, Labour's support in 1966 increased in all the social groups, but particularly among the middle class, with Labour's advance here being made to a large extent at the expense of the Liberals. At the same time, the underlying distribution of the votes in the various social groupings remained basically the same, and more long term comparisons suggest that these patterns have remained fairly constant over the last twenty-five years.

Although electoral divisions along class lines remain quite distinct, it is also the case that a minority (about 20%) of middle-class electors vote Labour, while a more substantial minority (about 30%) of working-class electors vote Conservative. These exceptions to rigid class voting alignments prevent a strictly Marxian interpretation of British electoral behaviour. The opponents of the nineteenth-century franchise extensions argued that as the working-class made up the vast majority of the population, any party that had complete, or almost complete, working-class electoral support could expect to be permanently in power. In fact, however, the retention of a large proportion of working-class support by the Conservative Party has prevented any such development in modern Britain. Also, the existence of a substantial working-class Conservative vote enables the Conservative Party to claim that it is more truly representative (at least at an electoral level) of the different social groups within the community than is the Labour Party, for while the middle-class Labour vote accounts for only a

[1] See below, p. 77.

small proportion (about 15%) of the total Labour vote, the working-class Conservative vote accounts for about 50% of the total Conservative vote. Thus the vital factor in electoral behaviour in Britain is the extent to which electoral support for the parties does *not* follow rigid class lines.

Various considerations can be advanced to explain these deviations from a strict class–party voting alignment in Britain.[1] The Conservative working-class vote is undoubtedly to some extent a product of feelings of deference among some members of the working class towards the Conservative Party. British society is notoriously more class-conscious and deferential in its political attitudes than are most comparable nations,[2] and clearly the Conservative Party has benefited from the view held by some working-class voters that the party's public school–Oxbridge–big business image gives it a monopoly of talent and of political expertise. At the same time, many Conservative policy attitudes are more attractive to members of the working class than are Labour attitudes. On subjects like capital punishment and crime generally, the 'firm' line that the Conservative Party tends to adopt can have more appeal for working-class voters than Labour's 'mild' or 'intellectual' approach. Further, the voting habits of many older working-class voters were formed in the years before the Labour Party emerged as one of the two main parties. In the nineteen-fifties the identification of Conservative Governments with the growth of material prosperity provided an additional basis for working-class Conservative support, although steady advances in material prosperity under Labour Governments would presumably lead to a compensating increase in Labour's working-class following.

Self-assigned social position can be very different from actual social position, and many actual members of the working class regard themselves as belonging to the middle class, and adopt middle-class attitudes (including political attitudes) as a consequence.[3] Also, the borderlines between social classes are

[1] See, for example, J. Bonham, *The Middle Class Vote*, London 1954; Rose, *Studies in British Politics*, Ch. 1; H. J. Eysenck, *The Psychology of Politics*, London 1954.

[2] See Alford, *Party and Society*, Ch. 6; E. A. Nordlinger, *The Working Class Tories*, London 1967.

[3] W. G. Runciman, ' "Embourgeoisement", Self-Rated Class and Party Preference', *SR* 1964, pp. 137–54.

inevitably blurred, and those situated on the social or economic borderline between the working class and the middle class often tend to adopt middle-class attitudes (such as voting Conservative) in an attempt to identify themselves with that class rather than with the working class. In this sense, voting Conservative can be seen as a means of gaining social prestige, and this is perhaps particularly the case among women. Pressure provided by family background, neighbourhood, and place of employment are also significant in this context. Working-class Conservative parents inevitably seek to persuade their children to vote Conservative. Surveys have suggested that a member of the working class who lives in a predominantly middle-class area is less likely to vote Labour than a worker who lives in a working-class area. Similarly, factory workers have been found to be more likely to vote Labour than workers who do not work in close proximity to large numbers of other workers. Surveys have also indicated that workers who do not belong to a trade union are less likely to vote Labour than are trade unionists. NOP found that in 1964, of all their analyses of the electors, whether by class, age, sex, locality, or religion, the most common characteristic of Labour voters was membership of a trade union, and 62% of all Labour voters had trade union connections.[1]

Demographic factors in voting behaviour can cut across class alignments, and thus help to explain the source of the working-class Conservative vote. As is revealed in more detail below,[2] women are more inclined to vote Conservative than are men, while middle-aged and older electors are more likely to vote Conservative than are the younger voters—and this applies to the working class as well as to voters in general. Similarly, with regard to regional and religious factors, Anglicans (including working-class Anglicans) have been found to be more likely than Nonconformists to vote Conservative, while electors (and thus workers) in areas like the midlands, south, and south-east of England, have been found to be more likely to vote Conservative than workers in, say, Wales, Scotland, or northern England. In Northern Ireland, religious divisions override class divisions.

[1] Butler and King, 1964, p. 296.
[2] p. 74.

Thus various factors can be advanced to explain the Conservative Party's working-class support, and many of these factors can also be used in reverse to explain the middle-class Labour vote. A member of the middle class whose parents were working class, or who lives in a predominantly working-class area, is more likely to vote Labour than someone with a completely middle-class background. Some members of the middle class, like school teachers or welfare officers, who are employed in working-class surroundings and are thus subject daily to working-class influences, are more likely to vote Labour than are members of the middle class who come in contact with no such influence. At the same time, many of the policy attitudes of the Labour Party that antagonize some sections of the working class, prove to be more acceptable to liberal-minded members of the middle class. Also, as is discussed below,[1] although the Labour Party derives its electoral support primarily from the working class, the middle class is in a majority within the Labour Party at a Parliamentary and Ministerial level, where policies are formulated.

During the nineteen-sixties, it was questioned whether major and permanent changes were taking place in the voting habits of the social classes.[2] During the nineteen-fifties Labour support declined, reaching its lowest electoral level in 1959. It was suggested that because (through the spread of affluence) the pro-Conservative middle class was growing in numbers, and the pro-Labour working class was becoming smaller, a permanent decline in Labour's voting strength was thereby inevitable. In 1964 (although not in 1966) NOP found that Labour support had declined further among the working class,[3] but at the same time in 1964, and again in 1966, Labour support rose markedly among the middle class.[4] It may be that these are merely temporary trends, perhaps counteracting the trends of the nineteen-fifties, or it may be that they represent a fundamental realignment of voting tendencies. It is too early as

[1] p. 87.
[2] See, for example, J. H. Goldthorpe and D. Lockwood, 'Affluence and British Class Structure', *SR* 1963, pp. 133–63; R. Fletcher, 'Social Change in Britain', *PQ* 1963, pp. 399–410.
[3] Butler and King, 1964, p. 297.
[4] See Table XII.

yet to say with any certainty, but it is clear that such changes as have taken place in voting patterns in recent elections have been towards a loosening rather than a hardening of strict class-party alignments.

*   *   *

Although socio-economic factors form the basis of party loyalties in Britain, other factors are clearly involved. Women are much more inclined than men to vote Conservative. Table XVI shows that in 1964 and 1966 Conservative support was considerably greater among women than among men, and Labour support greater among men. This is probably typical of all post-war elections, and perhaps all elections in the half century since women received the vote. It may be that women are more attracted than men towards the Conservative Party for social reasons, or it may be that they are more conservative

TABLE XVI

Voting Intention, 1964 and 1966 General Elections: by Sex and Age Group

1964	All	Men	Women	21–24	25–34	35–44	45–54	55–64	65 plus
Con.	43	40	46	39	40	38	43	45	51
Lab.	45	48	42	49	48	48	44	43	38
Lib.	11	11	12	11	11	13	12	12	10
Other	1	1	1	1	1	1	1	1	1
1966									
Con.	41	38	45	41	37	38	42	45	47
Lab.	49	52	45	51	55	51	47	46	43
Lib.	9	8	9	8	7	10	10	8	8
Other	1	2	1	—	1	1	1	1	2

Source: Based on tables in Butler and King, 1964, p. 296; Butler and King, 1966, p. 264

by nature than are men. On the other hand, women are not subject to the same extent as men to the pressures of factory working conditions and trade union membership, which are regarded as major factors determining Labour's electoral support. Also, women tend to live longer than men, and the older age groups tend to be relatively more Conservative than the younger age groups.

With regard to the relationship between age and voting patterns, Table XVI suggests that Labour support is greater among the younger voters (that is, voters under forty-five) than among the older age groups, with the Conservative pattern the reverse of this. These patterns seem to confirm the popular picture of radical youth and conservative old age. The more likely explanation, however, is that voting habits for a lifetime are fashioned in one's youth, and that differences that exist in party support between the age groups are not so much a result of changes in outlook that take place between youth and old age, but are rather a result of different generations forming, and retaining throughout their lives, strong attachments to one party rather than another. Thus the relative Conservative strength among the older age groups can be attributed to the political influences to which the members of this age group were subjected during their formative years, in the period of Conservative ascendancy and Labour and Liberal failure before 1939. Similarly, the greater level of support that the Labour Party enjoys among the younger voters can perhaps be attributed to the influence of the post-war period when Labour's political record has been much better than its record between the wars.

While religion is not a major political issue in Britain as a whole, in certain areas of Britain religion is a big factor (and in some cases is the biggest factor) in determining voting behaviour. In Wales, the strength of religious nonconformity accounts to some extent for Labour and Liberal success there, the Labour Party to some extent inheriting the Liberal Party's nineteenth-century nonconformist traditions. In Ulster particularly, where Catholic–Protestant divisions are marked, and in cities like Glasgow and Liverpool where large sections of the population are of Irish–Catholic extraction, religious factors cut across class factors in determining party alignments. Surveys in Glasgow, for example, found that Catholics of all social classes voted predominantly Labour, while working-class Protestants tended to vote Conservative in much greater proportions than in the United Kingdom as a whole.[1] In the rest of Britain, and especially in the south of England, religion is of less electoral significance, though some general relationship is evident between religion and voting patterns. In Bristol North East in 1955, for example, it was found that 62% of Conservative voters were Anglicans, compared with 42% of Labour voters, while 21% of Conservative voters were Roman Catholics or Nonconformists, compared with 29% of Labour voters.[2] Allowance has to be made for an overlap between religious and class factors, with Anglicans more than Nonconformists perhaps tending to be members of the middle class, but nevertheless, to some extent the relationship between religion and voting reflects the traditional picture of the Conservative Party as the party of the Established Church, and the Labour Party as the party of Nonconformity and of those of no religion.

It has already been noted that apart from Northern Ireland, regional issues do not play a major part in British national politics,[3] and that a feature of British elections is normally the uniformity of the swing from one party to another throughout the country. This is not to say, however, that support for each party is spread equally throughout the country, and (as is shown in Table XIV) there are clear differences in party strength from one region to another. The Ulster Unionists are dominant in Northern Ireland, and in 1970, as at every election since 1945, won a majority of seats there. In Great Britain in 1970, again as at every election since 1945, Labour won a much bigger proportion of seats in Scotland and Wales than in England. The differences in party strength between England, Scotland, and Wales are largely a result of Labour's urban strength and the Conservatives' rural dominance, which itself is a mirror of the socio-economic factors that are the basis of party support in Britain. Nevertheless, within the broad class alignments that are the basis of voting behaviour, some regional variations do exist. In 1961 the British Institute of Public

---

[1] I. Budge and D. W. Urwin, *Scottish Political Behaviour*, London 1966.

[2] R. S. Milne and H. C. Mackenzie, *Marginal Seat*, London 1958, p. 65.

[3] See above, pp. 13 and 56.

TABLE XVII

Factors in British Voting Behaviour

Main factors involved, in approximate order of significance	Labour voters	Conservative voters	Liberal voters
Trade union membership	Members	Non-members	Non-members
Social class	Working class	Middle class	Middle class
Income	Low	High	High
Age	Under 40s	Over 50s	Mixed
Sex	Men	Women	Both
Rural/urban	Urban	Rural	Rural
Region	Wales, Scotland N. England	N. Ireland, Midlands, South and East England	Wales, Scotland, South-west England
Religion	Nonconformist and no religion	Anglican	Nonconformist

Opinion found that the Conservative Party tended to get more working-class support in the south and south-west of England than elsewhere, while Labour got more middle-class support than elsewhere in Wales and the north-east of England.[1] On the other hand, the alignment between Labour and the working class, and between the Conservatives and the middle class, was found to be more pronounced in Yorkshire and East Anglia than in the rest of the country. Similarly, Liberal support varies quite markedly from region to region, and all six seats won by the Liberals in 1970 were in the 'Celtic Fringe' areas of north Scotland, Wales, and Cornwall. Thus the uniform character of British voting behaviour must not be exaggerated.

Floating Voters and Non-Voters

In the main, voting behaviour in Britain is habitual and ingrained, and elections are won and lost by the transfer of

[1] See Blondel, *Voters, Parties and Leaders*, p. 62.

allegiance of only a limited number of 'floating' voters.[1] Over
the eight general elections since 1945, which include the landslide Labour win of 1945 and the heavy Labour defeat in 1959,
Labour's share of the vote only fluctuated from 48·3% to
42·9%, and the Conservative share from 49·7% to 39·8%. The
size of the floating vote, however, is undoubtedly much bigger
than is suggested by these figures, and although it is very difficult to gauge the figure precisely, it has been authoritatively
claimed that as many as a quarter of the electorate change their
voting allegiance from one general election to another.[2]

Some floating voters are rational and reasonable persons who
are closely interested in political matters but are not committed
to one particular party, while others are people who are not
greatly interested in politics. Not all changes in voting habits
are represented by a straight transfer of loyalties from Labour
to Conservative, or vice versa. Someone who voted Conservative
in 1970 may well have abstained in 1966, or have voted for
a Liberal or some other minor party candidate. In Bristol
North East in 1955, for example, only one-fifth of the increase
in the Conservative poll came from Labour voters of 1951.[3]
Also, many people change their voting habits against the general
tide, and thus reduce the size of the overall swing. In addition
to the people who do change their party allegiance from one
general election to another, there are many people who may
well change their loyalties at a by-election or a local government election, and who may tell public opinion pollsters that
they intend to change their loyalties at a general election, but
who return to their original voting habits when polling day
arrives. Death and other factors produce a change in the
electoral register of about one-sixth every ten years, so that the
personnel of the Conservative vote in 1970 was substantially
different from the personnel of the 1945 or 1950 Conservative
vote. Thus behind the stability and consistency of British voting
behaviour, it is necessary to recognize the existence of the

[1] See R. S. Milne and H. C. Mackenzie, 'The Floating Vote', *PS* 1955,
pp. 65–8; W. H. Morris Jones, 'In Defence of Apathy: Some Doubts on the
Duty to Vote', *PS* 1954, pp. 25–37; R. J. Benewick (et al.), 'The Floating
Voter and the Liberal View as Representation', *PS* 1969, pp. 177–95.

[2] See Blondel, *Voters, Parties and Leaders*, p. 71.

[3] Milne and Mackenzie, *Marginal Seat*, p. 42.

floating voters, the 'almost floaters', and the presence of new voters on the electoral register each year.

Non-voters are often closely linked with the floating voters. In 1970 over a quarter of the electorate did not vote, and at general elections since 1945 the proportion of non-voters has ranged from 16% to 28%. Some abstentions can be accounted for by the limitations of the electoral register, which is inevitably out of date as soon as it is compiled, and by the Y voters who are included on the register but who cannot vote if the election is held before October 2nd.[1] These administrative factors can account for some 5% to 10% of the non-voters. Others can perhaps be accounted for by Liberals (or Communists or other minor party supporters) who prefer to abstain rather than vote for another party's candidate in constituencies which their party does not contest. It is difficult to measure precisely the effect of this factor, and certainly in 1970 there was no marked difference in turnout between constituencies in which Liberals stood, and constituencies contested only by Labour and Conservative candidates.

Some uncommitted electors abstain merely because they cannot decide whom to support. Others abstain because they are politically disillusioned, either permanently, like the idealists and the cynics, or temporarily, like some Conservatives in 1966 and some Labour supporters in 1970, who felt that on that particular occasion their party did not deserve their vote. Other abstentions can be accounted for by people who cannot be bothered to vote, perhaps because of bad weather on polling day, or because of some other similar consideration. Similarly, some people are prevented from voting by ill health or other accidental factors, although postal and proxy voting reduces the effect of this. Undoubtedly some people abstain because they feel that their vote is not needed as the election result is certain, either nationally or in their constituency. In more recent elections the forecasts of the opinion polls have probably added to this, especially in elections like 1966 and 1970, when a Labour victory seemed likely during the campaign. It may be that in 1970 the Conservatives benefited from an assumption among some Labour supporters that their party could win without their support. Again, a low turnout in safe constituen-

[1] For more details see above, p. 38.

cies can be partly a result of less activity on the part of party election machines in getting supporters to the poll. Finally, it may be noted that surveys have revealed that in general, abstentions are more numerous among women than among men, more numerous among the youngest age groups than among the middle-aged, more numerous among non-church-goers than among churchgoers, more numerous among the working class than the middle class, and more numerous among Labour supporters than among Conservatives.

Party Members and Activists[1]

Much less information is available about party members and activists than about voters. In addition, such studies as have been made of the backgrounds and opinions of members and activists, have revealed that considerable variations exist in party composition from one area to another. A Conservative constituency party in a northern industrial town, for example, can be very different in social composition and attitudes from a Conservative constituency party in northern Scotland or in Sussex. From the limited amount of information that is avail-able, it is thus difficult to make assumptions that could apply to the whole country, although some general conclusions can be drawn.

Although the Labour and Conservative parties are the biggest mass parties in the western world, the proportion of active party members is small, and it has been claimed that the pro-portion of active party members today is no greater than it was before 1867.[2] Of the 39,000,000 electors (25,300,000 of whom voted Labour or Conservative in 1970) some 3,000,000 are members of the Conservative Party, less than 1,000,000 are individual members of the Labour Party, and about 5,000,000 are affiliated members of the Labour Party through a trade union. Thus roughly 25% of the electorate are members of the Labour or Conservative Parties, while less than 1% are mem-bers of the Liberal Party. Membership of a political party, how-ever, need not entail political activity, while among the activists, participation may involve leadership through the holding of

[1] See D. R. Berry, *The Sociology of Grass Roots Politics*, London 1970.
[2] Rose, *Politics in England*, p. 93.

some office at a constituency, area, or national level, or it may merely involve frequent or infrequent attendance at party meetings. It has been estimated that of the 9,000,000 or so party members in Britain, only about 1,500,000 (4% of the electorate) take any part at all in party activities, and only about half of these take any regular part.[1] Thus, both parties have a large number of passive members. This is especially true of the Labour Party, with its big but largely inactive trade union membership. Among the 1,000,000 individual Labour Party members the *proportion* of active members is higher than among the 3,000,000 Conservative Party members, although the Conservatives still remain with the larger absolute number of activists.

The distinction which has been noted between the individual constituency party membership of the Labour Party and the affiliated trade union membership, manifests itself in a great number of ways within the party. The trade union membership is large but mainly passive, the individual membership is small but more active. Although trade unionists can 'contract out' of any affiliation with the Labour Party, many who have no real Labour Party sympathies do not bother to contract out, so that among the 5,000,000 affiliated party members there are many who are apathetic, and some who are hostile. The trade union membership is predominantly working class, while the individual membership contains a proportion of the middle class. To a large extent the trade union membership provides the party finances, while the individual membership provides the intellectual leadership. The individual members are often thought of as being more ideological in their political attitudes than the trade union members, who are seen as being largely concerned with bread-and-butter issues. Thus the original fusion of the unions and the socialist societies to form the Labour Party in 1900 is still reflected today in the composition of each local Labour Party.

It is sometimes assumed that if people are sufficiently interested in party politics to join one of the parties, the political attitudes of party members, and of party activists in particular, must tend to be more extreme than the attitudes of the mass of the party voters who are not sufficiently interested to join a

[1] Blondel, *Voters, Parties and Leaders*, p. 94. See also A. H. Birch, *Representative and Responsible Government*, London 1964, p. 193.

party. Studies of the political attitudes of party members, however, tend not to confirm this view. In Glossop, Derbyshire, it was found that Labour members tended to be slightly more 'left wing' than Labour voters, in that the party membership contained a higher proportion of supporters of CND and public ownership than was found among Labour voters, but extreme views were not dominant.[1] Among Conservative members there was no evidence that they were markedly more 'right wing' than Conservative voters. In Newcastle-under-Lyme, Staffordshire, a survey found that the Conservative members tended to be basically moderate in their attitudes, with Labour Party members being only slightly less so, despite being served by a left-wing Labour MP.[2] Studies of the type of resolution proposed by constituency party leaders at party conferences (which can perhaps be taken as indicative of the attitudes of party activists), also indicate that the constituency party leaders are not as extreme in their political attitudes as is often thought.[3]

Studies of the social structure of party membership have revealed that with the Labour Party the members tend to be drawn from the various social classes in much the same proportion as are Labour voters, with the working class being predominant and with the middle class being represented only by a minority. In Glossop for example, it was found that industrial workers made up 77% of Labour voters and 76% of Labour Party members, while business proprietors and professional or managerial workers accounted for 5% of Labour voters and 7% of Labour Party members. Similarly, in Newcastle-under-Lyme, it was found that 77% of Labour Party members were manual workers, 13% were clerical workers, and only 10% were business proprietors or professional or managerial workers. With the Conservative Party on the other hand, businessmen and professional and managerial workers tend to make up a much bigger proportion of party members

---

[1] A. H. Birch, *Small Town Politics*, London 1959, p. 82.

[2] F. Bealey, J. Blondel, and W. P. McCann, *Constituency Politics*, London 1965, p. 274.

[3] R. Rose, 'The Policy Ideas of English Party Activists', *APSR* 1962, pp. 360–71; K. Hindell and P. Williams, 'Scarborough and Blackpool: Analysis of some Votes at the Labour Party Conferences of 1960 and 1961', *PQ* 1962, pp. 306–20.

than of Conservative voters, and in Glossop they accounted for only 27% of Conservative voters, but 47% of Conservative Party members. White collar workers and industrial workers, on the other hand, made up 72% of Conservative voters in Glossop, but they were only 53% of Conservative members. Thus these surveys suggest that the electoral support that the Conservative Party has among the working class does not extend to the same extent to membership of the party, and at a membership level the Conservative Party is not as representative of the various social groups of the community as it is at an electoral level.

Many of the other differences of background that have been noted between Labour and Conservative voters are mirrored among party members. Just as Labour's voting strength is greater among men than among women, so it was found at Newcastle-under-Lyme that men made up 54% of Labour Party members, compared with 45% of Conservative members. Similarly, Labour's electoral strength among Nonconformists, and the Conservative support among Anglicans, is reflected to some extent in the fact that at Newcastle-under-Lyme 82% of Conservative Party members were Anglicans compared with 49% of Labour Party members, while only 28% of Conservative members were Roman Catholics or Nonconformists compared with 40% of Labour members. Similar trends were revealed by a survey in Greenwich.[1] In both parties, however, the party members tend to be drawn mainly from the older age group, and despite the extent of Labour's support among young voters, all the surveys suggest that the Labour Party does not have any markedly greater number of young members than does the Conservative Party. In some ways this perhaps reflects Labour's long-standing failure to develop a youth movement as successful as the Young Conservatives.[2]

Among the active Conservative Party officers, the middle class tends to be even more strongly represented than among the mass of Conservative members. In Glossop, the proportion of businessmen, professional men, and managerial workers was found to be 77% among Conservative Party activists, compared

[1] M. Benney, A. P. Gray, and R. H. Pear, *How People Vote*, London 1956.
[2] P. Abrams and A. Little, 'The Young Activist in British Politics', *BJS* 1965, pp. 315–32.

with 47% among party members, and 27% among Conservative voters. Similarly in Greenwich, 90% of Conservative Party officers were drawn from the middle class (that is, those in the top two of the British Institute of Public Opinion's socio-economic grades of Average Plus, Average, Average Minus, and D Grade). This compared with 77% of party members drawn from the middle class. Only 9% of Conservative Party officers in Greenwich were manual workers (Average Minus grade), and in Glossop only 8% of Conservative leaders were classed as industrial workers. Working-class deference towards the Conservative Party thus extends to the abdication of almost all control over the party's local affairs to the middle class. It was also found in Greenwich that although 57% of Conservative Party members were women, only 25% of the party officers were women.

The similarity between the social composition of Labour voters and Labour Party members is not repeated in the case of Labour Party activists, and the middle class tends to be better represented among Labour leaders than among the rank and file of Labour Party members. Although industrial workers accounted for three-quarters of Labour voters and party members in Glossop, they accounted for only one-third of the party leaders. White collar workers in Glossop were only one-sixth of Labour voters and members, but they accounted for a third of the activists. Professional and managerial workers made up another third of the activists, although they were less than one-tenth of Labour voters and members. Similar trends were found at Greenwich, although the workers made up a bigger proportion (almost half) of the activists.

Thus the social composition of both parties changes considerably from the electoral level to the local leadership level. In both parties the middle-class element forms a much bigger proportion of the local leaders than of the electors, and this tendency for the middle-class element to increase towards the top of the leadership hierarchy is continued among area and regional leaders. Having acknowledged this, however, the difference between the social composition of the two parties remains pronounced at the local leadership level. The vast majority of the Conservative middle-class activists are businessmen, while the Labour middle-class element consists primarily of professional and managerial workers. In particular, teachers and journalists tend to form a large proportion of Labour's local leaders, as they do of Labour MPs, and the Labour Party's intelligentsia is thus very different in composition from the middle-class leadership of the Conservative Party. The increased middle-class representation among the Labour Party's local leadership perhaps gives an overall impression of the mass membership of the Labour Party being led by the party's intellectuals. It must be emphasized, however, that in examining the social structure of the CLPs, only one half of the Labour Party structure is being dealt with. Although the trade unions play an important part in constituency party activities, they also remain as a separate part of the Labour Party structure at all levels of the party organization. The unions, which are of course overwhelmingly working class at a leadership level as well as a membership level, remain as a counterbalance to the middle-class intellectual element that emerges through the constituency parties.

It might perhaps be expected that in socio-economic respects the background of Liberal Party members would be closer to that of Conservative Party members than of Labour Party members. Certainly in Glossop it was found that the occupational background of Liberal Party members was predominantly middle class, and the proportion of industrial workers fell from 64% of Liberal voters, to 34% of party members and 6% of party leaders. Compared with Conservative activists, however, there was among Liberal activists a bigger proportion of professional, managerial, and white collar workers (61% to 30%), and a smaller proportion of businessmen (33% to 62%). At the same time, in Newcastle-under-Lyme men formed an even bigger proportion of Liberal members than of Labour members, and the Liberal Party had an even bigger proportion of Nonconformist members than did the Labour Party. Also, in Newcastle-under-Lyme the Liberals were the 'youngest' party, having a smaller proportion of members aged over 60, and a larger proportion aged under 30, than either of the other parties.

Parliamentary Candidates and MPs

Considerably more information is available regarding the relatively small number of party members who become Parliamentary candidates, and it is possible to examine their educational and occupational background in some detail. In recent elections about two-thirds of Conservative candidates had attended public schools. About half had attended Oxford or Cambridge Universities, while a much smaller proportion had been to other Universities.[1] It is perhaps significant that the proportion who had attended University is smaller than the proportion that had been to public schools, and it is the predominance of public school products that is the most characteristic feature of the social background of Conservative candidates, and also of Conservative MPs and Conservative Ministers. In contrast, in recent elections about a fifth of Labour candidates had attended public schools, while two thirds were from grammar or secondary schools. About half of Labour candidates in recent elections were graduates, the majority from Universities other than Oxford or Cambridge. This is clearly very different from the predominantly public school and Oxbridge pattern of Conservative candidates, but at the same time it is very different from the educational pattern of the mass of the population, of whom only about 3% attend public schools, and only 5% attend University.

Similar differences between the parties emerge with regard to the occupational background of the candidates. In making comparisons between occupational backgrounds, however, some allowance has to be made for the fact that the divisions into occupational groups must be somewhat arbitrary. A candidate may have had more than one occupation, and there is, for example, frequently a big overlap between business and the professions, and in particular between big business and the legal profession and the armed services. In this context, however, it is only the first occupation that is referred to. On this basis usually more than three-quarters of Conservative candidates are drawn from business or the professions, while only about 1% are workers. Of Labour candidates on the other hand, about a fifth are workers, and a half or two-thirds are from the

[1] See Butler and King, 1966, Ch XII.

professions or business. In so far as information is available regarding the religious convictions of the candidates, about a quarter of Labour candidates belong to 'Nonconformist' religious groups (in the broadest sense[1]), as compared with only an eighth of Conservative candidates. This mirrors the general impression gained at an electoral and party membership level of the links between religion and voting patterns, and between religion and party membership. The educational and occupational background of Liberal MPs tends to be much closer to the Conservative than the Labour pattern, with almost half coming from public schools, and some three-quarters being drawn from business or the professions.

As might be expected, many of the patterns that apply to the social backgrounds of the candidates of the respective parties are repeated in the case of the MPs. Thus the majority of the 330 Conservative MPs elected in 1970 had a public school and University education. About 20% attended Eton or Harrow, and a further 30% attended other public schools.[2] Of the rest, less than 1% had only an elementary school education. 53% of Conservative MPs had been to Oxford or Cambridge Universities, and a further 16% had attended other Universities. Of Labour MPs on the other hand, almost a fifth had only an elementary school education, half attended grammar or secondary schools, and less than a tenth attended public schools. A quarter of Labour MPs had been to Oxford or Cambridge Universities, and 40% had no University education.

Similarly, as is shown in Table XVIII, the vast majority of Conservative MPs elected in 1970 had middle class or upper class occupational backgrounds. Almost a third were company directors before entering Parliament, and over a fifth were barristers or solicitors. There were also a large number of farmers, landowners, authors and journalists, while managers, executives, administrators and other business occupations accounted for about 10% of the total. Only one of the 330 had a manual occupation. In marked contrast, almost a third of Labour MPs elected in 1970 were manual workers or party or Trade Union officers, and some 20% were teachers or lecturers.

[1] That is, Jews, Roman Catholics, and Quakers as well as Methodists and other Protestant Nonconformist groups. See Butler and King, 1966, p. 209.
[2] See 'The Times', *House of Commons 1970*, p. 257.

There were also larger proportions of engineers and clerical and technical workers among Labour than among Conservative MPs. At the same time, barristers, solicitors, managers, executives and administrators are to be found among Labour MPs in much the same proportion as among the Conservatives. On the whole, however, greater differences are to be found between the educational and occupational background of

TABLE XVIII

Occupational Background of MPs, 1970

	Conservative	Labour
Barristers, Solicitors	67	46
Journalists, authors	35	25
Lecturers, teachers	7	56
Medical	4	6
Civil service	2	3
Farmers, landowners	40	3
Company directors, brokers	129	4
Accountants	5	2
Managers, executives, etc.	17	23
Other business	24	20
Clerical and technical	4	11
Engineers	3	19
Trade union and party officials	7	36
Manual workers	1	37

Source: Based on a table in 'The Times', *House of Commons 1970*, p. 256, showing the occupations in which MPs are or have been engaged. For some MPs more than one occupation is listed.

Conservative and Labour MPs than were found between the candidates of the two parties. At the same time, there are considerable differences between the various elements that make up the PLP, although not between the members of the Conservative Parliamentary Party, who constitute a much more homogeneous social unit. With the Conservative Party the proportion of those with an 'exclusive' background (public school, Oxbridge, and the professions or business) was greater among the MPs than among the mass of the candidates. With the Labour Party, on the other hand, the proportion of those with a University education and a middle-class occupation was not as high among MPs as it was among the candidates. This is largely because trade union sponsorship of candidates means that a large proportion of working-class candidates with trade union connections acquire safe Labour seats, while a correspondingly large proportion of middle-class Labour candidates are left to contest the hopeless seats. The 'failure rate' among Labour's working-class candidates is thus much lower than among the party's middle-class candidates. This factor has been reduced somewhat, in that in the last ten years the unions have shown more willingness to sponsor candidates who have no actual union connections, although workers continue to account for the vast proportion of union sponsorships.

Despite its several diverse social elements, however, the PLP is still very far from being a mirror of society, and the middle class is represented in much bigger proportions among Labour MPs than among Labour Party members or voters, or among society as a whole. It may also be noted that the middle-class element in the PLP is increasing, and that the educational and occupational background of the two parties' MPs seem to be coming a little closer together. It can be seen from Table XIX that in the nineteen-fifties and 'sixties there was a noticeable increase in the proportion of University graduates and professional and businessmen within the PLP, while the proportion of working-class Labour MPs has declined. In the Conservative Party in the same period, the proportion of MPs drawn from the professions and business fell slightly, although this was because of a slight rise in the numbers drawn from other miscellaneous middle-class occupations, rather than from any increase in the number of working-class Conservative MPs. In comparisons like these between MPs elected in different years, some allowance has to be made for distortions which can occur from one election to another. A large proportion of the 'old guard' of both parties (Labour's trade unionists and the Conservatives' public school–big business elite) represent safe seats, and thus tend to be re-elected no matter how the party's fortunes may fluctuate from election to election. On the other hand, a big proportion of the 'new wave' of MPs of both parties are often in marginal seats, and thus lose their seats if the party

TABLE XIX

The Changing Social Structure of the Parties in Parliament
1951 to 1970

		1951	1959	1966	1970
University education	Lab.	41%	39%	51%	59%
	Con.	65%	60%	67%	69%
Working-class occupation	Lab.	37%	35%	30%	30%
	Con.*	—	—	—	—
Professions or business	Lab.	44%	48%	52%	54%
	Con.	77%	76%	75%	76%
Median age	Lab.	52	55	50	50
	Con.	47	48	48	48
Women MPs	Lab.	11	13	19	10
	Con.	6	12	7	15

* Less than 1% throughout

Source: Based on information given in Butler, 1951, Ch. 3; Butler and Rose, 1959, Ch. 10; Butler and King, 1966, Ch. 12; and 'The Times', *House of Commons 1970*.

suffers a heavy defeat—as did Labour in 1959 and 1970 and the Conservatives in 1966. Despite this, however, an overall picture can still be obtained, and the trends that have been noted as emerging between 1951 and 1970 are even more pronounced if comparisons are made with the MPs of 1945, or of before the war.[1]

The reduction in the proportion of working-class Labour MPs has to be deplored if it is felt that Parliament ought to be a more accurate mirror of the various strata of society. Not all

[1] J. F. S. Ross, *Parliamentary Representation*, London 1948, for a detailed examination of the backgrounds of MPs in the period 1918 to 1945.

would agree, however, that Parliament ought to be a micro-cosm of the nation, and it can be argued that the over-representation in Parliament of some sections of the community is highly desirable, as well as inevitable in the existing party and social system. It is uncertain what effect these changes will have upon the parties themselves, particularly on their electoral 'image'. The Conservatives could well lose some of their traditional deferential votes to a Labour Party that was losing its 'cloth cap' image, while by the same token the Labour Party could lose some working-class support. These speculative gains and losses are difficult to gauge accurately, however, while at the same time it is very easy to exaggerate the extent to which the social composition of the PLP is changing. Despite changes over the years, the two parties remain vastly different in the educational and occupational backgrounds of their MPs.

Other differences in the backgrounds of the MPs of the two parties may also be noted. The median age for Labour MPs elected in 1970 was 50, compared with 48 for the Conservatives, and 18% of Labour MPs were aged over 60 compared with just 10% of Conservative MPs. The Conservative Parliamentary Party thus tends to be 'younger' than the PLP, and this coincides with a general tendency for middle-class parties to be younger in composition than are working-class parties. In Britain this may be attributable in part to the fact that many Labour MPs, particularly the trade unionists, often had to serve a long apprenticeship in the Labour Movement before having their services rewarded with a seat in Parliament. In the Conservative Party, on the other hand, youth has been less of a barrier to a Parliamentary candidature, than have social and educational factors. It may be noted that between 1951 and 1964 there was no marked change in the median age of the MPs of the two parties, but in 1966 there was a big influx of Labour MPs aged under 40, and this brought the median age for Labour MPs a little closer to that of the Conservatives. About 60% of all MPs elected in 1970, however, were aged between 40 and 60, thus emphasizing that service in Parliament is very much a middle-aged occupation. It is thus misleading to think of Parliamentary service as a permanent career. While some MPs, particularly Labour MPs, may devote themselves almost completely to Parliamentary service over a period of many years, many others, and Conservative MPs in particular, tend to retain their professional or business contacts, and return to their former careers (or start a new career) after some years in Parliament. In the past, there have generally been more women among Labour than among Conservative MPs, but in 1970 fifteen Conservative women against only ten Labour women were elected.

The number of Liberal MPs is too small to justify any detailed comparisons with the two main parties. Nevertheless, it may be noted that of the 6 Liberal MPs elected in 1970, 3 attended public schools, all attended University (3 of them Oxbridge), and all had middle class occupational backgrounds. They were all male and five were aged under forty-five. They tended, therefore, to come closer to the pattern of Conservative MPs than of Labour MPs, and in this they followed much the same pattern as Liberal MPs elected for each Parliament since 1951.

*   *   *

From this examination of the social backgrounds of MPs, it is possible to discern three broad groups within the PLP. One group is made up of those MPs who had only an elementary or secondary school education, and who were manual workers before entering Parliament. A second group consists of the journalists, teachers, welfare officers, and various other white collar workers, who in the main were educated at grammar schools and provincial universities. In the main, they are sponsored by the constituency parties or the Co-operative Party,[1] rather than the unions, and they tend to be the youngest and shortest serving of Labour MPs. A third group is made up of those Labour MPs who are drawn from the older professions like the law and medicine, who often had a public school and Oxbridge education, and who also tend to be sponsored by the constituency parties. These groups are clearly not watertight compartments, and some Labour MPs do not fit precisely into any one group, but in general terms they do give a broad picture of the social structure of the PLP.

Various attempts have been made to examine the policy attitudes of the various elements within the PLP, and in

[1] See above, p. 47.

particular a survey of the attitudes of backbench MPs in the
1955–59 Parliament found some correlation between the three
groups of Labour MPs that have been outlined above, and
differences in attitude to party policies.[1] It was found that the
members of the first group (the trade union MPs) tended to
hold moderate, or 'right wing', views on ideological issues like
pacifism, anti-colonialism or humanitarian questions, but had
militant, or 'left wing', views on bread-and-butter issues such as
prices, wages, and taxation. The attitudes of the second group
(made up of the journalists, teachers, and other miscellaneous
white collar workers) tended to be the precise opposite of this,
being militant on ideological issues, but apathetic on bread-
and-butter issues. The third group (made up of the lawyers and
doctors) was found to be generally apathetic on bread-and-
butter issues, so that in this it was like the second group, but
the third group was also moderate, or 'centre', on ideological
issues.

Thus the survey found that the degree of militancy exhibited
by each group depended on the type of issue involved, so that
the divisions that emerged within the PLP were rather more
complex than the traditional simple divisions into left and right
wings. The militancy of the trade union group towards bread-
and-butter issues, and the apathy of the other groups towards
these matters, can be readily understood. Less obvious, however, are the differences in attitude between the second and
third groups. It has been suggested that journalists, teachers,
welfare officers, and the others who make up the second group,
are less conformist and disciplined in their attitudes towards
society, and thus towards ideological issues, than are MPs
drawn from the older professions, who make up a less extreme
element in society. Clearly, however, there is much room for
argument about this.

Within the Conservative Party in Parliament, it has been
noted how the differences in social background are much less
pronounced than they are within the PLP, and that the Conservative Party in Parliament is a remarkably homogeneous
unit. The survey of backbenchers' policy attitudes in the 1955–9
Parliament also revealed that there was no marked and con-

[1] S. E. Finer, H. B. Berrington, and D. J. Bartholomew, *Backbench
Opinion in the House of Commons, 1955–9*, London 1961.

sistent correlation between such differences as did exist among
Conservative MPs, and differences towards policy issues. One
correlation that was noted was that those Conservative backbenchers who were educated at Cambridge University tended
to be more favourably inclined towards policies of imperialism,
national sovereignty, and social democracy, thus following the
traditions of Disraeli's 'Tory Democracy', while those who were
educated at Oxford University tended to be more sympathetic
towards policies of internationalism, humanitarianism, and
domestic *laissez faire*. These distinctions, however, are clearly
too fine to be really significant.

Ministers

An examination of the social background of Labour and
Conservative Ministers can be made by comparing the composition of the Wilson Government at the dissolution in June
1970, with the Heath Government formed after the 1970 election.[1] This is done in Table XX. The Table reveals that among
Conservative Ministers, the proportion of public school and
Oxbridge products tends to be greater even than among the
mass of Conservative MPs. In the Heath Government in June
1970 the proportion of those with a public school education was
more than 80% of Ministers, and over 75% of Cabinet Ministers. Similarly, the proportion of those who had attended
Oxford or Cambridge was 69% of all Ministers and 83% of
Cabinet Ministers. Thus the proportion of Oxbridge products
steadily increases towards the top of the Conservative Party's
Parliamentary and Ministerial hierarchy. Similarly, the professional and business elements predominate among Conservative Ministers as they do among Conservative MPs, and in
June 1970 a majority of Cabinet and non-Cabinet Ministers
alike were drawn from the top professions and business. There
tends to be a greater proportion of professional men, and lawyers
in particular, among Conservative Ministers than among Conservative MPs, and a greater proportion among Cabinet
Ministers than among Ministers in general. At the same time,
the proportion of businessmen tends to be smaller among

[1] For earlier Labour Governments see J. Bonnor, 'The Four Labour
Cabinets', *SR* 1958, pp. 37–47.

Ministers than among MPs, and slightly smaller among Cabinet Ministers than among all Ministers. It must be emphasized again, however, that these comparisons between the professions and business can be misleading, as many professional men also have close and active connections with the business world.

With regard to Labour Ministers, there is a tendency for the public school and University element to increase towards the top of the Ministerial hierarchy, though this trend is much less pronounced than within the Conservative Party. In the Labour Government in June 1970 about a quarter of Cabinet and non-Cabinet Ministers had attended public schools, compared with a fifth of Labour MPs. At the same time, the proportion of Ministers with a grammar or secondary education was also high. The proportion of Oxbridge graduates rose from a quarter of Labour MPs, to a third of all Ministers and half of Cabinet Ministers, though the increase was at the expense of non-graduates rather than graduates of other Universities.

These educational patterns are reflected in the fact that the proportion of manual workers tends to be smaller among Labour Ministers than among the PLP as a whole, while the proportion of middle-class professional and white collar workers tends to be greater. This trend in favour of the professional and white collar element continues towards the top of Labour's Ministerial hierarchy, although many of the variations between the various levels of the Government shown in Table XX are perhaps too slight to be really significant, while variations can take place from year to year as Ministerial changes are made. Nevertheless, the general trends remain. The age differences that were noted as existing between Labour and Conservative MPs are mirrored in the age differences between the Ministers of the two parties. The median age for Conservative Cabinet Ministers in June 1970 was 52, and was 48 for the Government as a whole. The equivalent Labour figures were $56\frac{1}{2}$ and $50\frac{1}{2}$, although the Labour Government was then at the end of a Parliament. Thus, as might be expected, in both parties the younger MPs tend to be under-represented among the Ministers, though this is less true of the Conservative Party. As Ministers tend to be drawn mainly from the ranks of the older MPs, it might be expected that there would be quite a large turnover of Ministers, with Ministerial retirements being

TABLE XX

Social structure of the Wilson and Heath Governments, June 1970*

	Wilson Labour Government				Heath Conservative Government			
	Cabinet Ministers	Ministers Outside Cabinet	Junior Ministers	Total	Cabinet Ministers	Ministers Outside Cabinet	Junior Ministers	Total
Total Number	21	31	35	87	18	25	28	71
Median Age	56½	50½	44½	50½	52	51	43½	48
School	%	%	%	%	%	%	%	%
Eton			2·8	1·1	22·2	40·0	32·1	32·4
Other								
Clarendon	14·3	3·2	8·6	8·0	33·3	12·0	17·8	99·7
Other Public	14·3	25·8	8·6	16·1	22·2	40·0	32·1	32·4
Grammar, secondary	66·6	67·7	54·3	62·0	22·2	8·0	17·8	15·5
Elementary	4·8	3·2	25·7	12·6				
University								
Oxford	47·6	25·8	11·4	25·3	55·5	36·0	42·8	43·6
Cambridge	4·8	3·2	11·4	6·9	27·7	32·0	17·8	25·3
Other	33·3	41·9	25·7	33·4		12·0	14·3	9·8
None	14·3	29·0	51·4	34·5	16·7	20·0	25·0	21·1
Occupation								
Barristers, solicitors	14·3	22·6	14·3	17·2	33·3	32·0	21·4	28·2
Teachers, lecturers	38·1	12·9	22·8	22·9				
Journalists, authors	19·0	12·9	2·8	10·3	5·5	8·0	17·8	11·3
Medical		3·2	5·7	3·4				
Civil service	4·8	9·7	5·7	6·9	11·1	8·0		5·6
Business, commerce	9·6	9·6	5·7	8·0	22·2	28·0	32·1	28·1
Farmers, landowners			2·8	1·1	16·7	8·0	14·3	12·7
Military		9·7	2·8	4·6	11·1	12·0	10·7	11·3
Trade union or party officials	9·5	6·4	11·4	9·2				
Manual workers	4·8	6·4	17·1	10·3				
Others (housewives, etc.)		6·4	8·5	5·7		4·0	3·6	2·8

* That is, immediately before and immediately after the General Election. Junior Whips and appointments to Her Majesty's Household are not included.

Source: Based on information contained in the biographies of MPs in 'The Times', *House of Commons 1970*.

caused by age and ill health as well as by resignations and dismissals for political or personal reasons. Even allowing for these factors, however, the extent of the Ministerial turnover in the long period of Conservative rule from 1951 to 1964 was remarkably large. A total of four Prime Ministers, five Foreign Secretaries, and six Chancellors of the Exchequer served in this thirteen-year period. In the 1964–70 period there were three Foreign Secretaries, and only two Chancellors of the Exchequer. Finally, it may be noted that the Wilson Government in June 1970 contained seven women, one of whom (Mrs Castle) was in the Cabinet, while the Heath Government contained only three women, again one of whom (Mrs Thatcher) was in the Cabinet.

Thus the diverse social structure of the PLP, and the homogeneous social structure of the Conservative Parliamentary Party are reflected at Ministerial level. Even though the differences may not be as marked among Ministers as among MPs, and even though in some respects the social structures of the parties seem to be coming rather closer together, clear differences still remain.

Party and Society[1]

On the basis of this survey of the composition of the parties inside and outside Parliament, their social structure can perhaps be likened to a pyramid type of construction built in seven steps, with the voters, party members, party activists, Parliamentary candidates, MPs, Ministers, and Cabinet Ministers representing the seven steps. In both parties the middle-class element is much more in evidence at the top of the pyramid than at the bottom, and it constitutes a clear majority in the top levels of both parties, but apart from this general similarity the social pyramids of the two parties are clearly very different. The Conservative structure has a broad social base, in that in addition to the large middle-class Conservative vote the Conservative Party has a sizeable electoral following among the working class. The working-class element is much less in

[1] See also Guttsman, *The British Political Elite*; D. Marvick, *Policy Decision Makers*, New York 1960; D. R. Matthews, *The Social Background of Political Decision Makers*, New York 1964.

evidence among Conservative Party members, however, and is even less in evidence among the local activists. The upper- and upper-middle-class element within the Conservative Party becomes increasingly preponderant at the Parliamentary and Ministerial level, until at the top of the structure Conservative Cabinet Ministers tend to be drawn almost entirely from the most exclusive sections of society.

The Labour structure is considerably more complicated. It has a narrower social base than the Conservative Party, in that the Labour Party's electoral support is predominantly working class, with the middle class forming only a small part of the Labour vote. The same thing applies to party membership, but among Labour's local activists the middle-class element is much more in evidence, and constitutes a big majority among Labour's Parliamentary candidates. At a Parliamentary level, however, the trend in favour of the middle class is reversed, and the middle class forms a smaller proportion of Labour MPs than of Labour candidates. The pattern is further complicated at a Ministerial level, in that the middle-class element again increases towards the top of the Ministerial hierarchy. At the same time, the PLP has included over the years a growing element drawn neither from the upper middle class, nor from the trade unions, while the Conservative Party has also included a small proportion of MPs whose backgrounds were not exclusively upper middle class. In this way both parties are to some extent moving away from the dominance of their traditional elites, although the extent to which this is happening is all too easy to exaggerate.

4

The Political Parties

IN BRITAIN the constitutional role of the political parties is not recognized by statute, and an official facade is maintained of non-recognition of the parties. Until 1969 the official regulations relating to Parliamentary and local government elections did not refer to the parties, and ballot papers gave a candidate's name, address, and occupation, but not his party affiliation (the 1970 general election was the first at which party labels appeared on the ballot paper). Each candidate's personal election expenditure is limited by law, but not the expenditure of the parties on national publicity.[1] Entries in Hansard specify an MPs constituency, but not his party. In these and many others respects the existence of the political parties remains officially unacknowledged. Despite official non-recognition, however, the parties are the backbone of the modern political system. The mass parties represent the main link between the people and their political leaders. General elections today are primarily a contest between political parties, and to have any real chance of election a Parliamentary candidate has to have official party support. In Parliament an MPs' activities are dominated by the party Whips. The strength of a Government's position in Parliament, and the consequent stability of the British system of responsible government, is based to a very large extent on the predominantly two-party system, and the strength of Parliamentary party discipline.[2]

[1] See above, p. 53.

[2] For general works on the British parties see McKenzie, *British Political Parties*; Beer, *Modern British Politics*; I. Bulmer Thomas, *The Party System in Great Britain*, London 1953; S. D. Bailey, *The British Party System*, London 1953; A. Beattie, (ed) *English Party Politics* (2 vols) London 1970.

The Two-Party System

In many ways the most important feature of the British party system is the dominance of the two main parties.[1] This dominance is well illustrated by the 1970 general election results, when although numerous parties contested the election, the Labour and Conservative Parties between them won 617 of the 630 seats in the House of Commons. Numerous arguments, some less serious than others, have been advanced to explain two-party dominance.[2] It has been claimed, for example, that the two-party system in Britain (and the USA) is partly a product of the Anglo-Saxon love of order and efficiency, with the multi-party system of France and Italy being attributable to Latin temperament and lack of organization. The shape of the House of Commons, with MPs facing each other across a gangway, rather than being seated in a semi-circle, has even been suggested as a factor that contributes to the two-party orientation. Much more rationally, however, it can be argued that the two-party system results from a tendency for most political issues to resolve themselves (at least in Parliamentary terms) into a choice between two alternatives, with any compromise leaning towards one or other of the alternatives, and many features of the British political system tend to accentuate this tendency. With the British system of responsible government, issues in Parliament become a question of supporting or opposing the Government of the day, with this being further emphasized by the official recognition of Her Majesty's Loyal Opposition, and of the formal post of Leader of the Opposition. This situation tends to lead logically to a two-party system, with one party as the Government party and the other as the Opposition. At the same time, the electoral system undoubtedly operates to the advantage of the two main parties. Although many advocates of Party List and STV systems claim that there is no necessary correlation between these voting systems and the existence of a multiplicity of parties, the British system, with

[1] See L. Lipson, 'The Two Party System in British Politics', *APSR* 1953, pp. 337–59; L. Lipson, 'Party Systems in the United Kingdom and the Older Commonwealth', *PS* 1959, pp. 12–31.
[2] See Bulmer Thomas, *The Party System in Great Britain*, p. 83; M. Duverger, *Political Parties*, London 1964, p. 203.

its various features that produce a distortion between votes and seats, clearly militates against the minor parties.[1] Also, the expense involved in fighting a general election, and in organizing and administering a mass party, works to the advantage of the established order, as the Conservatives with the support of big business, and the Labour Party with the support of the trade unions, have financial resources with which no minor party can compete today.

In the case of Labour's emergence as a major party in the first quarter of this century, breaking into the established two-party ascendency of the Conservative and Liberal Parties, the financial and electoral difficulties were surmounted, but this could much less easily be repeated today. Labour's rise was dependent to a considerable degree on the newly realized wealth of the trade unions, particularly after the Trade Union Act 1913 restored to the unions the power (lost to them by the Osborne Judgement of 1910)[2] to use union funds to support a political party. At the same time, the fairly rapid attainment of a high level of electoral support was helped by the upheaval in the normal party alignments that resulted from the conflicts within the Liberal Party during and after the 1914–18 war. Without massive financial support, and without the break-up of the existing well-established party alignments, no existing minor party or new party could hope to repeat Labour's rise to power.

While recognizing the dominance of the Labour and Conservative Parties within the party system, it is necessary to appreciate the role played by the Liberal and other minor parties, with the consequent limitations that thereby apply to a rigid two-party interpretation of the system.[3] Only four of the eighteen elections of this century produced an overall majority of electoral votes for one party, the minor parties holding the balance of electoral votes between the two leading parties in the other fourteen elections. Today the Liberal Party is inevit-

[1] See above, p. 61.

[2] *Amalgamated Society of Railway Servants* v. *Osborne* [1910] A.C. 87 (HL).

[3] J. Rasmussen, *The Liberal Party: A Study of Retrenchment and Revival*, London 1965; J. Rasmussen, 'The Implications of the Potential Strength of the Liberal Party for the Future of British Politics', *Parl Aff.* 1961, pp. 378–90; L. G. Noonan, 'The Decline of the Liberal Party in British Politics', *J of P* 1954, pp. 24–39.

ably regarded as a minor party in comparison with the Labour and Conservative Parties, but it still retains a significant electoral following. At the 1970 election the Liberals polled 2,100,000 votes (7% of the total poll) but had only six candidates elected. The electoral system does not reward the minor parties with seats in the Commons in proportion to their share of the votes, and 'normal' party government, based on a clear party majority in the Commons, has operated without a break since 1945. Nevertheless, for a total of thirty years in this century the Government has been a Coalition or National Government, as in 1916–22, and 1931–45, or has been a Government drawn from one party but dependent upon the support of a third party, as in 1910–16, 1924, and 1929–31. Also, in the 1950–1 and 1964–6 Parliaments the Liberal MPs had an important place in the close party balance in the Commons. Having acknowledged this, however, it remains true that in most Parliaments since 1945 the Liberals have had only a minor role as the third party.

Numerous other minor parties, with varying degrees of significance, have appeared and disappeared over the years, but those that exist today have had so far only a limited electoral importance.[1] The Scottish and Welsh Nationalist movements provide permanent ethnic elements within the party system, but only three Scottish National Party candidates have ever been elected to Parliament (in by-elections at Motherwell in 1945 and Hamilton in 1966, and in the 1970 general election in the Western Isles) and only one Plaid Cymru candidate (in a by-election at Carmarthen in 1967). Despite high polls in by-elections, these parties (as yet) have had nothing approaching the success or impact of the Irish Party before 1922. In Northern Ireland today, the parties are essentially local in name and outlook, although the dominant Ulster Unionists, who won eight of the twelve Northern Ireland seats in 1970, support the Conservative Party at Westminster. At the same time, quite often in the past, divisions in one of the established parties led to the emergence of a new party or group. The Conservatives divided over the repeal of the Corn Laws in the eighteen-forties. The Liberals split over personal and policy issues in the

[1] G. Thayer, *The British Political Fringe*, London 1965; N. Harman, Minor Political Parties in Britain', *PQ* 1962, pp. 268-81.

eighteen-eighties, again during and just after the first world war, and yet again in the nineteen-thirties. The Labour Party lost its leader, a small group of MPs, and a number of voters in 1931.[1] The factions produced by these party divisions caused temporary complications within the party system, but fairly quickly the groups either disintegrated and faded from the scene, or were reabsorbed by one of the main parties. Since 1945 the two main parties have avoided any such final splits, though both have had their internal difficulties.

Occasionally a new political movement emerges with sufficient impetus to make some electoral headway, though the British Communist Party in the nineteen-twenties,[2] and the British Union of Fascists in the nineteen-thirties,[3] were unable to establish themselves in the way that the Labour Party did at the beginning of the century. In 1970 Communist candidates contested 58 seats, but all of them lost their deposits. Not since 1945 has a Communist candidate been elected, and in the main the Communist Party of Great Britain seeks to pursue its ends by other than electoral means. Other minor parties exist, and a handful of Democratic Party, National Front, British Movement, Mebyon Kernow (Cornish Nationalist movement), World Government and Socialist Party of Great Britain candidates contested the 1970 election, but with even less success than the Communists. The principle of 'leftism', to be found in some political systems, whereby a party of the left moves gradually to the right over the years, is then eclipsed or absorbed by the main party of the right, and thereby makes way for a more extreme party of the left (which is one possible interpretation of the replacement of the Liberals by the Labour Party as the 'radical alternative' to the Conservatives), has not yet manifested itself to the extent of the Labour Party being replaced by a new and more extreme Socialist Party.[4]

As a general rule, the new political movements today tend

[1] See below, p. 262.

[2] See H. Pelling, *The British Communist Party*, London 1958; J. Klugmann, *History of the Communist Party of Great Britain*, London 1969.

[3] C. Cross, *The Fascists in Britain*, London 1961.

[4] For comparative studies see Duverger, *Political Parties*; S. Neumann, *Modern Political Parties*, London 1956; S. J. Eldersveld, *Political Parties*, Chicago 1964; C. Leys, 'Models, Theories and the Theory of Political Parties', *PS* 1959, pp. 127–46.

to seek to work through the existing parties rather than in opposition to them. The general effect of this is that the two main parties (and the Liberal Party to a lesser extent) are made up of various organizational and social elements, and partly because of this complexity of structure the parties embrace innumerable different policy attitudes. While this is to some extent true of any political party, it is especially true of the parties in a basically two-party system, where extremist and moderate elements are accommodated within the established parties, rather than having an independent existence as separate parties in their own right. Thus the existence of a predominantly two-party system in Britain does not necessarily mean that numerous different policy attitudes are not to be found within the community—it merely means that numerous different policy attitudes are contained in the two parties. Thus in a sense, every Government in Britain is a 'coalition' of the several interests, elements, and attitudes that are covered by the broad umbrella of the Labour or Conservative Party label. One of the consequences of this is that on some issues there are greater differences of opinion within a party than there are between the parties. This complicates the application of the principle of collective responsibility, and the limitations of this doctrine in modern circumstances are discussed elsewhere.[1] The rigidity of the two-party system also produces on many issues an unnatural cleavage into black and white, when in fact numerous shades of grey should exist, and as a result minority opinions are often suppressed.

Both the main parties, while remaining nominally parties of the left and right, have been drawn into abandoning some of their more extreme policies partly because of their common desire to obtain the support of centre opinion and centre votes. To some extent this is the result of the rigidity of the two-party system, in that if the Liberal Party was more of an electoral force, or if there was some other third party to dominate the centre of the political spectrum in Britain, the Labour and Conservative Parties might move further to the left and right and might adopt more extreme policies, which (some would argue) would more truly reflect the real political attitudes of their supporters. The effect of such a development, particularly

[1] See below, p. 178.

on the relations between Government and Parliament, is of course open to speculation.

The Mass Parties

The two main stages in the history of the development of the party system into its modern form were first of all the appearance of 'groups' within Parliament in the seventeenth, eighteenth, and early nineteenth centuries, and then the growth of mass party organizations outside Parliament in the late nineteenth and early twentieth centuries.[1] With regard to the first stage of the development, however, the word 'party' has to be used with reserve, at least until the end of the eighteenth century, as these early alignments were merely based upon Parliamentary co-operation between groups of like-minded MPs. During the constitutional and religious conflicts of the seventeenth century, there emerged in Parliament two main elements, the Royalist or Court group, and the Parliamentary or Country group. The Court group became known as the Tories (a 'Tory' being an Irish brigand) because of the willingness of the King's supporters to use Irish troops to secure the succession of James II in 1679. Similarly, the Country group became known as the Whigs (the Whiggamores being Scottish Presbyterian rebels), and these names were retained throughout the eighteenth century. Group organization in Parliament in the eighteenth and early nineteenth centuries consisted of little more than informal meetings, often over dinner, between MPs of these groups. The late eighteenth century, however, saw the emergence of Whips in Parliament to organize MPs for debating and voting purposes, and the bitter controversies over the 1832 Reform Act led to a hardening of 'party' lines in Parliament.

It was during the nineteenth and early twentieth centuries that the names of the modern parties emerged. The Tory Party became generally known as the Conservative Party following Sir Robert Peel's declaration in his election address to the constituents of Tamworth in 1834, that Tory policy was to 'conserve' all that was good in existing institutions. The repeal of

[1] See I. Bulmer Thomas, *The Growth of the British Party System*, London 1965 (2 vols).

the Corn Laws in 1846 split the Conservative Party, one group led by Disraeli (the Protectionists) opposing the repeal, and another group in which Gladstone was prominent (the Peelites) supporting Peel's policy of extending free trade. The Peelites gradually merged with the Whigs and Radicals during the eighteen-fifties and 'sixties to produce a new Liberal Party.[1] In 1886, however, the issue of Irish Home Rule split the Liberals, Joseph Chamberlain leading a group who favoured the maintenance of Irish union with Britain, into a 'Unionist' alliance with the Conservatives. This was eventually acknowledged by the change of the Conservative Party's name in 1912 to the Conservative and Unionist Party. Finally, in 1900, in an attempt to get working-class representation in Parliament, the Labour Representation Committee was formed by an alliance between the trade unions and various socialist societies, including the Social Democratic Federation, and the Fabian Society. In 1906 the name was changed to the Labour Party, and between 1906 and 1922 the Labour Party grew to replace the Liberals as one of the two major parties.[2]

The great extension of the franchise that took place during the nineteenth century was linked directly with the second main stage in the evolution of the party system—the emergence of mass party organizations outside Parliament.[3] This process began with the 1832 Reform Act, although the Whig Parliamentary Candidates' Society had been formed before 1832 with the function of 'recommending' to the electorate particular candidates who favoured Parliamentary reform. After 1832 the political clubs, particularly the Tory Carlton Club, founded in 1832, and the Whig Reform Club, founded in 1836, became centres of party loyalties and organizations. Various local Registration Societies were formed after 1832 to persuade the new voters to support particular party candidates, while the growth in the use of election manifestos also dates from this period, the pattern being set by Peel's Tamworth Manifesto

[1] See J. Vincent, *The Formation of the Liberal Party 1857–68*, London 1966.
[2] See H. Pelling, *A Short History of the Labour Party*, London 1965; R. Miliband, *Parliamentary Socialism: A Study in the Politics of Labour*, London 1961; G. D. H. Cole, *Short History of the British Working Class Movement*, London 1948; F. Williams, *Fifty Years March: the Rise of the Labour Party*, London 1949; C. F. Brand, *The British Labour Party*, London 1965.
[3] H. J. Hanham, 'The First Constituency Party?', *PS* 1961, pp. 188–9.

of 1834. It was with the bigger franchise extension of 1867, however, that there occurred the main developments in local party organization outside Parliament, and the *national* organizations of the Liberal and Conservative Parties also date from this period. The Liberal Registration Association was founded in 1861, and in 1877 Joseph Chamberlain created the National Liberal Federation. Largely on Disraeli's initiative, the National Union of Conservative and Unionist Associations (as it is known today) was founded in 1867, and the Conservative Central Office in 1870. At the turn of the century the Labour Party organization was founded, though, in this case, with the organization outside Parliament preceding the emergence of the party in Parliament. From these beginnings the parties developed their organizations and increased their membership, until today the Conservative Party, with a membership of about 3,000,000, and the Labour Party, with some 6,000,000 individual and trade union members, are the biggest political parties in the world.

Various factors associated with the franchise extensions contributed to the emergence of these extra-Parliamentary organizations. One possible explanation is that the concept of 'popular democracy' contained in the franchise extension, demanded that machinery should be created to make MPs accountable to their supporters outside Parliament, and that the modern mass parties emerged because of this. While this may have been one of the factors involved, it is undoubtedly more accurate to say that the party organizations emerged primarily for more practical and less idealistic reasons. With a larger electorate a need arose for machinery to distribute party propaganda, and provide an organization for fighting elections. In Birmingham there was a particular need for electoral organizations because in 1867 an electoral experiment with the limited vote was introduced, the city being given three MPs but each elector having only two votes. Thus the Birmingham Liberal Association was formed in 1867 to organize (with great success as it turned out) the distribution of Liberal votes so as to achieve the election of all three Liberal candidates. The success of the Liberal organization in Birmingham proved to be an incentive to the creation of similar bodies elsewhere. The introduction of the secret ballot in 1872, and the imposition in the eighteen-eighties of limits on spending at elections, meant that electors had to be persuaded rather than bribed to support party candidates, and therefore a need arose for electoral organizations based on large numbers of voluntary workers. Also, the growth of literacy in this period meant that there was an increased demand for literature as a form of party propaganda, with a consequent need for people to distribute it, so that the party organizations outside Parliament can be said to have been developed primarily for electoral purposes.

*   *   *

The development of mass parties, based on a wide membership and a large organization outside Parliament, was deplored by some political writers of the time who argued that mass parties would lead inevitably to 'the tyranny of the masses'. Writing in 1902, Ostrogorski[1] argued that MPs were becoming enslaved by the extra-Parliamentary organizations and that there was a consequent loss of wise leadership and Parliamentary sovereignty. Other writers denied this, however, and claimed that the power structure of the mass parties was based on a pyramid, with a wide membership at the base, but with real power remaining with the leaders at the apex. A. L. Lowell in 1908[2] claimed that 'Plebiscitary Caesarism', or a facade of popular control hiding real authority in the hands of a few, was inevitable in the British parties, and he argued that the basis of the political system would continue to be that of 'government of the people, for the people, by the best of the people'. Robert Michels, writing in 1911,[3] claimed that the 'iron rule of oligarchy' meant that despite mass membership power in political parties would continue to be wielded by an oligarchic group of leaders. In the nineteen-fifties, R. T. McKenzie claimed that the need to work within the established system of Cabinet government had drawn the two parties into a common power structure, and although big differences between the parties may have existed in the past, the two

---

[1] M. I. Ostrogorski, *Democracy and the Organisation of Political Parties*, London 1902 (first English edition).

[2] A. L. Lowell, *The Government of England*, New York 1912.

[3] R. Michels, *Political Parties*, London 1911. See also J. D. May, 'Democracy, Organization, Michels', *APSR* 1965, pp. 417–29.

parties are 'overwhelmingly similar' in their internal distribution of power.[1]

Thus the question is raised of whether the extension of the franchise and the development of mass parties, has led in fact to the domination of MPs by the extra-Parliamentary organs of the parties, or whether power within the modern mass parties, and thus within the political system, remains with the Parliamentary leaders through an oligarchical power structure within each party. It can be argued, of course, that the answer to this question is different for each party, and that in Britain the Labour and Conservative Parties have developed entirely different power structures. The Conservative Party existed before the developments in the party system that came with the growth of the franchise, and because of this the party organization outside Parliament grew out of the Parliamentary party. The Labour Party, on the other hand, emerged after the big franchise extensions, and it can be claimed that these differences in origin have produced fundamentally different organizations, power structures, and attitudes within the two parties. Certainly, the parties' views of themselves often seem to suggest this. The Labour Party claims to be basically democratic in structure and attitude, while the Conservative Party often seems to suggest by word and action that it is desirable to delegate power to an oligarchy—though of course to a trustworthy oligarchy, and one that is subject ultimately to control by the party as a whole. It is thus necessary to examine the structures of the parties in some detail, to see whether basic differences do exist between them, or whether the seeming differences between the parties are merely a facade hiding a similar power structure.[2]

---

[1] McKenzie, *British Political Parties*, (1955 edition) p. 582. See also R. T. McKenzie, 'Power in British Parties', *BJS* 1955, pp. 123–32; W. J. M. Mackenzie, 'Mr McKenzie on the British Parties', *PS* 1955, pp. 157–9; S. Rose, 'Policy Decision in Opposition', *PS* 1956, pp. 128–38; R. T. McKenzie, 'Policy Decision in Opposition: a Rejoinder', *PS* 1957, pp. 176–82; G. Loewenburg, 'The British Constitution and the Structure of the Labour Party', *APSR* 1958, pp. 771–91; T. W. Casstevens, 'Party Theories and British Parties', *MJPS* 1961, pp. 391–9.

[2] See L. Epstein, 'British Mass Parties in Comparison with American Parties', *PSQ* 1956, pp. 97–125.

The Parties in Parliament[1]

Conservative Party. The Conservative Party embraces several organizational elements. Separate organizational structures are maintained by the Scottish Conservative and Unionist Association, the Ulster Unionists, and the National Liberals (a remnant of the pre-war National Government alliance between the Liberals and Conservatives). These different elements combine for Parliamentary purposes, however, and all are members of the 1922 Committee which forms the basis of Conservative organization in Parliament.[2] This body originated in a meeting of Conservative MPs at the Carlton Club in October 1922, which led to the fall of the Lloyd George Coalition and the emergence of Bonar Law as Prime Minister. The 1922 Committee is composed today of all Conservative backbenchers, and it excludes all Ministers when the party is in power. Its meetings are much less formal and less publicized than those of the PLP, and (in the Conservative tradition) votes are not taken, the views of the meeting being 'interpreted'. It has less formal power than the PLP, and there is no equivalent in the 1922 Committee to the election of Labour's Parliamentary Committee. Nevertheless, while its ability to influence party policy is perhaps less than that of the PLP, the power of the 1922 Committee to overthrow Conservative leaders has been amply illustrated this century. It is probably true to say, therefore, that the 1922 Committee has considerable power of appointment and dismissal of Conservative leaders, but that it exercises less control over the party leader when he is in power than is the case with the PLP and the Labour Party leader. There are various subject committees and regional groups of Conservative backbenchers, but again they tend to be less active and less vocal than their Labour counterparts. When the party is in opposition, a Shadow Cabinet (known as the Leader's Committee or the Consultative Committee) is appointed by the party leader, and these frontbench spokesmen act as chairmen of the backbench subject committees.

[1] For more detail see McKenzie, *British Political Parties.*

[2] See A. Butler, '1951–9 The Conservatives in Power', *PQ* 1959, pp. 325–35; G. Thomson, 'Parties in Parliament: The Conservatives', *PQ* 1963, pp. 249–53; R. Blake, *The Conservative Party From Peel to Churchill,* London 1970.

In direct contrast to the practice within the Labour Party, the Conservative Whip has not been withdrawn from any MP since 1945, though a number have voluntarily surrendered it.[1] The difference between the two parties in this respect may be because the decision to withdraw the Conservative Whip is made by the party leader, rather than by the Parliamentary Party as is the case with the Labour Party. However, there is less actual difference between the extent of the parties' control over their MPs than is suggested by this formal difference, and Conservative Party discipline is exerted, informally, as much through the local associations as through the 1922 Committee.[2] Conservatives claim, however, that the Whip has not been withdrawn since 1945 because their party has been more united than the Labour Party in this period, and because the Conservative Party does not fear party rebellions in the way that Labour fears another 1931. In the nineteen-fifties and 'sixties, rebellions tended to be by individuals rather than by 'wings' or groups, though the Suez Group of right-wing Conservative MPs were prominent in 1954 and 1956,[3] and the Common Market issue produced European and Commonwealth groups in the party in 1960. Lord Salisbury in 1957, and Thorneycroft, Powell, and Birch in 1958, resigned from Macmillan's Government over policy disagreements, while in 1963 Powell and Macleod refused to serve under Home. In opposition in 1965 and 1966 disagreements appeared within the party over the Rhodesian issue, and in 1968 Powell was dropped from the Shadow Cabinet because of his attitude on racial matters. On none of these occasions, however, did a major party split result.

The Labour and the Conservative Parties have basically the same method of selecting a leader, the effective choice being made by the MPs rather than by the party organization outside Parliament. Although individuals and bodies outside Parliament can make their views known to the MPs, there is provision in neither party for any form of primary election among the non-Parliamentary element. To choose a new Conservative leader today a ballot is held of all Conservative MPs,

[1] See L. Epstein, 'Cohesion of British Parliamentary Parties', *APSR* 1956, pp. 360–78.   [2] See below, p. 249.
[3] See L. Epstein, *British Politics in the Suez Crisis*, London 1964; L. Epstein, 'British MPs and Their Local Parties', *APSR* 1960, pp. 374–91.

and to be elected on the first ballot a candidate has to receive an overall majority of votes, and also has to receive 15% more votes than his nearest rival. If he does not achieve this, a second ballot has to be held two to four days later, for which the contestants have to be renominated, and for which new candidates can be nominated. To be successful in this second ballot a candidate merely has to have an overall majority of votes. If this is still not achieved, however, a third ballot is held, restricted to the three leading candidates of the second ballot, and with the voters indicating their first and second preferences on the ballot paper. After the votes have been counted, the third candidate is eliminated, and the votes that were given to him are redistributed, according to the second preferences, between the two remaining candidates. The successful candidate is then presented to a party meeting consisting of Conservative MPs, Peers, prospective candidates, and members of the National Union Executive Committee.

This process, which was promulgated only in February 1965, is thus highly complicated, though on the only occasion when it has been used so far, the practice was much less complicated than the theory might suggest. In July 1965, when Sir Alec Douglas-Home resigned as party leader, Edward Heath, Reginald Maudling, and Enoch Powell were nominated as contestants to succeed him. In the first ballot Heath received 150 votes, Maudling 133 votes, and Powell 15 votes, so that Heath did not have the required 15% lead. Before the second ballot was held, however, Maudling and Powell withdrew from the contest, leaving Heath as the choice to be duly approved by the party meeting. Before this election process was introduced in 1965, Conservative leaders were chosen by a method whereby a figure 'emerged' through a process of consultation within the party. The Whips and leading party figures sought the opinions of MPs and Peers, and of the party outside Parliament, and from these soundings the view of the party was ascertained and a leader evolved. In the changes of leadership in 1957 and 1963, however, the party had been subjected to much criticism, which in 1963 had extended to suggestions that the Monarch was associated with undesirable procedures.[1] Thus in 1965 the party changed its method of selecting a leader.

[1] See below, p. 261.

Once chosen, a Conservative leader in many respects seems to be in a more powerful position than a leader of the Labour Party. Unlike a Labour leader, a Conservative leader does not have to submit himself for annual re-election; when in opposition he is not faced by an elected Parliamentary Committee; he appoints personally the senior party officials, in particular the Chairman of the Party, the Chief Whip, and the Deputy Whip. While the significance of these formal factors can undoubtedly be exaggerated, it is probably the case that in policy making and general control over the party, he is subject to less control from the party inside Parliament than is a Labour leader. Thus an impression emerges of a Conservative Party power structure where more freedom and authority is delegated to the leader than is the case with the Labour Party, especially when the comparison is of the parties when in opposition. Nevertheless, it is also true that the Conservative Party does not hesitate to remove its leaders from power when it is felt that they have become a liability to the party. Of the nine leaders since 1902, four were undoubtedly removed from office by pressure from within the party. A. J. Balfour led the party from 1902 to 1911, when he was forced to resign by those right-wing members of the party who felt that his opposition to the Liberal Government was not strong enough. Austen Chamberlain, although never officially appointed to the post, was in fact Conservative leader from March 1921 to October 1922, but he was forced from power by members of the party who opposed continued Conservative participation in the Lloyd George Coalition Government. Neville Chamberlain, party leader and Prime Minister from 1937 to 1940, was forced to resign the Premiership in May 1940 as a result of a loss of support within the party, though he did remain as party leader for a short while after this. Sir Alec Douglas-Home led the party from 1963 to 1965, when he resigned as a result of pressures from within the party. The other five Conservative leaders since 1902 all retired through illness or through their own choice. Bonar Law, party leader 1911–21 and again 1922–3, retired through illness on both occasions. Baldwin, party leader 1923–37, and Churchill, 1940–55, both retired of their own volition although Baldwin, and Churchill to a lesser extent, were subjected at various times to pressures from within the party.

Eden, 1955–7, and Macmillan, 1957–63, both retired through illness, though both at a time when their position as leader was being questioned, and it may be doubted whether they could have remained in power if illness had not brought their retirement.

Thus of the nine Conservative leaders since 1902, four were clearly forced from office by party pressures, while two others may well have been saved from this only by illness. While the Conservative Party may be prepared to grant considerable powers of discretion to its leaders, it is clearly not prepared to allow a leader to remain in power if it is felt that he has not made the best use of his wide powers. Thus as long as he is successful (particularly in an electoral sense), a Conservative leader seems to be more powerful than a Labour leader, but if his leadership does not bring success for the party, a Conservative leader probably has less security of tenure than has a Labour leader. It may be that as the Conservative Party has been mainly in power this century, and the Labour Party mainly in opposition, the strain of holding the post of Prime Minister has contributed towards the turnover of Conservative leaders. It is probably more true to say, however, that the prestige attached to the office of Prime Minister is an asset in the leader's struggle to retain authority within the party, and that Labour leaders have retained their position despite the fact that they have been so long in opposition, not because of it.

Labour Party. In the organization of the Labour Party, an initial explanation must be given of the place of the Co-operative Party.[1] Founded in 1917 within the Co-operative Movement, the Co-operative Party supports the Labour Party in Parliament and outside, but retains a separate organization. There is an agreement for electoral co-operation between the two parties, and the Co-operative Party is affiliated to the Labour Party at a local level, but not at a national level. At the 1970 election eight Labour and Co-operative candidates were elected. On some particular issues affecting the Co-operative Movement the Co-operative Party MPs may disagree with the

[1] See B. Smith and G. N. Ostergaard, *Constitutional Relations Between the Labour and Co-operative Parties*, London 1960; T. E. Stephenson, 'The Role of Principles in a Democratic Organisation', *PS* 1964, 327–40; T. F. Carbery, *Consumers in Politics*, London 1968.

official Labour policy, but in the main the Co-operative MPs support the Labour Party line.

The PLP is composed of all Labour (and Labour and Co-operative) MPs, including Ministers when the party is in power and Shadow Ministers when the party is in opposition.[1] In 1924 an unsuccessful attempt was made to bring the PLP into line with the Conservative 1922 Committee by excluding Ministers or Shadow Ministers, thereby turning it into a purely backbench body. When in opposition the PLP normally meets once or twice a week, but generally only fortnightly when the party is in office. It has various backbench committees which discuss policy. These committees are vocal and influential when the party is in opposition, but are less so when the party is in power. When the Labour Governments were formed in 1924 and 1929, a Consultative Committee, consisting of twelve back-benchers and three Ministers, was set up to act as a link between the Government and its backbenchers. In 1945 a less formal Liaison Committee of six members was appointed, and in 1965 a similar informal body of eight members was set up. It is the function of this Committee to keep the Government informed of backbench opinion, and also to explain and rally support for Government actions.

When the party is in opposition, a Parliamentary Committee is elected by the members of the PLP, and this Committee forms the nucleus of the Opposition frontbench spokesmen.[2] The Committee consists of twelve members, elected annually by the PLP, plus the party leader, the chairman of the PLP (an office separated from that of party leader in 1970), the deputy leader, Chief Whip, and three Peers. It is sometimes claimed that the fact that the Committee is elected rather than chosen by the leader, places a limitation on the freedom of a Labour leader when in opposition that does not apply to a Conservative leader. In practice this seems not to be the case, however, as the leader does not necessarily give the chief

[1] See J. M. Burns, 'The Parliamentary Labour Party in Great Britain', *APSR* 1950, pp. 855–72; L. Epstein, 'Who Makes Party Policy? British Labour 1960–1', *MJPS* 1962, pp. 165–82; J. E. Powell, '1951–9 Labour in Opposition', *PQ* 1959, pp. 336–43; R. Hornby, 'Parties in Parliament 1959–63; the Labour Party', *PQ* 1963, pp. 240–8.

[2] See R. M. Punnett, 'The Labour Shadow Cabinet 1955–64', *Parl. Aff.* 1964–5, pp. 61–70.

shadow responsibilities to Parliamentary Committee members, nor, when the party comes to power, does he necessarily have to give Cabinet posts to those who hold shadow responsibilities. The election of the Parliamentary Committee does, however, provide an annual barometer as to the popularity of senior MPs.

There is generally more independence of spirit to be found among the PLP than among Conservative MPs, and consequently the Labour Whips have had to adopt a more stringent attitude towards the maintenance of party discipline.[1] To some extent this may be attributable to the fact that the Labour Party has been more often in opposition than in power, and certainly in their years in opposition from 1951 to 1964 there were a number of rebellions against the whip.[2] Towards the end of the Labour Government's period of office in 1951, Aneurin Bevan, Harold Wilson, and John Freeman resigned from the Government over financial and social welfare policy, and throughout the nineteen-fifties the party was divided over a number of fundamental issues, with a powerful 'Bevanite' group questioning official party policy, particularly with regard to defence and public ownership. Bevan resigned from the Shadow Cabinet in 1954, and was denied the whip in 1955. Labour disunity reached a peak after the 1959 election defeat, when Anthony Greenwood refused to serve in the Shadow Cabinet under Gaitskell, and he and Wilson challenged Gaitskell for the party leadership. Before Gaitskell's death in 1963, however, much of the party's unity had been restored. Within the PLP's Standing Orders the 'conscience clause' allows MPs to abstain from voting on matters of deep personal conviction.[3] Before 1946 this extended only to questions of religion and temperance, but today it is taken as having a broader meaning. The Labour whip is rarely surrendered (although Desmond Donnelly resigned the whip in January 1968), but on a number of occasions the whip has been withdrawn from some of the party's militant and vocal left-wing MPs.

[1] See R. E. Dowse and T. Smith, 'Party Discipline in the House of Commons—A Comment', *Parl. Aff.* 1962-3, pp. 159-64; R. K. Alderman, 'Discipline in the PLP 1945-51', *Parl. Aff.* 1964-5, pp. 293-305.

[2] See R. E. Dowse, 'The PLP in Opposition', *Parl. Aff.* 1959-60, pp. 520-9; L. Epstein, 'New MPs and the Politics of the PLP', *PS* 1962, pp. 121-9.

[3] See R. K. Alderman, 'The Conscience Clause of the PLP', *Parl. Aff.* 1965-6, pp. 224-32.

For the selection of a Labour Party leader, a ballot of the PLP is held in which, in order to be elected, a candidate has to receive an absolute majority of the votes. If no candidate receives an absolute majority, the bottom candidate drops out of the contest and a second ballot is held a week later, this process being repeated until a candidate secures an absolute majority. Thus in February 1963, in the election to choose a successor to Hugh Gaitskell, in the first ballot Harold Wilson received 115 votes, George Brown 88 votes, and James Callaghan 41 votes. As Wilson did not have an absolute majority, Callaghan dropped out, and in the second ballot a week later Wilson was elected with 144 votes to George Brown's 103. This method automatically eliminates the compromise third candidate, and if a great number of candidates offer themselves for election the process could drag on for several weeks, though in fact elections in the past have not extended beyond the second ballot. The Labour Party has not yet had to choose a new leader when it has been in office, but for such a situation a procedure exists whereby as many ballots of the PLP as may be necessary are to be held in one day.

*　　*　　*

Once he is elected, a Labour leader seems to be faced with more limitations on his power than is a Conservative leader. A Labour leader is subject to annual re-election, but in practice he is rarely opposed. In 1960 Gaitskell was opposed by Harold Wilson and in 1961 by Anthony Greenwood, but there was no contest throughout Attlee's twenty years as party leader. A Labour leader in opposition is faced by a Parliamentary Committee elected by the PLP, but in practice the existence of the Committee does not greatly restrict the leader's freedom to allocate frontbench responsibilities. Unlike the Conservative practice, a Labour leader does not appoint party officials, the Transport House organization being under the control of the party NEC. In reality, however, the influence of the leader on the NEC is normally strong. A Labour leader attends PLP meetings. Similarly, he attends the party's annual Conference, takes part in its debates, and is frequently subject to open criticism—as in particular was Hugh Gaitskell at the 1960 Conference. In some ways, however, participation in PLP meetings and Conference debates can be to the leader's advantage, in that he can face and overcome his critics. Certainly, the Conservative leader no longer appears at the Conference only on the final day, but since 1965 has adopted the Labour practice of daily attendance.

It is often argued that in formulating policy, a Labour leader and his senior colleagues are more restricted by the views of the PLP and the party outside Parliament than is the case with the Conservative Party. Certainly, for most of its history the Labour Party has been in opposition, thereby being concerned mainly with theoretical policies rather than with the harsh realities of office. Because of this and other factors, such as the egalitarian ideals of the party, the fear of bad leadership after MacDonald's 'betrayal' in 1931, and the unwillingness (at least in the past) to regard the party leader as a potential Prime Minister, the Labour Party in Parliament and outside has developed a more critical and less deferential attitude towards its leaders than is the case with attitudes within the Conservative Party. Despite this, however, whether in power or in opposition, Labour leaders have enjoyed a greater security of tenure over the years than have Conservative leaders. The Labour Party had a total of nine leaders before Harold Wilson. Between 1906 and 1921 the post of Parliamentary Spokesman (as the leader was then known) was held by five MPs (Keir Hardie, Arthur Henderson, G. N. Barnes, Ramsay MacDonald, and W. Adamson), each holding the office for two to three years, and each retiring of his own choosing. In 1921 J. R. Clynes became the leader, but with the election of a new group of Labour MPs at the 1922 election, Clynes was defeated in the leadership ballot by Ramsay MacDonald. The title of party leader was officially adopted in 1922, when Labour replaced the Liberals as the main opposition party, and MacDonald thereby became Leader of the Opposition. MacDonald's position within the party was further strengthened by Labour's 1923 election success, and his authority survived the fall of the 1924 Labour Government. As Prime Minister in 1924 and again in 1929, MacDonald was as omnipotent as any Conservative Prime Minister between the wars, but the events of 1931 inevitably produced a reaction within the party against strong leadership. MacDonald was succeeded as leader by Arthur Henderson who, like MacDonald, had led the party before 1914. Henderson retired after his defeat at the 1931 election, and was followed by George Lansbury, who served until he was forced to resign in 1935 in face of bitter criticism of his pacificist principles. Clement Attlee succeeded him, and although in 1935, Attlee was generally regarded as an unlikely choice, he remained leader until 1955, doing much to cure the party's distrust of strong leadership. As Prime Minister, Attlee ignored resolutions passed at the 1933 Conference demanding that when forming a Government a Labour Prime Minister should consult with the Parliamentary Committee, and when deciding when to ask for a dissolution of Parliament he should consult with the Cabinet and the PLP. On Attlee's retirement in 1955, Hugh Gaitskell was elected leader, as with Attlee before him and Wilson after him, on the second ballot. Gaitskell led the party only in opposition, and after the 1959 general election his leadership was subjected to severe criticism. He survived this criticism, however, and at the time of his death in 1963 he had restored his prestige. It is doubtful whether a Conservative leader could have survived in the way that Gaitskell did after 1959. Thus of the nine Labour leaders before Wilson, one died in office, five retired of their own accord, one broke with the party, and only two (Clynes and Lansbury) were forced to leave office by party pressures. Attlee was the longest-serving leader of any of the main parties in this century. The conclusion must be, therefore, that however much criticism a Labour leader may receive from the PLP and the party outside Parliament, and however much these bodies may seek to influence policy making, Labour leaders so far have had a much better record of security of tenure than have Conservative leaders.

The Parties Outside Parliament

Conservative Party. The main functions of the Conservative and Labour Party organizations outside Parliament are to nominate Parliamentary candidates, act as election-winning machines, providing a source of finance and party workers, and act as an educative force, producing and distributing party propaganda, particularly in an electoral context. In addition, they provide a means of communication between the Parliamentary leaders and the party supporters. For these purposes the Conservative Party organization outside Parliament is divided into two distinct sections, the amateur organization of the National Union, and the professional organization of the Conservative Central Office. Both bodies, and the party in Parliament, are, however, under the control of the party leader. The National Union of Conservative and Unionist Associations, formed in 1867, represents the mass membership of the Conservative Party, and is a federation of the various constituency associations throughout England and Wales. The Scottish Conservative and Unionist Association,[1] and the Ulster Unionist Association, represent separate but parallel bodies for Scotland and Northern Ireland, and these bodies and the National Union have a total membership of about 3,000,000, all on an individual basis. The nominal head of the National Union is the President, and he and the Chairman and the other officers are elected by the Central Council, the governing body of the National Union. The Central Council, which meets in London once a year, is composed of MPs, Peers, prospective candidates, representatives from the constituencies, principal officials of the Conservative Central Office, and the members of the Executive Committee of the National Union, making up a total membership of about 3,000. Its annual meeting is in effect a smaller version of the annual Conference.

The Executive Committee of the National Union is a body of some 150 members, made up of party officials (including the party leader) and representatives from the local areas. It meets every two months, but most of its functions are delegated to its General Purposes Sub-Committee of about 50 members, which meets monthly. The Executive Committee is also served by various advisory committees, including committees for Publicity and Speakers, Young Conservatives, Political Education, and Local Government. In addition to these committees there are others dealing with policy, finance, and Parliamentary candidates, composed primarily of party officials and MPs, and largely under the control of the leader, thereby removing from the National Union control over these vital aspects of party management.

[1] See D. W. Urwin, 'Scottish Conservatism: a Party Organisation in Transition', *PS* 1966, pp. 144–62.

At a regional level, the National Union has twelve Provincial Area Councils, which are made up of representatives from the constituencies in the area. At this level the party organization follows very closely that of the national structure, and each Area Council is served by officials, an Executive Committee, and various advisory committees directly parallel to the officials and committees that serve the Central Council. Within each area the party is organized into various Constituency Associations.[1] Each Association has a Chairman and other officers, an Executive Committee, which generally meets monthly and which is made up of representatives from the ward and local branches of the association, and a Finance and General Purposes Committee for day-to-day matters. Practically every Constituency Association is served by an agent, who is generally better paid than his Labour or Liberal counterpart. In addition to its fund-raising, propagandizing, and election-winning functions, the Constituency Association is responsible for the selection of Parliamentary candidates.[2] If a Conservative MP serves the constituency, the Association has to maintain links between the MP and the electorate, organizing meetings with constituents, public meetings, and other like activities for the MP. Within each constituency there are numerous ward or district branches, each with their own officers who serve on the constituency Executive Committee. It is on this final 'grass roots' level that the whole of the National Union's pyramid structure is based. The party relies for its finance on individual membership fees, on local and national fund-raising schemes, and also upon contributions received from business and commercial organizations.

The other main limb of the Conservative Party structure is the Central Office. This is the professional body, as opposed to the amateur National Union, and Central Office represents the central administrative structure which supervises the running of the local organizations. Central Office was established in 1870, after the creation of the Liberal Registration Association in 1861, and following the heavy Conservative defeat at the 1868 election. Today, Conservative Central Office is the most highly paid, and probably the most efficient organization of

[1] M. G. Clarke, 'National Organisation and the Constituency Association in the Conservative Party', PS 1969, pp. 345–7.   [2] See above, p. 45.

any of the British parties. The Chairman of the Party Organization, and other leading officers of the Central Office, are
appointed by the party leader, and are directly under his control. The leader's powers in this direction are the key to his
authority in the party, as the balance of power within the
Conservative Party structure lies overwhelmingly with Central
Office rather than the National Union. Attached to party headquarters are the Conservative Research Department (developed
particularly by R. A. Butler after 1945), and the Conservative
Political Centre, which produce literature for policy and propaganda purposes. In each of the twelve provincial areas there is
a Central Office Area Agent and an Area Office. This area
organization provides the means of Central Office supervision
of constituencies within the area, though at a constituency level
some degree of Central Office influence is also exerted through
the constituency agents.

*   *   *

The annual Conservative Party Conference has a potential
membership of some 5,600, made up of representatives from the
constituencies and from bodies like the Young Conservatives
and the Conservative Trade Union Council.[1] In fact, only
about half of this number generally attend. Those who do
attend are not instructed delegates, but speak and vote as they
think fit. This is claimed to be a democratic arrangement, but
it means that local constituency workers who do not attend
the Conference have no say in its deliberations. It is probably
true to say that in general the Conference is attended by the
most militant members from the constituencies, but nevertheless the Conference is characterized (certainly in comparison
with its Labour counterpart) by a readiness to accept the wishes
of the leadership. The Conference, which lasts some two to
three days, debates a vast number of issues, chosen by the
General Purposes Sub-Committee of the National Union, but
only rarely reveals any serious party divisions. At the 1950
Conference the leadership agreed unwillingly to accept the
Conference's proposed target of '300,000 houses a year' as an
election pledge, and in 1965 the Conference was critical of
party policy towards the Rhodesian independence issue, but

[1] See M. Shaw, 'An American Looks at the Party Conferences', *Parl. Aff.*
1961–2, pp. 203–12.

in the main the Conservative Conference is traditionally a united and deferential gathering, especially in the flush of electoral success, as in 1970. This annual display of party unity has done much, especially with the televising of party conferences, to enhance the image (however accurate an image) of the Conservative Party as a united and responsible body.

Thus a complicated national and local organization exists within the National Union and Central Office alike. To a large extent this is accompanied by a clear division of power between the central and local bodies, with the local associations being given a considerable degree of autonomy over their own affairs, including the selection of Parliamentary candidates. Nevertheless, despite this division of power, and despite the complicated nature of party organization, it must be emphasized that control over party affairs, in other than in purely local matters, rests firmly with the party leadership. The diversified formal structure of Conservative Party organization hides an actual power structure which concentrates power in the hands of the leadership, and of the party leader in particular. To a large extent this is achieved through the willingness of the constituency associations to leave policy matters largely in the hands of the leader and the Parliamentary party, and the overall supervision of the party machine primarily in the hands of the leader and Central Office. The main function of the party organization outside Parliament is thus not to control the party leaders, but to secure their election to Parliamentary power.

Labour Party. In many ways the most significant aspect of the structure of the Labour Party outside Parliament is the role that is played by the trade unions.[1] The Labour Party was formed in 1900 out of an alliance of trade unions and socialist societies, with the unions forming the dominant numerical and financial element. Today, affiliated membership through the unions accounts for about five-sixths of the total Labour Party membership of some 6,000,000, and the bulk of the Labour Party's funds are provided by the unions.[2] The Labour Party

[1] See M. Harrison, *The Trade Unions and the Labour Party since 1945*, London 1960; B. Hennessy, 'Trade Unions and the British Labour Party', *APSR* 1955, pp. 1050–67; M. Shanks, 'Politics and the Trade Unionist', *PQ* 1959, pp. 44–53.

[2] See M. Harrison, 'Political Finance in Britain', *J of P* 1963, pp. 664–85;

receives membership fees from individual constituency members, and from affiliated trade union members, with trade union affiliation fees accounting for more than four times the sum obtained through individual membership. The trade unions also contribute additional sums to the party's election-fighting fund, and to the finances of constituency parties that adopt trade union sponsored candidates. The consequent strength of trade union influence is reflected at various levels throughout the structure of the party.

The headquarters of the Labour Party are at Transport House, significantly the home of the Transport and General Workers Union, the biggest of the unions. The NEC of the Labour Party, which meets monthly, supervises the whole party organization outside Parliament.[1] The Labour Party General Secretary, and other senior members of the party bureaucracy, are appointed by and are answerable to the NEC, and not to the party leader as is the case with the Conservative Party. Since 1900 there have been only six party Secretaries, and while the first two (Ramsay MacDonald and Arthur Henderson) were powerful and independent figures within the party, the last four (James Middleton, Morgan Phillips, Len Williams and Harry Nicholas) have been rather more subject to NEC control. Under the Secretary, the Transport House organization is divided into various departments, including Research, Press and Publicity, and Finance, and these departments are supervised by various sub-committees of the NEC. The NEC is composed of 28 members. These are the leader and deputy leader of the party, twelve members elected by the trade union delegates to the annual party Conference, seven elected by the constituency party delegates, and five women members and the Treasurer elected by the whole Conference (where the trade union delegates have a majority of votes). The Secretary is also a member of the NEC, but he does not vote. The NEC elects a chairman and vice-chairman from its own number, and generally the longest-serving members are chosen.

Normally, MPs are in a small majority on the NEC, as

F. Newman, 'Reflections on Money and Party Politics in Britain', *Parl. Aff.* 1956–7, pp. 308–32.

[1] See R. T. McKenzie, 'The Wilson Report and the Future of Labour Party Organization', *PS* 1956, pp. 93–7.

usually most of the five women members, most of the seven members elected by the constituency parties, and at least some of the twelve members elected by the trade unions, are MPs. The domination of the composition of the NEC by trade union votes, and the overlap between the NEC and the PLP, are the most interesting features of the structure of the committee, and provide the key to the distribution of power within the Labour Party. In a notable dispute in 1945 with Harold Laski, then chairman of the NEC, Attlee emphasized the need for the Parliamentary leaders to be free from domination by the NEC or its chairman, and in the main the Parliamentary leaders do have this freedom. The party leader is able to overcome the formal limitations on his power, and is able to exert control over the NEC, through the support of the most powerful trade unions, which have been traditionally loyal to the party leadership. The authority of the Parliamentary leaders on the NEC has also been strengthened by the provision in the party constitution which makes members of the TUC General Council ineligible for membership of the NEC. In most cases the most prominent union leaders have preferred service on the General Council, leaving the second rank of union officials to serve on the NEC.

*　　　*　　　*

For purposes of regional organization, the Labour Party has eleven Regional Councils throughout England, Wales, and Scotland. This regional structure was established in 1938, and is weaker than Conservative area organization. The Regional Council, which meets annually, is made up of members drawn from the constituencies, trade union organizations, co-operative societies, and socialist societies within the region. These bodies are also represented on a federal basis on the Council's Executive Committee, which meets generally every two months. In each region there is a Regional Organizer, who has the task of supervising the party machine throughout the regions. The Regional Organizers are responsible to party head office rather than to the Regional Council, and this follows the pattern that applies within the Conservative Party. At a local level there is a committee for each ward or district, which join with the unions and other affiliated bodies to create a constituency organization.[1] The General Management Committee is the controlling body of this organization. As is the case with the annual Conference, the delegates from the affiliated organizations constitute a numerical majority on the GMC, but most attend its meetings only rarely. The GMC appoints an Executive Committee for day-to-day business, and there are various sub-committees of the Executive Committee for the several aspects of constituency affairs. Less than half of the constituencies have an agent, and at this level Labour organization is generally smaller, less wealthy, and less effective than Conservative organization. Although the constituencies are largely free to manage their own internal affairs, they are subject to rather more central control than is the case with the Conservative Associations.

The annual Labour Party Conference generally lasts for five days, the bulk of the time being devoted to debating resolutions proposed by the NEC or the delegates. It has a smaller attendance than the Conservative Conference. Each trade union, affiliated organization, and constituency association is entitled to send one delegate for every 5,000 of its party members, and these delegates, plus various ex-officio members of the Conference, make up a total potential attendance of about 2,500. In fact, the actual attendance is usually only about 1,100. The unions in particular normally send only about half the numbers they are entitled to, and they are generally outnumbered by the constituency delegates. The constituency delegates are also usually much more vocal than those union delegates who do attend. However, the union delegates have a much greater voting strength than those from the constituencies, as each delegation has a 'block vote' equivalent to the total number of party members that it is representing. As the unions account for the bulk of the membership of the Labour Party, they control the bulk (about five-sixths) of the votes at the Conference.

There is no general rule as to how far Conference delegations receive prior instructions from their unions and associations on how to vote on the various Conference issues, but in most cases the decisions are made by the delegations themselves. A

[1] See H. J. Hanham, 'The Local Organization of the British Labour Party', *WPQ* 1956, pp. 376–88; J. Blondel, 'The Conservative Association and the Labour Party in Reading', *PS* 1958, pp. 101–19.

delegation may divide its total number of votes if it so wishes, but it is an accepted convention that the various delegations cast their votes as a block. The six biggest unions (Transport and General Workers, National Union of Mineworkers, Amalgamated Engineering Union, National Union of General and Municipal Workers, National Union of Railwaymen, and Union of Shop Distributive and Allied Workers) account for about half of the total Conference votes, while the TGWU alone accounts for as many votes as all the constituencies put together. The voting power of the big unions is thus vital to the control of Conference decisions, and as a rule the party leadership has been able to rely on the big unions for support at Conferences. In the nineteen-sixties, under the leadership of Frank Cousins and Jack Jones, the TGWU was less prone to support the party leadership than when Ernest Bevin and Arthur Deakin were the union's leaders, but it nevertheless remains generally true that the party leadership has been able to control Conference decisions largely through the backing of some combination of the biggest unions.

A picture is often presented of the union delegates representing the right wing of the party, and the constituency delegates the left wing, with the ever-moderate union leaders supporting the party leadership against left-wing extremists. As a generalization, however, it is probably more true to say that on most Conference issues the left wing of the party draws its support in the main from a minority of trade unions and a minority of constituency associations, while the right wing is represented by the majority of unions and the majority of constituency associations alike. There are clearly exceptions to this general rule, but as is suggested by studies of the type of Conference resolutions proposed by the various delegations, it is probably a more accurate generalization than any straight division into trade unions versus constituency associations.[1]

The Conference, as well as being a rally and an annual meeting ground for MPs and party workers, has the twin functions of debating and proposing principles of party policy,

[1] See R. Rose, 'The Policy Ideas of English Party Activists', *APSR* 1962, pp. 360–71; K. Hindell and P. Williams, 'Scarborough and Blackpool: An Analysis of Some Votes at the Labour Party Conferences of 1960 and 1961', *PQ* 1962, pp. 306–20.

and of debating and approving the details of policies that have
been drawn up by the PLP and the NEC. The precise interpretation and extent of these powers, however, has frequently
caused controversy in the past. The whole question of the
extent to which the organization outside Parliament is able to
influence Labour Party policy issues, is to a considerable degree
bound up with the interpretation of the precise nature of the
power and authority of the Conference. It has been noted
above that the party leader and his senior Parliamentary
colleagues are generally in a position to control the NEC, and
it has also been noted that with the support of the majority of
the big unions, the leadership is able to control conference
decisions on most occasions. It is less clear, however, to what
extent the NEC, the PLP, and the party leader are limited in
their power when the Conference passes policy resolutions of
which the leadership does not approve. On the one hand it has
been claimed that the Conference is 'the final authority of the
Labour Party . . . [It] lays down the policy of the party, and
issues instructions which must be carried out by the Executive,
the affiliated organizations, and its representatives in Parliament and on local authorities.'[1] It has also been authoritatively
claimed that a Labour Minister is 'tied and bound' by a Conference decision.[2] In practice, however, the Parliamentary
leaders have sought to retain the power to decide policy issues
themselves, regardless of Conference decisions. As early as 1907,
Keir Hardie and Arthur Henderson resisted Conference attempts to 'instruct' Labour MPs to introduce particular legislation, and insisted on the right of MPs to decide legislative
priorities. More recently, at the 1960 and 1961 Conferences,
Hugh Gaitskell defended the right of the Parliamentary leaders
to decide policy issues irrespective of Conference decisions,[3] and
in 1968 when the Conference opposed (by a majority of five to
one) the Government's prices and incomes policy, Harold
Wilson declared that he would note the decision but could not
accept it as an instruction.

[1] C. R. Attlee, *The Labour Party in Perspective: and Twelve Years Later*,
London 1949, p. 93.

[2] Attlee, Labour Party Annual Conference Report, 1954. Quoted in
McKenzie, *British Political Parties*, p. 598.

[3] S. Haseler, *The Gaitskellites: Revisionism in the British Labour Party 1951–64*,
London 1969.

As well as the argument that for practical reasons the Parliamentary leaders should be the ones to decide precisely what legislation a Labour Government should seek to introduce, the doctrine of Parliamentary Sovereignty makes it unconstitutional for the Conference to attempt to dictate to the PLP, and MPs claim that they should be free from outside party pressures in the same way that Burke's interpretation of the MP's role demands that he be free from constituency pressures.[1] It is probably true to say that the Conference was intended to play a much more important part in party affairs than it does at present, and it is probably also true that to outside observers and Conference delegates alike, it seems to have more power and influence than it actually does have. When a Labour Government has been in power the Conference has possibly been even more submissive to the wishes of the Prime Minister than has the Conservative Conference to Conservative Prime Ministers. It is when the Labour Party has suffered a setback, as at the 1918, 1931, and 1959 elections, that there have occurred open disputes between the Conference and the party leadership, and it is at times such as this that the Conference emerges as a limiting force on the authority of the leader. Though the extent of these limitations can be exaggerated, they remain as a factor that marks some difference between the power structures within the Labour and Conservative Parties.

Liberal Party. In most essential features the structure of the Liberal Party is very close to that of the Conservative Party. The leader of the party is elected by the Liberal MPs, and he becomes the effective head of the whole party. The number of Liberal MPs has been so small in recent years that Liberal organization in Parliament can be very informal, but Liberal MPs and Peers are allocated to 'shadow cabinet' responsibilities. The Liberal Party Organization outside Parliament is headed by a President and officers elected by the annual Assembly. The Assembly is attended by MPs, Peers, party officials, and representatives from the constituencies, making a total of about 800. This body elects representatives to the Liberal Council, a body of some 150 members, which meets quarterly and which decides policy issues when the Assembly is not in session. The Council delegates authority to an Execu-

[1] See below, p. 249.

tive Committee which meets monthly, and this body in turn elects an Organizing Committee which controls party head-quarters and is responsible for day-to-day matters. In addition, there is a Liberal Party Committee which is composed of the fifty or so senior figures and officers of the Liberal Party in and out of Parliament. This Committee is responsible for the overall supervision of Liberal Party affairs, but its existence does not remove autonomy from the Parliamentary Party. At a local level the constituency associations are organized in much the same way as the Conservative and Labour Parties, with an Executive Committee controlling affairs. The local party has, if anything, more independence from central control than is the case in the Conservative Party. At a regional level there are Area Federations, and party headquarters appoint or-ganizers in the Areas, and agents in some of the constituencies.

Conclusion

In Chapter 1 there were noted certain basic differences in the political attitudes of the two main parties, and in Chapter 3 much more significant differences were noted in their social structures. In contrast, in this chapter the emphasis has been on the basic points of similarity that exist between the parties in their organizational structure. In both parties the centre of power lies with the Parliamentary Party and the Parliamentary leaders rather than with the party organizations outside Parlia-ment, thus disproving Ostrogorski's worst fears. In both parties the selection of the leader is made by the Parliamentary Party. In both parties power within the extra-Parliamentary organiza-tion lies with the national organization rather than with the regional or constituency parties. At the same time, in both parties the constituency parties maintain considerable in-dependence in their internal affairs, including the selection of Parliamentary candidates.

Having acknowledged these basic similarities, however, it must be emphasized that on many points of detail the two parties differ quite considerably. A Labour leader, certainly when in opposition and perhaps when in power, is more limited in policy matters by his Parliamentary colleagues than is a Conservative leader. At the same time, Labour leaders seem to enjoy greater security of tenure. The Conservative organization outside Parliament is subject to the personal control of the leader to a greater degree than is the case with the Labour Party. The Labour Conference is generally livelier, more critical, and at least when the party is out of office, is rather more of a limitation on the authority of the Parliamentary leaders than is the case with the Conservative Conference. The Labour organization outside Parliament is more centralized than that of the Conservative Party, though in this respect the degree of difference is only slight. The distinction between the Conservative Central Office and the National Union is less blurred than the distinction between the professional and amateur parts of the Labour Party structure. More significant than any of these considerations, however, the overwhelmingly important place occupied by the trade unions in the Labour Party, with all the effects that this has on party membership, finance, and internal balance of power, has no parallel in the Conservative Party, and represents much more than a mere difference of detail.

5

Pressure Groups

THE BASIS of the electoral system in Britain is territorial representation, whereby an MP serves a geographical constituency, rather than functional representation, whereby members of the legislature are elected directly by sectional interests based on social, economic, ethnic, or some alternative groupings within the community. Nevertheless, some sections of the community are directly represented within the British political system by the activities of pressure groups. Through the trade unions, employers' associations, religious and educational bodies, recreational and welfare societies, and innumerable organizations capable of exerting political pressure, the opinions and interests of sections of the community are brought to bear on the political process. At the same time, the political parties indirectly represent social and economic interests within the state. MPs are drawn from various sections of the community, and while representing a geographical constituency, one MP may also be a member (and thus potentially a representative) of a trade union, while another may be associated with an industrial or commercial interest. In practice, therefore, functional representation exists side by side with territorial representation.

Pressure Group Politics

Pressure group politics has been defined as 'the field of organized groups possessing both formal structure and real common interests, in so far as they influence the decisions of public bodies',[1] or alternatively, ' . . . in so far as they seek to

[1] W. J. M. Mackenzie, 'Pressure Groups in British Government', *BJS* 1955, p. 137.

influence the process of government'.[1] In detail this means influencing the formation, passage through Parliament, and administration of policy by means of contact with Ministers and civil servants, the political parties, individual MPs, and the public. In Britain today there are literally thousands of organized groups of varying size, structure, functions, and influence, from the Confederation of British Industries and the TUC on the one hand to local social and cultural groups on the other, although as a political study, interest lies primarily with those bodies that seek to affect public policy, for as long as they do so. Pressure groups are not themselves political parties as they do not seek political power over the whole process of government. They are concerned with only a limited aspect of the field of public policy, and their efforts are more concentrated and perhaps more effective as a result. The term 'pressure group' is sometimes objected to because it implies coercion, and because these bodies have functions other than the influencing of public policy. Thus the term 'lobby' is used as an alternative.[2]

Pressure groups are by no means a new phenomenon, although detailed academic interest in pressure group politics in Britain is comparatively recent.[3] The Convention of Royal Burghs in Scotland, which can be traced back to the fourteenth century, is generally regarded as the oldest surviving pressure group in Britain. In the eighteenth century there emerged a number of political associations that agitated for the reform of Parliament.[4] These associations were largely unsuccessful, but the Committee for the Abolition of the Slave Trade, formed in 1807, was a much more successful body. In the middle of the nineteenth century the lack of party cohesion allowed scope for activity by pressure groups in Parliament, and the Anti-Corn Law League was an outstandingly successful pressure group in this period. Later in the nineteenth century there emerged a close identification between the Liberal Party and the temperance movement, while the Conservative Party formed (and

[1] J. D. Stewart, *British Pressure Groups*, London 1958, p. 1.
[2] S. E. Finer, *Anonymous Empire*, London 1965, for the use of this term.
[3] See W. J. M. Mackenzie, 'Pressure Groups: the Conceptual Framework', *PS* 1955, pp. 247–55, for an early analysis.
[4] E. C. Black, *The Association*, Harvard 1963, for details of these bodies.

retains) close ties with brewing interests.[1] At the turn of the century the Labour Party emerged as a combination of various pressure groups from the trade union and socialist movements.

Though pressure groups are not a new phenomenon, they are a growing force in British politics. In a collectivist age when government activity spreads more and more into the spheres of social welfare, industry, and economic planning, the state is inevitably drawn into closer direct contact with more people, and more groups of people, thus giving a greater impetus to the activities of organized groups. Similarly, as the work of government extends into technical fields, the administrators have to turn for expert advice to bodies outside the Civil Service, again creating opportunities for pressure group influence. Each pressure group that emerges tends to produce a counter pressure group, thereby causing a snowball effect. The ease of communication within society today, with more and more advertising through the mass media, and the growth in the efficiency and respectability of 'public relations', means that pressure groups have greater facilities for influencing public opinion. In this respect it is often claimed that in many ways Britain is the most 'organized' country in the world, with much more scope for activity by pressure groups than in the USA.[2]

Certain features of the British political system contribute to this. The unitary nature of the British system, with the concentration of constitutional authority in the hands of the central government, means that pressure groups can direct their activities towards the machinery of a single central government.[3] At the same time, there is in Britain a historical tradition of contact between MPs and outside bodies, which helps to legitimize the close contact that exists in Britain today between the parties and some pressure groups. After the ideological disputes of the 1945–50 Parliament, the emphasis on details rather than ideological principles in British politics since 1950 has provided pressure groups with a fruitful field in which to work.[4] By the

[1] J. M. Lee, 'The Political Significance of Licensing Legislation', *Parl. Aff.* 1960–1, pp. 211–28.

[2] S. H. Beer, 'Pressure Groups and Parties in Britain', *APSR* 1956, pp. 1–23, for comments on this. See also S. H. Beer, 'Representation of Interests in British Government', *APSR* 1957, pp. 613–51.

[3] See R. T. McKenzie, 'Parties, Pressure Groups, and the British Political Process', *PQ* 1958, pp. 5–16.   [4] See above, p. 24.

very nature of their function pressure groups can be much more effectively concerned with the details of policy than with general principles, and thus the 'politics of details' of the nineteen-fifties and 'sixties enabled the influence of pressure groups to increase. To a certain extent, however, the politics of details is the result as well as the cause of increased pressure group activity, in that the growing awareness of Conservative Governments of their dependence on the TUC, and the parallel awareness of Labour Governments of their dependence on business interests, means that neither major party can be as ideologically extreme as perhaps it once was.

It may also be argued, however, that the more discontent that exists in a community, the more scope there will be for pressure group activity. Thus it has been claimed[1] that pressure groups in Britain are today less numerous than they were in the first decade or so of this century, when the nation was bitterly divided over a number of social, political and constitutional issues. However, while the Suffragettes, advocates of home rule for Ireland, and other major cause groups active in the nineteen hundreds were largely concerned with issues of principle, pressure groups today are more concerned with details and administration, and are perhaps more powerful and successful (if less vocal) as a result.

Classification of Pressure Groups

Pressure groups can be classified into categories according to their general structure and organization, the nature of the interest they represent, the authority that they seek to influence, and the methods they use to achieve their ends.[2] An initial distinction can be made between sectional interest groups (like the Automobile Association or the Institute of Directors), which exist for other purposes as well as lobbying, and cause groups (like the League against Cruel Sports or the National Viewers and Listeners Association), which are bodies created specifically to lobby on behalf of some cause, and have no function other than this. Cause groups are the oldest type of pressure group,

---

[1] See Stewart, p. 5.

[2] For a detailed examination and classification see A. M. Potter, *Organized Groups in British National Politics*, London 1961.

and the political activities of sectional interests are a much more recent phenomenon. Sectional interest groups are generally formed initially for some purpose other than lobbying, and their role as a political pressure group often remains a relatively minor aspect of their activities. Because they are something more than pressure groups, and because they are often able to provide the Government with expert advice, sectional interest groups are quite likely to be consulted by the Government in matters affecting their members, provided that they are authoritative and representative of their interests. They have a potential membership limited to the sectional interest they represent, and their percentage membership is an important factor in determining their strength and authority. For example, some 90% of farmers are members of the National Farmers Union, so that this body can claim to be highly representative and authoritative when speaking on behalf of the interests of farmers.[1] In contrast, only about 10% of the war wounded are members of the British Legion, so that this body cannot claim to be highly representative of wounded veterans. Unity of purpose is also an important factor. The TGWU has the largest membership of any trade union in Britain, with $1\frac{1}{4}$ million members. Because 'General Workers' covers so many categories of employment, however, and the TGWU contains so many diverse elements, a unified purpose is often lacking, and the NUM, though smaller in membership (690,000 members), is capable of much more concerted action because it is concerned only with one class of workman and one employer.

Any sub-division of sectional interests into categories according to the interests they represent, must to a very large extent be arbitrary, but a basic four-fold classification can be made into business groups, labour groups, professional groups, and miscellaneous groups. The business groups include the vast number of industrial, commercial, and managerial bodies like, for example, the Institute of Directors, the Confederation of British Industries, the British Bankers' Association, the Association of British Chambers of Commerce, the National Federation

[1] See P. Self and H. Storing, *The State and the Farmer*, London 1962; J. R. Pennock, 'Agricultural Subsidies in England and America', *APSR* 1962, pp. 621–33; R. W. Howarth, 'The Political Strength of British Agriculture', *PS* 1969, pp. 458–69.

of Building Trade Employers.[1] The labour groups are primarily the TUC and the individual Unions, with 'the big six'
most powerful unions having a combined total of nearly $4\frac{1}{2}$
million members—almost half of the trade unionists in Britain.[2]
The Co-operative Movement, under the leadership of the Co-
operative Union, can also be included among the Labour
groups, although there is not the same concentration of influence in the Co-operative Movement as in the TUC. While
many business groups tend to be associated with the Conservative Party, and labour groups are formally affiliated to the
Labour Party, the professional groups are largely free from
direct ties with any one particular party. Bodies like the British
Medical Association, the Society of Civil Servants, and the
Association of University Teachers are not affiliated to a
political party, and remain aloof from close and formal party
ties. There are also a multiplicity of miscellaneous groups
which may be further subdivided under various other headings.
There are welfare groups (the Royal Air Force Association),
ethnic groups (the New Zealand Society), church groups (the
Free Church Federal Council), property groups (the National
Federation of Property Owners), and any number of other
groupings.

Cause groups are formed for no other purpose than to promote some particular objective, such as the abolition of capital
punishment, the preservation of rural England, the reform of
the electoral system, or the introduction of a simplified alphabet,
and such groups disband or change their nature if their objective
is achieved.[3] Thus the National Union of Societies for Equal
Citizenship changed into the National Union of Townswomen's
Guilds once the Suffragette cause was won by 1928. Such bodies
are less likely than sectional interest groups to be consulted by
the Government, unless, like the Howard League for Penal
Reform, they are able to offer specialized advice on technical
matters. Cause groups tend to be organized as a committee,

[1] See S. E. Finer, *Private Industry and Political Power*, London 1958;
S. E. Finer, 'The Political Power of Private Capital', *SR* 1955, pp. 279–84,
and 1956, pp. 5–30; S. E. Finer, 'The Federation of British Industries', *PS*
1956, pp. 61–85; F. G. Castles, 'Business and Government: A Typology of
Pressure Group Activity', *PS* 1969, pp. 160–76.

[2] W. Paynter, 'Trade Unions and Government', *PQ* 1970, pp. 444–54.

[3] A. M. Potter, 'Attitude Groups', *PQ* 1958, pp. 72–82.

often with a large but passive membership, or with supporters rather than members. A certain distinction may be noted among cause groups between what may be termed 'interested parties' and 'promoters of good causes'. Aims of Industry and the Economic League, bodies which seek to promote the interests of private enterprise, are composed primarily of individuals who have a direct financial interest in the prosperity of private enterprise. On the other hand, bodies like the Royal Society for the Prevention of Cruelty to Animals, or the National Society for the Prevention of Cruelty to Children, seek to promote 'good causes'. The dividing line between interested parties and the promoters of good causes is an arbitrary one, however, and to some extent both elements are to be found in most groups, though in differing degrees. Cause groups can be listed under numerous different categories, and there are, for instance, animal welfare groups (the League against Cruel Sports), religious and moral groups (the Lord's Day Observance Society), social health groups (the National Society for Clean Air[1]), internationalist groups (the English Speaking Union), and feminist groups (the Fawcett Society). As with the classification of sectional interests, however, this is an arbitrary and incomplete categorization, and is intended only to illustrate the wide variety of bodies that exist.

Pressure Group Activity

The methods by which pressure groups seek to influence the process of government vary from country to country according to the nature of the political system, but in Britain it is possible to distinguish between pressure group activity directed towards the executive, towards Parliament, and towards the public.[2] Of these three levels of activity, pressure on the Government and the Civil Service is the most direct and most important sphere of influence, as the concentration of constitutional authority in the hands of the central government, and in the executive machine particularly, means that pressure on Parliament and the public is used only as a means of indirectly

[1] J. B. Sanderson, 'The National Smoke Abatement Society and the Clean Air Act', *PS* 1961, pp. 236–53.
[2] J. H. Millett, 'British Interest-Group Tactics: a Case Study', *PSQ* 1957, pp. 71–82.

influencing the Government. Also, the most likely success for pressure groups is in the field of administrative and legislative detail, and here it is influence with the executive that is most valuable.

In Britain there is a direct overlap between pressure group politics and party politics, in that there is a close link between some pressure groups and the two main political parties.[1] The general influence of the trade unions over the Labour Party is clear. The Labour Party is a product of the trade union movement, and today twelve of the twenty-eight seats on the party's NEC are filled directly by the unions. Roughly one-third of the Labour MPs elected in 1970 were directly sponsored by the unions, and many others had trade union links.[2] Direct sponsorship means that 80% of the election expenses of the candidate are paid by the union, and contributions are also made to the constituency party's funds. In this and other ways the trade unions provide the Labour Party with most of its finance, while the votes of the trade union delegates are a vital factor in disputes at the Labour Party Conference. Similarly, the Co-operative Movement is linked directly with the Labour Party through the Labour and Co-operative Party. The links between the Conservative Party and the business community are also strong, though less formal than the Labour Party's ties with the unions. More than 90% of Conservative Members of Parliament have industrial, commercial or farming links, and there is considerable interchange of personnel between the business world and the Conservative Party in Parliament.[3] Even though candidates may not be sponsored or officially supported, business and commercial pressure groups have a stake within the Conservative Party merely because they have members or former members among the ranks of Conservative MPs, and the Conservative Party receives considerable financial contributions from big business.

Thus there is an important relationship between the main parties and powerful sectional interests within the community. When their party forms the Government, particular advantages

[1] For an appraisal of this see Beer, *Modern British Politics*.

[2] See above, p. 87.

[3] For details see A. Roth, *The Business Background of MPs*, London 1967; R. Rose, *Influencing Voters*, London 1967, Ch. 5 to 7.

can accrue to these interests, just as can disadvantages when their party is in opposition. However, the dependence of both parties when in power today upon co-operation with trade union and business interests alike, perhaps tends to nullify this factor to a large and growing extent. A Labour Government, for example, needs the co-operation of both employers and employees in a prices and incomes policy, so that the party's special relationship with the unions has to be tempered by close co-operation with business interests. Similarly, the trade unions' ties with the Labour Party do not prevent the unions from being able to influence Conservative Governments when they are in office, nor do they guarantee favourable treatment for the unions from a Labour Government.

What has been referred to as 'quasi-corporatism',[1] the inter-dependence between the Government and many outside bodies, means that many interests have regular and direct dealings with the executive machine. In that respect, contact with the executive may be all that is needed to secure a pressure group's ends, but even when wider activity is thought to be necessary, a pressure group will often approach the executive as a first step before seeking to influence Parliament or public opinion. Pressure at Government level can be discreet and hidden, and with pressure group politics a valid general principle is that most noise equals least success.

The Government relies upon outside bodies for technical advice and information, for co-operation in the framing of legislation, and for help in the administration of policy. There exist numerous permanent advisory committees to provide the Civil Service with expert information, and pressure groups provide members for these committees.[2] The Ministry of Agriculture, for example, relies heavily upon the NFU for membership of some fifty agricultural advisory committees, from the Bees' Diseases Advisory Committee to the National Food Survey Committee. Expert advice is given in return for the recognition of interests. The Government consults with interested parties before legislation is produced, and the information provided by these interests is often essential in the preparation

[1] Beer, *APSR* 1956, p. 7.
[2] Political and Economic Planning, *Advisory Committees in British Government*, London 1960, for details.

of a Bill. Pressure groups cannot be made aware of the precise text of a Bill before it is revealed to Parliament, as this would be a breach of Parliamentary privilege, but the general proposals have often to be revealed in order to secure co-operation from interested parties. The Government cannot ignore bodies that execute legislation, as with local government organizations like the County Councils Association and the Association of Municipal Corporations over the reform of local government. This factor is especially important with the growth of delegated legislation. Some bodies actually administer legislation on behalf of the Government; for example, the Law Society administering Legal Aid, and the Royal Society for the Prevention of Accidents acting as a Government agent. This type of direct involvement in the process of legislation or administration is open only to bodies that are able to speak authoritatively on behalf of some association, trade, profession, or interest in the community. This is an incentive to amalgamation between groups of like nature, and to the concentration of authority within an organization. In this respect the doctors, through the BMA, are more cohesive and better organized, and are thus more likely to be consulted by the Government, than are the teachers with their numerous factious organizations. In this context a pressure group has to be responsible if it is to retain its influence within the executive machine, and this can place limitations upon its ability to conduct campaigns to influence Parliament or the public, if this becomes necessary.

In addition to the formal machinery for contact between the Government and outside bodies, pressure groups are able to exert influence upon individual Ministers and civil servants in less formal ways. Many Ministers are themselves members or former members of pressure groups, and these groups are thereby able to exert influence upon Ministers in much the same way as they can upon individual MPs with whom they have connections. Here a Minister may be divided between loyalty to the Government and loyalty to the interest group, as perhaps was the Minister of Technology, Frank Cousins, in 1966, over the Wilson Government's incomes policy. There is often informal contact between Ministers, top civil servants, and the leaders of many pressure groups, so that 'the personal touch' is of great significance in this context. As with direct participation in the process of government, this form of influence is open to only a limited number of interests, and this perhaps represents the most criticized aspect of pressure group activity in Britain. It cannot be known, for instance, how many Ministers or civil servants are influenced in their contact with powerful business pressure groups by the possibility of acquiring top posts in industry or commerce at some later date.[1]

*   *   *

The second level of pressure group activity is through Parliament. Bodies that do not have the direct links with the departments of state that are enjoyed by some pressure groups, have to seek other means of establishing contact with the parties or with individual MPs.[2] In the main they seek to infiltrate the established parties rather than promote independent candidates dedicated solely to the interests of one pressure group, as today independent candidates stand little or no chance of election, and even if elected would be swamped by the party machines in Parliament. Candidates supporting individual interests sometimes do seek election, particularly in by-elections, but their object as a rule is merely to secure publicity for their cause, and they generally receive only a small number of votes. Pressure groups without direct party ties may still attempt to influence one party in particular, or they may attempt to infiltrate both main parties equally. The National Union of Teachers, for example, is allowed by its Constitution to offer official support at a general election to four candidates from each of the main parties, although in practice far more Labour MPs than Conservative MPs are ex-teachers.[3] Other groups ignore the party organizations as such, and seek to influence individual MPs regardless of their party affiliations, often recruiting existing MPs into their ranks, perhaps as honorary office holders.

Even where this degree of contact does not exist between a pressure group and MPs, the pressure group can still exert influence by offering 'votes for causes' at elections. Some

[1] See D. C. M. Platt, 'The Commercial and Industrial Interests of Ministers of the Crown', *PS* 1961, pp. 267–90.

[2] F. Noel-Baker, ' "The Grey Zone"—the Problem of Business Affiliations of MPs', *Parl. Aff.* 1961–2, pp. 87–93.

[3] R. A. Manzer, *Teachers and Politics in England and Wales*, London 1970.

constituencies are dominated by a particular interest, such as the car workers' vote in Coventry, or the anti-coloured vote in Smethwick in 1964. Often, interest groups send questionnaires to the candidates at an election to ascertain their views on particular issues, but in the 1929 general election there were so many questionnaires in circulation that the parties made a formal agreement to ignore many of them. To some extent the degree of pressure to which an MP is subject in this way depends on the size of his majority, MPs in marginal seats being more susceptible to such pressures. Between elections, however, pressure groups are still free to 'lobby' backbench MPs and Ministers alike, and even if a candidate does not have a direct affiliation with the interest that dominates his constituency, he has to take some heed of this interest between elections. Pressure groups often use gimmicks to draw attention to their cause, and they may organize a mass lobbying of an MP by his constituents, or a mass demonstration at Westminster. Contact can be made by letter and telegram. On December 17th 1946, MPs received 2,500 telegrams in opposition to the nationalization of road haulage (although to no avail), while on one occasion a vast number of valentine cards were sent to MPs in the cause of equal pay for women.[1] Dinners, gifts, expense-free tours in Britain and abroad, and other perhaps rather dubious forms of contact through the 'personal touch' can also be employed. Ultimately pressure groups and individuals with grievances can withdraw electoral support from an MP, but it is very easy to exaggerate the influence that pressure groups have in individual constituencies. Also, to threaten to withdraw electoral support from an MP as a means of persuasion is a breach of Parliamentary privilege. In 1947 the Civil Service Clerical Association was censured by the House of Commons' Committee of Privileges for threatening to withdraw official support from W. J. Brown, Independent MP for Rugby, who was sponsored by the Association. It was deemed that pressure of this kind on an MP was undesirable and unconstitutional.

Within Parliament, groups such as the Parliamentary Panel of the Institute of Directors exist as a focus for pressure group interests. Some pressure groups hire the services of professional

[1] See A. M. Potter, 'The Equal Pay Campaign Committee', *PS* 1957, pp. 49–64.

lobbyists, called Parliamentary Agents.[1] Other interests, like
the NFU, have local Parliamentary correspondents to maintain
contact with their local MPs. By these various methods pressure
groups can prevail upon MPs to use the Parliamentary timetable to call attention to their interests.[2] Question Time, the
daily Adjournment Debate, Private Members' time, and other
parts of the Parliamentary timetable can be used for this purpose. Amendments to Government Bills can be made at the
instigation of pressure groups, with the Confederation of British
Industries and other business groups being particularly active
with regard to the passage of the Finance Bill through the
Commons each year. The Committee stage of this and other
Bills, when the details of the legislation are under consideration,
provides scope for the furtherance of a pressure group's cause,
and this form of pressure group activity is perhaps second in
importance only to direct contact with the executive. Pressure
groups have the greatest chance of influencing legislation in
Parliament when the normal party alignment is broken. If there
is dissension among Government backbenchers with regard to
a particular piece of Government policy, this can be exploited
by the opponents of the policy. Thus in the 1964-6 Parliament
the interests opposed to steel nationalization benefited from the
dissent among Labour backbenchers over the Government's
proposals. Similarly in 1957 a combination of the Labour
Opposition and some Conservative backbenchers persuaded the
Conservative Government to postpone the operating date of
the Rent Act, to the satisfaction of the tenants' interest groups.
In the passage of legislation through Parliament the Government may make concessions to the views of interested parties in
order to placate the interest groups, or through fear of losing
electoral or financial support. On the other hand, it may be that
during the passage of a Bill the Government may become con-
vinced that the pressure group's case is a valid one.

*   *   *

The final level of pressure group activity is through public
opinion, in the hope that this will lead ultimately to influence

[1] D. C. M. Yardley, 'The Work and Status of the Parliamentary Agent',
Parl. Aff. 1964-5, pp. 162-6.
[2] J. H. Millett, 'The Role of an Interest Group Leader in the House of
Commons', *WPQ* 1956, pp. 915-26.

on Parliament, or directly on the government. This is the most conspicuous but at the same time the least rewarding activity. In the main it is undertaken as a last resort, as pressure directly on the executive (or if this is not possible, pressure directly on Parliament) can bring results much more quickly and much more cheaply. Also, interest groups that have established contacts with the executive have to present an image of responsibility if these contacts are to be maintained, and this can inhibit contact with the public through publicity campaigns. Some bodies, however, particularly cause groups, have to resort to pressure on public opinion because they have only limited means of lobbying at Government or Parliamentary level.

With publicity campaigns that seek to influence public opinion, it is necessary to distinguish between the long-term educational campaign and the short-term propaganda campaign. Bodies such as Aims of Industry and the Economic League have conducted campaigns over a long period designed to educate public opinion in favour of free enterprise, and similar work in defence of Socialism has been attempted by the Fabian Society.[1] The National Union of Teachers has attempted over a long period to present a favourable picture of the teaching profession. The object of such long-term campaigns is gradually to cultivate in the minds of the public an image, favourable or unfavourable, of private enterprise, economic planning, nationalization, trade unions, a particular profession, or whatever the cause may be.[2] The short-term propaganda, or 'fire-brigade' type of campaign, seeks to achieve particular *ad hoc* goals in a shorter space of time, and by means of much more concentrated activity. Thus in the late nineteen-forties, and before the 1959 and 1964 general elections, campaigns against the nationalization of the iron and steel industry were mounted by the steel firms, while during the elections of 1950 and 1951 the cartoon figure of Mr Cube was used in a campaign against the nationalization of the sugar corporations. The success of such short-term campaigns, however, often depends on the imminence of a general election.

[1] J. F. Milburn, 'The Fabian Society and the British Labour Party', *WPQ* 1958, pp. 319–39.
[2] H. H. Wilson, 'Techniques of Pressure: Anti-Nationalization Propaganda in Britain', *POQ* 1951, pp. 225–43.

The methods that are used in long- and short-term campaigns are similar, though the fire-brigade type of campaign generally uses more gimmicks. Press advertisements offer a wide scope for such campaigns, and the press is all the more important because TV and radio cannot be used for these purposes in Britain. The Institute of Public Relations, formed in 1948, has widened the scope of advertising, with prestige advertising being more widely undertaken. Some industrial and business concerns issue publications which present an image of an advanced and progressive enterprise, Unilever's *Progress* being one such publication. Direct contact with the public can be achieved through meetings, demonstrations, petitions, and public opinion surveys. In 1946 dentists were urged to present to their patients the case against state medicine—the dentist's chair being seen as a highly effective place for influencing public opinion. Much propaganda, deliberate and accidental, on behalf of the Campaign for Nuclear Disarmament, has been achieved through novels, films, and plays.[1]

These different forms and different levels of pressure group activity are not necessarily mutually exclusive. An interest group may be engaged in negotiations with a Government department about the details of legislation, and at the same time be attempting to influence MPs and public opinion against that piece of legislation. There can be conflict within a pressure group, the rank and file calling for a public campaign while the leaders seek to pursue only the more discreet methods.

Pressure Groups in Action

The BMA is an example of a pressure group that has an important place in the machinery of central government.[2] The BMA was originally a research body, but increased state activity in the field of public health has meant that it has been drawn into closer contact with the executive. Membership of the BMA grew from about 50% of the medical profession in 1900 to more than 80% today, so that it is highly representative

[1] F. Parkin, *Middle Class Radicalism: the Social Bases of the British Campaign For Nuclear Disarmament*, London 1968.

[2] See H. Eckstein *Pressure Group Politics*, London 1960; H. Eckstein, 'The Politics of the British Medical Association', *PQ* 1955, pp. 345–59.

and has no serious rivals within the profession. As the Ministry of Health is largely a technical department (or 'civil servants department'), dealing in the main with technical details, there is considerable scope for influence by an authoritative and representative medical body such as the BMA which can provide a considerable amount of technical information for the Ministry. The Association has not been very successful in influencing major policy decisions, however, and over the National Insurance Act 1911 and the National Health Service Act 1946, the BMA was largely ignored by Lloyd George and Aneurin Bevan. The BMA has been much more successful in influencing the administration of the principle of state medicine, and after 1946 Bevan and successive Ministers of Health were much more willing to consult the BMA over the detailed implementation of the health scheme.

In its contact with the Ministry, the BMA works through its Council, officers, and specialized committees, the power structure within the Association concentrating authority in the hands of the officers. Despite hostility over the question of pay, relations with the Ministry are good, and as is typical of pressure group politics at this level, neither side wishes to jeopardize this. No MPs are sponsored, and there is no alignment with a political party, though there is a non-party Parliamentary Medical Group. Contact with the public is also limited, the only major 'campaign' being in the form of threats to withdraw from the Health Service. More than half of the members of the BMA voted in favour of this in 1946, and the threat was revived again in 1962, 1964 and 1970 over pay, but it may be questioned whether this is a really practical means of gaining public support.

*　　*　　*

The Independent Television Authority Act 1954 was essentially a triumph for pressure group activity by the radio and TV industry, advertising interests, and finance houses.[1] After 1945 the BBC was criticized in some quarters on account of its monopolistic and non-commercial basis. There were demands for a commercial radio and TV concern to compete with the BBC. The 1945 Labour Government favoured the existing system,

[1] See H. H. Wilson, *Pressure Group*, London 1961.

and the Beveridge Committee on Broadcasting set up in 1949 was opposed to the idea of a commercial rival for the BBC. Even when the Conservative Government was formed in 1951 there was at first no obvious alignment between the Government and commercial radio and TV interests, and the Conservative leadership seemed either to favour the existing system or to be non-committal. There was soon a rapid change. A Conservative backbench group was formed, led by John Profumo and Ian Orr-Ewing, to agitate for commercial broadcasting. At the same time, Lord Woolton was put in charge of Government broadcasting policy, and as he was one of the few members of the Government who actively favoured commercial TV, the door was open for influence by 'the group'. Churchill was concerned primarily with foreign affairs, and was content to leave domestic matters to other members of the Government, while the narrow Parliamentary majority on which the Government was based perhaps made Ministers more open to outside pressure.

Two main pressure groups emerged, the National TV Council, led by Christopher Mayhew (a Labour MP and at that time a BBC personality), to oppose commercial TV, and the Popular TV Association, in which Lord Derby was prominent, to agitate for commercialism. There followed a campaign to convert the Conservative Government to commercialism, and at the same time a 'grassroots' campaign was aimed at public opinion. The Government and most Conservative backbenchers were persuaded to accept commercial TV during 1953, and a White Paper was introduced in November 1953, and then a Bill in January 1954. The Bill passed the Commons despite vigorous Labour opposition, but was only passed through the Lords with the assistance of Conservative 'backwoodsmen' after Lord Hailsham had led strong opposition to the measure.

Thus in this particular instance pressure group activity was directed towards public opinion on the one hand, and the top levels of the Conservative Government on the other. As the issue involved was one of principle rather than details, contact with the Civil Service was not necessary. The episode shows how quickly a pressure group can achieve its ends if it can convert to its cause influential elements in the Government of the day. Once the Conservative Government was committed to the cause of commercial TV, Parliament and the legislative process proved to be no barrier, and the delaying power of the Lords was not applied in this instance.

*   *   *

The Murder (Abolition of the Death Penalty) Act 1965, which suspended the operation of the death penalty for an experimental period of five years, came after many years of activity by abolitionist cause groups, and represents a triumph for pressure group politics.[1] As early as 1810 the Society for the Diffusion of Knowledge upon the Punishment of Death was formed as a reaction against the big increase in the use of the death penalty. This society was followed by many others in the nineteenth century which sought, with some success, to reduce the number of capital crimes. In the revival of reformist interest in capital punishment after 1918, the Howard League for Penal Reform was formed in 1921.[2] The Howard League's concern was with all forms of legal reform, and it has formed over the years a close relationship with the Home Office. Thus, like the BMA, it must maintain a responsible attitude, and this inhibited its activities in public campaigns against the death penalty. On the other hand, the National Council for the Abolition of Capital Punishment, formed in 1925, and its successor, the National Campaign, formed in 1955, though less wealthy and less well established than the Howard League, were concerned only with capital punishment and were able to mount campaigns without worrying about Home Office attitudes. The counter-lobby was badly organized in the main, but as it was made up primarily of the Home Office, prison officers, and sections of the Conservative Party, its powerful position made up for this.

As this was an emotional not a technical issue, largely beyond party politics, pressure group activity was directed towards public opinion (which for most of the period after 1945 opposed abolition), and towards individual MPs. Neither Labour nor

[1] See James B. Christoph, *Capital Punishment and British Politics*, London 1962; James B. Christoph, 'Capital Punishment and British Party Responsibility', *PSQ* 1962, pp. 19–35; E. O. Tuttle, *The Crusade Against Capital Punishment*, London 1962.

[2] See G. Rose, *The Struggle for Penal Reform*, London 1962; G. Rose, 'Some Influences on English Penal Reform 1895–1921', *SR* 1955, pp. 25–43.

Conservative Governments were prepared to take abolition upon themselves, but on occasions they did allow time and free votes in the Commons for the consideration of Private Members' proposals for abolition. Thus ultimately the success of the abolitionist cause depended at least on the neutrality of the Government of the day. In 1948 a free vote was allowed in the Commons on an abolitionist amendment to the Criminal Justice Bill, although the Home Secretary, Chuter Ede, was opposed to abolition. The amendment was carried, but was rejected by the Lords, and the Government was not prepared to oppose the Lords' action. In 1956 a Private Member's Bill, introduced by Sidney Silverman, passed the Commons, but again the Lords opposed abolition. On this occasion the Conservative Government introduced their own compromise Bill, retaining capital punishment for some crimes. Finally, in 1965 a Private Member's Bill, again introduced by Sidney Silverman, was accepted by the Commons and the Lords with the tacit approval of the Labour Government, and in 1970, after an experimental period of five years, the provisions of the Act were put onto a permanent basis.

*   *   *

As a result of pressure group activities, the form of the Race Relations Bill, introduced by the Labour Government in 1965, was altered quite considerably during its passage through Parliament.[1] In 1964, when still in opposition, Harold Wilson called upon the Society of Labour Lawyers to prepare a Race Relations Bill to make illegal racial discrimination and incitement to racial hatred in public places. The Labour lawyers advocated the application of criminal law sanctions to those guilty of racial incitement, and this was approved by the Labour Party's NEC and was incorporated in the Bill when it was presented initially to Parliament. Among some Labour lawyers and some backbench Labour MPs the view emerged that criminal law sanctions were too rigid and therefore too limited in application, and moves were made to replace criminal law sanctions by conciliation machinery, supported by legal sanctions when necessary. Such machinery could be

[1] See K. Hindell, 'The Genesis of the Race Relations Bill', *PQ* 1965, pp. 390–405.

applied to a much wider field of racial problems. The Campaign against Racial Discrimination (CARD) sought to persuade backbenchers of both parties, the Society of Labour Lawyers, and the Cabinet sub-committee in charge of the Bill, that conciliation machinery was practical and was preferable to criminal law sanctions. The views of CARD were widely publicized in the press, and many Labour MPs expressed dissatisfaction with the Government's restrictive attitude towards the immigration question.

At first the Minister co-ordinating Government policy on immigration, Maurice Foley, and the Home Secretary, Sir Frank Soskice, supported the attitude of the Home Office advisory committee, which was that changes in the Bill were not practical. However, the activities of CARD in Parliament and in the press produced a change in attitude in the Cabinet sub-committee, and at the Committee stage in the Commons conciliation machinery was substituted for criminal law sanctions as the means of dealing with racial incitement.

Pressure Group Politics: an Assessment

Pressure groups can be seen as performing a valuable function within the political system in a number of ways. Pressure group activity allows participation in the decision-making process between elections, and this is perhaps particularly important in a situation (as in Britain) of Government domination of Parliament. A bigger proportion of the population is active in pressure groups than in the political parties, and this has led Professor S. E. Finer to make the claim that 'For better or for worse such self-government as we now enjoy today is one that operates by and through the Lobby.'[1] In return for the acknowledgement of their interests, and for the influence and status that comes through involvement in the process of Government, pressure groups provide information, administrative co-operation, and public and political support. It can be argued that those who are most closely affected by Government activity should be most closely consulted, and should be able to influence policy. Indeed pressure groups are indispensable to the executive for the part they play in policy making and in

[1] Finer, *Anonymous Empire*, p. 120.

administration. Thus pressure groups draw people into the process of government and at the same time break down party domination of the political process, bringing to the fore issues, like capital punishment, which might otherwise lie outside the sphere of party politics.

The basic objection, however, to the influence of pressure groups is that not all sections of the community are equally capable of exerting influence. Though virtually everyone is able to join an organization that can influence the process of government to some degree, some organizations are clearly more powerful than others. Consumers, for example, lack the formal contact with the centres of political power that is enjoyed by business and commercial interests. The rich, the powerful and the well-organized can acquire an excessive degree of influence, and sectional interests can thereby override national interests. The 'concurrent majority' as represented by the powerful pressure groups, is seen as having too much power as compared with the 'numerical majority' as represented in Parliament.[1] Thus the rise in the importance of pressure group politics has led to the emergence of a new hierarchy of political influence, based on the organization of group interests, producing what has been described as a 'new Medievalism',[2] whereby a person is politically important only in so far as he belongs to a group. The leadership of pressure groups is often unrepresentative and authoritarian, as it has to be powerful if it is to be in a position to negotiate. Thus secrecy in decision making is to a large extent inevitable. In so far as the most powerful pressure groups are mainly concerned with administrative details rather than ideology and broad policy, any growth in pressure group politics at the expense of party politics must lead to the subordination of principles to argument over details. In these various respects, therefore, pressure group politics, as opposed to party politics, are perhaps to be deplored.

However, various factors within the political system balance and limit the power of pressure groups. Within the central government the independence and political neutrality of the Civil Service acts as something of a counterbalance to political pressure of all kinds, including the activities of interest groups.

[1] ibid., p. 108.
[2] Mackenzie, *BJS* 1955, p. 146.

The collective view of the Cabinet can counter influence on individual Ministers, while the pressure that may be exerted on individual MPs is countered by the forces for party unity. Parliamentary debates can be used to give publicity to seemingly dubious relationships between interest groups and an MP or Minister, a party or a Government. In this respect the Parliamentary privilege of free speech is important. Despite the close and direct ties that exist between some interest groups and the political parties, party politics can at times be seen to be in direct conflict with pressure group influence. If a pressure group seeks to influence one party particularly, as do the trade unions and big business, it encounters concerted opposition from the other main party. If, on the other hand, it seeks to infiltrate both main parties, as do bodies like the RSPCA and other 'non-political' organizations, the pressure group can expect to be only one of the lesser forces and influences within the parties. In Britain no pressure group is capable of dominating both main parties, although many powerful groups do have considerable influence on Governments of all political complexions. Each lobby tends to be faced by a counter-lobby, the emergence of a new pressure group tending to produce a rival group, although not necessarily of equal strength. The brewers are matched with temperance interests, the League against Cruel Sports with the fox hunters, the Lord's Day Observance Society with advocates of a continental Sunday. Sometimes there is hostility and conflict between groups pursuing similar ends, as with the AA and the RAC, or CND and the Committee of 100. Often two conflicting forces emerge within one political party, as with the emergence of pro-European and pro-Commonwealth groups in the Labour and Conservative Parties in 1962, 1967 and 1970, over the question of Britain's relations with the Common Market. It does not necessarily follow that rival interests are equally matched, but a certain natural balance of forces does emerge, as between the trade unions and big business.

Pressure groups that have contacts with the executive have to be responsible and co-operative if they are to remain influential, and this applies to the most powerful interests. Wholly exceptional in this respect were the direct clash between the TUC and the Government in the General Strike of 1926, and the conflict between the National Farmers' Union and the Government over agricultural policy in 1943-4. The general concept of 'the public interest' or 'the general good of the nation' acts as a counter to pressure group influence, a pressure group's case being considerably weakened if it can be shown by the Government or by its opponents to be a threat to national interests. Thus in recent years the trade unions have suffered through bad publicity given to industrial strikes. Much pressure group advertising is designed, like the steel industry's campaign in 1959 and 1964, to convey the impression that the interests of one section of the community coincide with the interests of the nation as a whole.

Despite these limitations, critics of the existing degree of power enjoyed by pressure groups argue that changes should be made within the political system to reduce the scope for pressure group influence. It is argued that the structure of the Civil Service should be reformed to bring into the service more specialists and technical experts, and thereby reduce the need for advisory committees through which pressure groups have so much influence. Opponents of the power that the trade unions have in the Labour Party have argued for a reduction in the union numbers on the party's NEC, and for a weakening of union voting power at party Conferences. It has been suggested also that primary elections should be introduced as the means of choosing party candidates so as to weaken trade union influence at this level. Legal limitations on the right to strike have also been advocated as a means of generally limiting the power of the trade unions. Similarly, the opponents of big business have claimed that there should be more publicity given to the connections between the Conservative Party and the business world. It has been demanded that MPs should be forced to reveal their interests and connections in the way that Ministers do, and for this purpose a 'Register of Connections' has been suggested (the Liberal Party has such a register for its own MPs). However, just as important as present and past connections, are the positions that MPs and Ministers may hope to take up on leaving Parliament. This type of potential influence can only be restricted by increasing the existing limitations on former Ministers taking up appointments with commercial concerns with which they had dealings as Ministers.

These and many other proposals for reducing or publicizing pressure group influence have been made from time to time. Before the salary increases given to MPs in 1964 it was argued that higher salaries would make MPs less dependent upon outside interests, but it is as yet too early to judge whether the 1964 increase has had such an effect. Similarly it is difficult to ascertain whether the revelation of contributions by firms to political party funds will in any way reduce the influence of big business upon the Conservative Party. These and any other similar changes, foreseeable in the near future, can have only a minor effect on the power and influence of pressure groups in the political system.

part three

Government and Parliament

6

The Constitution

THE ESSENTIAL feature of the Constitutional machinery of
British government is the formal concentration of authority,
rather than any separation or diffusion of powers. The various
legal features of the Constitution, combined with the practical
features of the party and Parliamentary systems, give to the
Government of the day, and particularly to the Prime Minister,
a power and control over the Constitutional machinery that is
not to be found in systems where Constitutional checks and
balances are designed to prevent any one element in the government process from exercising too much power. The features of
the Constitution that help to create this concentration of
authority are its antiquity and its unwritten, flexible, and
unitary nature, and in each of these respects the British Constitution is often contrasted with that of the USA.

The Unwritten Constitution[1]

The British Constitution is old by any standards, in that the
origins of the present system can be traced back at least to the
period after the Norman Conquest.[2] The political system has
evolved slowly, and Constitutional developments have tended

[1] For works on the Constitution see A. V. Dicey, *Introduction to the Study of
the Law of the Constitution*, London 1959; Sir Ivor Jennings, *The Law and the
Constitution*, London 1959; E. C. S. Wade and G. G. Phillips, *Constitutional
Law*, London 1960; O. Hood Phillips, *Constitutional and Administrative Law*,
London 1962; D. C. M. Yardley, *Introduction to British Constitutional Law*,
London 1964. See also J. D. B. Mitchell, 'The Flexible Constitution', *PL*
1960, pp. 332–50; O. Hood Phillips, *Reform of the Constitution*, London 1970.
[2] For the history of Constitutional development see J. E. A. Jolliffe, *The
Constitutional History of Medieval England*, London 1961; D. L. Keir, *The
Constitutional History of Modern Britain*, London 1964.

to come only gradually. It is necessary to emphasize, however, that though many of the institutions of the present system of government in Britain have medieval origins, the role that these institutions play is constantly changing as the substance of the Constitution evolves. The danger of stressing and perhaps glorifying the ancient origins of some Constitutional features is that these features are thereby credited with more significance and influence than they actually merit.

Partly because of its ancient origins, the British Constitution is largely unwritten and unsystematic, in the sense that there is no Fundamental Law of the Constitution and there has been no attempt to codify the various rules and conventions that make up the Constitution. The sources of modern Constitutional practice are thus numerous and varied. The Constitution has some written aspects, just as the written Constitution of the United States has been modified by some unwritten conventions, but the parts of the British Constitution that are written, such as Acts of Parliament relating to Constitutional machinery, do not require any special legislative process for enactment. The Act of Settlement 1701, the Parliament Acts 1911 and 1949, the Representation of the People Act 1949, the various Local Government Acts, and the Peerage Act 1963, are all examples of legislation that creates or modifies some aspect of the Constitution. Also in this category can be included Constitutional documents such as Magna Carta 1215, and the Petition of Rights 1628. Some classic writings on the Constitution have acquired the status of Constitutional documents themselves. Probably the most authoritative of such works is Erskine May's *Treatise on the Law, Privileges, Proceedings, and Usage of Parliament*.[1] This is the classic guide to the procedure and privileges of Parliament, and is constantly referred to by Speakers of the House of Commons in the formulation of their rulings on questions of privilege and procedure. Also (although to a much lesser extent) A. V. Dicey's *Law of the Constitution*[2] has acquired over the years an authority that makes it more than merely a commentary on constitutional practice.

The exercise of the Royal Prerogative forms another aspect of

[1] Sir T. Erskine May. *Treatise on the Laws, Privileges, Proceedings, and Usages of Parliament*, London 1964 (17th edition).

[2] 10th edition, London 1964.

Constitutional practice. The power to declare war, make treaties, pardon criminals, and dissolve Parliament are vital functions performed by Royal Prerogative, and are executed through Orders in Council or through proclamations and writs under the Great Seal. Today, these functions are performed by Ministers acting on behalf of the Monarch, so that this gives to Ministers a sphere of activity in which the authority for the decision comes from the Crown rather than from Parliament. Decisions made by the Courts form a further source of Constitutional authority, many of the privileges of Parliament being based on nineteenth-century judicial decisions. Thus the decision in the case of the Sheriff of Middlesex in 1840 established the principle that Parliament had the right to punish its own members for a breach of privilege, no other legal authority being necessary,[1] while the judgement of Mr Justice Stephen in *Bradlaugh* v. *Gossett* in 1884 established the supremacy of Parliament over the Courts in all matters concerning the internal affairs of Parliament.[2]

The bulk of Constitutional practice, however, is based on conventions that have emerged and evolved through time. Doctrines such as the impartiality of the Speaker of the House of Commons, the collective responsibility of the Cabinet, and the individual responsibility of Ministers,[3] are not based on statutes, documents, or judicial decisions, but on the acceptance of a general practice over the years. Conventions are continually evolving, and there is no guide as to what forms a Constitutional convention other than what is generally regarded as normal practice at any given time. Lord Salisbury, for example, was Prime Minister from 1895 to 1902, but today it is generally accepted that the Prime Minister must serve in the House of Commons, and thus in 1963 Lord Home had to disclaim his Peerage on becoming Prime Minister. In Britain, proper Constitutional conduct merely involves the interpretation of such written documents as there are, and the acceptance of the current conventions. There is no special machinery for Constitutional amendment, and the absence of Constitutional Courts to adjudicate on Constitutional conflicts gives the British

[1] Court of Queen's Bench 27.1.1840.
[2] Queen's Bench Division 9.2.1884.
[3] See below, p. 178.

Constitution great legal flexibility. The Constitution can be adapted to new developments unhampered by legal formalities, and the Constitution is so adaptable and fluid, precisely because its sources are diverse and old. Thus the old, unwritten, and flexible characteristics are all interrelated.

Unitary Government

The other main legal feature of the Constitution is that it is unitary, there being only one sovereign body in the state. The central government, taking its authority from Parliament, is constitutionally supreme, and the local government machine is merely an agent for the central government. Within the unitary structure of the Constitution, however, some areas do enjoy a degree of regional independence, but nowhere does this extend to the creation of a federal relationship. Northern Ireland, while it sends MPs to Westminster, has its own Parliament, made up of Senate and House of Commons, and its own Cabinet and Governor-General, although one of the anomalies of this arrangement is that while Northern Ireland enjoys this degree of freedom from interference by Westminster MPs, Northern Ireland's representatives at Westminster remain free to deliberate on the domestic affairs of Great Britain. In 1920 this was envisaged as applying to the whole of Ireland, but it was rejected by the south in favour of full independence. While in internal matters Northern Ireland is virtually self-governing, the relationship between Northern Ireland and Westminster is not a federal one in that Northern Ireland is ultimately subject to the legislative supremacy of Westminster, and the power enjoyed by the Northern Ireland Parliament and executive could be withdrawn by the United Kingdom Parliament. The Channel Islands and the Isle of Man have their own Parliaments, and like Northern Ireland they are largely self-governing in internal affairs. Nevertheless, they also are ultimately subject to the legislative supremacy of the United Kingdom Parliament, even though they are not represented at Westminster.

Scotland enjoys a considerable degree of administrative devolution in that the Scottish Education, Agriculture and Fisheries, Development, Home and Health Departments are

TABLE XXI

Legislative, Executive and Administrative Devolution Within the United Kingdom

	MPs at Westminster	Own Parliament	Own Cabinet	Own Department of State
England	*			*1
Scotland	*			*
Wales	*			*
Northern Ireland	*	*	*	
Isle of Man		*	*	
Channel Islands		*	*	

¹ That is, the Home Office.

situated in St Andrews House, Edinburgh. The 1603 union of the crowns of England and Scotland left separate Parliaments for the two countries, but the 1707 Act of Union dissolved the Scottish Parliament, and Scotland has since sent representatives to Westminster. In the House of Commons, however, the Scottish Grand Committee (made up of all MPs representing Scottish constituencies, plus ten to fifteen other MPs to secure a reflection of the balance between the parties in the Commons as a whole) debates the Scottish Estimates, Scottish affairs in general, and the Second Reading of Bills relating exclusively to Scotland. The Committee Stage of Scottish legislation is taken in a special Standing Committee on which there is a majority of MPs from Scottish seats. The administration of Welsh affairs is centred in Whitehall, although there is a Welsh Office in Cardiff. In 1957 the post of Minister of State for Wales was created, attached to the Ministry of Housing and Local Government, and in 1964 there was appointed a Secretary of State for Wales with a seat in the Cabinet. There is also a Welsh Grand Committee, and a Welsh Standing Committee on similar lines to the Scottish Committee. Such administrative or legislative devolution as exists in Britain, however, does not destroy the essentially unitary nature of the Constitution, with the United Kingdom Parliament retaining ultimate sovereignty over the whole of Great Britain and Northern Ireland.

The Evolution of Parliament and the Cabinet

The evolutionary nature of the British Constitution is well illustrated by the history of Parliament and the Cabinet.[1] Parliament emerged after 1066 from the Magnum Concilium, or Great Council, of the Norman Kings of England, although even before this, the Saxon Kings had been advised by an assembly of wise men, the Witangemot. The Norman Great Council was made up of the barons who, under the feudal system, held land directly from the King. It met three or four times a year when summoned by the King, and its task was to give advice and support to the King and to provide money when he was unable to live from his own finances. During the thirteenth century the King found it increasingly difficult to live off his own money, or the money provided by the barons, and in years when the King was particularly short of finance members of the new rich trading classes were added to the baronial members of the Great Council. In 1213 King John summoned four knights from each county, selected by the Sheriff, and in 1254 Henry II summoned from each county two knights who were chosen by their colleagues. In 1265 Simon de Montfort summoned as well as the knights from the counties two burgesses from the independent towns with Royal charters, and in the 1295 'Model Parliament' of Edward I, barons, knights, burgesses, senior clergy, and lower clergy were all summoned on the principle that 'what touches all should be approved by all'.

The influence of Parliament, and particularly of the Commons, grew during the fourteenth century with the growing reliance of the Monarch on the taxes paid by the trading classes. The principle was established that taxation would only be granted after grievances had been redressed, and this principle remained the basis of Parliamentary development during the fifteenth and sixteenth centuries. The growth in Parliament's influence led inevitably to conflict between the Monarch and Parliament over the extent of Parliament's powers, and this culminated in the constitutional conflicts of the seventeenth century. After Royal attempts to rule without Parliament, the 1688–9 settlement established a 'separation of powers' between

[1] For the history of Parliament see A. F. Pollard, *The Evolution of Parliament*, London 1964; K. R. Mackenzie, *The English Parliament*, London 1959. See also Sir R. S. Rait, *The Parliaments of Scotland*, Glasgow, 1924.

the executive authority of the Monarch and the legislative power of Parliament, but Constitutional developments in the eighteenth and nineteenth centuries led to a complication of this situation, with Ministers drawn from Parliament exercising more and more executive authority on behalf of the Monarch. Thus the earlier Constitutional conflicts between the King and Parliament were followed in the modern period by conflicts between Parliament and Governments drawn from Parliament.

As with Parliament, the origins of the Cabinet can be traced back to the period following the Norman Conquest.[1] All Monarchs, even in medieval times, tended to surround themselves with close advisers, and very often with one adviser in particular. The Norman Kings looked for advice to the Curia Regis, a gathering of leading figures within the Magnum Concilium. During the thirteenth century the Curia Regis developed into the Privy Council composed of Royal officials like the Justiciar, the Chancellor, the Treasurer, and the Secretary (later to be known as the Secretary of State), and the medieval Monarchs relied on the Privy Council for advice on administration and the implementation of policies. By the middle of the seventeenth century the Privy Council had grown into a body of thirty or forty members, and an inner committee of advisers emerged, known variously as the Junto, Cabal, or Cabinet Council. Under William and Mary, and then Queen Anne, the Privy Council remained nominally as the body of King's advisers, but more and more influence passed to the Cabinet Council of about ten advisers.

In its turn, this body grew in numbers, and during the course of the eighteenth century there emerged a smaller group within the Cabinet Council known at different times as the Lords of the Committee, the Select Lords, or the Inner Cabinet of senior advisers. By the middle of the eighteenth century the full Cabinet Council had ten to thirteen members, while the Inner Cabinet had from five to eight members. The King tended to refer primarily to the Inner Cabinet, and it thus grew in status. It superseded the larger body, and in its turn became known as the full Cabinet. By 1832 this Cabinet had grown to about thirteen members, and to about fifteen by the middle of the century. This was a result partly of the growth in the number of

[1] For a history of the Cabinet see Mackintosh, *The British Cabinet.*

administrative departments, and partly a result of Parliamentary demands for all government agencies to have heads in Parliament so that they could be held responsible to Parliament. Thus the emergence of the Cabinet was based essentially on the growth of a smaller body out of a large one.

Among the King's advisers there often tended to be a predominant figure, and in medieval times this was often the Chancellor. Even after 1660 Clarendon under Charles II, and Harvey and Godolphin under Queen Anne, were powerful figures. It is only with Sir Robert Walpole, however, towards the middle of the eighteenth century, that the title of Prime Minister is used to describe the King's chief Minister. Walpole, appointed First Lord of the Treasury in 1721, at first shared power with Townshend, but with Townshend's retirement in 1729 Walpole became supreme, and remained so until his resignation in 1742. The power that Walpole possessed between 1729 and 1742 stemmed largely from his personal influence with the Monarch, but also from the fact that as First Lord of the Treasury he had the national finances at his disposal for patronage purposes, and in the eighteenth century this became essential for the management of Parliamentary elections on the King's behalf. The ability to secure through bribery the return of the King's candidates at elections gave Walpole power and influence in the Court. Similarly, he was able to command support in Parliament, and it is the fact that he was the direct link between the Monarch and Parliament that distinguishes Walpole from previous Royal advisers, and justifies his description as the first Prime Minister. After 1717 the Hanoverian Monarchs tended less and less to attend Cabinet meetings, largely because they preferred to consult their Ministers informally. This added to the influence that Walpole and his successors were able to exert as the link between King, Cabinet, and Parliament, while later in the century the Cabinet strengthened its authority in face of the Monarch and Parliament by presenting Cabinet decisions as a common view through the doctrine of collective responsibility.

*   *   *

The acceptance of the responsibility of Ministers to Parliament as well as to the King, forms the other main aspect of

Cabinet development in Britain. The essential feature of this was the emergence of the principle that the King's Ministers *could* be drawn from Parliament, and then later that they *must* be drawn from Parliament (or must become members of one of the Houses). At first, limitations were placed on the right of members of the House of Commons to hold Ministerial office for fear that the Monarch might exercise too much influence over the Commons through the power of patronage. Thus the Act of Settlement 1701 contained a clause that excluded entirely from the Commons anyone who held an office of profit under the Crown. Had this rigid separation of the executive from the legislature been implemented to the full, the whole nature of British Constitutional development would have been fundamentally altered. The exclusion of Ministers from Parliament might limit executive control over the legislature, but by the same token it would limit the capacity of the legislature to influence the executive. Before the 1701 Act could be brought into operation, however, the attitude of the Commons softened, and the Succession to the Crown Act 1705 (re-enacted after the union with Scotland as the Regency Act 1707) drew a distinction between some posts which members of the Commons could not hold, and others to which members of the Commons could be appointed, subject to the provision that any such Ministers resign their House of Commons seats and seek re-election in by-elections.

This system operated throughout the eighteenth and nineteenth centuries, though some junior posts were excluded from the re-election requirements, and the list of posts that members of the Commons could not hold was gradually whittled away. The Reform Act 1867 also modified things slightly by allowing Ministers to change from one post to another without involving re-election. In the main, however, the appointment of an MP to a Ministerial post was automatically followed by a by-election to re-establish his place in the House. Legislation in 1919 and 1926 finally got rid of the re-election requirement. The Re-election of Ministers Act 1919 declared that re-election was not necessary in the case of Ministers who were appointed in the first nine months of any Parliament, while an amending act in 1926 abolished the requirement entirely.

Today it is accepted that Ministers must be members of one

of the Houses of Parliament. At times someone from outside
Parliament is appointed to Ministerial office and is then found a
seat in the Commons through a by-election (as with Frank
Cousins in 1965), or is given a Peerage (as with Lord Mills in
1957, and four Labour Ministers in 1964). In such cases, however, membership of one of the Houses must be attained, and in
1965 Patrick Gordon Walker had to resign his post as Foreign
Secretary after failing to be elected to the Commons in a by-
election.

The modern Cabinet system demands, however, that as well
as being drawn from Parliament, Ministers individually and
the Cabinet and whole Government collectively must have
the support of the majority of the members of the House of
Commons, with the resignation of the Government or the dissolution of Parliament being required if this support is lost.
Support for the Government in the House of Commons has been
achieved by different factors at different times. In an attempt
to maintain harmony with Parliament, the Monarchs after 1688
tended to choose as Ministers some figures who were influential
in the Commons. In 1694 and 1708 the Cabinet was composed
entirely of Whig Ministers, and in this can perhaps be seen the
beginning of party ties as the basis of Government strength in
the Commons. However, in the eighteenth century, support for
the Cabinet in the Commons was assured largely because the
Monarch and his Prime Minister could use patronage and
financial bribery to manipulate elections so as to produce a
House of Commons favourable to the Cabinet. The Reform Act
1832, by extending the franchise and destroying the rotten
boroughs, destroyed this Royal control over elections, and in
the modern context, largely since the growth of mass parties
after the 1867 franchise extension, the support of the House of
Commons for the Government has been assured primarily by
the strength of party discipline and the working of the modern
party system. In the middle of the nineteenth century, however, with the elimination in 1832 of Royal manipulation of
elections, but before the emergence of the modern party system,
support was based on a number of factors, including personalities, some degree of party loyalty, and the fear of MPs that
unless an alternative Government was available, defeat for the
Government would lead to dissolution. It is only this com-

paratively short period of some forty years following the first
Reform Act that represents Parliament's 'Golden Age', when
Governments were made and unmade largely at the will of
individual MPs.

Government and Parliament Today[1]

The doctrine of the Sovereignty or Supremacy of Parliament
means the absolute legal power of Parliament to make or un-
make any law whatsoever, Parliament being the Crown, Lords
and Commons in Parliament assembled. The four essential
features of the doctrine are that there is no higher legislative
authority; no court can declare Acts of Parliament to be in-
valid; there is no limit to Parliament's sphere of legislation; and
no Parliament can legally bind its successor, or be bound by its
predecessor. Thus there are no limits to Parliament's sphere of
legislative authority, other than those of physical possibility and
practical politics.[2] Combined with the unitary nature of the
Constitution, Parliamentary Sovereignty means that the ultimate authority of the Westminster Parliament in all respects
extends to the whole of the United Kingdom. Thus whoever
controls Parliament has unlimited legislative authority. Though
in strict terms Parliament means Crown, Lords and Commons,
in practical terms Parliament means the House of Commons,
in that the power of the Crown is limited by convention, and
the power of the House of Lords by statute and convention.[3]
Thus it may be said more truly that whoever controls *the House
of Commons* has unlimited legislative authority, other than in
those rare cases when the power of the Crown or the Lords is
invoked to oppose the Commons.

The practical working of the Cabinet system and the two-
party system in Britain means that this control over the House of
Commons is exercised by the Government of the day. The
Government is drawn from the Commons and the Lords, and is
maintained in power by the support of the majority of the
members of the Commons. The two-party system, in the

---

[1] See Mackintosh, *The British Cabinet*; Lord Morrison, *Government and
Parliament*; Sir Ivor Jennings, *Cabinet Government*, London 1959; A. B. Keith,
The British Cabinet System, London 1952.
[2] See below, pp. 184 and 419.   [3] See below, Ch. 9.

context of the existing electoral system, means that generally one party has an overall majority in the Commons, while the strength of party discipline means that in most circumstances party support for the Government is guaranteed. The Government is thus in a dominant position of control over the House of Commons, and thus (in most circumstances) over the whole of Parliament. In this situation the Government is omnipotent. The unwritten, flexible, and unitary nature of the Constitution, and the doctrine of Parliamentary Sovereignty, mean that the Constitution can be readily amended, and any legislative change is legally possible. Thus the Government in 1914 assumed almost dictatorial powers through the Defence of the Realm Act, and in 1939 through the Emergency Powers Act. In 1965 the Bill giving the Government wide powers to deal with the Rhodesian rebellion was passed through all of its stages in less than twenty-four hours. The Government controls and dominates the Parliamentary timetable, and the rules of the House of Commons (the Standing Orders) can be altered by the House itself. By Act of Parliament the Government can perpetuate the life of the Parliament (and thus its own life), as happened during the two world wars. If the Government is beaten in the House of Commons, it can ask for a reversal of the decision at a later date. Thus with a secure majority in the Commons, a Government, in legal and Parliamentary terms, can achieve anything.

There is some argument as to precisely what factors produce the great strength of party loyalty on which the Government's security of tenure is based. MPs can be seen as having a positive loyalty to their party, perhaps based on the feeling that the party is being well led and is pursuing satisfactory policies, or, less idealistically, on the principle that the other parties offer a worse alternative. Linked with this is party loyalty based on the need to present an image of unity in order to improve the party's electoral chances. Alternatively, party loyalty can be seen as being a product of the personal fear that rebellion might lead to expulsion from the party, or at least to setbacks in a political career. While Sir Winston Churchill was an example of someone who quarrelled with his party on many occasions, and twice changed completely his party loyalty, excessive tendencies to rebellion are seen in the main as a handicap to political advancement. The increased professionalization of politics in this century has probably increased the tendencies towards conformity among MPs.

The traditional interpretation of the strength of the Government's position in the House of Commons, is the very fact that the Government is itself drawn from the Commons and needs the support of the Commons in order to remain in power. This seeming weakness of the Government's position is seen as its real strength, in that rebellion against the Government is deterred by the fact that a defeat for the Government would lead in most circumstances to a dissolution of Parliament, and a general election.[1] The natural dislike of MPs for general elections makes them unlikely to precipitate such an event. Thus the strength of the Government's position is widely seen as resting upon the threat that dissolution would follow from a major defeat in the House. Some of these assumptions may be questioned, however. In the first place it is doubtful whether the threat of personal defeat plays a big part in preventing MPs from precipitating a general election, as most MPs are in safe seats.[2] Little personal expense is incurred by MPs at elections today, and the majority suffer only slight discomfort during the campaign. Thus considerations of personal defeat would not seem to be of major importance, although the fear that a general election might allow the Opposition Party to gain power is perhaps a strong force for loyalty among Government MPs, with the Prime Minister's power of patronage also being of vital significance here. It can also be argued that the dissolution threat is not an effective means of securing backbench loyalty because MPs realize that a Prime Minister dare not seek a dissolution and face the electorate with a party that seemed to be divided. However, while a Prime Minister might not voluntarily seek a dissolution in these circumstances, he might have no option but to dissolve if his Government suffered a defeat on a major issue.

Thus there can be advanced as possible reasons for the maintenance of party loyalty these several factors of positive loyalty to a party and its policies, the desire to present a party image of

[1] See W. G. Andrews, 'Some Thoughts on the Power of Dissolution', *Parl. Aff.* 1959–60, pp. 286–96; W. G. Andrews, 'Three Electoral Colleges', *Parl. Aff.* 1960–1, pp. 178–88; G. Marshall and G. C. Moodie, *Some Problems of the Constitution*, London 1961, Ch. 3.

[2] See above, p. 44.

unity, the fear of the effects of rebellion upon a political career, and the threat of a dissolution which might lead to an electoral defeat for an MP or his party. In all of these considerations the role of the party Whips is the crucial one, acting, as they do, as the machinery through which party discipline is enforced, or through which concessions are made to enable individual MPs to dissent from the party line on some particular issue. Undoubtedly, factors will vary from one MP to another, a young ambitious MP representing a marginal constituency being motivated by factors different from an older and well-established backbencher serving a safe seat. What forms the overriding consideration, however, remains open to argument, though whatever its cause, the effect of strong party discipline, combined with the tendency for general elections to produce a clear overall majority for one party, is to produce Governments secure in their control of the House from one election to another.

*   *   *

Given the strength of party discipline in the Commons today, what Parliamentary factors limit the power of the Government? One consideration is that the 'normal' situation of a Government based on a clear party majority does not emerge in every instance, and a majority for a Government can be achieved in a number of different ways. A Government may be a Coalition with the support of all the parties in the Commons, as with the two wartime Coalitions, or of just some party elements, as with the National Government formed in 1931. A Government can be formed from one party but with the support necessary for a majority in the Commons coming from more than one party, as with the Liberal Government of 1910–15 and the Labour Governments of 1924 and 1929–31. Coalition Governments are always liable to disintegrate, and minority Governments tend to be unstable, but are inevitable if a general election does not produce an overall majority for one party. Of the nineteen elections of this century, fifteen did produce an overall majority in the Commons for one party (though Labour's majorities in 1950 and 1964 were very small), while in the elections of 1910 (January and December), 1923, and 1929 no party won an overall majority.

Even when the Government is based on a clear majority, the 'rules of the game' and the 'customs of the House' demand that the Opposition cannot be ignored or steam-rollered, and this is not merely to avoid bad public reactions. To a large extent the effective working of the Parliamentary machine is dependent upon the co-operation and mutual accommodation of the Government and Opposition Whips. A Government with a very small majority in the Commons could have this destroyed in by-elections. This did not happen in the 1950–1 or 1964–6 Parliaments with the minute Labour majorities, and such an occurrence would have been unprecedented, but the possibility was always there for Attlee and Wilson. Also, Governments secure in the Commons can be destroyed by an internal Cabinet split, as happened with the Unionist Government in 1905, the Coalition Governments in 1916 and 1922, and the Labour Government in 1931. Ultimately a Government could conceivably be overthrown by a defeat in the House of Commons caused by a breakdown in party loyalty on the backbenches. However, in practical terms no Government with a clear party majority in the Commons has been destroyed by a defeat in a division in the House since Gladstone resigned after a defeat on the Finance Bill in 1885. This forms the basis of the claim that today Governments are not created and destroyed by the House of Commons, as they were in the nineteenth century, but by the electorate at general elections, and by the leaders of the party that is in power between elections.

As can be seen from Table XXII, on most occasions this century the change of Government came as a result of factors unconnected with defeat in the House or the loss of Parliamentary confidence. Cabinet discord was responsible for the fall of the Government in 1905, 1916, 1922, and 1931. In 1929, 1945, 1964 and 1970 the Government was beaten at a general election towards the end of a full Parliament. In 1915 the Government gave way to a wartime Coalition. In 1902, 1908, 1923, 1935, 1937, 1955, 1957, and 1963 the Prime Minister was replaced, between elections, by another member of the Government. There were four other occasions this century (in January 1924, October 1924, 1940, and 1951) when the House of Commons was involved in some respects in the fall of the Government, though there were complicating factors on each

TABLE XXII

Governments and Prime Ministers this Century

Prime Minister			Reason for the change of Government A. Voluntary retirement of the Prime Minister (that is, for health or similar reasons) B. Electoral defeat C. Resignation of the Prime Minister or the whole Government for reasons other than electoral defeat D. Wartime emergency
Salisbury	Con.	1895–1902	A
Balfour	Con.	1902–5	C
Campbell-Bannerman	Lib.	1905–8	A
Asquith	Lib.	1908–15	D
Asquith	Coalition	1915–16	C
Lloyd George	Coalition	1916–22	C
Bonar Law	Con.	1922–3	A
Baldwin	Con.	1923–4	B
MacDonald	Lab.	1924	B
Baldwin	Con.	1924–9	B
MacDonald	Lab.	1929–31	C
MacDonald	National	1931–5	A
Baldwin	National	1935–7	A
Chamberlain	National	1937–40	D
Churchill	Coalition	1940–5	C
Churchill	Con.	1945	B
Attlee	Lab.	1945–51	B
Churchill	Con.	1951–5	A
Eden	Con.	1955–7	A
Macmillan	Con.	1957–63	A
Home	Con.	1963–4	B
Wilson	Lab.	1964–70	B
Heath	Con.	1970	

occasion. In the 1923 general election the Conservatives lost their overall majority, but remained the largest single party. Baldwin did not resign at once, but met Parliament in January 1924, only to be beaten by the combined Liberal and Labour votes in the Commons. Thus, technically the Government was overthrown by the House of Commons, but in fact the Government's fate had been sealed at the general election, and the defeat in the House was largely a formality. In October 1924 MacDonald asked for a dissolution (and lost the consequent election) when the Labour Government was beaten in a division in the Commons. However, the MacDonald Government was a minority Government, dependent on the support of the Liberals, which was not forthcoming on the occasion of the Government defeat.

In 1940 the Chamberlain Government fell after a censure debate in the Commons on the Government's handling of the war. The Government was not defeated in the division, but its majority was so much smaller than its normal majority, and criticism of Chamberlain was so severe in the debate, that the Prime Minister felt obliged to resign. However, this was a peculiar wartime situation, and a Conservative Prime Minister and Government was merely replaced by another Conservative Prime Minister and a Conservative dominated coalition. It has also been argued that Chamberlain's resignation came as a result of the pressure of public opinion rather than the House of Commons division.[1] In 1951 Attlee asked for a dissolution after his Government (left with an overall majority of only six at the 1950 election) had been subjected to eighteen months of vigorous Opposition pressure. The Government lost the consequent election, and there has been much argument as to whether Attlee need have sought a dissolution when he did.[2] Attlee was not forced to seek a dissolution as a result of any specific Government defeat, and in the final analysis the Government could have carried on. Indeed, it can be argued that the 1950-1 Parliament, and more particularly that of 1964-6, illustrate how a Government can survive in the Commons with a very small majority, provided that it avoids as far as possible issues that are likely to cause dissent among its own backbenchers. This suggests that a Government with a very small majority is in some ways more secure than a Government with a large majority, potential rebels being less likely to show dissension if the Government appears to be in a precarious position.

[1] See Jennings, *Cabinet Government*, p. 478. See also J. S. Rasmussen, 'Party Discipline in War-Time: the Downfall of the Chamberlain Government', *J of P* 1970, pp. 379–406.
[1] See Hoffman, *The Conservative Party in Opposition, 1945-51*, Ch. 7.

Despite these four instances, it remains true that on no occasion this century has a Government based on a workable party majority been overthrown by the House of Commons. The January 1924 incident merely involved a technicality, in that Baldwin's defeat in the Commons was inevitable after his overall majority had been destroyed at the election, while in October 1924 the Government party was in a minority in the House, and in 1940 and 1951 the Government's fall did not come as a result of any specific defeat in a division in the Commons. While October 1924, 1940, and 1951 illustrate how the House of Commons can still be involved in the circumstances surrounding the fall of a Government, the general principle remains that today Governments are made and unmade by the electorate and the party leaders rather than by the House of Commons.

*   *   *

The degree of Government control over Parliament today produces varying reactions. On the one hand, Parliamentarians deplore the situation and describe it as 'Cabinet dictatorship' or 'executive despotism', and argue that today the power, efficiency, and prestige of Parliament is unacceptably low. They argue that the strengthening of the Government's position in relation to Parliament in this century, and particularly since 1945, has produced a situation in which Parliament is merely a rubber stamp for Government decisions, with Parliamentary activity in many instances being ineffective and pointless. It is claimed that the dominance of the party Whips means that minority opinions are lost, that new ideas are stifled by excessive conformity, and that as a result there is less colour in Parliament and less public interest in politics. This is presented as being the negation of democracy, with the executive being given virtually dictatorial power in between general elections. Thus demands are made for a reduction in the extent of Government control over Parliament.

Undoubtedly, dissatisfaction with Parliament's role is based to some extent on party political considerations. In the period of the Labour Government from 1945 to 1951, charges of executive despotism came mainly from right-wing critics who said that Parliament was being steam-rollered by 'Socialist Dictators'. In the period from 1951 to 1964, however, right-wing critics were less vocal, and dissatisfaction with Parliament's power was expressed mainly by left-wing commentators who saw opposition in Parliament as being fruitless in face of the long uninterrupted period of Conservative rule. No doubt an extended period of Labour rule into the 'seventies would have revived right-wing concern over Parliament's role. As well as these partisan considerations, however, there is in Britain an excessive attachment to Parliament, and to the tradition and ceremonial that surrounds it,[1] which can lead to a misunderstanding of the role that Parliament played in the past and plays today, and which can produce a misinterpretation of the whole political system in Britain. The change that has taken place in Parliament's role since the brief Golden Age of Parliamentary power in the middle of the nineteenth century is popularly regarded as a decline, whereas from a different standpoint this may be regarded merely as an evolution in Parliament's role as the whole political system has evolved. References have been made above to the value of 'strong government' that results from a powerful executive, and to the need for speedy and efficient government in the modern world.[2] A Parliament that is capable of making and unmaking Governments at will, can produce near anarchy, as was illustrated to some extent in the French Fourth Republic. Governmental stability is essential for long-term policy making, and as the details of administration must be considered in the formulation of policy, and as the Government alone has access to the administrative facts of life, the Government should be in a position to control the legislative process.

Also, the extent to which the Government controls Parliament is often exaggerated, and in fact Governments are limited and controlled by their own backbenchers to a greater extent than is normally revealed by public debate. Government defeats in Parliament are rare, partly because the Government knows what Parliament will accept, and therefore only introduces measures that it knows to be acceptable. Thus to say that the Government is never beaten in Parliament misses the point to some extent, as influence can be exerted behind the scenes. Party unity and docility in public, often hides discord

[1] See below, p. 224.   [2] See p. 65.

and rebellion behind the scenes. Certainly, the extent of backbenchers' subservience to the Whips varies considerably from one situation to another. As a general rule, it is probably true to say that there is more independence exhibited by back-benchers when their party is in opposition than when it is in office, while within the Government party backbench inde-pendence is generally greater when the Government has a secure majority than when it has a small one, and greater when the party has been in office for some time than when it newly comes to power.

Finally, it may be noted that even though Parliament may not be able to make and break Governments in the way that it did in the mid-nineteenth century, and even though the fate of the Government today is normally determined by a general election rather than by a vote in Parliament, the evolution of the British system of government has left Parliament with the vital function of criticizing and publicizing Government activi-ties. Thus the modern role of Parliament is not to seek to overthrow the Government, but is rather to reveal the actions of the Government, and the implications of its policy, for the ultimate judgement of the electorate. Given the acceptance of this role for Parliament, it can nevertheless still be argued that Parliament does not perform this role as adequately as it might, and that a reform of Parliamentary procedure is re-quired to enable it to better perform its function as a publicist.[1] This attitude to Parliamentary reform, however, accepts the basic principle that Parliament cannot and should not destroy the Government, but that Parliament's task within the machin-ery of government is to uncover and advertise to the elec-torate the activities of the executive.

Ministerial Responsibility

The term 'responsible government' can be applied to the British system in three main respects.[2] First of all, it may be regarded as a characteristic feature of the British system that Governments act in a responsible manner, in the sense that they do not abuse the wide legal powers that they possess as a result

---

[1] See below, p. 245.
[2] See Birch, *Representative and Responsible Government.*

of the various features of the Constitution which concentrate considerable power in the hands of the Government of the day. In this sense, responsible government means trustworthy government, and is a general description of the British political culture. Secondly, responsible government can be taken to mean that the Government is responsive to public opinion, and acts in accordance with what it judges to be the wishes of the majority of the people. There is a certain overlap between this meaning and the first meaning, in that today we assume that in order to be regarded as trustworthy, a Government has to be responsive to public opinion. There can be a conflict between these meanings, however, in that at times a Government may have to ignore current public opinion if it is to act in what it regards as the long-term interests of the people. The third and most specific meaning of responsible government is that the Government is accountable to Parliament. This meaning is based first of all on the principle that Ministers are drawn from Parliament, and secondly on the principle that the Government has to have the support of the majority of the members of the House of Commons. The modern application of this third meaning of responsible government has been considered above, but it is necessary here to consider two doctrines that stem from it—the principles of collective Government responsibility and individual Ministerial responsibility to Parliament.[1]

The doctrine of collective responsibility means that all members of the Government are collectively responsible for the successes or failures of the Government, and all Ministers, not just the departmental Ministers concerned, must collectively share moral responsibility for its policies. Implicit in the doctrine is the notion that all Ministers are bound to support Government decisions before the public, Parliament, and the party, and at the very least must refrain from openly criticizing Government policy. This doctrine also implies that a Minister who dislikes a particular Government policy must reconcile his differences or resign from the Government. The principle is perhaps aptly summed up by Lord Melbourne's comment to his Cabinet colleagues that 'it doesn't matter much what we say but we must all say the same thing'.

[1] See G. Marshall, 'Ministerial Responsibility', *PQ* 1963, pp. 256–68; Marshall and Moodie, Ch. 4.

Collective responsibility had its origin in the need for Ministers in the eighteenth century to present a united front to the Monarch on the one hand, and to Parliament on the other. Today, collective responsibility enables the Government to present a common face to its party supporters inside Parliament, to the party outside Parliament, and to the electorate generally—the maintenance of a united Government front being an essential prerequisite of the preservation of party discipline in the House, and to the answering of Opposition and public criticism of Government policy. In this respect it also serves as a means of suppressing differences of opinion within the Government itself. The doctrine applies to all Ministers, from senior Cabinet Ministers to junior Ministers. It would also seem to apply to the unpaid Parliamentary Private Secretaries, in that in 1965 Mr Frank Allaun, Parliamentary Private Secretary to the Colonial Secretary, resigned his post because he could not accept Government policy towards the crisis in Vietnam, and in 1967 the Prime Minister forced a group of Parliamentary Private Secretaries to resign when they declined to support specific aspects of Government economic policy. On some issues where there is no clear party line, the members of the Government are sometimes allowed to join in the 'luxury' of a free vote, uninhibited by the party Whips or by the doctrine of collective responsibility. Even on some occasions when backbenchers are allowed a free vote, however, the Government's collective view is often made clear. The Government is expected to give a lead on practically all issues, and for the Government not to do so can be seen as an abdication of its duty.

In the National Government formed in 1931 there was an open 'agreement to differ' among Ministers in their attitude towards tariff policy.[1] The Government contained Conservative, Liberal, and Labour members, who had fundamentally opposed attitudes towards the question of protective tariffs, and this was felt to be justified in order that the Government might maintain its broad all-party nature. Such an open agreement could not normally be justified, however, as it interferes with the Government's collective accountability to Parliament, and rather like a free vote it provides a cloak for Government responsibilities. A public rejection of collective responsibility in

[1] For comments see Jennings, *Cabinet Government*, p. 278.

this way could only have been possible in a Coalition Government, and in fact the agreement only operated from January to September 1932, when the free-traders primarily concerned (Snowden, Samuel, and Sinclair) resigned from the Government.

Although in strict theory today the doctrine of collective responsibility demands support from all Ministers for Government policies, there are obvious practical difficulties in applying such a principle in modern Governments which contain about one hundred members. The British parties, and thus to some extent British Governments, are made up of many diverse elements. When in Opposition, all parties reveal internal conflicts. A party that seemed to be united in office often shows clear divisions and disagreements when it leaves office, and these are not all due to the process of self-examination that tends to follow electoral defeat. It is safe to assume, therefore, that within any Government there will be a number of important policy disagreements which are not publicly revealed, and it is necessary to discount the notion that collective responsibility involves genuine agreement by all Ministers on all aspects of Government policies. Certainly, in the eyes of the public some Ministers are held to be 'more responsible than others', and thus open to more blame (or in some cases, more praise) than their colleagues. The 'Guilty Men at Munich' in 1938, and the 'Suez Ministers' in 1956, were small groups of Ministers who received particular blame for the Government's policies. Similarly, individual Ministers often attract criticism rather than the whole Government, and in 1963 and 1964 Ernest Marples, as Minister of Transport, received particularly severe criticism from motorists, while the Chancellor of the Exchequer is always singled out for particular criticism in times of wage restraint. The Government can often use individual Ministerial unpopularity as a means of escaping from collective responsibility. Thus in 1935 Sir Samuel Hoare was sacrificed when the foreign policy agreement he had negotiated with France proved to be highly unpopular with the public. This was a direct breach of collective responsibility, in that the Government rejected Hoare's policy after previously committing themselves to support it. Similarly, in 1962 Selwyn Lloyd was asked to resign after his incomes policy, which had previously been endorsed by the whole Government, proved to be unpopular and ineffective.

The degrees of responsibility that exist within the Government for particular policies, are thus often known to the public, and are sometimes used as a means of sacrificing one Minister in order to relieve the whole Government of responsibility. A general basis of unity has to be maintained, however, in that if disagreements become too acute, and become too well known to the public, the Government's Parliamentary and electoral security is threatened. To this end, collective responsibility, despite its practical limitations, remains as a device that is used to curb excessive disagreements among Ministers, and hide such disagreements as do exist, in order to prevent them from being exploited by the Opposition, and by dissident elements within the Government party.

*   *   *

The doctrine of individual responsibility has a number of meanings. In the legal sense it means that the Minister, not the Monarch, is responsible for a particular aspect of governmental activity, and in this sense it is the logical expression of the principle that the Monarch exercises his powers only on the advice of Ministers. In relation to Parliament, Ministerial responsibility means that the Minister has to answer, in the informative sense, for the activities of the department of which he is in charge. He has to answer questions and contribute to debates in Parliament, providing information about the sphere of activity for which he is responsible. Further, as outlined above, individual Ministerial responsibility can mean that within the doctrine of collective Government responsibility an individual Minister is particularly responsible for his own department or his own sphere of activity. Theoretically this can be taken to mean that the Minister, and not his departmental officials, is responsible for the mistakes made by the department, with the Minister's resignation being necessary in the event of a serious error by the Minister's department.

The precise extent of a Minister's responsibilities in this direction is not clear, nor are the consequences of the acknowledgement by Ministers of responsibility for departmental errors. It has been argued that the Minister is held to be responsible and accountable for all mistakes by his subordinates, even though the Minister may not have known about them, and could not have prevented them. Thus Sir Ivor Jennings talks of 'the responsibility of the Minister for every act done in his department',[1] while Lord Morrison has said that the Minister 'must accept responsibility as if the act were his own'.[2] In a statement to the House of Commons in 1954, however, Sir David Maxwell Fyfe, then Home Secretary, claimed that a Minister could not be held responsible for departmental actions that he did not know of, and of which he did not approve.[3]

Although many Ministers are asked to resign because they are generally unsuitable, resignation in acknowledgement of specific Ministerial errors is rare, there being only twenty in the hundred years from 1855 to 1955.[4] Of these, four were for personal mistakes by Ministers, as with Dalton's Budget leak in 1947, six were because the Cabinet repudiated a specific Ministerial policy, as with Hoare's resignation in 1935, and ten were for departmental errors not necessarily made by the Ministers themselves. A number of factors are responsible for the comparative rarity of such Ministerial resignations. The Minister may be shielded by the collective responsibility of the whole Government. Similarly, a small group of Ministers can assume a collective responsibility, making it difficult to apportion specific blame, as with the Treasury, the Ministry of Defence, and the service departments over the large profits made by the Ferranti firm out of defence spending in 1963. Even when criticism is clearly levelled at one Minister, as with the Minister of Food, John Strachey, over the failure of the groundnut scheme in 1947, the Prime Minister may support the Minister and help him to weather the storm. Alternatively, the Minister may be moved to another department in a Ministerial reshuffle, as were Shinwell after the fuel crisis of 1947, and Callaghan after the 1967 devaluation. A Minister who does resign may, of course, return to the Government in another post at a later date, as did Hoare, Dalton, and Selwyn Lloyd.

Thus there is a clear overlap between individual Ministerial responsibility and collective Government responsibility, in that

[1] *Cabinet Government*, p. 499.   [2] *Government and Parliament*, p. 329.
[3] 530 H. C. Deb. 5S. 1289.
[4] S. E. Finer, 'The Individual Responsibility of Ministers', *Pub. Admin.* 1956, pp. 377–96. See also G. K. Fry, 'Thoughts on the Present State of the Convention of Ministerial Responsibility', *Parl. Aff.* 1969–70, pp. 10–20.

at times a Minister's individual responsibility is used as a means of avoiding the Government's collective responsibility for an error, while on other occasions an individual Minister can be shielded behind the collective responsibility of the whole Government. As the scope of government activity grows, and as the size of Governments tends to increase, Ministers must inevitably find it increasingly difficult to keep in touch with the technical details of their departments' work, while it also becomes harder to keep the Government as a collective body responsible for the whole range and depth of executive actions. Thus both doctrines become more and more difficult to apply in their strict meaning, and there must inevitably be a large and growing difference between their theory and practice.

Constitutional Authority and Political Power

In this chapter, emphasis has been placed on the almost unlimited Constitutional authority of Governments in Britain. At the same time, however, in practical terms a Government's power is restricted by numerous factors. Politics is essentially the art of the possible, and numerous practical difficulties, including foreign crises, balance of payments difficulties, industrial unrest, and economic crises at home, can all interfere with a Government's plans, and limit its ability to fulfil its policies. Government aims are also limited by what is administratively possible, and policies that are worked out in opposition often turn out to be administratively impractical when the party comes to power.[1] Ultimately, of course, a Government is limited in what it can achieve by the threat of rebellion or public non-co-operation, but long before this stage is reached, the pressure of public opinion limits to a considerable extent what a Government can achieve. Precisely what constitutes public opinion and how it makes itself felt, is difficult to define, but several forces, including the press, radio and TV, the local organs of the political parties, and pressure groups, all help in the formulation of public attitudes, and at the same time provide media for the expression of these attitudes.[2] In so far as a

[1] See Chapter 14 for a more detailed comment upon these factors.
[2] For a discussion of some of these factors see H. Durant, 'Public Opinion Polls and Foreign Policy', *BJS* 1955, pp. 149–58; K. Younger, 'Public

Government wishes to win the next general election (it being assumed that a Government wishes to remain in office), it cannot afford to ignore entirely in the years before the election, the opinions that are expressed by pressure groups, the press, and all the other outlets for public attitudes.

To quote examples of widely unpopular actions that Governments could take, or have taken in the past, detracts from the essential fact that in the main, Governments do not abuse the wide Constitutional powers that they do possess. The essential features of the British political culture are those of co-operation and trust on the part of the people, and moderation on the part of Governments. Thus a picture emerges of British Governments having almost unlimited legal power, but exercising this power in a spirit of moderation. They are not limited in the scope of their activities by written Constitutional checks and balances, but rather by various practical considerations, by the nature of British society, and by an unwritten code of behaviour. It has been said of the British Constitution that it is 'no more than the current notion of politicians about proper conduct'.[1] This essentially vague and nebulous feature of the British political system, with the consequent differences between what the Constitution theoretically allows and what is actually practised, means that the British system can be easily misinterpreted. It is thus necessary to emphasize the very real check that is imposed on the activities of Governments by the traditional acceptance of the need for moderate, popular, and reasonable government.

Opinion and Foreign Policy', *BJS* 1955, pp. 169–75; D. C. Watt, 'Foreign Affairs, the Public Interest, and the Right to Know', *PQ* 1963, pp. 121–36. See also G. Marshall, 'The Constitutional Status of "The People" ', *Parl. Aff.* 1956–7, pp. 148–54; B. Crick, ' "Them and U": Public Impotence and Government Power,' *PL* 1968, pp. 8–27.

[1] D. E. Butler, *The Study of Political Behaviour*, London 1959, p. 17.

7

The Structure
of Government

WITHIN THE machinery of government in Britain today, the
Government and the Cabinet are not synonymous terms. The
Government is an all-embracing term, covering the various
grades of Ministers and junior Ministers, with varying shades
and degrees of authority, who go to make up the political side
of the executive. The Cabinet, a product of convention rather
than statute, is a committee of the Government, chosen by the
Prime Minister, and made up of the twenty or so senior Ministers who meet together for four or five hours each week to
supervise and co-ordinate the work of the whole Government
machine.

Government Structure

The general term 'Minister' covers a number of categories.[1]
The various departments of state are each presided over by a
Minister or a Secretary of State, the distinction between the
two being largely historical, though the Secretaries of State
do tend to be in charge of the most important departments.
Some departments are headed by Ministers who carry ancient

[1] For a detailed analysis of government structure see F. M. G. Willson
and D. N. Chester, *The Organization of British Central Government*, London
1957. See also F. M. G. Willson, 'The Organization of British Central
Government 1955-61 and 1962-4', *Pub. Admin.* 1962, pp.159-206, *and*
1966, pp. 73-101. For more general comments see H. R. G. Greaves,
'British Central Government 1914-56', *PQ* 1957, pp. 383-9; W. A. Robson,
'The Reform of Government', *PQ* 1964, pp. 193-211.

titles, but who have the same status and salary (£8,500) as other Ministers and Secretaries of State. In this category is the Chancellor of the Exchequer, and the more recently created post of Chief Secretary to the Treasury (although he is not head of a department). In addition, there is the Attorney-General, the Solicitor-General, the Lord Advocate, the Solicitor-General for Scotland, and the Lord Chancellor who, as the chief law officer, has a salary of £14,500 (£500 more than the Prime Minister). There are a number of non-departmental posts that have historical significance and at one time carried important duties, but which today are largely free from specific responsibilities. The Prime Minister's official post of First Secretary to the Treasury comes into this category, as do the posts of Lord President of the Council, Lord Privy Seal, Paymaster-General, and Chancellor of the Duchy of Lancaster. Today these offices are either held in conjunction with some other Ministerial office, or are included in the Government in order that the holder may perform some general function within the Government. A Minister without Portfolio is also sometimes included for this purpose. These various categories of full Ministers come to a total of about forty posts, and only about half of these are included in the Cabinet at any one time. The others are classified as 'Ministers outside the Cabinet'.

Each departmental Minister is assisted by one or two junior Ministers who have the title of Parliamentary Secretaries, while Secretaries of State have Parliamentary Under Secretaries of State to assist them. The distinction between Parliamentary Secretaries and Parliamentary Under Secretaries is again largely that of title, and they have the same salary of £3,750. At the Treasury the junior Minister is the Financial Secretary, while the titles carried by the Chief Government Whip and his five or six senior assistants are Parliamentary Secretary to the Treasury and Lord Commissioners.

A third group in the Ministerial hierarchy is made up of Ministers of State, who are subordinate to Ministers and Secretaries of State, but who have more status and salary (£7,625 or £5,625) than the other junior Ministers. This office of Minister of State was introduced in its modern form in 1955, and was at first confined to departments with wide geographical commitments that involved a Minister being away from London

TABLE XXIII

Structure of the Heath Government, June 1970

Office or Department	Secretary of State	Minister	Minister of State	Parlia-mentary Secretary
Prime Minister		1*		
Lord President of the Council		1		
Lord Privy Seal		1		
Chancellor of the Duchy of Lancaster		1		
Paymaster-General		1		
Lord Chancellor		1		
Attorney-General		1		
Lord Advocate		1		
Solicitor-General		1		
Solicitor-General for Scotland		1		
Agriculture, Fisheries and Food		1		1
Civil Service		1*		1
Defence	1		1	3
Education and Science	1			2
Employment and Productivity	1		1	1
Foreign and Commonwealth	1		1	2
Home Department	1		2	1
Housing and Local Government		1	1	3
Overseas Development		1		
Social Services	1		1	2
Posts and Telecommunications		1		
Public Buildings and Works		1		1
Scotland	1		1	3
Technology		1	2	2
Board of Trade		1	1	1
Transport		1		1
Treasury		2†	1	7‡
Wales	1		1	
	8	20	13	31

* The Prime Minister was also Minister for the Civil Service
† Excluding the Prime Minister   ‡ Excluding four Assistant Whips

for long periods. For this reason Ministers of State tended to be Peers, whose day-to-day presence in Parliament was not as essential as it was for members of the Commons. More recently, the post of Minister of State has been extended to a number of other departments. In its broadest sense the Government also includes the Parliamentary Private Secretaries who act as unpaid assistants to Ministers, fulfilling the role of secretary and general assistant in Parliamentary matters.[1] A classic line of promotion would be through the various levels of Parliamentary Private Secretary, Parliamentary Secretary or Under Secretary, Minister of State, non-Cabinet Minister, Cabinet Minister, senior Cabinet Minister, and ultimately Prime Minister. It is unlikely, however, that promotion would be as laborious or as precise as this. Sometimes appointments are made to full Ministerial office, and perhaps even Cabinet office, without any previous junior Ministerial experience, especially if a party comes to power after a long period in opposition. Alternatively, some members of the Government may never rise above the rank of junior Minister.[2]

*   *   *

The overall size of the Government (excluding Parliamentary Private Secretaries) has more than doubled this century, rising from about forty-five in the Governments of Balfour, Campbell-Bannerman, and Asquith before 1914, to more than one hundred in the Wilson Government formed in 1964. In 1970, however, Heath formed a Government of less than eighty members, as part of a general policy to reduce the size of the Whitehall machine. The danger of excessive executive domination of the legislature is one of the problems involved in a large executive machine. In the House of Commons elected in 1964, for example more than half of the Labour MPs held posts either as Ministers,

[1] See R. K. Alderman and J. A. Cross, 'The Parliamentary Private Secretary', *PS* 1966, pp. 199–207.

[2] See P. W. Buck, 'The Early Start Towards Cabinet Office 1918–55', *WPQ* 1963, pp. 624–32; P. W. Buck, 'MPs in Ministerial Office 1918–55 and 1955–9', *PS* 1961, pp. 300–6; D. J. Heasman, 'Parliamentary Paths to High Office', *Parl. Aff.* 1962–3, pp. 315–30; F. M. G. Willson, 'Routes of Entry of New Members of the British Cabinet 1868–1958', *PS* 1959, pp. 222–32; F. M. G. Willson, 'Entry to the Cabinet 1959–68; *PS* 1970, pp. 236–8.

junior Ministers, or Parliamentary Private Secretaries. The eighteenth-century Parliamentary fear that the Monarch would dominate Parliament if the King's Ministers were drawn from Parliament, is thus echoed today in the fear of Government domination of Parliament, and this led to criticism of the trend that in the 'fifties and 'sixties produced a marked increase in Ministerial numbers in the Commons. Although members of the Commons appointed to Ministerial office no longer have to secure re-election to the Commons, there do exist statutory limits on the number of Ministers allowed to serve in the Commons at any one time. One of the first pieces of legislation introduced by the new Labour Government in 1964 was the Ministers of the Crown Bill, which sought to increase the number of Ministers allowed to sit and vote in the House of Commons. Legislation was necessary because the new ministries and posts created in the Wilson Government increased the number of Ministers serving in the Commons beyond that allowed by existing legislation.

The Ministers of the Crown Act 1937 specified that only eighteen out of twenty-one senior Ministers could serve in the Commons at any one time, so that if all twenty-one posts were filled, at least three had to be held by members of the Lords. The twenty-one senior posts were listed in the Act and were those posts which normally would carry Cabinet status. In addition, it was stipulated that not more than twenty junior Ministers could sit in the Commons at any one time. During the war, under the provisions of the emergency legislation, these figures were exceeded, while many of the new Ministerial posts created after the war were specifically excluded from the restrictions of the 1937 Act. In 1941 the Select Committee on Offices and Places of Profit Under the Crown recommended that only sixty Ministers in all should serve in the Commons.[1] Taking account of this recommendation, and of the changes that had taken place since then, the House of Commons Disqualification Act 1957 declared that not more than twenty-nine senior Ministers listed in the Act, and not more than seventy Ministers in all, could serve in the Commons at one time. These figures were not exceeded by Macmillan or Home, despite the increase in the size of the Conservative Governments between 1957 and

[1] The Herbert Committee Report, H.C. 120 of 1941.

1964. When the Labour Government came to power in 1964, however, the number of new Ministerial posts created meant that new legislation became necessary. The 1964 Act increased from seventy to ninety-one the total number of Ministers allowed to serve in the Commons, and abolished the limit on the number of senior Ministers that could be drawn from the Commons. The figure of ninety-one fixed by the Ministers of the Crown Act as the maximum number of Ministers that could be drawn from the Commons, was below the total number of Ministerial posts in the Wilson Government, so that the Act recognized the principle that some posts should be filled by members of the Lords.

Cabinet Structure[1]

In 1918 the Committee set up to review the machinery of government in Britain (the Haldane Committee) officially defined the functions of the Cabinet as:[2]

1. The final determination of policy to be submitted to Parliament:
2. The supreme control of the national executive in accordance with the policy prescribed by Parliament: and
3. The continuous co-ordination and delimitation of the activities of the several Departments of State.

Thus, in short, the role of the Cabinet is that of a central directing force within the machinery of government, making the most important decisions of policy, supervising the execution of that policy, and in general co-ordinating the work of the whole executive machine.

With this role in mind, a Prime Minister has to consider and balance a number of factors when forming his Cabinet. If too many Ministers are included in the Cabinet it becomes an unwieldy body, and conflicts with the general principle that the task of decision making is most effectively performed by a small body. If too few Ministers are included, it becomes difficult for the Cabinet to keep in touch with the other members

---

[1] For a detailed historical analysis see Hans Daalder, *Cabinet Reform in Britain 1914–63*, London 1964; P. Gordon Walker, *The Cabinet*, London 1970.

[2] Report of the Machinery of Government Committee, Cd. 9230 (1918).

of the Government and with the departments of state, as well as with the Government backbenchers and the party outside Parliament. Some departmental posts such as Foreign Secretary, Chancellor of the Exchequer, Home Secretary, would be included in any conventional Cabinet. Added to these are the most important posts of the day, and also some posts, such as perhaps the Secretaries of State for Scotland and Wales, which are included largely for reasons of prestige or regional representation. Balanced with these departmental posts must be some Ministers free from departmental ties who can undertake the tasks of policy co-ordination, long-term planning, and general administrative functions not attached to specific departments. Posts like Lord Privy Seal, Lord President of the Council, Chancellor of the Duchy of Lancaster (which today are largely of historical and ceremonial significance), can be included in the Cabinet in order that their holders may perform non-departmental functions. Under Macmillan in 1962, for example, Lord Hailsham, as Lord President of the Council, was responsible for sport, science, and north-east affairs, as well as being leader of the House of Lords.

Personality factors inevitably play a vital part in Cabinet making, in that the Prime Minister has to include among his Ministers men of standing within the party, regardless of their potential Ministerial ability. This is perhaps particularly important in face of the several diverse elements within the British parties. Thus in 1964 Harold Wilson included in his Cabinet Ministers drawn from various sections of the party, including 'militants' like Frank Cousins and Barbara Castle, alongside 'moderates' like Sir Frank Soskice and Lord Longford. Similarly in 1957 Macmillan included in his Cabinet left and right wingers like R. A. Butler and Lord Salisbury (although Salisbury later resigned from the Government), and Heath's Cabinet in 1970 was drawn from various 'wings' of the party. The Prime Minister has also often to decide whether a particular party extremist would be a bigger threat to party unity in or out of the Cabinet, in that it is sometimes possible to 'buy' silence and conformity from a potential rebel by giving him the responsibility of Ministerial office, and this perhaps influenced Attlee's inclusion of Aneurin Bevan in his Cabinet, and Wilson's inclusion of Cousins.

TABLE XXIV

Cabinet Posts January 1957–June 1970

	Jan. 1957	Oct. 1959	Oct. 1963	Oct. 1964	June 1970
Prime Minister	✓	✓	✓	✓	✓
Lord Chancellor	✓	✓	✓	✓	✓
Lord President of the Council	✓	*2	*3	✓	✓
Lord Privy Seal	*2	*3	✓	✓	✓
Duchy of Lancaster	✓	✓	✓		✓
Chancellor of the Exchequer	✓	✓	✓	✓	✓
Secretary of State:					
Foreign	✓	✓	✓	✓	✓
Home	*2	✓	✓	✓	✓
Colonies	✓	✓	*4	✓	
Commonwealth	✓	*2	*4	✓	
Scotland	✓	✓	✓	✓	✓
Economic Affairs				*1	
Social Services					✓
Minister of Education†	✓	✓	✓	✓	✓
Minister of Defence†	✓	✓	✓	✓	✓
Minister of Agriculture	✓	✓	✓	✓	✓
Minister of Labour	✓	✓	✓	✓	
Minister of Housing and L.G.	*1	*1	*1	✓	✓
Minister for Welsh Affairs†	*1	*1	*1	✓	✓
President of the Board of Trade	✓	✓	*5	✓	✓
Minister of Transport	✓	✓	✓	✓	
Paymaster-General		✓	*2		
Minister of Power	✓	✓	✓	✓	
Minister of Aviation		✓			
Minister for Science		*3	*3		
Chief Secretary to the Treasury			*2		
First Secretary of State				*1	
Minister Without Portfolio			✓‡	✓	
Minister of Public Building and Works			✓		
Minister of Health			✓		
Secretary of State for Industry			*5		
Minister of Technology				✓	✓
Minister of Overseas Development				✓	
Secretary of State for Employment					✓
Number of Posts	20	22	28	24	18
Number of Ministers	18	19	23	23	18

† Replaced by Secretary of State in October 1964
Where a Minister held more than one post, the posts are marked by an asterisk and a number, e.g. in January 1957 the Home Secretary was also Lord Privy Seal.
‡ In October 1963 Home appointed two Ministers without Portfolio.

The problem of what is the ideal size for the Cabinet in order that it may be representative of all sections of the Government and the party, and yet avoid being unwieldy, largely resolves itself into the question of whether the Cabinet should contain all Ministers, most Ministers, or merely a few very senior Ministers. In the nineteenth century this question largely solved itself, in that it was possible to include all Ministers and still keep the Cabinet a reasonably small and workable unit. Before 1867 Cabinets generally contained thirteen to sixteen members, and in 1914 it was still possible, with a cabinet of twenty, to include virtually all full Ministers. Even in 1939, Chamberlain's Cabinet of twenty-three excluded only a few minor posts. Since 1945, however, the vast increase in the range of Government activities, and the consequent increase in the number of departments and Ministers, has meant that if all Ministers were to be included today, the Cabinet numbers would be in excess of forty. It has been argued that a Cabinet of this size, containing all full Ministers, is a logical and desirable development, with Cabinet Committees and an informal Inner Cabinet of senior Ministers fulfilling the specialized function of detailed discussion of policy.[1] This view, however, has not been widely canvassed. Since 1945 no Prime Minister has attempted to include all Ministers in his Cabinet, and a clear distinction has been made between Cabinet and non-Cabinet Ministers. Within the concept of the Cabinet composed of not all Ministers but of most of them, opinions vary as to what is the ideal number to include. Lord Morrison has advocated a Cabinet of sixteen to eighteen members;[2] D. N. Chester, eighteen to twenty;[3] Harold Laski, little more than fifteen members;[4] Harold Wilson, fifteen to twenty members[5]—though his actual Cabinet formed in 1964 had twenty-three members. Cabinets since 1945 have in fact ranged from sixteen to twenty-three members, with a general tendency over the years for them to increase in size. In 1970, however, Heath reversed this trend with a Cabinet of only

---

[1] See R. V. Clements, 'The Cabinet', *PS* 1965, pp. 231–4.

[2] *Government and Parliament*, p. 44.

[3] Sir John Anderson (ed.), *British Government Since 1918*, London 1950, p. 36.

[4] H. J. Laski, *Reflections on the Constitution*, London 1962, p. 178.

[5] BBC Publications, *Whitehall and Beyond*, London 1964, p. 26.

eighteen members, and of only seventeen after the Ministerial
re-shuffle in October 1970. The balance between departmental
and non-departmental posts, and the actual Ministerial offices
included in the Cabinet, have varied from one Government to
another.

*   *   *

As well as Cabinets composed of all Ministers or most
Ministers, a third possible type of Cabinet is that composed of
only a few 'Super Ministers'. Such a Cabinet of perhaps half
a dozen members could be made up entirely of non-departmental Ministers who could act solely as co-ordinators and
planners, or it could be composed of the six or so senior departmental Ministers, or it could be made up of a mixture of the
two types of Minister. The Cabinet formed by Lloyd George
when he became Prime Minister in 1916 was composed of only
five Ministers, four of them without specific departmental
duties, and in 1918 a fifth non-departmental member was
added. Departmental Ministers and service chiefs were often
called upon to attend War Cabinet meetings, however, and it
has been calculated that in the final year of the Cabinet's life
a total of 248 non-Cabinet personnel attended its meetings.[1]
With the outbreak of war in 1939, Neville Chamberlain formed
a Cabinet of nine members, including four non-departmental
Ministers. When Churchill succeeded him in 1940 he
formed a Cabinet composed of himself, the Foreign Secretary,
and three Ministers without departmental duties. In August
1942 Churchill increased the Cabinet size to eight by adding
three more departmental Ministers. The conflict that arose
within the Cabinet between Ernest Bevin as Minister of Labour,
and Lord Beaverbrook as Minister of Production, illustrates
the problems that can arise in a small Cabinet made up of
senior departmental Ministers, and a change to an entirely
non-departmental Cabinet was urged on Churchill, but to no
avail. It is probably true to say, however, that Churchill's
Cabinet was based more on personalities than on theories of
departmental or non-departmental Cabinets.

As well as these actual examples of small Cabinets, theoretical

---

[1] Daalder, *Cabinet Reform in Britain 1914–63*, p. 54.

support for the idea of Super Ministers came from the Machinery of Government Committee in 1918.[1] The Committee reported on the theoretical principles of Cabinet Government and their practical application, and it advocated a Cabinet of ten to twelve Super Ministers, though it avoided the question of whether or not they should be departmental Ministers. Super Cabinets have been advocated in other academic studies, and L. S. Amery proposed a small Cabinet of six non-departmental Ministers to decide broad policy, with departmental committees for administrative supervision under the chairmanship of Cabinet Ministers.[2]

Thus the concept of a Super Cabinet involves firstly the question of whether a small Cabinet of six or so members is to be preferred to the conventional larger Cabinets, and secondly, if a small Cabinet is preferred, whether or not it should be composed of Ministers free from departmental duties. Theoretical proposals and the wartime precedents offer different examples of attempts to resolve these questions. The basic argument used by those who favour the concept of a Super Cabinet, is that with the gradual increase in the number of Ministers both inside and outside the Cabinet, the present system is getting out of hand, and rather than attempting to adapt the existing machinery to the new conditions, there is a need for radical re-thinking about Cabinet structure and functions. It is often argued that under the present system the policy-making function of the Cabinet is being neglected as a result of the pressure of departmental business on Cabinet Ministers. As Ministers are increasingly bound up with the details of their own departments, they have less and less time to devote to the general supervision of the whole field of government. Thus it is maintained that it is necessary to distinguish more clearly between policy making and administration, and to create a new category of Super Ministers who would, with the Prime Minister, devote their attention primarily to broad policy, leaving the details of administration largely to Ministers outside the Super Cabinet.

In favour of a Super Cabinet it can be said that a small unit

[1] Cd. 9230 (1918). See also Hans Daalder, 'The Haldane Committee and the Cabinet', *Pub. Admin.* 1963, pp. 117–36.

[2] L. S. Amery, *Thoughts on the Constitution*, London 1964.

is a much more efficient decision-making body than a large one, and that a small Cabinet could meet more often and deal with business much more expeditiously than the existing Cabinets of twenty or more members. With a small composite Cabinet, linked with the rest of the Government through a system of committees, the number of departmental and junior Ministers could increase without affecting Cabinet size. At present a Prime Minister may have difficulty in finding twenty or so men whose abilities merit a place in the Cabinet, and many are included who are not really fitted for the policy-making role. Similarly, a small Cabinet composed only of senior Ministers would dispense with the need to include in the Cabinet prestige posts such as the Secretaries of State for Scotland and Wales. As with the wartime Cabinets, and as indeed with the present system, non-Cabinet Ministers could be called to attend Cabinet meetings when their presence was required, so that the small Cabinets need not become too remote from the rest of the Government. The problem of the size of the Cabinet is also very closely bound up with the question of Prime Ministerial authority, in that a Cabinet made up of six senior Ministers would be a much more effective check on the individual power of the Prime Minister than is the present system. The idea of a Super Cabinet is thus favoured by those who argue that the Prime Minister's authority within the present system is excessive and ought to be curbed.

The idea of a Super Cabinet, however, can be objected to on a number of grounds.[1] It is not always practical to separate the functions of policy making and administration in the way envisaged with a Super Cabinet, and such a body could become too far removed from the administrative facts of life, and too theoretical in its thinking. Similarly, a Cabinet of only a few senior Ministers could become too far removed from the rest of the party, from the rest of the Government, and from Parliament. The present difficulties experienced by the Cabinet in keeping in touch with the party, and with junior and non Cabinet Ministers, would be magnified. The authority of Ministers who were not included in the Cabinet would be reduced, and this could lead to an increase in 'back-stairs' influences, in that civil servants might be tempted to approach

[1] See, for example, Laski, *Reflections on the Constitution*, Chs. 8, 9, and 10.

Cabinet Ministers directly, rather than through their departmental Minister. The wartime Cabinets which are quoted as examples of small Cabinets working effectively, are not necessarily good precedents, in that what is successful in wartime conditions may not work in peacetime. In wartime, Ministers, Parliament, and the political parties are prepared to delegate power to a few powerful figures, and as the wartime Governments were coalitions, they were not precedents for *party* government through a small Cabinet. With a coalition of three parties, six or so leading figures may present themselves, but with one party it may well be easier to find twenty men of moderate ability, than six men of really outstanding ability. Also, while the wartime Cabinets were theoretically small, in Lloyd George's Cabinet meetings additional Ministers and service chiefs were normally present, while in Churchill's Government the Lord President's Committee acted almost as a second Cabinet responsible for home affairs.

*   *   *

Thus the existing system, with all its limitations, is perhaps a more practical system than that of a Super Cabinet. In practice it may be that the two systems are not so very different. Even with a Super Cabinet other Ministers would at times attend Cabinet meetings, and within the existing system most Governments tend to contain a group of senior Ministers who have more authority than their colleagues, and upon whom the Prime Minister particularly relies—although whether the Prime Minister's closest colleagues can be said to make up a formal 'Inner Cabinet' is a matter of debate. Certainly, the work of any Government falls into the four general categories of external affairs, defence, home affairs, and financial and economic affairs, and the Ministers in charge of these fields must inevitably form an inner group of particularly influential Ministers. Further, most Governments over the past fifty years seem to have contained their inner circles. In MacDonald's two Labour Governments for example, Clynes, Henderson, Snowden, and J. H. Thomas were particularly influential, and in the 1931 crisis, MacDonald, Snowden, and Thomas worked particularly closely together—to the detriment of the collective responsibility of the Cabinet. The 'Guilty Men' of Chamberlain's Government in the prelude to the second world war were Lord Halifax, Hoare, Simon, and Chamberlain himself, and as with Mac-Donald in 1931, the advent of a crisis seemed to produce more frequent consultations between senior Ministers. Attlee relied particularly on Bevin, Cripps, and Morrison, and later on Ede, Griffiths, and Morrison. Churchill, despite the impression of personal rule, had his circle of particular friends during the war, and in his 1951 Government he often met for informal 'conversations' with his chief Ministers and friends. In the Eden Government the men particularly responsible for the Suez policy were Eden, Macmillan, Anthony Head, Lord Hailsham, and Selwyn Lloyd, with Butler being close to the Prime Minister at other times. Macmillan seems to have relied on Lord Home, Butler, Macleod, and Selwyn Lloyd, for much of the time. Bonar Law and Baldwin, however, are thought to have had no Inner Cabinet. In 1964, when still in opposition, Harold Wilson declared that he was opposed to the idea of chief advisers meeting as an Inner Cabinet,[1] but in 1969 he formed a 'Parliamentary Committee' of six senior Cabinet Ministers, plus himself as chairman, and this was widely interpreted as representing the formal creation of an Inner Cabinet. It may be that a similar group will emerge in the Heath Cabinet. The precise extent of a Prime Minister's reliance upon advisers must vary from Government to Government, but the extent to which he does rely upon his senior colleagues bridges the gap between the structure of the existing Cabinet system and the idea of a small Super Cabinet.

The Prime Minister and the Cabinet

Writing in 1867, Walter Bagehot, in *The English Constitution*,[2] declared that the two characteristic features of Cabinet Government in Britain were, firstly, that the Cabinet was a collective executive body, and secondly, that it was drawn from Parliament and was answerable to Parliament (rather than directly to the electorate) for its authority and very existence. This, argued Bagehot, was in direct contrast with Presidential

[1] *Whitehall and Beyond*, p. 27.
[2] Fontana Library edition, London 1963, pp. 59-81.

Government in the United States where the executive was the single figure of the President, who was elected directly by the people and was thus not responsible to the legislature. It is often argued, today, however, that Constitutional developments in Britain in the last one hundred years have largely removed from our system the classic features attributed to it by Bagehot. The modern relationship between the Government and Parliament has been discussed above, but there remains the question of the relationship between the Prime Minister and the other members of the Cabinet and the Government.

The traditional description of the Prime Minister's role in the Cabinet is that of *primus inter pares*, but it is widely claimed today that the power of the Prime Minister within the Cabinet is such that he is much more than 'first among equals'.[1] The general basis of the Prime Minister's authority is wide, and this was true in the past as well as today. As the Monarch's principal adviser, he is the chief inheritor of the Monarch's powers and prerogatives. The Prime Minister personally advises the Monarch on the date of the dissolution of Parliament, and this matter is not discussed in the Cabinet, though it is not clear to what extent the Prime Minister would consult his colleagues informally.[2] The Prime Minister has wide powers of patronage, including the appointment and dismissal of Ministers. In 1962 Macmillan dismissed a third of his Cabinet, and in an age when professional politicians predominate, the Prime Minister's ability to affect directly the careers of ambitious MPs inevitably gives him considerable power and authority. The distribution of general patronage through the Honours List gives the Prime Minister an influence in many sectors of national life. To a certain extent Lloyd George's abuse of patronage discredited the whole system, and since 1922 a Committee of the Privy Council has vetted all proposed awards, but patronage re-

---

[1] See Mackintosh, *The British Cabinet*; A. H. Brown, 'Prime Ministerial Power', *PL* 1968, pp. 28–51 *and* 96–118; G. W. Jones, 'The Prime Minister's Power', *Parl. Aff.* 1964–5, pp. 167–85; R. W. K. Hinton, 'The Prime Minister as an Elected Monarch', *Parl. Aff.* 1959–60, pp. 297–303; D. J. Heasman, 'The Prime Minister and the Cabinet', *Parl. Aff.* 1961–2, pp. 461–84. See also A. King (ed), *The British Prime Minister*, London 1969; Byrum E. Carter, *The Office of Prime Minister*, London 1956.

[2] See above, p. 33.

mains a valuable political weapon in the Prime Minister's hands.[1]

Within the structure of the Government the Prime Minister has a special place, in that he has no department of his own and he acts as co-ordinator in chief. In the past, departmental responsibilities were sometimes combined with the Premiership. Lord Salisbury was Foreign Secretary 1895–1900 as well as being Prime Minister. Asquith, when Prime Minister in 1914, also temporarily assumed the post of Minister of War. Baldwin was Chancellor of the Exchequer as well as Prime Minister as a temporary expedient in 1923, and MacDonald in 1924 assumed the office of Foreign Secretary. Attlee, 1945–6, and Churchill, 1940–5 and 1951–2, combined the Premiership with the post of Minister of Defence. Wilson, and then Heath, assumed responsibility for the new Civil Service Department, created in 1968. These, however, may all be regarded as exceptions to the general rule. The Prime Minister has the special authority that goes with being Chairman of the Cabinet. As votes are not taken at Cabinet meetings, the Prime Minister's power to sum up in Cabinet discussions is very important, though the ability to handle Cabinet meetings must, like any chairmanship, vary from one Prime Minister to another. The Prime Minister also enjoys the natural authority that goes with being party leader, although MacDonald's position in the National Government in 1931, and for a while Churchill's position in the wartime Coalition, were exceptions to this.

These several aspects of the Prime Minister's position within the political system are all of quite long standing, most of them emerging during the constitutional developments of the nineteenth century. A number of more recent developments, however, have added to the Prime Minister's historically based power. In many ways the structure of the Government machine in recent years can be likened to a pyramid with the Prime Minister at the apex. The junior Ministers, the non-Cabinet Ministers, the Cabinet Ministers, the senior Cabinet Ministers, and finally the Prime Minister at the top can be seen as representing an ascending structure of power, with the Prime

[1] See K. Sainsbury, 'Patronage, Honours and Parliament', *Parl. Aff.* 1965–6, pp. 346–50; P. G. Richards, *Patronage in British Government*, London 1963.

Minister performing an ever-increasing role as supervisor and co-ordinator of the whole machine. Similarly, the Prime Minister can be seen as the head of a Civil Service elite of Permanent Secretaries who, since 1920, have moved from department to department, answerable not so much to individual departments as to the Treasury and the Prime Minister.[1] The Prime Minister vets all appointments to top Civil Service posts in order to prevent friction between the Minister and his Permanent Secretary. Thus, as with the Ministerial hierarchy, the Prime Minister can be seen as the head of the permanent administrative structure.

Departmental Ministers are today more bound up with departmental duties than at any time in the past, so that the planning and co-ordinating function of government is left increasingly in the hands of the few non-departmental Ministers of the Cabinet, and the Prime Minister in particular. In this sense the role that the Cabinet played in the nineteenth century, of discussing and deciding on general policies, has to a large extent given way to the more automatic function of approving policies that are largely decided elsewhere. The inability of departmental Ministers to probe into the details of their colleagues' departmental work, suggests that policies receive Cabinet approval largely on the strength of an alliance between the departmental Minister concerned and the Prime Minister. The Prime Minister is no longer tied to the Commons as Leader of the House.[2] Asquith separated the offices of Prime Minister and Leader of the Commons in 1915 when he appointed Lloyd George to this office, and this precedent was followed with Bonar Law and Austen Chamberlain as Leader of the Commons under Lloyd George's Premiership, and with Clynes and then Baldwin under MacDonald, and Morrison under Attlee. Since 1945 no Prime Minister has attempted to combine the two roles, and thus the Prime Minister is left with more time to devote to his task of co-ordinating the Government machine.

This century has seen the development of a Secretariat to record Cabinet decisions, and in both world wars the Secretariat performed much more than a purely secretarial role.[3] Since 1945 the Secretariat has developed as a body of officials

[1] See below, p. 319.   [2] See below, p. 219.
[3] See below, p. 211.

largely under the Prime Minister's control, and this has provided the Premier with a staff of his own. When a Prime
Minister wishes to take particular note of a department or a
Minister, he can create a special Cabinet Committee to perform the task of supervision. Normally the Prime Minister takes
a special interest in the supervision of the Treasury, and Budget
policy is decided primarily by the Prime Minister and the
Chancellor of the Exchequer, rather than by the Cabinet.
The Prime Minister also normally involves himself with foreign
affairs, sometimes to the exclusion of the Foreign Secretary's
own authority. Lord Salisbury, 1895–1900, and MacDonald in
1924 were literally their own Foreign Secretaries. Prime Ministers and Foreign Secretaries who were generally regarded as
working closely together were Chamberlain and Lord Halifax,
Churchill and Eden, Macmillan and Home, Wilson and
Stewart. On the other hand, Chamberlain and Eden, and
MacDonald and Henderson, did not seem to work harmoniously
while Ernest Bevin under Attlee is usually quoted as an example
of a Foreign Secretary who was allowed considerable freedom
to pursue his own policies. In the main, the nature of international relations today, with 'summit meetings' of heads of
state and the need for speedy military decisions in an atomic
age, means that the Prime Minister's involvement in foreign
affairs is personal and direct. The effect of two world wars on
the machinery of Cabinet government was to concentrate
power in the hands of the Prime Minister and his immediate
advisers, and to some extent this increased authority must inevitably have been retained in the return to peacetime conditions.[1]

In general elections today the emphasis tends to be on the
'image' of the Prime Minister (and the Opposition Leader) and
the appeal that is personally made to the electorate. It has been
claimed that in 1964 and 1966 the Labour Party won and the
Conservatives lost the elections largely because of the impression, or lack of an impression, made by their leaders.[2] The
effect of the mass media on elections has been to concentrate
the electorate's attention on personalities, and the personalities

[1] See J. Ehrmann, *Cabinet Government and War 1890–1940*, London 1958;
Lord Hankey, *Government Control in War*, London 1945.
[2] See above, pp. 50 and 67.

of the party leaders in particular. This process, perhaps beginning with Gladstone's Midlothian Campaign in 1880, and
culminating with the impact of television on general elections
since 1959, has had the effect of increasing the influence that
a successful leader can exert over his own party, in that the
leader has become the hub of the party's electoral appeal and
the centre of party loyalty. This must inevitably make easier
the Prime Minister's task of retaining the loyalty of his party's
MPs in Parliament.

*   *   *

These several developments in the political process can all be
advanced as factors that have increased the individual authority
of the Prime Minister in this century. At the same time, there
are various other considerations which still limit the power of
the Prime Minister. The Prime Minister's authority has no
legal basis, in that it is not based on statute, and his constitutional role is purely that of principal adviser to the Monarch.
Whatever may be the power of Prime Ministers when in office,
their security of tenure does not seem to be particularly strong.
Of the thirteen Prime Ministers between 1902 and 1964, only
Churchill, Baldwin (twice), and MacDonald returned to office
after once losing it. Asquith and Churchill each served for a
total of nearly nine years as Prime Minister, but most tenures
of office were much shorter than this, and the average was
under five years. Between elections the Prime Minister is
dependent upon the support of his Ministers and his party to
an extent that a popularly elected leader is not. This support
can be withdrawn and very often is. The Prime Minister can
survive the resignation of a leading Minister, as did Macmillan
in 1957 with Lord Salisbury's resignation, and in 1958 with the
resignation of Thorneycroft, Powell, and Birch, but a Prime
Minister can be forced from office when faced with a substantial body of discontent in his Cabinet or his party. The
resignations of Asquith in 1916, Lloyd George in 1922, Mac-
Donald in 1935, and Chamberlain in 1940 came primarily as
a result of discontent within the Government, while Eden in
1957 and Macmillan in 1963 were widely criticized within the
party before illness brought their resignations.

The wide powers of appointment and dismissal that the

Prime Minister enjoys are nevertheless limited by personal and practical factors. Cabinet and Government composition is complicated by factors of maximum and minimum numbers, the temperament and party standing of potential Ministers, the availability of talent, and even geographical considerations. The Prime Minister must consider the views of the Whips and of his chief colleagues, while some men are of sufficient ability or party standing as to be able virtually to choose their own posts. Ministers themselves choose their own junior Ministers and Parliamentary Private Secretaries. A party that has been out of office for some time may be short of Ministers with adequate experience. If a Prime Minister wants to appoint someone from outside Parliament to Ministerial office, a seat in the Commons can perhaps be found, or a Peerage conferred, but the Prime Minister has to be sure that as well as administrative ability, the Minister has the ability to deal with the political hurlyburly of Parliamentary life, particularly if a seat is found in the Commons rather than the Lords. It is debatable to what extent the Prime Minister's power to dismiss Ministers extends to his closest colleagues. Certainly, in 1962 Macmillan sacked one-third of his Cabinet, including the Chancellor of the Exchequer, but it can be argued that in general there is an inner circle of senior Ministers with a security of tenure that a Prime Minister would find very difficult to shake. This, and the several other factors already noted, can be quoted as restrictions upon the Prime Minister's absolute powers of appointment and dismissal.

With regard to the personality cult in modern elections, 1945 is often quoted as an example of an election when the undoubted prestige and personality of Winston Churchill did not bring electoral advantage for his party, and in 1950 the Conservatives consequently played down the personality of their leader. The 1970 election perhaps comes into this category as well. The importance of a good image can rebound on a party leader, in that just as a good image may be an electoral advantage, so a bad image can be fatal to a leader's standing within his party. Before their resignations, the prestige of Eden, Macmillan, and Home within the Conservative Party had probably suffered because it was thought that their electoral image was to the disadvantage of the party.

The power exercised by Lloyd George and Churchill during the two wars was in some ways exceptional, and it is easy to exaggerate the extent to which this wartime authority was carried over into peacetime. It is possible to find in the nineteenth century evidence of Prime Ministers who dominated their parties and their Governments. Disraeli's purchase of the Suez Canal shares for Britain in 1878, without prior Cabinet approval, can be advanced as a major example of the exercise of individual authority, while Disraeli and Gladstone together dominated their parties and the whole of the political arena for almost twenty years. It can further be claimed that no modern Prime Minister has had the authority and control over the whole government process that was enjoyed by Sir Robert Peel in the eighteen-forties, and that the extent of modern government is such that no Prime Minister can be expected to grasp all the intricacies of his Ministers' work. Despite the development of the Cabinet Secretariat as a body of officials largely at the Prime Minister's disposal, no modern Premier can hope to dominate all aspects of policy and administration in the Peelite tradition. Today a Prime Minister's activities are bound to be limited and specialized to a certain extent, and some Foreign Secretaries like Ernest Bevin, or some Chancellors of the Exchequer under Prime Ministers like Churchill and Home, who were not economists, can be largely free to pursue their own activities without direct interference from the Premier. Also, as has been noted above, the presence within every Cabinet of a group of senior Ministers (whether or not they form an 'Inner Cabinet') who are of particular authority in the Government and the party, means that there is formed a counter-balance to the individual power of the Prime Minister.

Thus while it is generally agreed that the Prime Minister's powers are today great, and in many respects are growing, a number of reasoned arguments are advanced by academic writers and practising politicians alike both for and against the proposition that the increase in Prime Ministerial authority in recent years extends to a basic change in the system of Cabinet Government. On the one hand R. H. S. Crossman argues that '. . . The post-war epoch has seen the final transformation of Cabinet Government into Prime Ministerial Government . . .',[1]

[1] Introduction to *The English Constitution*, p. 51.

and J. P. Mackintosh claims that ' . . . Now the country is governed by a Prime Minister, his colleagues, junior ministers and civil servants with the Cabinet acting as a clearing house and court of appeal'.[1] On the other hand, Lord Morrison has written that the Prime Minister ' . . . is not the master of the Cabinet', and he ' . . . ought not to, and usually does not, presume to give directions or decisions which are proper to the Cabinet or one of its Committees'.[2] Morrison's rejection of the idea of Prime Ministerial government is echoed in the writings of some academic authorities who present a picture of the Prime Minister as a powerful but not overwhelmingly supreme figure, with the Cabinet remaining as a collective executive body.[3] Despite these fundamental disagreements, the nature of the Prime Minister's relations with his Cabinet depends to some extent on the individuals involved, Churchill and Wilson representing a very different type of Prime Minister from Attlee and Home. Further, it should be pointed out that it is misleading to talk of the increase in the Prime Minister's power giving him 'Presidential' authority. Because of the various factors that were noted above as concentrating Constitutional authority within the British system (particularly the unitary nature of the Constitution and the unification rather than the separation of powers), the power of the Prime Minister, no matter how much he may be limited by the Cabinet, is necessarily greater than that enjoyed in many Presidential systems of government. Certainly, the Prime Minister's power is greater than the authority of the President within the United States system, where the federal nature of the Constitution and the separation of powers raise barriers to the President's authority which do not exist for Prime Ministers in Britain.

Government Co-ordination

In recent Governments the problem of keeping the Cabinet in touch with other Ministers and junior Ministers has been tackled in different ways. A degree of co-ordination can be

---

[1] *The British Cabinet*, p. 524.   [2] *Government and Parliament*, p. 52.
[3] See D. N. Chester's comments in Sir John Anderson (ed.), *British Government since 1918*. See also D. N. Chester, 'Who Governs Britain?', *Parl. Aff.* 1961–2, pp. 519–27.

achieved by amalgamating departments, as with the amalgamation of the Ministry of Agriculture and Fisheries with the
Ministry of Food in 1955, and the amalgamation of the Colonial
and Commonwealth Offices in 1967.[1] Similarly, co-ordination
can be achieved by making one Minister responsible for two
departments, as with the appointment of one Secretary of State
for Colonial and Commonwealth affairs from 1962 to 1964.
There are clearly limits to this type of Ministerial reorganization, however, and it involves an increased burden on the
Minister which could make him less effective as a result. It is
merely piecemeal reorganization, and although the Haldane
Committee in 1918 recommended a wholesale reorganization
of the departments, no such reform has yet been attempted.
Another way to co-ordinate departments is to create the formal
post of co-ordinator, without a department of his own, to
supervise and co-ordinate the work of a number of other Ministers. Thus in 1936 a Minister for the Co-ordination of Defence
was appointed, and in his 1951–5 Government Churchill
experimented with a number of Overlords to supervise various
departmental Ministers. Alternatively, a new department can
be formed, as with the creation of the Ministry of Defence in
1947 to co-ordinate the Service Departments.[2] By these means
it is possible to leave out some Ministers from the Cabinet by
including only the co-ordinating Minister, although the creation of a new Ministerial post, with or without a department,
adds to the original problem of an ever-increasing Government
machine.

In the main, however, the co-ordination of the Government
departments in Britain today is achieved through a system of
Cabinet committees. The origins of the system of Cabinet
standing committees can be traced back to the Committee of
Imperial Defence, which was formed in 1902 as a permanent
committee to supplement the Cabinet's general responsibility
for defence.[3] Cabinet committees had been formed before this

[1] See M. Beloff, 'The Foreign and Commonwealth Services', *Pub.
Admin.* 1964, pp. 415–22; B. Miller, 'The Colonial Office and the Estimates
Committee', *Pub. Admin.* 1961, pp. 173–80.
[2] See F. M. G. Willson, 'Defence Organization—1958 Style', *Pub. Admin.*
1958, pp. 385–90.
[3] See F. A. Johnson, *Defence by Committee*, London 1960; F. A. Johnson,
'The British Committee of Imperial Defence', *J of P* 1961, pp. 231–61.

to deal with particular questions, but this was the first standing committee of the Cabinet. The Defence Committee was retained during and after the first world war, though with a frequently changed name and status, and in 1919 there was also created a Home Affairs Committee. More standing committees emerged in the inter-war period, and with the second world war an extensive committee system was adopted as the basis of the means of co-ordinating the expanding Government machine. This committee system was retained by Attlee in 1945, and he had some fifteen committees composed of Cabinet and non-Cabinet Ministers, and presided over by a senior member of the Cabinet. The essence of the system as it has operated since 1945 has been that of informal co-ordination, with the chairmen and members of the committees not generally being named, and being responsible only to the Cabinet, and not to Parliament, for their role as committee chairmen. Despite its anonymity, the chairmanship of a Cabinet committee involves a lot of work, and the need to include in the Cabinet sufficient men capable of filling the role is one of the factors that a Prime Minister has to bear in mind when forming his Government.

*   *   *

Apart from the Cabinet committees, the most ambitious post-1945 experiment in the co-ordination of Government departments was the system of 'Overlords' introduced by Churchill in his 1951–5 Government. In October 1951 Churchill formed a Cabinet of sixteen Ministers, including six Peers, three of whom were Overlords with the task of co-ordinating various departments. Lord Leathers was Minister for the Co-ordination of Transport, Fuel and Power; Lord Cherwell, as Paymaster-General, was to co-ordinate scientific research and development; Lord Woolton, as Lord President of the Council, was to co-ordinate the work of the Ministry of Agriculture and Fisheries and the Ministry of Food. Churchill, as Minister of Defence as well as Prime Minister, was at first responsible for the co-ordination of the service departments, but in January 1952 Lord Alexander was made Minister of Defence, increasing the number of Overlords to four. Sir John Anderson was to have been given a Peerage and the post of Chancellor of the Duchy of Lancaster to co-ordinate Treasury, Board of Trade, and Ministry of Supply policy, but he declined.

The object of the scheme was to group and co-ordinate the departments by some means other than the Cabinet committee system, and to reorganize the nature and structure of Cabinet composition. A number of weaknesses of the scheme soon emerged, however. In the first place, although the presence of the co-ordinating Ministers meant that five Ministers (Agriculture and Fisheries, Food, Transport, Civil Aviation, and Fuel and Power) did not need to be in the Cabinet, these Ministers had not been in the Attlee Cabinet in 1951 either (apart from the Minister of Agriculture and Fisheries), and in fact the Lord Leathers appointment made up for this saving of one departmental Minister. Churchill did reduce his Cabinet size by holding the post of Minister of Defence himself, but this only meant a Cabinet of sixteen members as compared with Attlee's Cabinet of seventeen in 1951, and by December 1952 Churchill had increased his Cabinet numbers to nineteen.

A second fundamental criticism of the experiment was that whereas the chairmen of the Cabinet committees had been unannounced, the Overlords held formal posts, and this led to confusion as to who was the responsible Minister, the Overlord or the departmental Minister. Attlee argued that the task of co-ordination was best achieved within a Government, without resorting to a formally announced post. He claimed that with Churchill's system, both Parliament and the civil servants were confused over the question of who was the responsible Minister. The position was further confused by some of the Ministers themselves when they made mutually conflicting statements about their responsibilities. The situation was again complicated by the fact that the Overlords were indeed Lords and were thus not answerable to the House of Commons. The Opposition attacked this as a threat to the authority of the House of Commons, and argued that it added to the general confusion over the respective responsibilities of the Ministers.[1]

Early in 1952 there was a transport crisis involving a decision not to extend to the rest of the country increases in rail fares that had been made in the London area, and there was some

[1] See Morrison, *Government and Parliament*, Ch. 3, for more detailed comments.

doubt as to who was responsible for Government policy in this matter, Lord Leathers as Overlord, or the Minister of Transport. After this, the experiment was gradually abandoned. Lord Woolton's duties faded gradually away, Lord Leathers' post disappeared in September 1953, and Lord Cherwell's in November 1953, and Churchill returned to the system of Cabinet committees for the co-ordination of policy. It has been suggested that one reason for the failure of the experiment was that of personalities.[1] In Attlee's Government the co-ordinators in the Cabinet were men of high standing within the party, and thus had considerable authority over the other Ministers. The Overlords, on the other hand, depended more upon Churchill's own authority within the Government and the party, which perhaps was not as dominant as it had been in wartime. Further, had the co-ordinators been drawn from the Commons, their authority might have been greater, and the pattern of responsibility rather more clear. As well as this, however, there remained a fundamental difference between informal co-ordination within the Government through unnamed Ministers, and the formal co-ordination that Churchill attempted through his openly announced co-ordinating Ministers.

The Cabinet Secretariat

Before 1914 no minutes of Cabinet meetings or records of Cabinet decisions were kept, though occasionally written memoranda were made, as with the request to the Queen in 1870 to abolish the purchase of Commissions, and the requests made to Edward VII and George V during the Constitutional crisis in 1910, for the creation of Liberal Peers.[2] In 1916, under the pressure of wartime conditions, the Secretariat that under Sir Maurice Hankey had served the Committee of Imperial Defence, was transferred by Lloyd George to the wartime Cabinet, and was retained throughout the war. In 1918 the Haldane Committee recommended that it be retained in peacetime, and despite the claim that it was a threat to the principle of Cabinet secrecy, the Secretariat was retained after the break-up of the Coalition Government in 1922, though with a cut in

[1] Daalder, *Cabinet Reform in Britain 1914–63*, p. 119.
[2] See below, p. 269.

staff from 144 to 38.[1] Today the Secretariat is an essential part
of the Cabinet system, and is even more necessary as a result
of the development of the system of Cabinet committees.[2]

Since 1916 the post of Secretary to the Cabinet has been filled
only by Lords Hankey, Bridges, Normanbrook, and the present
Secretary, Sir Burke Trend. Until 1962 the Cabinet Secretary
was also one of the two joint Permanent Secretaries to the
Treasury, but in the reorganization of the Treasury in 1962
the Secretary of the Cabinet was relieved of his other Treasury
duties.[3] The 'number 10 network' of secretarial organization and
communication is widely recognized as being ultra-efficient. The
Secretariat helps in the co-ordination of Government business
in that it keeps non-Cabinet Ministers informed of Cabinet decisions, prepares the ground for Cabinet meetings by circulating memoranda beforehand, and performs this function also for
the committees of the Cabinet. As well as this general function
of co-ordination, it has been argued that the Secretariat should
be developed to serve more as a personal agency for the Prime
Minister, with staff being drawn from other departments and
from outside the Civil Service, to keep the Prime Minister
better informed and free from the departments for his information.[4] Its size, scope and authority could be developed to allow
it to become more like Churchill's wartime personal advisers,
and Lloyd George's 'Garden Suburb', which was a body of
advisers, housed in the garden of 10 Downing Street, acting as
a personal office for the Prime Minister, additional to the main
Secretariat. There are indications that the Secretariat may be
developed by the Heath Government. The danger of such a
development, however, is that a powerful 'White House Office'
under the Premier's personal direction could lead to friction
with the departments, and could mean the duplication of much
work by the Secretariat and the individual departments. The
extent to which it is desirable to develop the Secretariat along
these lines also depends largely on the desirability of developing
the personal authority of the Prime Minister.

Despite the work of the Secretariat in preparing an agenda

[1] Daalder, *Cabinet Reform in Britain 1914–63*, p. 60.
[2] R. K. Mosley, *The Story of the Cabinet Office*, London 1969.
[3] See below, p. 285.
[4] See Harold Wilson's comments in *Whitehall and Beyond*, p. 19.

and drawing up minutes or 'conclusions' of Cabinet meetings, Cabinet proceedings remain essentially secret. The conclusions of Cabinet meetings are bare and factual, and in a sense are a distortion of the truth, in that all discussion is summarized and clarified. The agenda and conclusions are circulated to all Cabinet Ministers, but remain top secret. This Cabinet secrecy is based formally on the Privy Councillor's Oath, the Official Secrets Act, and the Constitutional principle that Cabinet decisions are advice to the Monarch, so that Royal permission is required for their disclosure. In practical terms, however, the essence of Cabinet secrecy is that free discussion is possible only in secret, and only through the secrecy of Cabinet discussion can any semblance of collective responsibility be maintained. Complete secrecy is limited by the guidance that is sometimes given to the press, and by the revelations that occasionally appear in the writings of former Cabinet Ministers, especially when in a Cabinet crisis like that of 1931, Ministers are anxious to have their attitudes clarified. Also, 'un-attributable leaks' occur, and, for example, the press and public became aware of clear divisions in the Labour Cabinet in 1969 over Government policy towards the trade unions. From these sources it is possible to gain some idea of the nature of the internal workings of the Cabinet.

The agenda for Cabinet meetings, and any papers that are to be dealt with, are circulated beforehand so that prior consideration can be given to the issues. In this way Cabinet approval is no doubt often a formality, while Cabinet meetings are very often merely a report on progress and a forum for inter-departmental disputes. The Chancellor of the Exchequer and the Law Officers see the Cabinet papers before other Ministers in order to look for legal and financial snags. Formal votes are not taken in Cabinet meetings, partly because the Ministerial hierarchy means that opinions have to be weighed as well as counted. The meeting comes to general agreement under the guidance of the Prime Minister's chairmanship, but the nature of Cabinet meetings, and the method of reaching decisions, must depend upon the Prime Minister and his handling of his colleagues—a factor that must inevitably vary according to the personalities involved. Cabinet Ministers have attested to the grandeur of the Cabinet room and to the importance of the Prime Minister's role, while non-Cabinet Ministers have revealed that it can be an awesome experience to be 'summoned' to Cabinet meetings. Senior civil servants are occasionally called upon to attend, especially Foreign Office and Treasury officials, and service chiefs, and their presence, and the permanent presence of the Cabinet Secretary and his assistant, must inevitably reduce the party political content of Cabinet discussions.

Despite the vast increase in the scope of Government activity in this century, the volume of work undertaken by the Cabinet has not markedly increased. The Cabinet meets normally only twice a week, for two or three hours at a time, though in times of crisis there may be longer and more frequent meetings. The nature of the work undertaken by the Cabinet has changed considerably, however, with the full Cabinet inevitably being much less concerned with details and much more concerned with making and approving top-level decisions. This change in the nature of Cabinet proceedings has been made possible only through the work of the Secretariat in preparing and circulating material for Cabinet meetings, through the delega-tion of much work to Cabinet committees and individual Ministers, and through informal contact between the Prime Minister and other Ministers outside full Cabinet meetings.

8

Parliament:
I. The House of Commons

PARLIAMENT is made up of three distinct elements: the Monarch, the House of Lords, and the House of Commons. The legal doctrine of Parliamentary Supremacy, whereby Parliament is the supreme legal authority, vests sovereign legislative power in these three branches acting together (the King or Queen in Parliament), except in the case of measures passed under the terms of the Parliament Acts 1911 and 1949, whereby the assent of the House of Lords is not required. In practical terms, however, the role of the Monarch in Parliament is largely formal, and in a number of respects the legal power and political authority of the House of Lords is subservient to that of the Commons. Today, the Commons, composed of the 630 elected representatives of the people, is the dominant element in Parliament, so that in almost all practical (though not legal) respects Parliament and House of Commons are interchangeable terms.

Functions and Timetable of the Commons

Within the general outline that has been given in Chapter 6 of the place of Parliament within the machinery of government, a more precise examination may be made of the detailed functions of the House of Commons.[1] Initially, however, a distinction must be made between the House of Commons as a

---

[1] For general works on the House of Commons and Parliament see P. G. Richards, *Honourable Members*, London 1964; Sir Ivor Jennings, *Parliament*, London, 1957; A. H. Hanson and H. V. Wiseman, *Parliament at*

collective body, and MPs as individuals, as different individual
MPs fulfil vastly different roles within the House. Some MPs
are Ministers, and others are official frontbench Opposition
spokesmen, while among Government and Opposition MPs
alike, some are regarded (or regard themselves) as potential
Ministers, and their activities and attitudes in the House are
likely to be vastly different from those MPs who accept a role
as permanent backbenchers. Among backbenchers there are
those who are loyal supporters of the party leadership, while
others are almost permanently in rebellion against their leaders,
and rebellion by a normally loyal party man is likely to be
more telling than a rebellion by a number of permanent rebels.
Also, on both sides of the House it is possible to note various
House of Commons 'types'. Some MPs, for example, specialize
in a knowledge of Parliamentary procedure, and some devote
the bulk of their time to the service of the House by joining the
Speaker's Panel, the Services Committee and its sub-committees
which supervise the House of Commons Library and catering
arrangements, or other similar bodies. Other MPs concentrate
their activities on furthering unlikely and obscure causes, while
others fill the role of Parliamentary characters. Some use the
House of Commons to further their own business interests, or
perhaps to gain a knighthood or some similar honour, while yet
others act almost exclusively as spokesmen for some pressure
group.

One function that is common to all MPs, however, is their
responsibility to their constituents. In this capacity the MP
deals with problems and grievances raised by individual constituents, and here the MP's role is rather like that of a general
welfare officer. The MP may pursue a constituent's cause
publicly through question or debate in the House, or the matter
may be dealt with informally and inconspicuously behind the
scenes. For some MPs this form of activity occupies the bulk
of their time, and a number of backbenchers spend practically

Work, London 1962; Lord Campion, *Parliament: a Survey*, London 1963;
H. V. Wiseman, *Parliament and the Executive*, London, 1966; Eric Taylor, *The
House of Commons at Work*, London 1965; A. H. Hanson and B. Crick (eds),
The Commons in Transition, London 1970. See also D. N. Chester, 'The
British Parliament 1939–66', *Parl. Aff.* 1965–6, pp. 417–45; G. Marshall,
'Parliament and the Constitution', *PQ* 1965, pp. 266–76; A. H. Hanson,
'The Purpose of Parliament', *Parl. Aff.* 1963–4, pp. 279–95.

the whole of their Parliamentary careers doing conscientious and efficient work on behalf of their constituents, without ever hitting the Parliamentary headlines. This is one aspect of an MP's activity that is often overlooked, and yet it is an aspect that is of increasing importance in face of the extension of state activity into more and more fields.[1]

As a collective body, the main role of the House of Commons is as a publicist and critic of Government activities, though within this overall role it is possible to distinguish between three forms of Parliamentary activity. In classical Constitutional terms the functions of the Commons are to legislate, to approve the granting of finance to the Government, and to examine and criticize the activities of the Government. The legislative function of the House of Commons (as of the House of Lords) extends to the introduction of legislation, and the approval of all legislation before it becomes law. Today, however, Government domination of the Commons' timetable, and the assured Government majority in the House, means that the legislative function of the Commons is limited mainly to the discussion, perhaps the amendment, and then the final approval of Bills that are introduced by the Government, although Private Bills and Private Members' Bills remain as exceptions to this. The details of the financial powers of the House of Commons are examined elsewhere,[2] but it may be noted here that as with other Government legislation, the granting of supply and the approval of the Government's financial proposals are largely automatic today, financial debates being used primarily as a further opportunity to comment in general upon Government activities. Thus the deliberative function of the Commons, the probing and criticism of the Government actions, is today not limited merely to questions and general debate, but is exercised also through the examination of Government legislation and financial proposals.

* * *

A Parliament, in the sense of a Parliamentary period, lasts

---

[1] See R. Fulford, *The Member and His Constituency*, London 1957; R. E. Dowse, 'The MP and His Surgery', *PS* 1963, pp. 333–41. See also Sir A. P. Herbert, *I Object!*, London 1958; Sir A. P. Herbert, *Independent Member*, London 1958. [2] See below, Ch. 10.

for a maximum of five years before it is dissolved and a general election held (unless, as during the two world wars, the life of the Parliament is extended by special legislation). Each Parliament is divided into sessions, which are terminated by prorogation, and each session is self-contained, in that uncompleted business cannot be carried over from one session to another.[1] Until 1920, sessions generally began in February, but today sessions normally run from October to October. In election years when the election is not held in October (as in 1966 and 1970), this pattern is upset, and an especially long or short session is necessary in order to return to the October prorogation. The legislative business of a normal session is usually completed by the end of July, before the long summer recess begins, but in order that Parliament may be recalled if necessary during the summer, with the minimum of procedural fuss, Parliament is not prorogued until the end of the summer recess in October or November, and the new session then begins almost at once.

The House of Commons generally sits for about 160 days in each session, and there has been no marked increase in this number as compared with the inter-war years. The average length of each day's sitting, however, has increased slightly as compared with pre-1945 sessions, so that today the Commons does spend slightly more hours in session than it did in the past. The House sits from 2.30 p.m. to 10.30 p.m. from Monday to Thursday, and from 11.0 a.m. to 4.30 p.m. on Fridays. In 1967 morning sessions were introduced on Monday and Wednesday mornings as an experiment, but now the House sits in the mornings only rarely, in order to deal with un-finished business from the previous evening. Normal hours can be exceeded on days when certain types of business are being discussed, and on any day if the House agrees to suspend Standing Orders. The last Saturday sitting was on November 3rd 1956, during the Suez crisis, and the last Sunday sitting was on September 3rd 1939.

This distribution of time is often seen as inadequate. It is

---

[1] For Parliamentary procedure see Lord Campion, *Introduction to the Procedure of the House of Commons*, London 1958; J. Redlich, *The Procedure of the House of Commons*, London 1908; R. A. Chapman, 'The Significance of Parliamentary Procedure', *Parl. Aff.* 1962-3, pp. 179-87.

suggested, for example, that the House should sit for at least another fifty days in each session; that there should be more frequent and longer morning sittings; and that the sittings should be spread more evenly over the year, with perhaps a mid-week recess rather than the long holiday recesses.[1] Such proposals are criticized, however, on the grounds that they would impose too great a burden on members of the Government, this being one of the problems involved in a system of government where Ministers are members of the legislature. Morning sittings for each day of the week are opposed because they might interfere with the work of the Standing Committees, which at present meet in the mornings, and longer hours are also objected to by those who argue that MPs should retain interests, and even employment, outside the House. Thus, here, as in so many aspects of the activities of the Commons, the question is raised of whether the role of an MP should or should not be a full-time one.

Each day's sitting in the Commons begins, appropriately enough, with prayers, and this is followed (except on Fridays) by Question Time which lasts an hour. After Question Time a number of matters may be dealt with, including Ministerial statements, Urgency Motions, and the formal First Reading of Bills. Then follows the main business of the day (the Orders of the Day), be it legislation, finance, or the consideration of some motion. The final half-hour of the sitting is devoted to the Adjournment Debate, when backbenchers can raise constituency or personal grievances. In the main, Fridays are devoted to Private Members' Bills and Private Members' Motions, though this can vary from session to session. On other days the business to be considered is determined by the two frontbenches. The Leader of the House of Commons and the Government Whips

---

[1] For general works on Parliamentary reform see B. Crick, *The Reform of Parliament*, London 1964; Hansard Society, *Parliamentary Reform 1933–60*, London 1961; M. Foot, *Parliament In Danger!*, London 1959; A. Hill and A. Whichelow, *What's Wrong With Parliament?*, London 1964; A. H. Hanson, 'The Labour Party and House of Commons Reform', *Parl. Aff.* 1956–7, pp. 454–68; P. Bromhead, 'How Should Parliament Be Reformed?', *PQ* 1959, pp. 272–82; S. A. Walkland, 'A Liberal Comment on Recent Proposals for Parliamentary Reform', *Parl. Aff.* 1962–3, pp. 338–42; B. Crick, 'The Prospects for Parliamentary Reform', *PQ* 1965, pp. 333–46; H. V. Wiseman, 'Parliamentary Reform', *Parl. Aff.* 1958–9, pp. 240–54.

consult with the Opposition Whips about the timetable and try to meet Opposition wishes, but the final control of the timetable lies with the Government.

In 1800 Government time involved only one day per week, but this was increased to two days in 1837, three days in 1892, and four days in 1902, while Governments with a particularly heavy programme have in some sessions suspended private members' business altogether. Excluding the daily Question Time and Adjournment Debate, roughly 35% of the time of the House is normally devoted to the consideration of motions, roughly 45% to the consideration of Government legislation, and roughly 5% is taken up in incidental business.[1] Thus about 85% of the House's time is devoted to matters determined by the Government and Opposition frontbenches. The 15% that remains for backbenchers' topics is made up of ten or so days for Bills and ten or so days for motions, with some of the time that is devoted to the consideration of the Annual Estimates, and part of the first day's debate on the Speech from the Throne, also being devoted to private members' topics. Backbenchers criticize this distribution of time as devoting too much attention to matters raised by the two frontbenches, at the expense of constituency matters. From another standpoint, the timetable can be criticized for devoting too much time to the consideration of Government legislation, and the Finance Bill in particular, as these debates often involve long hours spent on points of detail which are incomprehensible to most MPs and outside observers. The details of legislation and of finance would probably be better considered in committee away from the floor of the House, with more time thereby being made available for general debates on broad issues and principles of policy. The main function of the House, of drawing the attention of the public to Government activities, can be much better achieved by debating issues and principles, rather than by examining financial and legislative details. Any attempt to reduce the time devoted to legislative details on the floor of the House, however, would necessarily involve further modifications in the committee system.

[1] For an analysis of the Commons' timetable over several sessions see Lord Campion, *Introduction to the Procedure of the House of Commons*, Appendix III.

Parliamentary Procedure

The principles governing the conduct of business in the House
are based partly on the 'practice of the House' (which consists
of conventions and traditions of behaviour which have developed over the years), and partly on Standing Orders, which
are the written rules that have been formulated in the modern
period, particularly over the past century. The interpretation
and application of the various conventions and Standing Orders
is the responsibility of the Speaker or his deputy, and in this
task he is aided by 'the Bible' of Parliamentary practice, Erskine
May's *Law, Privileges, Proceedings and Usage of Parliament*, which
is regularly brought up to date by succeeding Clerks of the
House.[1]

The office of Speaker originated when the Commons elected
one of their own number to report proceedings to the Monarch.[2] Sir Peter de la Mare in the 1376 Parliament is usually
regarded as the first Speaker, but it was not until the Constitutional struggles of the seventeenth century that the Speaker
emerged as the champion of Parliamentary rights against Royal
authority. The independence of the Speaker was established
in the eighteenth and nineteenth centuries, when he was given
a salary (now £8,500) and a pension, and was required to
sever his party connections on taking office. The convention
also emerged in the nineteenth century that the Speaker was
not opposed at a general election, but this has not always been
observed this century. A special Speaker's constituency of St
Stephen's, made up only of MPs, has been advocated at various
times, but it has been resisted partly on the grounds that if the
Speaker was not re-elected to office he would be without a seat
in the House. The Speaker serves for a full Parliament, and
since 1935 all Speakers have been reappointed if they so desired.
The choice of Speaker is not normally contested, as this would
be seen as weakening his impartiality, and any disagreements
over the choice of Speaker are generally settled by the Whips

[1] 17th edition, 1964. See above, p. 160.
[2] See P. Laundy, *The Office of Speaker*, London 1964; P. Laundy, 'The
Speaker of the House of Commons', *Parl. Aff.* 1960–1, pp. 72–9; J. E. Powell,
'A Speaker Before "The First" ', *Parl. Aff.* 1964–5, pp. 20–2; J. A. Cross,
'Deputy Speakers and Party Politics', *Parl. Aff.* 1964–5, pp. 361–7; W. S.
Livingston, 'The Security of Tenure of the Speaker of the House of
Commons', *Parl. Aff.* 1957–8, pp. 484–504.

TABLE XXV
Sessional Timetable 1964–5

	House of Commons	House of Lords
Legislation	64½	60½
Government Bills introduced in Commons	46	36
,, ,, ,, ,, Lords	3	7
Private Members' Bills introduced in Commons	13	4½
,, ,, ,, ,, ,, Lords	1½	13
Opposed Private Bills	1	
General debates	46	55½
Initiated by Speech from the Throne	6	5
,, ,, Government or Opposition Motions	21½ ⎫	5½
,, ,, Private Members' Motions	11½ ⎭	
,, ,, Adjournment Motions for a Recess	4	
,, ,, Motions for Papers*		37½
,, ,, Questions		6
,, ,, Statutory Orders	3	1½
Finance	60½	1
Finance Bill	26½	1
Budget statements	6	
Consolidated Fund Bills	3	
Supply Days	25	
Incidental business	6	7
Opening of Parliament	1	1
Oath taking	2	2
Tributes to statesmen†	2	3
Prorogation	1	1
Total sittings	177	124
Total hours	1,534	609
Average length of sittings	8 hrs 40	4 hrs 54
Longest sitting	23 hrs	9½ hrs

* A procedure, peculiar to the Lords, that reserves for the proposer the right to have the last word in the debate

† Death of Sir Winston Churchill and Lord Woolton

behind the scenes. In 1951, however, there was a division on the choice of Speaker for the first time since 1895, and the 1951 situation was further unusual in that the choice of a new Speaker had to be made immediately after a general election rather than in the middle of a Parliament. ·

As well as being responsible for the maintenance of order and the general conduct of debates, the Speaker has control over such matters as the acceptance or rejection of Urgency Motions, motions for the Closure, the selection of amendments for debate, and the limitation of supplementary questions at Question Time. The Speaker is also the initial judge of whether there has been a breach of House of Commons privilege, though in matters of privilege the ultimate judges are the House itself and the Committee of Privilege.[1] Most of the 'ancient and un-doubted rights and privileges' of the House are now largely of historical significance, having arisen from a desire in the past to protect MPs from outside interference (primarily Royal interference), and from a desire to allow freedom of speech and activity in the House. Thus Parliamentary privilege includes freedom of speech, so that MPs cannot be prosecuted for sedition or sued for libel or slander for anything said in the House or reported in Parliamentary publications. The House is also protected from criticism that affronts 'the dignity of the House', and can deal internally with matters affecting its own privileges and conduct. In 1947 Garry Allighan was expelled from the House on account of critical articles he had written about Parliament, and at times, outside offenders against privilege are summoned to the House and reprimanded.

Privileges of the House also include the right of access to the Crown through the Speaker; the general right to have its activities favourably construed by the Monarch; the right to judge cases of electoral malpractice (though today this is handled by High Court Judges); the right to fill casual vacancies (which gives the Whips of the party that holds the seat the right to determine by-election dates); and the right of freedom from civil arrest, which in its practical application today means freedom from jury service and subpoena.

[1] G. Marshall, 'Privilege and "Proceedings in Parliament" ', *Parl. Aff.* 1957–8, pp. 396–404.

While these privileges were perhaps desirable in the constitutional conflicts of the past, it may be questioned whether
these are necessary today.[1] The ancient Parliamentary privileges are also often linked in criticism and ridicule with the
time-honoured ceremonial of Parliament, such as the Speaker's
traditional reluctance to take office; the ceremonial attached
to the opening of a new Parliament; Black Rod's summoning
of the Commons to the Lords to hear the Royal Assent to
legislation; the Royal Assent being given in Norman French;
the references to MPs in debates by their constituencies rather
than their own name; the reference to Honourable, Right
Honourable, Honourable and Gallant, and Honourable and
Learned Members. All of these aspects of traditional Parliamentary practice are frequently attacked as time-wasting and
useless mumbo-jumbo. Certainly it can be questioned how the
Government can expect British industry and the nation as a
whole to 'modernize', when Parliament is itself steeped in out-
moded practices which are far from harmless in that they reduce
Parliament's desire to reform itself. The emphasis on the historical origins and traditions of Parliament can be linked with the
survival of the House of Lords, and with the tradition that
surrounds the Monarchy, as being characteristic of Britain's
unhealthy preoccupation with the past, and with the prestige of
ancient institutions. Thus, characteristically, when the House of
Commons was destroyed during the second world war, a new
building was constructed to resemble the old building as closely
as possible, without adequate seating facilities for all MPs.

The defenders of 'the glory of Parliament', however, reject
these criticisms and claim that Parliament's traditional practices
are a colourful part of a Parliamentary and national heritage
of several hundreds of years, which (they claim) produces
respect for Parliament and the dignity of its proceedings.[2] They
argue that the ancient practices of Parliament serve in general
to emphasize the stability and continuity of the political system,

[1] Lord Kilmuir, *The Law of Parliamentary Privilege*, London 1959;
D. C. M. Yardley, 'The House of Commons and its Privileges since
the Strauss Affair', *Parl. Aff.* 1961–2, pp. 500–10; C. Seymour Ure, 'Proposed Reforms of Parliamentary Privilege', *Parl. Aff.* 1969–70, pp. 221–31.

[2] See, for example, H. Boardman, *The Glory of Parliament*, London 1960;
S. Gordon, *Our Parliament*, London 1964; Sir H. Dunnico, *The Mother of
Parliaments*, London 1951; H. King, *Parliament and Freedom*, London 1962.

and that in countries where such traditions do not exist, they are often invented. The debate is an old and frequently repeated one, and is linked very closely with the debate over the ceremonial value of the Monarchy. To some extent the debate cuts across party lines, though in general Conservative MPs tend to be more 'traditionalist' in outlook, while Labour and Liberal MPs tend to be less so. The issue has more point, however, at a time when the reform of the Parliamentary timetable and procedure is being canvassed, as in many respects the practical work of Parliament cannot be reformed without cutting away much of the traditional ceremonial.

The Legislative Process

The legislative function of Parliament embraces various types of Bill. There is an initial distinction between Public Bills, which concern the whole community, Private Bills, which affect only a section of the community (be it a local authority, a business company, or an individual), and Hybrid Bills, which are Public Bills that are classified by the Speaker as having a particular effect on one section of the community (like the 1969 Transport (London) Bill which allowed the Greater London Council to take control of the London transport system). Further, there are Provisional Order Confirmation Bills, which are Private Bills introduced by the Government to confirm the granting of land or the delegation of power to a local authority. Most Public Bills are Government Bills, introduced by a Minister as official Government policy, but Public Bills may also be introduced by backbench MPs as Private Members' Bills.

These formal classes of legislation can be further sub-divided according to their precise source. Government Bills may stem from the party electoral programme, particularly after a general election, and especially if a party has been out of office for some time and comes to power with a big legislative programme. Such legislation tends to attract attention because it is often contentious, but in the main this type of legislation forms only a small part of a Government's legislative programme for a session. Some Government Bills, like the Finance Bill and the Consolidated Fund Bills, have to be introduced every session. A Government may also be called upon to introduce emergency

legislation to meet an immediate crisis at home or abroad, while
the findings of Select Committees, Royal Commissions, or other
committees of enquiry may produce a need for legislation.
Pressure groups may be able to influence a Government to
introduce a particular piece of legislation, while 'departmental
Bills' can stem from the administrative needs of the departments of State. Legislation that applies to England and Wales
has sometimes to be introduced separately for Scotland, and
some Bills arise from the need to supplement the work of
previous legislation. Similarly, Consolidation Bills are frequently
introduced to gather existing legislation into one general statute,
so that these various factors inevitably reduce the party political
content of a Government's legislative programme. Private
Members' Bills also may have various sources, and a Bill may
be the result of the initiative of the MP concerned, or one backbencher may persuade another to introduce a measure on his
behalf. A pressure group may persuade a backbencher to
introduce a Private Member's Bill, while the Government or
Opposition Whips may prevail upon a backbencher to adopt a
Bill that they wish to see introduced but cannot accommodate
in Government time.

Whatever its source, however, to become law a Bill has to be
approved by both Houses of Parliament (other than under the
terms of the Parliament Acts 1911 and 1949), and must receive
the Royal Assent. Bills may be introduced first into either
House, though politically controversial legislation, financial
legislation (particularly the annual Finance Bill and Appropria-
tions Bill), and electoral legislation begins in the House of
Commons. The procedure for Public Bills is basically the same
in both Houses. The Bill is drafted by Parliamentary Counsel,
and if it is a Government Bill, before it is presented to Parliament its proposals will be examined by the Cabinet, a Cabinet
committee, the department of state concerned, and any sectional interests who may be affected. These discussions behind
the scenes may be continued during much of the Bill's passage
through Parliament, and in many cases they are of more
practical significance for the Bill's fate than is the Parliamentary
process.

The Bill is introduced into one of the Houses and is given
a formal First Reading. It is then printed, and normally after

two or three weeks the Second Reading debate takes place, when the general principles and merits of the Bill are considered. The Second Reading can be taken on the floor of the House or in a Standing Committee. The opponents of the Bill may choose not to vote against it at this stage (especially in the Lords), but may seek to make amendments at the committee stage. If the Bill involves the spending of public money, it is accompanied by a financial resolution which is considered after the Second Reading. The Bill goes to a Standing Committee for detailed consideration, clause by clause, though for some Bills this stage is taken in a Committee of the Whole House. The Report stage then follows, when the amendments made in committee are considered and perhaps altered, but if further detailed amendments are sought, the Bill has to be returned to the Committee. With non-controversial Bills the debate at the Report stage can be dispensed with. Finally, the Bill is debated once more in general terms, with only verbal amendments allowed, and is given a Third Reading. The Bill then passes to the other House, where the process is repeated. Any amendments made in the second House have to be considered by the original House, and deadlock may result. Generally, however, agreement is reached, and Bills are rarely lost at this stage. Finally, the Bill goes for Royal Assent, given either by the Monarch in person or more usually by Lord Commissioners.

A committee now exists to take the Second Reading of non-controversial Bills. The Second Reading of all Scottish Bills can be taken in the Scottish Grand Committee if the House agrees, and it is sometimes proposed that the Second Reading of all Bills should be taken in committee, as long as there was no objection from the House. This would save time on the floor of the House, and the Bills would probably be much better considered in committee, although more standing committees would be needed to deal with the extra committee work, with a consequently greater strain on the Whips.

All Bills are sessional, in that if they are not passed in one session they cannot be taken up in the next session from where they left off. Thus in the 1969–70 session a number of Government Bills were lost as a result of the 'early' dissolution (see Table XXVI). The timetabling of legislation is arranged by the Leader of the House in consultation with the Opposition

Whips. In the Commons, all the stages of a Bill can be taken on one day, as was illustrated with the Rhodesia Bill in 1965, and though the Lords' Standing Order No. 41 prevents two stages being taken on one day, in practice this Standing Order is frequently suspended. In the Commons, machinery exists to overcome attempts to disrupt the timetable. The Closure (first applied voluntarily by Speaker Brand to end a $41\frac{1}{2}$-hour sitting, January 31st to February 2nd 1881) can end a debate at any stage if the Speaker accepts a Motion of Closure supported by a hundred members. Secondly, 'the Guillotine', or closure by compartments, also introduced in 1881, enables the Government to allocate a specific timetable for the consideration of each section of a Bill, and a logical extension of this would perhaps be a Rules Committee to timetable the committee stage, or perhaps all stages of all Bills.[1] Thirdly, 'the Kangaroo', introduced in 1909, gives the Speaker the power to select for consideration a few representative amendments from a long list, in order to prevent repetitive debating. These three devices apply to the committee stage as well as to debates on the floor of the House.

*   *   *

In most sessions, Public Bills are divided equally in numbers between Government Bills and Private Members' Bills, but whereas Government Bills are almost certain to be passed, the majority of Private Members' Bills are lost.[2] During this century the number of Private Members' Bills introduced in each session has gradually fallen, though the number that are successful in each session has not declined, so that the 'failure rate' among Private Members' Bills has been reduced somewhat. An MP who wishes to introduce a Bill is faced with a number of problems. In the first place, little time is available. Sixteen Fridays (when sittings only last five hours) are normally allocated to Private Members' Bills each session. The Government may allocate extra time for a Bill, but this depends on the Government's

[1] J. Palmer, 'Allocation of Time: the Guillotine and Voluntary Time-tabling', *Parl. Aff.* 1969–70, pp. 232–47.
[2] See P. Bromhead, *Private Members' Bills*, London 1956; E. Davies, 'The Role of Private Members' Bills', *PQ* 1957, pp. 32–9.

goodwill. One Standing Committee, however, gives precedence to Private Members' Bills. A ballot at the beginning of the session determines which MPs will be given time. Many enter the ballot without having a Bill to promote, and then adopt some measure (perhaps on the advice of the Whips) if they are successful in the ballot. It has been suggested that MPs should have a Bill before being allowed to enter the ballot, or that the ballot should be abolished and precedence given to Bills that received most support among MPs, perhaps in the form of MPs' signatures appended to the Bills.

If an MP is successful in the ballot, and if he overcomes the problems of drafting the Bill, he may have difficulty in maintaining a quorum of forty members for a non-controversial measure. Alternatively, if his Bill is controversial he may find that it is obstructed. The usual means of killing a Bill is to talk it out, perhaps because it is controversial itself, or perhaps because it is due to be followed by a controversial measure on which some MPs wish to avoid a debate. Between the wars, Private Members' Bills tended to be more controversial and party political than they are today, and they were often used as a means of harrying the Government, but this is less the case today. A further complication for a backbencher is that he cannot initiate a Bill, the main purpose of which is financial, and any Bill that involves the spending of public money has to be accompanied by a financial resolution introduced by a Minister. Any Bill that passes all its stages in the Commons has a very good chance of being given time in the Lords, but Bills that have passed first through the Lords cannot always be accommodated in the more crowded Commons' timetable.

In addition to Private Members' Fridays, other means of introducing a Bill are open to MPs. Any member at any time may ask the House for leave to introduce a Bill for an unopposed Second Reading, but this is killed at once if there is any objection. Further, under the 'Ten-Minute Rule', at certain limited times in the week's timetable, a backbencher may make a ten-minute speech in defence of a Bill he wishes to introduce. This is followed by a ten-minute speech in opposition, and then a vote on whether the Bill may be introduced. Few Bills do materialize from this procedure, however, and it is used mainly to draw attention to an issue, though without much real hope of legislative success.

Thus there are great difficulties facing backbenchers who seek to introduce legislation, and there is some doubt as to the overall value of Private Members' time. Most Bills deal only with petty matters, and the standard of debate is generally poor. With an overcrowded timetable the time that is devoted to Private Members' Bills could perhaps be better used in considering Government policies, and during the wars, and from 1945 to 1948, Private Members' time was suspended. Today the main function of MPs is to criticize Government legislation and Government policy, rather than introduce legislation themselves. Backbenchers are able to propose amendments to Government Bills, and many amendments can have the force of separate legislation. Further, for some MPs the sole value of Private Members' time is that it occupies Fridays, and thus enables them to go home for a long weekend beginning on Thursday night.

In defence of Private Members' Bills, however, it is undoubtedly the case that there are some types of issues, like animal welfare, some legal matters, and moral questions, about which Governments will not legislate for fear of offending some sections of the community. Thus important Private Members' Bills have been the Matrimonial Causes Act 1937,[1] the Obscene Publications Act 1959, the Murder (Abolition of the Death Penalty) Act 1965, the Termination of Pregnancy Act 1967, and the Divorce Reform Act 1969. Similarly, Private Members' Bills may reveal otherwise unpublicized issues and thereby stimulate the Government into action, as with the 'clean air' campaign. In this sense Private Members' legislation is another means of publicizing Government activity or inactivity. Private Members' time can also be defended as being one of the rare occasions when Parliament is acting largely free from the control of the Government and the Whips, though at times the Government Whips persuade backbenchers to introduce measures than cannot be accommodated in the official Government legislative programme. Ultimately, however, the question is whether it is worth while spending time debating legislative proposals that in the main are comparatively insignificant, or

[1] See A. P. Herbert, *The Ayes Have It*, London 1937.

whether it would be better to devote the time to a fuller discussion of Government policies.

*   *   *

Private Bills are promoted in the main by local authorities which seek to acquire powers additional to those granted by general legislation, or by private firms and interests that wish to acquire land or property.[1] Many matters which in other countries might be settled by the Law Courts, are in Britain settled by an approach to Parliament. As with Public Bills,

TABLE XXVI

Legislation 1968–9 and 1969–70

	Total Introduced		Passed one House but not Enacted		Enacted	
	1968–9	1969–70	1968–9	1969–70	1968–9	1969–70
Government Bills	55	63	1	7	51	38
Non-Government Bills	105	90	1	2	12	15
Private Members'						
Ballot	27	27	0	1	5	6
Ten Minute Rule	39	22	0	1	4	1
S.O. No. 37	25	27	0	0	1	3
Private Peers	14	14	1	0	2	5

Source: based on a table contained in I. F. Burton and G. Drewry, 'Public Legislation: A Survey of the Session 1969–70'; *Parl. Aff.* 1969–70, p. 313.

Private Bills must pass both Houses and receive the Royal Assent to become law, and the procedure involves three Readings, a committee stage, and a Report stage. In practice, however, the procedures for Public and Private Bills are very different, and almost all of the work on Private Bills is done in committee, or before the Bill ever reaches Parliament. Private Bill proposals have to be advertised widely in the press, and are presented to Parliament as a petition. The Bill is examined by the Examiners of Petitions for Private Bills to see that Standing Orders are complied with, and it is allocated to the Commons

---

[1] See H. V. Wiseman, 'The Leeds Private Bill 1956', *Pub. Admin.* 1957, pp. 25–44; 'Promotion of Private Bills by Local Authorities', *Pub. Admin.* 1960, pp. 72–3.

or Lords for introduction. Greater use is made of the Lords today than in the past, and about half of the Bills begin in the Lords. Any petitions opposing the Bill must be presented by the end of January, and after this the Bill is given a formal First Reading, and a Second Reading when its principles are debated. It then goes to the Private Bill Committee, composed of only four MPs, where, as in legal procedure, witnesses are called, evidence is examined, and legal counsel make pleas for and against the Bill. This process may last four or five days. Bills that are unopposed go to the Unopposed Private Bill Committee, made up of five MPs. Then follows a Report to the House, Third Reading, and transfer to the other House where the procedure is repeated.

A joint committee of both Houses has been suggested for Private Bills, as has a committee to take the Second Reading. A more drastic reform that would make much private legislation unnecessary, would be to set up a committee with the authority, when petitioned, to grant to local authorities powers that had already been granted to other local authorities. As it is, however, less use is made of Private Bills than in the past. In the eighteenth and nineteenth centuries the enclosure movement and the purchase of land by the railway companies was largely achieved through Private Bills. Today, however, Government legislation has wider scope than in the past, while the cost of private legislation is often prohibitive, in that it sometimes involves several thousands of pounds, and alternative procedures exist which are cheaper, speedier, and more convenient. A Provisional Order Confirmation Bill can be used to confirm the granting to a public or private authority of some power that has previously been examined and approved by a public enquiry and by the Government department concerned. This is a cheap and effective procedure, in that the dispute is largely settled before reaching Parliament. A similar procedure is to lay before Parliament a Statutory Order granting powers to a public or private authority. Opponents or individual MPs are allowed a month in which to petition against the Order, and if this happens a joint committee of both Houses considers the issues involved. This is an expeditious process, in that opponents must take the initiative if they wish to object to the Order.

Finally in this context may be noted the procedure for Hybrid

Bills.[1] They follow the same course as Public Bills, except that they are presented to the Examiners of Petitions for Private Bills who decide whether Private Bill Standing Orders are applicable, and have been complied with. Also, after Second Reading, the Bill goes to a small Select Committee where a procedure is followed that is similar to that of the Private Bill Committee. The Bill then reverts to the normal Public Bill procedure.

Questions and Debates

As well as the detailed probing into Government policy that is achieved during the passage of Government legislation, the Commons' function of publicizing executive action is achieved through the questioning of Ministers in the House, through the consideration of Government policy in general debates, and through the work of the committees of the House. There are a number of different ways in which MPs can ask questions of members of the Government.[2] Ministers can be questioned orally in Question Time in the Commons on Mondays to Thursdays from 2.30 p.m. to 3.30 p.m. Alternatively, questions may be submitted for a written answer in Hansard, and in addition, any oral questions that are not dealt with in Question Time are given a written answer. About twenty-five questions each day are submitted for written replies, and there has been no marked increase since written answers were introduced in 1902. Private Notice Questions on urgent matters may be submitted for oral answer on the same day, but the Speaker determines whether the matter is urgent enough to merit this, and in fact not many are granted. In addition to these public questions, MPs can write to Ministers for information, and this form of activity is on the increase.[3]

[1] See G. W. Jones, 'A Forgotten Right Discovered', *Parl. Aff.* 1965–6, pp. 363–72.
[2] D. N. Chester and N. Bowring, *Questions in Parliament*, London 1962; P. Howarth, *Questions in the House*, London 1956; N. Johnson, 'Parliamentary Questions and the Conduct of Administration', *Pub. Admin.* 1961, pp. 131–49.
[3] K. E. Couzens, 'A Minister's Correspondence', *Pub. Admin.* 1956, pp. 237–44; D. Thompson, 'Letters to Ministers and Parliamentary Privilege', *PL* 1959, pp. 10–22.

The daily question hour is essentially a product of the Parliamentary system of government, with Ministers drawn from and answerable to Parliament. The practice developed in the nineteenth century, partly as a result of the activities of the Irish MPs in the eighteen-eighties, who were determined to draw attention to the Irish problem, but also as a result of the increased awareness of MPs of their responsibilities to their constituents, and of the growth in the extent of state activity. As well as increasing the number of questions asked in the House, however, the growth in the scope of governmental activity increased other pressures on Parliamentary time, and legislation, general debates, and questions competed for priority. In 1901 Government business was delayed by the number of questions asked in the Commons, and thus in 1902 Balfour introduced a procedure for questions, which, as modified in 1906 and on occasions since then, has survived as the basis of the existing procedure.

Today, Question Time is limited to one hour (there being no increase or reduction in this time since 1906), and at least two days' notice of a question must be given. Generally about 60 to 100 questions are submitted for oral answer each day, and about 50 of them are answered in the hour, though this can vary according to the time allowed by the Speaker for each answer. There is a limit on the number of questions that each MP can ask, and since 1960 this limit has been two questions per day, as compared with eight per day in 1909. In fact, however, Question Time tends to be dominated by a few MPs, with Labour members generally asking more questions than Conservative members, whether a Labour Government is in office or not. There is no limit (other than the Speaker's discretion) on the number of supplementary questions that may be asked, and supplementaries are not limited to the original questioner. In 1908 some 42% of the questions were followed by supplementaries, while more recently the proportion has been over 90%. It is, of course, debatable whether it is better to have a few questions answered in detail, with perhaps even a short debate on five or six questions each day, or whether it is better to have a lot of questions answered briefly with distinct limits on supplementaries.

On Tuesdays and Thursdays, fifteen minutes of the hour are

devoted to questions to the Prime Minister. Other Ministers answer questions in turn on a complicated rota system, that attempts to ensure that each Minister will appear fairly regularly. A particular Minister can be 'sheltered', however, by his supporters putting down a large number of questions for the Minister who precedes him on the rota. MPs also often hand in a question well in advance to try to ensure that it will be high on the list, or perhaps in order to exclude other questions, although questions may not now be submitted more than three weeks in advance. The Speaker determines whether a question is 'out of order'. As general guides, a question must be concerned with fact and not merely opinion, it must be an enquiry and not a statement, and it must be couched in 'proper' language. A question must be within a Minister's sphere of responsibility, and there can be disagreement over the precise extent of a Minister's responsibility, as with disputes over Ministers' responsibilities with regard to the public corporations.[1]

Questions may be motivated by a number of different considerations. An MP may seek information that he cannot otherwise obtain for himself, but in such a case a question for a written answer or a letter to a Minister is often best, as this allows for a more detailed answer. MPs argue, however, that this type of enquiry would be less necessary if the House had better research facilities. An oral answer is most likely to be sought not so much for information, but in order to voice a grievance or embarrass the Minister. Similarly, an oral question, or the threat of an oral question, can be used to stimulate action by a Minister. Not all questions are hostile, however, and a question may be asked by Government backbenchers in order to reveal Government achievements, while some questions are asked merely in order to gain publicity for the questioner. Question Time generally receives good coverage in press reports of Parliament as it tends to be livelier and more topical than some Parliamentary proceedings,[2] and

[1] See below, p. 360.

[2] For relations between Parliament and the press in general see A. Butler, 'The History and Practice of Lobby Journalism', *Parl. Aff.* 1959–60, pp. 54–60; P. Bromhead, 'Parliament and the Press', *Parl. Aff.* 1962–3, pp. 279–92; A. E. Musson, 'Parliament and the Press', *Parl. Aff.* 1955–6, pp. 277–88.

also because it comes early in the day and thus can be reported in the evening and morning newspapers. A supplementary question can turn a seemingly innocent enquiry into a much more meaningful issue, and Question Time is very much a battle of wits between Ministers and questioners, with some Ministers clearly being much more adept than others at dealing with questions. A Minister can be evasive, or can decline to answer 'in the public interest', but excessive reliance on this would eventually discredit the Minister. An MP who is not satisfied with an answer can seek to develop the issue through an Adjournment Debate, an Urgency Motion, or by further questions. It has been suggested that Question Time is inadequate as it operates at present, and that Ministers should be regularly questioned by a standing committee instead of (or as well as) by individual MPs on the floor of the House. It has also been suggested that a Prime Ministerial or Ministerial Press Conference should be introduced in Britain, on the lines of the American Presidential Press Conference, to supplement Parliamentary questioning. Despite its limitations, however, Question Time remains as a vital weapon that MPs have for probing the activities of the executive.

*   *   *

Government policy and actions can be the subject of general debates on various different occasions during the Parliamentary session. At the beginning of each session the Queen's Speech, containing the Government's legislative proposals, is followed by five or six days of debate. The first of these days is devoted primarily to speeches by backbenchers on constituency issues, but the other days are spent in debating more specific aspects of Government policy as agreed by the Whips. In addition, a further fifteen or so days in a normal session are devoted to general debates on topics chosen by the Government, after consultation with the Opposition. The Government sometimes uses these debates to test the attitude of the House and the public on some aspect of policy, perhaps as contained in a Government White Paper, and this may be used as a preliminary to future legislation. Motions of censure also come into this category, and the Government will always find time for such a motion. The twenty-six Supply Days spread throughout the year, when theoretically the House debates the Government's financial estimates,[1] are in fact spent in general debates on broad Government policy as reflected in the Government's spending proposals. For these debates the topics are chosen by the Opposition.

Ministerial statements after Question Time cannot develop into full-scale debates, but very often lengthy statements and counter-statements continue for half an hour or so, though this tends to be a somewhat untidy procedure. Under Standing Order No. 9, however, the House may adjourn in order to debate 'a specific and important matter that should have urgent consideration'.[2] This motion is proposed after Question Time, and needs the support of forty members and the agreement of the Speaker. Such debates last for three hours, and then the business of the day resumes from where it was interrupted. Originally the Speaker allowed the House to decide whether a matter was sufficiently urgent to merit such a procedure, but today the Speaker decides for himself. Until 1967 very few such debates were granted, there being only four from 1940 to 1950, and only eight from 1950 to 1960. Since 1967, however, the Standing Order has been interpreted more liberally, and there have been more such debates than in the past. The Government may propose the adjournment of the House at the beginning of the day's business in order to debate a particularly urgent matter. The historic debate in 1940 that led to Chamberlain's resignation was of this type, but such debates are even rarer than Urgency Motion debates.

These are all occasions when MPs have an opportunity to debate Government policy, but the topics are controlled by the two frontbenches. In these debates backbenchers are at a disadvantage when wishing to speak, in that Privy Councillors are given precedence over other MPs. Also, the Whips may discourage backbenchers from speaking in order that the frontbenchers may present the party case, and Government backbenchers are probably in the worst position of all in this respect. The Speaker usually allows minority opinions to be heard,

---

[1] See below, p. 286.

[2] See H. V. Wiseman, 'Private Members' Opportunities and Standing Order No. 9', *Parl. Aff.* 1958–9, pp. 377–91; W. H. Greenleaf, 'Urgency Motions in the Commons', *PL* 1960, pp. 270–84.

however, so that Liberal MPs have an advantage here. There are other occasions when backbenchers are given the chance to raise their own topics. Four Fridays per session are allocated to Private Members' Motions, MPs being selected by ballot. A number of motions are allocated to each day, though in practice only one is generally dealt with. Very often, Government policies rather than constituency topics are raised, and many MPs enter the ballot merely to prevent it being dominated by their opponents. It has been suggested that it would be better to have twenty-eight half days rather than fourteen full ones, and that instead of a ballot to decide who raises an issue, topics should be chosen according to the support they have among MPs.

The final half-hour of each day's sitting is devoted to an Adjournment Debate on a topic initiated by a backbencher, on the historically based principle that the House should not rise without debating outstanding grievances. Since the introduction of morning sessions, they also have ended with an Adjournment Debate. The MPs to raise topics in an Adjournment Debate are chosen partly by ballot and partly by the Speaker. The matters raised are primarily constituency issues, and often arise from unsatisfactory answers at Question Time. The Adjournment Debate is a useful means of probing executive action, in that the enquiries can be more detailed than at Question Time. The Minister has to state his case more fully, and it is harder to evade the issue than it is in Question Time. The debate often fails to attract attention, however, because the House tends to be empty by the end of the day, and except on Fridays the debate comes too late to receive good press and news coverage. Accordingly it has been suggested that the debate should be moved to a different time, perhaps to the middle of the sitting, though the Adjournment Debate in the morning sessions has gone some way towards meeting this. In addition to the daily Adjournment Debate, the final day before the House adjourns for the recess at Christmas, Easter, Whitsun and summer, is devoted to general debates on topics decided by the Speaker in consultation with the Whips.

The Committee System

Much of the work of the House, both legislative and delibera-tive, is done through committees, though in many ways the House of Commons' committee system could be revised and developed to advantage.[1] There is a clear distinction between the committees that exist to consider legislation, and those that exist for purposes of general enquiry. The committee stage of all legislation is taken either in a Standing Committee or a Committee of the Whole House. A Committee of the Whole is made up of the House minus only the Speaker and the mace —the symbol of Royal authority. Originally the House met as a committee in this way in order to exclude the influence of the King through the Speaker, while in the eighteenth century the practice also developed of allowing all who wished to do so to attend Select Committee meetings, so that on occasions these committees were made up of virtually the full House. Today the significance of a Committee of the Whole is not merely historical, in that the rules of debate and the general atmosphere in a Committee of the Whole are less formal than in the House with the Speaker. The Bills that are taken in a Committee of the Whole are either 'one-clause Bills' which can be passed very quickly, or Bills of first-class constitutional importance, though this is clearly a definition that is open to interpretation. In addition, the money resolution that accompanies any Bill that proposes an increase in public spending, is considered between the Second Reading and the committee stage by the House sitting as a Committee of the Whole. As well as this legislative function, some aspects of financial procedure are also considered by the whole House.

The Committee stage of most Bills, however, is taken in one of the Standing Committees. These Committees also take the Second Reading of some Bills. The first Standing Committee emerged at the end of the last century, and in most sessions before 1945 three to five Standing Committees were normally

---

[1] See K. C. Wheare, *Government by Committee*, London 1955; M. Ryle, 'Committees in the House of Commons', *PQ* 1965, pp. 295–308; D. Pring, 'Standing Committees in the House of Commons', *Parl. Aff.* 1957–8, pp. 303–17; A. H. Hanson and H. V. Wiseman, 'The Use of Committees by the House of Commons', *PL* 1959, pp. 277–92.

appointed. Today there are eight, including one where precedence is given to Private Members' Bills. Each committee is made up of sixteen to fifty members chosen in proportion to party strength in the House (though a Government with a small majority may exaggerate its majority on the committee), and according to their expert knowledge of the piece of legislation to be considered. A committee may deal with a number of Bills in a session, and until 1960 each committee had a nucleus of twenty members with an additional thirty or so who were chosen according to the Bill to be considered. Since 1960, however, only the chairman has been permanent throughout the session, and all other members have been chosen because of their knowledge of the particular Bill to be dealt with.

The proportion of MPs involved in the work of the Standing Committees is not large, and informed estimates vary from about seventy to about two hundred in any one session. The increase in MPs' salaries in 1964 was designed partly to produce more full-time members who would be ready for committee service. The committees meet in the mornings, generally for two-and-a-half-hour sessions. The Government may be defeated in committee because its majority is comparatively small, and because most committee work is concerned with details which cut across party lines, rather than with principles. Also, the fate of the Government is not threatened by defeat in a Standing Committee. The Opposition can delay the Government's legislative programme at the committee stage, but to speed committee work the Closure, the Guillotine, and the Kangaroo can all be applied.

The committee stage of all Bills relating exclusively to Scotland is taken in a special Standing Committee made up of thirty MPs for Scottish seats and twenty others chosen for their interest in the particular Bill, or in order to achieve on the committee a reflection of the party balance of power in the House.[1] Also for Scottish affairs there is the Scottish Grand Committee, made up of all seventy-one MPs for Scottish constituencies, plus an additional ten to fifteen MPs to maintain the balance of the parties. The Scottish Grand Committee deals with the Second Reading of Scottish Bills (unless the House votes to

[1] See J. H. Burns, 'The Scottish Committees of the House of Commons, 1948–59', *PS* 1960, pp. 272–96.

keep them on the floor of the House), and it spends six days per session considering the Scottish Estimates, and two days on general Scottish debates. A similar committee exists for Welsh affairs. Also for legislation may be noted the Opposed and Unopposed Private Bill Committees, composed of four and five members respectively, which deal with the committee stage of private legislation, and the joint committees of Lords and Commons for the committee stage of some non-contentious legislation. Joint committees may also be used as committees of enquiry.

As well as the Standing Committees for legislation, there are a number of Select Committees appointed to enquire into some aspect of executive activity. These may be *ad hoc* Select Committees, set up from time to time for some enquiry that is specific and limited in its extent, or they may be sessional Select Committees, like the Public Accounts Committee or the Select Committee on Estimates, which are set up at the beginning of each session, and which are in effect permanent features of the House of Commons' committee system. *Ad hoc* Select Committees, which are limited in their membership to fifteen MPs, are used less today than in the nineteenth century, when much legislation resulted from their enquiries. Between 1867 and 1900 there were, on average, thirty-three Select Committees appointed each year, but between 1945 and 1961 the average was only fifteen a year.[1] They have been replaced in the main by Royal Commissions, departmental committees of enquiry, and judicial enquiries. Where they are appointed, Select Committees are most useful for enquiries into subjects where there are no clear party alignments.

The sessional Select Committees, however, are of growing significance in the work of the House. The PAC, the SCE, the Statutory Instruments Committee, and the Select Committees on Nationalized Industries, Science and Technology, Scottish Affairs, Overseas Aid, Parliamentary Commissioner, Education and Science, and Race Relations (the last six created since 1967) are committees of enquiry which supplement the Commons' general examination of some aspect of executive activity. Their task is to enquire and then report to the House, drawing attention to any irregularities in their specialized fields of

[1] Crick, *The Reform of Parliament*, p. 94.

enquiry. There are other sessional Select Committees which contribute to the administration of business in the House. The Select Committee on Procedure, composed of ten MPs, examines proposals for the reform of Parliamentary procedure.[1] The Committee of Selection, made up of eleven MPs in proportion to party strength in the House, arranges the composition of the various committees. The Committee of Privileges, made up of fifteen of the most experienced members of the house, examines cases of alleged breach of Parliamentary privilege. The day-to-day running of the House is assisted by the Select Committee on Services, which helps the Speaker to organize Hansard and other official publications, and which is responsible for the catering facilities in the House. It is the only Select Committee with executive powers. In addition to these various official committees of the House, there are a number of committees within each party in the House, chief of which are the 1922 Committee and the PLP,[2] while also in this context may be noted the all-party backbench committees like the Parliamentary and Scientific Committee[3] or the Temperance Group.

*   *   *

The main criticism that is levelled against the committee system as it operates at present is that it does not achieve adequate specialized enquiry into the activities of the departments and the various aspects of Government policy, and that in this respect it is inferior to the specialized committee system that operates, for example, in the United States' Congress. Apart from the few sessional Select Committees, the House of Commons lacks specialist probing committees. The Standing Committees deal exclusively with legislation, and do not indulge in general debate, though Standing Orders permit the consideration of business other than legislation, and in 1919 experiments were made in referring the Estimates to them. The composition of the Standing Committee varies from one

[1] See H. V. Wiseman, 'Procedure: the House of Commons and the Select Committee', *Parl. Aff.* 1959–60, pp. 236–47; C. J. Boulton, 'Recent Developments in House of Commons Procedure', *Parl. Aff.* 1969–70, pp. 61–71.

[2] See above, p. 111. See also R. Body, 'Unofficial Committees in the House of Commons', *Parl. Aff.* 1957–8, pp. 295–302.

[3] S. A. Walkland, 'Parliament and Science', *Parl. Aff.* 1963–4, pp. 308–20, *and* pp. 389–402, *and* 1964–5, pp. 266–78.

Bill to another, so that although a committee may have specialist knowledge of the particular measure being considered, the Standing Committees do not represent a permanent specialist element in the committee system. It is frequently suggested, therefore, that the committee system should be reformed, either by turning the existing Standing Committees into permanent specialist bodies with the power to debate general policy as well as examine legislation (as with the Scottish Grand Committee), or by leaving the Standing Committees as they are at present and creating extra Select Committees on the lines of the committees appointed since 1967, like Race Relations, Science and Technology, and Overseas Aid.[1]

There have been numerous proposals on these lines, with variations as to the details of the form that the committees should take and the powers they should have. It has been suggested for example that specialist committees could take the Second Reading of all Bills, and when not considering legislation they could examine the Estimates, debate general policy, and perhaps take the initiative in proposing legislation. It has also been suggested that such committees could have the power to examine witnesses, civil servants, and Ministers, while some proposals extend to the Ministers being chairmen of the committees. One committee per department has been advocated, while more modest proposals have sought to group the departments into four or five categories with a committee for each one. Recently, however, the most frequent suggestions have been for committees for defence, and Commonwealth and foreign affairs,[2] while as an alternative it has been suggested that sub-committees of the Estimates Committee should be developed as specialist bodies.

Numerous arguments can be advanced in favour of a greater number of specialized committees. Expert views can be developed through continued service on one committee dealing with one subject, and as well as developing the knowledge and critical powers of MPs, this serves as a good training ground for Ministers. The executive could benefit from better-informed

---

[1] M. Partington, 'Parliamentary Committees: Recent Developments', *Parl. Aff.* 1969–70, pp. 366–79.

[2] D. R. Shell, 'Specialist Select Committees', *Parl. Aff.* 1969–70, pp. 380–404.

MPs, and the departments would be kept more alert. The House of Commons is always slow to delegate to committees, and falls behind many other legislatures in this respect, but as modern government is so detailed and complicated, some degree of delegation is inevitable today. The existing sessional Select Committees, and particularly the PAC, are examples of specialist committees that work effectively, and the Standing Committees originally created in the eighteen-eighties were designed as specialist bodies. Also, committees on these lines would cut across party affiliations to some extent, and this would be seen by many as being a desirable thing for the party system and for the House of Commons.

Critics of the idea of specialized committees argue, however, that specialization in itself need not necessarily be advantageous, in that this can very often lead to narrowness of outlook. Committees to examine the Estimates and debate general policy are also criticized from the executive's point of view as being too great a burden on Ministers, while it is sometimes claimed that a greater number of such committees would in fact actually weaken Parliament's power to criticize the executive by linking Parliament too closely with the executive and executive decisions. Certainly, to draw parallels with the United States Congress can be misleading, as Parliament's role in the system of government is very different from that of Congress. From the practical point of view, any increase in the number of committees would cause staffing problems, though there is less force in this argument if service as an MP is regarded as being a full-time occupation. As far as the examination of legislation is concerned, the existing committee system is more specialized than is generally realized, and even though the Standing Committees do not have a permanent membership, their members are specialized in the particular piece of legislation that is before them at any one time. Ultimately, however, the arguments for and against the development of a more specialized committee system are bound up with the question of how far it is desirable to weaken the hold that Governments have at present over the House of Commons, and on this fundamental question there is a wide disagreement.

Parliamentary Reform

In recent years considerable dissatisfaction has been expressed with the role that Parliament plays in the process of government, and there have been numerous proposals for a reform of Parliament. With the question of Parliamentary reform, however, a distinction has to be made between, on the one hand, fundamental reforms to the nature of the Constitution, which are designed to give Parliament greater freedom from Government control, and on the other hand, reforms of the procedure of Parliament. Within this second category there is a further distinction between reforms designed to make Parliament a better critic of the Government, and reforms designed to enable the Government to get its measures through Parliament more easily. Among the fundamental Constitutional reforms are proposals (dealt with elsewhere)[1] for a reform of the electoral system to reduce the chances of a party getting an overall majority in the House; a reform of the power of the House of Lords so that it may provide a bigger check to Governments that are dominant in the House of Commons; changes within the parties to reduce the subservience of MPs to the party Whips; and changes to allow devolution of authority from Whitehall and Westminster to regional authorities. Such sweeping reforms, however, would on the whole seem to have less chance of success than some of the proposed reforms to the internal procedure of Parliament. Most significant of these are proposals for the introduction of a more specialized committee system; alterations to legislative procedure to allow more work to be transferred from the floor of the House to committees; a revision of the distribution of time between the various classes of business; reforms to Private Members' time, and other such changes. These various proposals have been examined earlier in this chapter, but in addition there are numerous other suggestions that have been made from time to time to improve the overall efficiency of Parliament.

The present method of voting in Parliament is often criticized.[2] A division involves MPs marching through the respective

[1] See Chs. 2, 4, 9 and 13.

[2] See L. Wolf-Phillips, 'Parliamentary Divisions and Proxy Voting', *Parl. Aff.* 1964-5, pp. 416-21.

division lobbies for 'Ayes' and 'Noes', a process that takes about ten minutes. It is a time-consuming process and in most cases it is a futile exercise, with Government majorities assured on all but the most exceptional occasions. Over the Finance Bill in 1951 there was a total of about four hours spent in the division lobbies, and in the 1909 session there were 895 divisions, equivalent to about eight days and nights in the lobbies. An alternative would be mechanical voting, with each MP having a seat with a voting device, but in the existing House of Commons there are not enough seats to accommodate 629 MPs at once. Votes could be recorded *en bloc*, with the Whips voting on behalf of all their party's MPs unless the MP declared to the contrary, but this tacit acceptance of an MP's subservience to the Whips would offend many. Divisions held only at fixed times of the day would remove the need for MPs to be on hand at other times, though this would make the voting process even more artificial than it is at present. Most practical of all would seem to be a much wider application of the principle of pairing (whereby an Opposition absentee is paired with an absentee from the Government), or of proxy voting on behalf of MPs who were ill or absent from the House. Even this, however, would offend the principle that voting in the House is a personal responsibility, but it would end the need for the sick, the lame, and the dying to attend vital divisions.

An increase in salary is often advocated as a means of improving the quality of MPs, and thereby increasing the overall efficiency of Parliament. In the early days of Parliament, Knights of the Shire were paid four shillings per day, and Burgesses two shillings per day for attending Parliament, as attendance was then regarded as a burden and as a favour to the King. This practice soon ended, however, and payment for modern MPs dates only from 1911, when they were given a salary of £400 a year. This was raised to £600 in 1937, £1,000 in 1946, and after small increases in 1954 and 1957, to £3,250 in 1964. Since 1969 they have also been allowed £500 to cover secretarial costs. The arguments used to support and oppose the introduction of payment in 1911 have been largely reproduced over every salary increase for MPs since then. It is always argued in defence of salary increases that higher salaries would attract men of greater ability; that MPs are more open to undesirable pressures if they are badly paid; that service as an MP should be a full-time occupation, with adequate professional salary rewards; and that only lawyers, journalists, trade union officials, company directors, and the self-employed, can be MPs and at the same time maintain outside employment. It is argued that if the House is to function effectively, it should be composed of full-time MPs drawn from all sections of the community.[1]

Higher salaries are always resisted, however, on the grounds that MPs should not be full-time but should have outside connections. It is argued that there is a tradition of public service which does not demand high financial rewards, and that high salaries attract people to Parliament 'for the wrong reasons'. By increasing the trend towards professionalism in politics, it is claimed that higher salaries produce more career-minded politicians who subordinate principles to expediency, and to submission to the party Whips. It is also said that high salaries deter retirement, and thus help to maintain a high average age for MPs, though the solution to this factor would be to continue to pay MPs' salaries, in whole or in part, after retirement. To some extent the issue is a party political one, the Liberal and Labour MPs generally being sympathetic to the principle of adequate remuneration, while Conservative MPs in general have been more inclined to regard membership of the Commons as a service and as a part-time occupation. As an alternative to an increase in basic salaries, additional fees could be paid for committee work, or a subsistence allowance paid to MPs whose homes are not in London. Also, MPs' salaries could be tied to a Civil Service grade so that the pay of MPs would rise automatically with Civil Service pay, thereby removing some of the controversy from the issue.

The general accommodation provided for MPs in the House is inadequate in many respects, and hardly conducive to the efficient performance of MPs' tasks.[2] The House of Commons that was built after the last war improved on pre-war conditions slightly, and there have been further improvements and

[1] P. W. Buck, *Amateurs and Professionals in British Politics 1918–59*, London (and Chicago), 1963.

[2] See A. Barker and M. Rush, *The Member of Parliament and His Information*, London 1970.

extensions since then, including free postage and 'phone calls from the House, but MPs are still not provided with adequate desk or office facilities, or secretarial assistance. In these respects the 'Mother of Parliaments' compares unfavourably with the legislatures of the USA, Canada, Australia, and New Zealand, though it is superior to many European legislatures. Free secretarial assistance, more office space, and cheap accommodation for those whose homes are not in London, are often asked for, as are better research facilities in the library of the House of Commons. Many Parliamentary questions and letters to Ministers would be unnecessary if the library gave MPs greater access to information about the departments of state.[1] Such a development is resisted, however, partly because of the expense and partly because of doubt as to the constitutional desirability of this.

Finally, it may be questioned whether Parliament's task of publicizing Government activities would be aided if Parliamentary proceedings were televised or broadcast.[2] The State Opening of Parliament has been televised, and there are numerous television and radio programmes which comment on Parliament, but there are no live transmissions of Parliamentary proceedings. The televising of Parliamentary proceedings on a special channel, or a programme of selected parts of the day's proceedings, might make the public more aware of Parliamentary activities and would thus further Parliament's publicizing function. The televising of Parliament might produce better attendance in the House and better speeches, but it might also lead to greater exhibitionism and a tendency to play to the cameras. It could also remove some of Parliament's mystique (for good or ill) and this is perhaps a major reason why the Commons, on a free vote in November 1966, rejected a proposal for the televising of proceedings for an experimental period, even though a Select Committee had reported in favour of such an experiment. The House of Lords, however, continued with plans for the televising of its proceedings.

[1] See D. Menhennet, 'The Library of the House of Commons', *PQ* 1965, pp. 323–32.
[2] See C. Seymour Ure, 'An Examination of the Proposal to Televise Parliament', *Parl. Aff.* 1963–4, pp. 172–81; C. Seymour Ure, 'Parliamentary Privilege and Broadcasting', *Parl. Aff.* 1962–3, pp. 411–18.

The MP and his Constituents

In any system of representative government problems can arise regarding the nature of the relationship between the representatives and the electorate in between general elections. Once elected, are representatives free to speak and act according to their own consciences, subject only to the need to act in such a way as to secure their re-election to office, or must they behave more like delegates or agents than true representatives, acting on instructions issued by their constituents? In Britain this problem manifests itself particularly in the question of the relationship between an MP and his constituency party. In theoretical terms it is generally accepted that an MP is indeed a representative who decides issues according to his own judgement, who speaks and votes in Parliament as he wishes, who cannot be forced to resign, and who is protected by the doctrine that it is a breach of Parliamentary privilege for a group of constituents, or any other body, to seek to limit an MP's freedom of speech. An MP is, of course, limited in his freedom by his ties with his Parliamentary party, and he has to bear the consequences of any actions that offend this body. These, however, are ties that exist within Parliament and within the principle that MPs, individually or as members of a Parliamentary party or group, are representatives who are free to make such rules as they think fit to govern their Parliamentary activities.

Nevertheless, assuming that an MP wishes to be returned to office at the next election, he has to bear in mind the consequences of any actions that may offend his constituents, and this is the essential basis of the democratic principle of representation. In addition to this general electoral control, however, the MP's constituency party association, and the executive committee and officers in particular, have the power to influence the conduct of MPs to an extent that often leads MPs to complain of dictation from the constituency.[1] A local party association sometimes censures an MP for an action that he has taken, or remarks that he has made, and an MP is sometimes called upon to attend an association meeting to explain his conduct. Most important of all, however, the constituency party can refuse to readopt the sitting member as the official

---

[1] See above, p. 112.

party candidate for the next election, and as a candidate stands little chance of being elected without official party support, it is often claimed that in practical terms there is little real freedom left for MPs. It is even sometimes argued that the electoral dependence of candidates upon their party is such that an MP is morally obliged (if not Constitutionally obliged) to resign his seat if he breaks with his party between elections.

The problem is not a new one.[1] In the seventeenth and eighteenth centuries in some constituencies a number of Political Associations were formed that sought to impose instructions on MPs, and in their turn many MPs freely pledged themselves to pursue particular policies in Parliament on behalf of their constituents. There was a reaction against this, however, epitomized by Edmund Burke's declaration to the voters of Bristol in 1774 that he represented the whole nation as well as his own constituents. Burke argued that ' . . . You choose a member, indeed; but when you have chosen him, he is not a member of Bristol, but he is a member of Parliament.'[2] In recent years there have been a number of examples of MPs in conflict with their constituency parties, and Burke's theme has often been echoed. Nigel Nicolson, elected Conservative member for Bournemouth East and Christchurch in 1955, offended his constituency party by voting in favour of the abolition of capital punishment in February 1956, and by abstaining in a vote of confidence on the Conservative Government's Suez policy in November 1956.[3] A meeting of the local Conservative Association criticized these actions and demanded his resignation, but Nicolson refused to resign, arguing that he was a representative who was free to decide on issues as he thought fit. The Association chose a new prospective candidate, but he resigned after a year, and the Conservative Central Office intervened and arranged a ballot of the Association to choose between Nicolson and some unnamed alternative. Nicolson was narrowly beaten in the ballot and he agreed not to stand at the next election.

[1] C. Leys, 'Petitioning in the Nineteenth and Twentieth Centuries', PS 1955, pp. 45–64.

[2] Edmund Burke in a speech to the electors of Bristol, 3.11.1774.

[3] See Nigel Nicolson, People and Parliament, London 1958; L. W. Martin, 'The Bournemouth Affair: Britain's First Primary Election', J of P 1960, pp. 654–81; L. Epstein, 'British MPs and their Local Parties: the Suez Cases', APSR 1960, pp. 374–91.

Stanley Evans, Labour MP for Wednesbury, was involved in a similar dispute at the same period.[1] He also abstained in a vote of confidence on the Conservative Government's Suez policy in November 1956, and the Wednesbury Labour Party sought his resignation. Unlike Nicolson, however, Evans complied with the request. More recently, Dr Donald Johnson, elected Conservative MP for Carlisle in 1955, criticized Macmillan's handling of the Profumo affair in 1963, and expressed dissatisfaction with his own role as an MP, and this led the local Conservative Party to choose a new prospective candidate. Johnson sought a meeting of the party association in order that he might air his grievances, but when this eventually took place the meeting rejected him. Johnson decided, however, to contest the seat at the 1964 election as an Independent Conservative candidate, and the Conservatives lost the seat to Labour partly because of Johnson's candidature.

J. H. McKie, Unionist MP for Galloway for many years, was more successful in his struggles with his local party. He stood as an Independent Unionist candidate against official Unionist and Labour candidates at the 1945 election, and he won the seat. He was later accepted back into the party fold, and at the 1950 election he fought and won the seat as the official Unionist candidate. Similarly, Sir David Robertson, elected as Unionist MP for Caithness and Sutherland in 1950, resigned the party whip in January 1959 and fought and won the seat at the 1959 election as an Independent Unionist, although he was not opposed by an official Unionist candidate. He sat throughout the 1959–64 Parliament as an Independent Unionist, and though he did not seek re-election in 1964, he supported another Independent candidate for Caithness and Sutherland who, however, was not elected.

In the 1970 general election S. O. Davies won Merthyr Tydfil as an Independent Labour candidate. Davies had represented the constituency since 1934, and at the age of eighty-three he resisted pressure from the constituency association to give up the seat. Although the association selected another official candidate, Davies opposed him and triumphed with a majority of almost 25%.

As a general rule it is MPs of moderate opinions in both the

[1] See Lord Morrison, *Government and Parliament*, p. 364.

main parties who seem most likely to antagonize their local party, perhaps because the local party activists may tend to be more extreme in their views than their MPs, or perhaps because moderate opinions held by an MP can be taken as indicating sympathy with the opposing party. Also, an MP is in a stronger position if an election is imminent, and if the constituency is a marginal one, as then the local party will presumably be anxious to avoid a public dispute with the MP. An MP can also generally win his fight if the national party supports him against the local party. Thus Major Lloyd George, with Conservative Central Office support, triumphed over his local party in Newcastle North in 1951, and Mrs Braddock, with Transport House backing, won Liverpool Exchange for Labour in 1955, despite the presence of another Labour candidate supported by the local party. On many occasions, however, the MP comes into conflict with the local party precisely because he has rebelled against the Parliamentary Party Whip, and at times the national party uses the local party to censure a rebel MP. On these occasions there is a clear overlap between pressure on MPs by the party Whips, and pressure on MPs at a constituency level, although on many other occasions the national party often declines to interfere at all in a local dispute, thereby acknowledging local party autonomy.

9

Parliament:
II. The Monarchy and
the House of Lords

THE MONARCHY

THE ORIGINS of the Monarchy in Britain can be traced back to the ninth century, with the unification of England under one King. The authority of the Crown was extended to Wales and Ireland by conquest, and in 1603 the thrones of England and Scotland were united in the one person of James I of England and VI of Scotland. The royal succession goes back to the Saxon King Egbert, and its continuity has been broken only once, by the republican period in the mid-seventeenth century. Today the Monarch is also Head of the Commonwealth, though the title and status of the Monarch varies in different parts of the Commonwealth.

Value of the Monarchy

The essential feature of the development of the Monarchy over the centuries has been its adaptability to changing patterns of political power, and in particular in the last three hundred years, its evolution into a Constitutional Monarchy.[1]

[1] For general works on the Monarchy today see Kingsley Martin, *The Crown and the Establishment*, London 1963; Sir C. Petrie, *The Modern British Monarchy*, London 1961. See also Sir H. Nicolson, *George V*, London 1952; Sir J. Wheeler-Bennett, *George VI*, London, 1958. F. Hardie, *The Political Influence of the British Monarchy 1868–1952;* London 1970; J. Murray-Brown (ed), *The Monarchy and Its Future*, London 1969.

While Britain is not unique as a Constitutional state with a Monarch as head of state, a number of alternatives exist regarding the nature of the head of state within a Constitutional system of government. In the first place, a clear choice presents itself between a largely ceremonial figurehead, and a head of state who is also the political head of government. The United States, and France under the Fifth Republic, dispense with a purely ceremonial figurehead, and combine the ceremonial role with that of political head of the government, whereas Britain has the Monarch as a non-political figurehead and 'steering-wheel' within the Constitution. Even with a non-political head of state, however, there is a republican alternative, in that in the Fourth French Republic, Presidents Auriol and Coty played a largely ceremonial role, while the Premier was the political head of the government. Similarly, in the West German Federal Republic today the President is head of state while the Chancellor is the political head of the government.

There was a republican movement in Britain in the middle of the last century, when the cost and practical value of the Monarchy were questioned, but the movement failed, and Queen Victoria's reign ended in a blaze of Monarchical fervour. Today Britain remains as one of the few surviving Monarchies in Europe. The Monarchies of Britain, Belgium, the Netherlands, Denmark, Norway, and Sweden (and the Grand Duchies of Luxembourg, Liechtenstein and Monaco), have survived largely because they have been adapted (though to differing degrees) to a Constitutional system of government. Among the existing Monarchies, however, it is possible to make a distinction between the Monarchies of Scandinavia, and the distinctly more aloof and 'splendid' Monarchy in Britain, and the 1953 Coronation epitomized the British Monarchy as the 'Rolls Royce' of Monarchies.[1] Had Edward VIII not abdicated in 1936, there might have been an evolution of the Monarchy into a form more akin to the Scandinavian model, but George VI and Elizabeth II have sought to preserve much of the Monarchy's remoteness and mystique.

Thus as head of state Britain has a Monarch, fulfilling a

[1] See E. A. Shils and M. Young, 'The Meaning of the Coronation', *SR* 1953, pp. 63–81; N. Birnbaum, 'Monarchs and Sociologists', *SR* 1955, pp. 5–23.

largely ceremonial role as a constitutional figurehead, but distinctly more aloof and 'royal' than the other surviving Monarchies of Europe. There are undoubtedly a number of merits in this arrangement. In numerous ways it is desirable to separate the political and ceremonial aspects of public life. With a separate ceremonial head of state the political leader is freed from the need to embark on goodwill trips abroad or to perform other formal roles, and he thus has more time to devote to his political responsibilities. In this respect the British Prime Minister has an advantage over the United States' President. Also, without a separate figurehead, the political President, despite the fact that he is a party political figure, inevitably appears as the centre of national loyalty and acquires a certain aura as a result. This gives him an electoral advantage over his opponents, which can perhaps be seen as undesirable in a democratic system. In Britain on the other hand, although the Prime Minister appears to a certain extent as a national figure as well as a party figure, the Crown remains as the centre of national loyalty. Thus it is possible to 'damn the Government but cheer the Queen', perhaps with greater national cohesion as a result, and certainly with less electoral advantage for the Prime Minister.

The Monarch is a more personalized and attractive symbol of national unity than the vague concept of the State, the flag, or even a President, and the hereditary system at least solves the problem of succession. The selection of a truly independent national figure as a republican figurehead can be difficult. In Britain there can even be disputes over the choice of a Speaker of the House of Commons—perhaps the closest we get to an independent non-Monarchical figure within the Constitutional machinery. Once chosen, a republican head of state is always more open than a Monarch to accusations of party political bias, as was revealed with Presidents Auriol and Coty in the French Fourth Republic. Also, given average ability, the continuity in office that comes from the hereditary system can produce experience, and Prime Ministers have spoken of the value of the political advice given by some Monarchs. The ceremonial that surrounds the Monarchy is largely harmless, and at best has the positive merit of emphasizing national traditions and historical values, while the glitter of the Monarchy is a feature of British national life that is often envied abroad. These various arguments can also be used to defend the Monarchy in its present form, with the emphasis on mystique and ceremonial, which makes it different from the other European Monarchies. The Monarchy is also one of the factors that helps to strengthen Commonwealth ties, and in so far as it is desirable to preserve the Commonwealth, it is necessary to emphasize the role of the Monarchy as a symbol of unity.[1] In a sense, this is an echo of Disraeli's successful attempt to promote British nationalism and Imperial unity through Queen Victoria's role as Empress of India, and the evolution of the British Monarchy from being Head of the Empire to being Head of the Commonwealth has been achieved remarkably smoothly, and with considerable ingenuity.

The Monarchy has many critics, however, who argue that it is a definite liability within the political system. They criticize the hereditary system from the practical point of view of being no real guarantee of merit (and many Monarchs in the past were undoubtedly rather dubious specimens), while from a general standpoint they condemn the hereditary principle as being undesirable in a democratic system. Many critics also see the Monarchy as the centre of the class system in Britain, and claim (with some justification) that the continued existence of the Monarchy helps to promote deference, snobbery, and an acceptance of outdated traditions and values. The cost of the Monarchy is often criticized, though it is extremely difficult to arrive at a clear conclusion as to the actual cost to the state. In 1761 George III surrendered the Crown Lands to the nation in return for an annual income from Parliament, and this arrangement has been renewed at the beginning of each reign. Today the Crown Lands of some 292,000 acres are administered by the Crown Commissioners, and the annual profit, estimated at about £2,500,000, goes to the state. Parliament grants an annual Civil List of £475,000, but there are a number of additional items of royal expenditure, the precise cost of which is not clear. Allowances are paid to the Queen Mother, the Duke of Edinburgh, and other members of the Royal Family. Revenue from the Duchies of Cornwall and Lancaster (about £90,000 a

---

[1] See G. C. Moodie, 'The Crown and the Commonwealth', *Parl. Aff.* 1957–8, pp. 180–203.

year) goes to the Prince of Wales after his eighteenth birthday. Departments of state cover many aspects of royal expenditure, the Ministry of Public Building and Works being responsible for the maintenance of the royal castles, and the Defence Departments for the Queen's Flight and the royal yacht.

The royal family has a large personal fortune which is not diminished by death duties. Queen Victoria handed down more than £2,000,000, and in addition there are valuable royal collections of jewellery, stamps, and pictures. Estimates as to the total value of the royal family's personal wealth vary from £10,000,000 to £60,000,000. One informed estimate[1] as to the royal 'Balance Sheet' is that the Monarchy costs the nation about £2,000,000 per year, so that on this estimate the Monarchy is a costly institution, and critics argue that a republic would be much cheaper. On the other hand, this is in many ways an artificial estimation, in that the Monarchy has a value, even as a tourist attraction, that offsets much of its cost, so that in some respects the Monarchy is a good national investment.

Constitutional Role of the Monarch

The Crown is the personification of the state, and is the supreme legal authority in Britain. The doctrine of Ministerial Responsibility means that the Monarch acts on the advice of Ministers, but the precise extent of the independent powers of the Monarch is one of the aspects of the unwritten British Constitution that still provides scope for argument among Constitutional lawyers. In external affairs the Royal Prerogative includes the power to declare war, make treaties, and cede territory, these powers being exercised by the Prime Minister and the Defence and Foreign Ministers. As the head of the judiciary and the source of judicial authority, the Monarch appoints judges and dispenses mercy, but only on the recommendation of the Prime Minister, the Home Secretary, or the Scottish Secretary. As 'the fountain of honour' the Monarch appoints diplomats and senior ranks in the forces, and confers titles, again on the advice of the Prime Minister. In the past, the Monarch's power to create Peerages was the ultimate means of securing a

[1] Anthony Sampson, *The Anatomy of Britain Today*, London 1965, p. 22. See also Martin, *The Crown and the Establishment*, p. 134.

majority in the House of Lords for the Monarch's Ministers, but such action has not been threatened since 1911 and seems inconceivable today. As an integral part of Parliament, the Assent of the Monarch is required as the final stage of the legislative process, but not since Queen Anne refused to accept the Scotch Militia Bill in 1703 has the Royal Assent been denied. In 1913 it was argued in some quarters that the Monarch could and should refuse to accept the highly controversial Irish Home Rule Bill, and theoretically the Monarch could still refuse to grant the Royal Assent, but this would hardly seem to be practical politics today.[1]

In two spheres, the granting of a dissolution and the appointment of a Prime Minister, there have been this century a number of Constitutional controversies involving the role of the Monarch. Parliament is dissolved by the Monarch on the request of the Prime Minister, but it has been argued that in practical as well as theoretical terms the Monarch retains the right to refuse the Prime Minister's request, and also that the Monarch has the right to dissolve Parliament without receiving a request from the Prime Minister.[2] George V was involved in a major controversy over the power of dissolution in 1913, at the height of the controversy over Irish home rule. The Liberal Government's Bill to grant home rule to Ireland had been twice rejected in the Lords, but was presented to Parliament for the third time (under the terms of the Parliament Act 1911)[3] in 1913. The Unionist Opposition, supported by Sir William Anson, A. V. Dicey, and other prominent Constitutional lawyers, argued that the Monarch should dissolve Parliament in order that the electorate might 'pronounce' on this controversial Bill, even though the Prime Minister (Asquith) did not want a dissolution.[4] They claimed that a dissolution was politically desir-

---

[1] See G. C. Moodie, 'The Crown and Parliament', *Parl. Aff.* 1956–7, pp. 256–64.

[2] See D. J. Heasman, 'The Monarch, the Prime Minister and the Dissolution of Parliament', *Parl. Aff.* 1960–1, pp. 94–107; K. Sainsbury, 'The Constitution—Some Disputed Points', *Parl. Aff.* 1961–2, pp. 213–43; G. C. Moodie, 'The Monarch and the Selection of the Prime Minister', *PS* 1957, pp. 1–20.

[3] See below, p. 269.

[4] For the detailed arguments used in this controversy see Jennings, *Cabinet Government*, Appendix III. See also Nicolson, *George V*, Chs. 14 and 15.

able and constitutionally justified, in that the Monarch retained the right to dissolve Parliament at his discretion, especially at a time when civil rebellion was threatened as a result of Government actions. Other Constitutional experts, however, denied the Monarch's right to dissolve Parliament in these circumstances, against the wishes of the Prime Minister. They argued that the right of dissolution on the Monarch's own initiative had been killed by non-use, and that practical politics made it impossible. Parliament was not dissolved in 1913, and the home rule issue was swamped by the outbreak of war in 1914, but the episode illustrates the problems that can be raised for the Monarch in cases of Constitutional interpretation.

George V was involved in a less heated dispute over the dissolution in 1918, when, with the end of the war in November 1918, Lloyd George requested a dissolution in order that his Coalition Government could be extended into peacetime, with electoral approval for the making of the peace. George V was opposed to a dissolution at the end of 1918 because he felt it to be inopportune. He claimed that the Government was pledged to make the peace treaty before holding an election, and that problems would be involved with soldiers serving abroad, and with the service voters and newly enfranchised women voters making the election result unpredictable. Lloyd George's view prevailed, however, and the election was held in December 1918, producing a big win for the Government.

George VI and Elizabeth II seem to have escaped involvement in controversial dissolutions. Theoretically the position of the Monarch could be important if a Government refused to resign after losing the confidence of the Commons on a major issue. There is no Constitutional machinery to overthrow a Government that has refused to resign, other than by the dissolution of Parliament on the Monarch's own initiative (or eventually by the refusal of Supply by the Commons). There is no precedent as a guide as to what would happen in these circumstances, but this is a highly speculative situation and it is venturing into the realms of Constitutional fiction to see the Monarch achieving today what could not otherwise be achieved by the pressure of public opinion or the threat of civil revolt.

*　　　*　　　*

The Constitutional principle with regard to the appointment of the Prime Minister is that the choice is made by the Monarch, but again acting on the advice of the retiring Prime Minister or other authoritative figures. The last occasion when the Prime Minister was appointed on the Monarch's own initiative was in 1894, when Queen Victoria chose Lord Rosebery rather than Spencer or Harcourt. Today there is no difficulty in the selection of the Prime Minister if the reigning Government is successful at a general election, as the Prime Minister then remains in office, as happened in 1950, 1955, 1959, and 1966. Similarly, no problem arises if the Government is beaten at a general election and the main Opposition party emerges with a clear majority, as happened in 1945, 1951, 1964 and 1970. When a Prime Minister dies or retires between general elections both the Labour and Conservative Parties now have machinery for electing a new party leader who would then be the Monarch's choice as the new Prime Minister. These procedures have operated to date only when the parties have been in opposition, and the Conservative procedure was adopted only in 1965. Before this, the death or retirement of a Conservative Prime Minister between elections meant that the Monarch was sometimes associated with controversies over the choice of Conservative Prime Ministers, and this was particularly the case in 1923, 1957, and 1963.

In the spring of 1923 Bonar Law was forced by ill-health to retire as Prime Minister, and Baldwin and Lord Curzon emerged as rivals to succeed him.[1] Lord Curzon appeared to have a better claim than Baldwin, but in the event the King sent for Baldwin. It is not clear why Curzon was overlooked. One factor that complicated the issue was that Bonar Law declined to advise the King as to his successor. It seems that he expected Curzon to be chosen, but he would not speak in his favour and advised the King to consult Lord Salisbury. The Monarch did seek the advice of Lord Salisbury and Lord Balfour, while L. S. Amery and W. C. Bridgeman, two prominent members of the Government, gave their advice to Lord Stamfordham, the King's Private Secretary. There were suggestions

---

[1] For details see R. Blake, *The Unknown Prime Minister*, London 1955, pp. 513–34; Amery, *Thoughts on the Constitution*, pp. 21–2; Nicolson, *George V*, pp. 375–9.

that the Monarch was misled into believing that Bonar Law favoured Baldwin. Lord Stamfordham informed Curzon that the reason for his exclusion was the fact that he was a Peer, but it is possible that the Peerage issue was used merely as an excuse, and that Curzon was passed over because of personal factors. Whatever the reason, however, the Monarch was caught up in unsavoury party machinations.

Again in 1957 the Monarch was involved in a certain amount of controversy over the succession to the Premiership. In January 1957 Eden resigned as Prime Minister on the grounds of ill-health. It was widely assumed that R. A. Butler would succeed him, as he had presided over Cabinet meetings in Eden's absence and was the most experienced member of Eden's Government, but Harold Macmillan was in fact appointed. It is not clear what advice, if any, was given to the Queen by Eden, but Churchill and Lord Salisbury were consulted and spoke for Macmillan. Cabinet Ministers were consulted individually by Lord Salisbury and Lord Kilmuir, while backbenchers were sounded by the Chief Whip (Edward Heath). Some backbenchers, however, have denied ever being consulted, and have claimed that Macmillan's selection was a conspiracy. It has also been suggested by Sir Ivor Jennings[1] that the party was prepared to follow either Macmillan or Butler, and that the Queen made a genuine personal choice between them. This seems difficult to support, however, and it appears clear that Churchill and Lord Salisbury stressed that Macmillan was to be preferred, but as in 1923, the episode caused speculation over the role of the Monarch, and involved the Crown in what appeared to be doubtful proceedings.

In 1963 the selection of Home as Prime Minister proved to be even more controversial than that of Macmillan in 1957. On October 10th 1963 Macmillan unexpectedly announced that owing to ill-health he intended to resign. The contenders to succeed him were R. A. Butler, Lord Hailsham, Lord Home, Reginald Maudling, Edward Heath, and Iain Macleod, with Butler and Hailsham seeming to have the best chance. The emergence of Home thus came as a surprise to most observers, and again brought attention to bear on the whole process of selection, including the role of the Monarch. It has been

[1] Jennings, *Cabinet Government*, p. 28.

claimed that after soundings had been taken among Ministers, backbenchers, Peers, and constituency workers, Home was selected, not necessarily because he was most people's first choice, but because he was overwhelmingly the least objectionable.[1] Macmillan is said to have acted as a single funnel of opinion for the Queen, and to have recommended Home to her as the clear choice of the party. Critics have said, however, that the soundings conducted within the party were not fairly conducted, and were designed primarily to exclude Butler. It was even suggested in some quarters that the Queen and Macmillan 'conspired' to secure Home's selection against the wishes of the majority of the Cabinet and the party as a whole.[2] However ill-informed these accusations may have been, and no matter how fair the process of consultation might have been in fact, the process *seemed* to be dubious in 1963, as it did in 1923 and 1957. This inevitably involved speculation as to the role and impartiality of the Monarch in the selection process, and helped to persuade the Conservative Party to change its method of choosing a leader.[3] The existence today of the Labour and Conservative Parties' procedures for electing their leaders does not in itself affect the Constitutional prerogative of the Monarch, in that the Monarch remains free to choose whoever may be regarded as suitable. Nevertheless, in practice it seems inconceivable that the Monarch would now choose as Prime Minister anyone who had not first been elected party leader, provided that in a crisis time was allowed for the election to take place.

It is possible, however, that the Monarch could still play more than a merely formal role in the selection of a Prime Minister in a Parliamentary situation where it was not clear which party could form a Government. In 1931 George V was drawn into the constitutional and political crisis involving the fall of the MacDonald Labour Government and the formation of the National Government.[4] In August 1931 the Labour

[1] See R. Churchill, *The Fight for the Tory Leadership*, London 1964; Sampson, *Anatomy of Britain Today*, p. 34.

[2] See Paul Johnson, *New Statesman*, 24.1.64.

[3] See above, p. 112.

[4] R. Bassett, *1931 Political Crisis*, London 1958; S. Webb, 'What Happened in 1931', *PQ* 1932, pp. 1-17; H. Dalton, '1931', *PQ* 1958, pp. 356-65; Nicolson, *George V*, p. 465.

Government could not agree over the measures to be taken to deal with the economic crisis, and MacDonald took the Government's resignation to the King. No party had an overall majority in the Commons, and there was no clear alternative Government. A dissolution seemed to be impossible because of the immediacy of the economic crisis. A meeting was held on August 24th between the King and the party leaders (MacDonald, Baldwin, and Lord Samuel), and from this meeting MacDonald emerged with the task of forming a National Government. The Conservatives and some Liberals supported MacDonald, but only three former Labour Ministers and a handful of Labour MPs followed him, and he was deprived of his leadership of the Labour Party. George V was criticized for his role in the formation of the National Government, and it was said that either the King realized that the Labour Party would not follow MacDonald, in which case he was wrong to accept him as Prime Minister, or alternatively, the King was used by Baldwin and Lord Samuel in order to escape from their responsibilities. Either way the Monarch does not emerge with credit, and the episode illustrates how the Monarch can be involved in bitter party conflict when the normal Parliamentary situation breaks down.

Although the crisis of August 1931 was undoubtedly exceptional in its origins and its consequences, it is still conceivable that a Monarch could again be faced with a situation where no party won an overall majority of seats in the Commons, and it was not clear which party or combination of parties was capable of forming a Government. In such a situation the Monarch's role in the selection of the Prime Minister could still have practical significance. Having acknowledged this, however, it must be stressed that on the whole today the practical significance of the Monarch's Constitutional functions is slight. Too great an emphasis on historical precedent and Constitutional theorizing can produce a distorted and exaggerated picture of the Monarch's role in the practical working of the political system. In that sense Bagehot's description of the ceremonial aspects of the Monarch as a cloak for real power, is perhaps still applicable. No doubt the regular consultations that take place between the Prime Minister and the Monarch can have practical significance if the Monarch is vital and well informed, and it is true that the real political power of Monarchs tends to come to light only after their deaths, in biographies and memoirs. Nevertheless, the real justification for the retention of the Monarchy has to be sought outside the field of the Monarch's theoretical function as a Constitutional steering-wheel.

THE HOUSE OF LORDS

As with the Monarchy, and as with so many aspects of the British Constitution, the problem with regard to the House of Lords is that of adapting it to a modern political system.[1] Most recently, the Wilson Government sought (though without success) to adapt and 'modernize' the Lords through a full-scale reform of both composition and powers. A second chamber can fulfil a number of roles within a modern Constitutional system of government. It can represent territorial interests within the community, as does the Senate in the United States federal system. In a situation where the lower house is largely controlled by the Government, a second chamber can act as a limiting force on the power of the Government, operating either as a popular check, obstructing the Government's work when it feels that it is acting contrary to the wishes of public opinion, or alternatively as a conservative check, obstructing the Government if it seems to be paying too much attention to popular opinion and is proposing ill-conceived and purely popularity-seeking measures. Yet again, the second chamber can be seen not as an obstructive force, but as a body designed merely to ease the legislative and deliberative burden of the lower house. The House of Lords has never filled the Senatorial role of representing territorial interests, but at different times in its history the Lords has been seen as performing these other functions.

Composition of the House of Lords

The two main aspects of the problem of the House of Lords have been its composition and its functions, the two aspects

---

[1] See P. Bromhead, *The House of Lords and Contemporary Politics*, London 1958; S. D. Bailey (ed.), *The Future of the House of Lords*, London 1954; Crick, *The Reform of Parliament*, pp. 100–46.

being inevitably closely bound together. Basically the problem has been that of composition, the House of Lords being a large and unwieldy body, based on the hereditary principle, with a guaranteed majority for the Conservative Party. The reforms proposed by the Wilson Government in October 1967, but abandoned eighteen months later, included a reduction in the size of the second chamber, and an ending of its hereditary basis. Today, there are over one thousand Peers eligible to sit in the Lords. Of these, about nine hundred are hereditary Peers, about one hundred and fifty are Life Peers created since the Life Peerages Act 1958, and nine are Lords of Appeal.[1] Until 1963 the Scottish Peers elected for each Parliament sixteen representative Peers to sit in the Lords, but the Peerage Act 1963 opened membership of the Lords to all Scottish Peers. In addition, there are twenty-six Spiritual Peers of the Established Church of England—the Archbishops of York and Canterbury, the Bishops of London, Durham, and Winchester, and the twenty-one senior Bishops in order of appointment to their Sees. Although the total membership makes the House of Lords the largest legislative assembly in the world, actual attendance is low. At the beginning of each Parliament, Peers receive a Writ of Summons to attend the Lords, and those who do not reply are excluded from attending the House for the rest of the Parliament. Even among those who do reply to the Writ of Summons, however, the majority attend only infrequently or not at all. The daily attendance on average is rather less than two hundred, while only about one hundred and fifty are regularly engaged in the work of the House. In operation, therefore, the Lords is thus a small and intimate body, though attendance can be much greater when controversial issues are being dealt with.

In the early years of the nineteenth century the number of Whigs and Tories were fairly evenly balanced in the Lords. Tory strength declined after the divisions in the party in 1846, but with the split in the Liberal Party in the eighteen-eighties, the Conservatives secured a clear dominance in the Lords, and in this century neither the Liberal Party nor the Labour Party has been able to match Conservative numbers in the Lords. Probably about half of the one thousand Peers support the

[1] G. Drewry and J. Morgan, 'Law Lords as Legislators', *Parl. Aff.* 1968–9, pp. 226–39.

Conservative Party, while about a third have no pronounced party ties.[1] Among those who attend regularly, the Conservative preponderance is perhaps not so great, but the vast number of infrequent attenders ('the backwoodsmen') remain as a reservoir of potential support for the Conservatives. The House of Lords at present, however, contains one Communist Peer (Lord Milford), so that in one sense the Lords is more representative than the House of Commons.

The Conservative domination of the House of Lords created obvious difficulties in the past for Labour and Liberal Governments. Until 1911 the two Houses of Parliament had virtual legislative equality, except that the most important Bills tended to be introduced in the Commons, and the power of the Lords was limited with regard to financial legislation. It had been recognized as early as the seventeenth century that the Lords could not *initiate* or *amend* financial legislation, and it was claimed in House of Commons resolutions in 1860 that the Lords could not *reject* financial legislation, although the validity of this last claim was questioned. Non-financial legislation was not protected by privilege, however, and in the event of conflict between the Government and the Lords, the ultimate remedy lay in the creation by the Monarch of enough new Peers sympathetic to the Government to swamp the hostile majority in the Lords. This had been done in 1713 in order to secure approval in the Lords for the Treaty of Utrecht. It was threatened in 1832 in order to secure the passage of the Reform Bill through the Lords, and was threatened again in 1911 in order to secure acceptance for the Parliament Bill. This remedy, however, was a somewhat cumbersome means of dealing with obstruction in the Lords, and in this century Liberal and then Labour Governments have been faced with the task of devising some more workable method of solving the problem presented by Conservative dominance in the Lords.

The most obvious way for Liberal or Labour Governments to deal with the problem would have been to reform the composition of the Lords so as to remove the permanent Conservative

---

[1] For details of the composition of the House of Lords, and of the party political affiliations of Peers, see *Dod's Parliamentary Companion* (published annually). See also Vincent, *Parl. Aff.* 1965–6; A. Wedgwood Benn, *The Privy Council as a Second Chamber* (Fabian Tract 305), London 1957.

majority. A major reform of composition was not attempted, however, largely it would seem because of the fear that as long as the Lords retained the power to obstruct legislation, a reformed and thereby strengthened House of Lords would emerge as a serious rival to the House of Commons. Thus to date, the only changes in composition that have been made are the Life Peerages Act 1958 and the Peerage Act 1963 (both passed by a Conservative Government) which made only minor adjustments of composition. The main way in which the problem of the House of Lords has been tackled has been by the reduction of the obstructive powers of the Lords through the Parliament Acts 1911 and 1949, so as to make the anomalies of composition of less consequence. Even in 1967, when the Labour Government did produce proposals for a major reform of composition, these were accompanied by proposals for a further reduction in the powers of the second chamber.

Over the years there have been numerous proposals for a full-scale reform of composition. The Preamble to the Parliament Act 1911 declared that it was merely a temporary measure until a full-scale reform of composition could be undertaken, and in 1917 a Conference was held under the chairmanship of Lord Bryce to examine the possibilities of a full-scale reform of the Lords. The Conference produced a detailed report in which it was advocated that the second chamber be completely reconstructed, with the new membership based primarily on election by the House of Commons of prominent members of the community, whether they were Peers or not.[1] The Bryce Conference also advocated the creation of a permanent Conference Committee, drawn from both Houses, to settle disputes between the Commons and the second chamber, but nothing was done to implement these proposals. Similarly in 1948, during the controversy over the second Parliament Bill, another all-party Conference examined the role of the second chamber and reached agreement on certain principles for a reform of composition.[2] The Conference Statement declared that no party should have a permanent majority in the Lords, and that heredity should in itself be no qualification for membership. It

[1] Report from the Second Chamber Conference, Cd. 9038 (1918).
[2] Agreed Statement of the Conference of Party Leaders on the Parliament Bill, Cmd. 7380 (1948).

was proposed that Lords of Parliament be appointed to serve in a newly constituted second chamber, and that Peers who were not Lords of Parliament should be eligible for the Commons. It was proposed also that women be eligible for membership of the second chamber, and that there should be payment for attendance and disqualification for non-attendance.

Action on these proposals did not result, however, as the Conference could not agree on the precise powers that the second chamber should possess. Nevertheless, some of these proposals were incorporated in the Life Peerages Act 1958, which created a new category of Life Peers and Life Peeresses, whose titles were not hereditary.[1] The 1958 Act also established the payment of three guineas (now £6·50) per attendance in the Lords. The Act was designed as a means of infusing new life into the House of Lords, though the Labour Opposition criticized the measure as an attempt by the Conservative Government to give new authority to the Lords, while avoiding the basic problem of the hereditary element. About a hundred and fifty Life Peerages have been created since 1958, and they have become prominent among the active members of the Lords.

While the 1958 Act introduced a new element into the Lords, the Peerage Act 1963 allowed hereditary Peers to disclaim their titles (and thus become eligible for membership of the House of Commons).[2] The Act was largely the result of the publicity given to the plight of unwilling heirs to titles by the activities of Anthony Wedgwood Benn, who in 1960 inherited the title of Lord Stansgate and consequently was forced to give up his seat in the Commons.[3] The Peerage Act 1963 allowed existing hereditary Peers twelve months in which to disclaim their titles, and allowed future heirs to titles twelve months in which to disclaim (or one month if they were members of the Commons when they inherited their titles). The hereditary principle remained intact, however, as the Act specified that the title could pass, on the Peer's death, to his heir, unless he also chose to disclaim. In the first twelve months' operation of the Act, only eight Peers chose to disclaim, but among the eight

[1] See B. Crick, 'The Life Peerages Act', *Parl. Aff.* 1957–8, pp. 455–65.
[2] See P. Bromhead, 'The Peerage Act and the New Prime Minister', *Parl. Aff.* 1963–4, pp. 57–64.
[3] See above, p. 44.

were Lord Home and Lord Hailsham, who were able to disclaim at the time of the Conservative Party leadership crisis in
1963. However, the Act did not lead to a great exodus from the
Lords, and the general effect of the 1958 and 1963 Acts was to
leave almost untouched the original basic problem of composition.

Power of the House of Lords

While the composition of the House of Lords has been changed
only slightly, its power and functions have altered considerably
this century. The Asquith Liberal Government in 1911 introduced the first legislation to limit the power of the Lords,
against a background of great political and Constitutional controversy.[1] The House of Lords had rejected the 1909 Finance
Bill, thereby raising the question of the Lords' power with
regard to financial legislation. Asquith dissolved Parliament,
and when the Liberals won the consequent election in January
1910 (though with a greatly reduced majority) the Lords
accepted the Finance Bill. Nevertheless, the Government decided to proceed with a full-scale reform of the powers of the
second chamber. A second election was held in December 1910,
and again the Liberals won a narrow victory. The Government introduced the Parliament Bill and secured its passage
through both Houses, though only as a result of the threat to
create sufficient Peers to give the Government a majority in the
Lords. The Parliament Act 1911 contained three main provisions dealing with the maximum length of Parliaments, the
power of the Lords with regard to financial legislation, and the
power of the Lords with regard to ordinary legislation. The
Septennial Act 1716 was amended to make five years rather
than seven years the maximum length of a Parliament. A
Money Bill (defined in the 1911 Act as a Bill certified by the
Speaker as a Bill containing *only* financial clauses) was to become law, with or without the approval of the Lords, one month
after being sent to the Lords. Any other Bill that passed the
House of Commons in three successive sessions (whether in the
same Parliament or not) was to become law without the assent
of the Lords, provided a period of two years elapsed between

[1] See R. Jenkins, *Mr Balfour's Poodle*, London 1954.

the Second Reading of the Bill in the Commons in the first session, and the Second Reading in the Commons in the third session.

The reduction in the length of Parliaments to a maximum of five years, has to be seen in relation to the other terms of the Act. As the general effect of the Parliament Act was to tilt the Parliamentary balance of power in favour of the Government-dominated House of Commons, at the expense of the Lords, more frequent elections would bring greater electoral pressure to bear on the Commons. Also, a delay power of two years was of more value to the Lords in a five-year Parliament than in a seven-year Parliament, so that the reduction in the length of Parliaments was a form of 'self-denying ordinance' by the Liberal Government. The definition of a Money Bill in the Parliament Act is a very narrow one, and is much narrower than what is understood by financial legislation in normal Parliamentary procedure. Much financial legislation fails to qualify for the Speaker's certificate because it contains administrative as well as financial clauses. Only about half of the annual Finance Bills introduced since 1911 have received the certificate,[1] but since 1911 the Lords have treated certified and non-certified financial legislation with equal respect.

The main terms of the 1911 Act, relating to non-financial legislation, did not remove the Lords' power of veto, but merely provided a means of overcoming the veto after a delay of two years. The machinery was soon tested when the Lords opposed the Irish Home Rule Bill and the Welsh Church Disestablishment Bill in 1912. The Bills were reintroduced in the next two sessions, but the outbreak of war in 1914 led to the postponement of their enactment until after the war. The Temperance (Scotland) Bill, also introduced in 1912, was opposed by the Lords in its first session, but was accepted the next year, while the Plural Voting Bill, introduced in 1913, and opposed by the Lords, was not reintroduced in 1914 because of the war. The Education Bill of the 1929–31 Labour Government was rejected by the Lords, and the Government's Representation of the People Bill was severely amended, and these Bills would possibly have been reintroduced and passed by the Parliament Act procedure if the Government had survived. The only Bill to

[1] Jennings, *Parliament*, p. 417, for more details.

have an uncomplicated passage by the Parliament Act procedure was the second Parliament Bill, introduced in 1947 and passed finally in 1949. This measure came as a result of the fear of the Attlee Labour Government that the Lords would obstruct the Bill to nationalize the iron and steel industry, which the Government was not in a position to introduce until 1948. Thus in 1947 the Government introduced the Parliament Bill which sought to amend the 1911 Act so that any Bill which passed the Commons in two successive sessions (instead of three) was to become law without the assent of the Lords, provided that a period of one year (instead of two) elapsed between the Second Reading in the Commons in the first session and the Second Reading in the Commons in the second session. The House of Lords was naturally opposed to the Bill, and it did not receive the Royal Assent until 1949, under the terms of the original Parliament Act. A provision was included in the 1949 Act to make its terms retrospective, and applicable to any Bill then being passed under the terms of the 1911 Act, so that the Iron and Steel Bill, which was introduced in 1948, could be delayed for only a year. In fact, however, the Iron and Steel Bill was accepted by the Lords after the Government had compromised on its provisions.

Thus the 1949 Act enabled a Government to overcome obstruction in the Lords after a delay of one year from the date of a Bill's Second Reading in the Commons (though in fact this meant a delay of only nine months, as generally some two or three months elapse between the Second Reading of a Bill in the Commons and its First Reading in the Lords). The delaying power has not been used on many occasions since 1911, and has not been used at all since 1949. In 1967 the Government proposed a further reduction in the delaying power, but the proposal was later dropped. The infrequent use of the delaying power has been partly because since 1911 there have been few Governments in power that did not have the support of the Conservative Party, and thus of the majority of the members of the Lords. The main significance of the Parliament Acts, however, has not been the actual use of the machinery for overcoming obstruction in the Lords, but rather the existence of the machinery as a deterrent to obstruction by the Lords. As was illustrated in the first years of the 1945–50 and 1966–70

Parliaments, there is little point in the Lords rejecting measures that are bound to become law after the delay period has elapsed. Since 1945, however, obstruction by the Lords has also been deterred by the knowledge that a Labour Government might abolish the House of Lords if it sought to obstruct major Government legislation.

It may be questioned whether there is any merit in allowing the second chamber to have even a nominal delaying power. In its defence, and thus in defence of the role of the second chamber as an obstructive body, it is sometimes argued that when (as is normal today) a Government dominates the Commons through a secure party majority, the second chamber remains as the only real Parliamentary limitation on the Government's power, and it is claimed that there should be some Parliamentary check upon Governments, additional to that imposed by the House of Commons. It is perhaps conceivable that a Government might risk losing a general election in order to force through a particularly controversial piece of legislation, and in the last year of a Parliament the delaying power of the Lords could be used as a deterrent to such an action. Thus to a large extent the question of the delaying power of the Lords is bound up with the concept of the mandate, with the Lords' delaying power being seen as a means of opposing legislation for which the Government has no mandate. The main objection in the past to the retention of the delaying power has been that the Lords only perform their obstructive function against non-Conservative Governments, and since 1911 all controversial Conservative legislation has been accepted without any delay. It remains to be seen whether a major reform of composition could produce a less partisan second chamber. More generally, however, the validity of the concept of the mandate, on which much of the justification of the Lords' delaying power is based, is open to question, and if restrictions on Government power are to be sought, this perhaps should be through a reform of the popularly elected House of Commons rather than through the hereditary second chamber. Also, while the delaying power has been little used, and while a year or nine months is not a long period of delay, clearly some essential legislation could be destroyed by a delay of even a few months.

*   *   *

Although there is this clear disagreement over the value of the delaying power, there is less disagreement regarding the other functions of the House of Lords, and in recent years it has undoubtedly fulfilled a useful function in easing the legislative burden of the House of Commons. In every session a number of non-controversial Bills are introduced in the Lords (such as the 1969 Family Law Reform Bill), and the detailed work done before they are passed to the Commons. The Lords also deals initially with the majority of Private Bills that are introduced each session. Bills that have been passed too quickly through the Commons can be re-examined in the Lords, and amendments made along lines that are acceptable to the Government. Tributes have been paid in this respect to the work of the Lords on the heavy legislative programme undertaken by the Attlee Government of 1945.[1] The timetable of the Commons often does not allow adequate time for general debate, and although debates in the Lords do not normally attract as much publicity as those in the Commons, it is preferable to have matters raised in the Lords than not raised at all. Debates in the Lords are often of a high standard, with contributions from elder statesmen. The timetable of the House of Lords is divided almost equally between legislation and general debates, though in recent sessions rather more time has been devoted to legislation.[2] In the consideration of legislation, the Lords spend roughly twice as much time on Bills sent from the Commons as on Bills initiated in the Lords. In all, the Lords generally sit for about 120 days per session, some thirty days less than the Commons. Daily sittings, on average, last about four and a half hours, again shorter than in the Commons, although since 1945 the length of the sittings in the Lords has tended to increase. The main difference between the timetable of the Lords and the Commons, however, is that the Commons spend almost one-third of their time on financial legislation and debates, while the Lords spend only three to four days per session on financial matters.

Thus in the functions of initiating and revising legislation, and in general debate, the Lords can supplement the work of the Commons and thereby disprove the argument that if a second

[1] Lord Morrison, *Government and Parliament*, Ch. 9.
[2] See above, p. 222. See also R. M. Punnett, 'The House of Lords and Conservative Governments', *PS* 1965, pp. 85–8.

chamber agrees with the lower house it is thereby superfluous. The Lords also has a role to play as a seat for some Government Ministers, and in every Government there are a number of posts filled by Peers.[1] By the limitations placed on the number of Ministers allowed to serve in the Commons by the Ministers of the Crown Act 1937, the House of Commons Disqualification Act 1957, and the Ministers of the Crown Act 1964, statutory recognition was given to the fact that if all Government posts are filled, some Ministers must be drawn from the Lords. The desirability of limiting the number of Ministers in the House of Commons is one reason for allocating some Government posts to members of the Lords, but membership of the Lords does confer a number of practical advantages on Ministers. A Peer has no constituency duties, and his attendance at debates and votes is not essential, so that he has more time to devote to Ministerial duties than does a member of the Commons. This is a factor that is perhaps most significant for a Government that has only a small majority in the Commons. In spite of the 'escape route' provided by the Peerage Act 1963, it may safely be assumed that the Peerage will not be stripped of all talent, and that the Lords will continue to contain hereditary Peers of Ministerial calibre. At the same time, the Lords is also useful as a seat for Ministers, in that any figure who is called upon to serve in the Government, but who does not wish to enter the party political fray of the House of Commons, can be raised to a Peerage and thereby made eligible for Ministerial office. Thus Sir Percy Mills was given a Peerage in 1957 to enable him to take up the post of Minister of Power in Macmillan's Government, while Lords Bowden, Caradon, Chalfont, and Gardiner were given Life Peerages in 1963 and 1964, and were thereby made eligible for Ministerial office in the Wilson Government. On the whole, however, not a great deal of use has been made of this means of recruiting non-party men into the Government, despite the fact that the Life Peerages introduced in 1958, and the disclaiming of titles allowed by the 1963 Act, have made elevation to the Lords more acceptable to those who might otherwise be unwilling to inflict an hereditary title on their heirs.

[1] See R. M. Punnett, 'Ministerial Representation in the House of Lords', *Table* 1961, pp. 67–71, *and* 1964, pp. 69–80.

The Future of the Second Chamber[1]

The general attitude of Conservative Governments towards the House of Lords in this century has been to defend its obstructive powers, and advocate minor reforms of composition in order to make it more respectable and thus more justifiable in the use of its existing powers. Liberal and Labour Governments, on the other hand, while gradually removing the obstructive powers of the Lords, have failed to deal with the question of a major reform of composition, and in the main have opposed mild reforms of composition as being irrelevant to the real problem. Abolition of the Lords has not been attempted by any Labour Government, partly it would seem because the second chamber is recognized as being capable of performing useful legislative and deliberative functions, especially for Labour Governments which tend to have heavier legislative programmes than Conservative Governments. Thus it is when a Labour Government is in power that the second chamber is most useful as a constructive legislative body, but in the past it has been precisely then that the Lords, with its permanent Conservative majority, has been most likely to be in conflict with the Government.

The future of the House of Lords seems uncertain. It could be abolished, leaving Parliament as a single-chamber legislature, but the value of the Lords as a revising body would seem to militate against abolition. At the same time it seems unlikely that a future Conservative Government would attempt to increase the obstructive powers of the Lords. The abortive attempt at reform made by the Government in 1967–9 could have achieved a lasting settlement, with a smaller second chamber, no longer based on the predominantly hereditary principle, being left with an obstructive power that amounted to a nominal delay. Certainly the need for a 'once-and-for-all' settlement is clear. Already in this century there have been four Acts of Parliament relating to the powers and composition of the

[1] See Lord Chorley, 'The House of Lords Controversy', *PL* 1958, pp. 216–35; V. Weare, 'The House of Lords—Prophecy and Fulfilment', *Parl. Aff.* 1964–5, pp. 422–33; H. Burrows, 'House of Lords—Change or Decay?', *Parl. Aff.* 1963–4, pp. 403–17; B. Crick, 'What Should the Lords Be Doing?', *PQ* 1963, pp. 174–84.

Lords, and the House of Lords is thus a good example of an element within the Constitution that has unwritten origins, but which has frequently been amended by written statutes. In this respect it can be argued that the House of Lords has received in the past, and continues to receive today, a degree of attention that is out of all proportion to its current significance.

part four

The Workings
of Government

10

The Treasury
and National Finance

THE CONTROL of national finances involves, first of all, control over the proposals for Government expenditure, and secondly, control over the raising of revenue to pay for this expenditure. These processes are theoretically quite distinct, and separate procedures exist for the supervision and control of the two processes by Parliament, the Treasury, and the Government as a whole. In fact, however, control of expenditure and of revenue are inextricably bound up together, in that (as with personal spending) Government spending is inevitably limited by the extent of the potential income.

The Principles of National Finance[1]

A basic principle of national finances is that all taxation is paid into a common fund, the Consolidated Fund (or Exchequer Account), and all expenditure is met from this fund. Before 1787 taxes were levied for specific purposes, and Parliamentary control was more complete through the appropriation of taxes for particular purposes. In 1780, however, the Commissioners of Public Accounts were set up to review the receipt

[1] See U. K. Hicks, *Public Finance*, London 1955; H. Dalton, *Principles of Public Finance*, London 1954; A. R. Prest, *Public Finance in Theory and Practice*, London 1960; A. T. Peacock and D. J. Robertson, *Public Expenditure: Appraisal and Control*, London 1963; A. T. Peacock and J. Wiseman, *The Growth of Public Expenditure in the United Kingdom*, London 1961. See also E. A. Collins, 'The Price of Financial Control', *Pub. Admin.* 1962, pp. 289–310; T. H. Caulcott, 'The Control of Public Expenditure', *Pub. Admin.* 1962, pp. 267–88.

and spending of public monies, and they recommended that there should be one fund into which all revenue should flow, and from which all supply should be drawn. This was duly achieved through the Customs and Excise Act 1787, and in 1866 the Consolidated Fund Act merged the English and Irish Funds into one. Departments with some form of revenue can use some of this as an 'appropriation in aid' to set against their expenditure, but this has to be specified in the estimates, and any excess beyond the specified amount has to go to the Consolidated Fund.

National finances are administered on an annual basis. Surpluses and deficits are accounted for annually, rather than being carried over into the next financial year, and deficits are met by borrowings, while surpluses are used to help to reduce the National Debt. Income Tax has to be renewed each year, at the latest one month after the end of the financial year on April 5th, thereby ensuring that there is annual Parliamentary consideration of taxation. Similarly, most expenditure is approved on an annual basis. After 1688 money for the army was granted on an annual basis, but civil expenditure was met from the Civil List which was granted for the whole of the Monarch's reign. This system broke down during the eighteenth century, when Parliament was frequently called upon to meet deficiencies in the Civil List, and by 1832 the various civil departments were removed from the Civil List, leaving this purely as an item of royal expenditure. Exceptions to the annual basis of expenditure are provided by the Consolidated Fund Services, which are voted once and for all and do not require annual renewal. These items include the interest and management costs of the National Debt, subsidies to Northern Ireland, the Civil List, the salaries of the Speaker, Leader of the Opposition, the Judges, the Comptroller and Auditor-General, the Parliamentary Commissioner, the Governor of Northern Ireland, and other miscellaneous matters. The Consolidated Fund Services generally account for about 10% of annual expenditure. A further practical breach in the principle of annual supply is that the Government can, and increasingly does, incur financial liabilities for future years on long-term projects, although if these projects stem from legislation, then Parliament's approval of the projects will have been granted. Not all such projected spending does stem from legislation, however, and in these cases Treasury control and general Ministerial responsibility remain as the only safeguards. Nevertheless, in 1970 the Government broke away from the principle of annual financing to some extent, and published a White Paper outlining the proposed expenditure over the next five years. These proposals, amounting to some £50,000,000,000, were thus open to debate in Parliament. For emergency situations, there is a Civil Contingencies Fund, fixed in 1955 at £55,000,000. Any department that draws upon the Fund has later to replenish it through its own estimates.

Revenue from taxation is regulated annually by the Government's 'Budget' proposals. The Budget is primarily concerned with raising enough revenue to balance the national finances on an annual basis, but in addition, the Budget is an economic and political weapon. The raising of revenue is only one purpose of taxation, and Customs Duties, for example, may be designed to protect home industry from foreign competition, while direct taxes may be used as a means of redistributing wealth. Particularly since 1940, the Budget has been used as a means of influencing the national economic situation through Government financial policy. There can be conflict between the desire to influence the national economy by means of a particular taxation policy, and the need to balance the Budget on an annual basis. Thus from the economic policy point of view the need to balance Government income and expenditure each year is sometimes looked upon as an undesirable irrelevance.

The classic theory behind the annual control of finances is that all proposals for expenditure and taxation are initiated only by Ministers of the Crown (a principle established in the eighteenth century), while Parliament, and more particularly the House of Commons, has to approve these proposals. As has been noted elsewhere,[1] finance was fundamental to Parliament's development, and it was the inability of the Norman Kings to live off their own finances that led to the original summoning of Parliament to consent to taxation proposals. From this, Parliamentary authority developed with the prin-

[1] See above, Ch. 6. See also P. Einzig, *The Control of the Purse*, London 1959.

ciple that Parliament would not consent to taxation proposals until its grievances were redressed, so that the British Parliament emerged and developed as a result of practical financial considerations, rather than for the more idealistic principles that lay behind the development of some other legislatures. Today the House of Commons retains the traditional financial powers of, firstly, the right to consider and approve the Government's proposals for expenditure, including the detailed appropriation of the money to its specific purposes; secondly, the right to check the Government's spending through the accounting process; and thirdly, the right to grant taxation to meet the cost of the Government's expenditures. The degree of control that Governments exert over the Commons today, however, means that in practice the House does not 'control' the Government's financial policies any more than it 'controls' the Government in any other aspects of its activities. Today the main control over a Government's financial policy lies with the Government itself, and particularly with the Treasury. Ministers are as anxious as other MPs to keep down taxation levels, and in fact MPs today tend to encourage rather than discourage spending (and therefore higher taxation) to a greater extent than in earlier years. Thus the role of the Commons as the guardian of the public purse has to a large extent been superseded, ultimately by the electorate, and immediately by the Government's own desire to keep public expenditure within acceptable limits.

A Government's desire to limit expenditure may spring from a wish to follow a definite policy of 'retrenchment' in spending through a reduction in state activity. In the late nineteenth century Gladstone attempted to follow a retrenchment policy in an attempt to ease the burden on the taxpayer, and he was defeated in the Cabinet in 1874 and 1894 because he wished to make cuts in Government expenditure. Lord Randolph Churchill fought a similar battle within the Conservative Party at about the same time, and his son took up the cause for a short while in the early years of this century. The heavy military and social service expenditure of the 1905-14 Liberal Governments, however, and then the 1914-18 war with further massive military spending, destroyed any success that Gladstone might have had in limiting public expenditure. After the war, attempts were made to cut back on Government spending, and the 1922 Geddes Committee on National Expenditure[1] advocated whole-sale cuts in departmental spending. In 1931 the crisis within the Labour Government arose primarily over the question of how to make cuts in national expenditure.[2] All this was reversed, however, by the need to re-arm in the late nineteen-thirties, followed by the further wartime increase in Government spending. In the immediate post-1945 period there was not the same reaction against massive public expenditure as there had been after 1918, apart from attempts to reduce defence expenditure, which were successful for only a while. The Conservative Government elected in 1970, however, is committed to a policy of cutting back public expenditure, and the first steps in this policy were taken in the autumn of 1970, with the announcement of various departmental economies.

More generally, however, limitations on Government spending stem from a desire to avoid wastage and inefficiency, and from the wish to pursue a spending and taxation policy which will be acceptable to the electorate (especially in an election year), and which will not be harmful to the immediate needs of the economy. In this context, the purpose behind the annual process of preparation by the departments, and the Treasury, of detailed expenditure and taxation proposals, and the presentation of these proposals to Parliament for scrutiny, is partly to give a further opportunity for a general examination of Government policies. The object is also, however, to give Parliament a chance to aid the Treasury and the departments themselves in their task of discovering wastage and inefficiency in the policies of the Government, and in the structure of the government machine.

The Role of the Treasury

The Treasury has a key place, not only in the control of national finances, but in the machinery of government as a whole. The Treasury has evolved over the years from the

[1] Reports of the Committee on National Expenditure, Cmd. 1581, 1582, 1589 (1922).
[2] See above, p. 263.

medieval post of Lord Treasurer.[1] The first stage in the emergence of the Treasury as a department of state came when Burghley, Lord Treasurer from 1572 to 1598, appointed a Secretary to assist him, and this was followed in the reign of James I by the appointment of six Privy Councillors to assist the Lord Treasurer. After this, the post of Lord Treasurer lost its significance and eventually disappeared, and in 1667 Charles II appointed a Commission to perform the Lord Treasurer's work. Of this body, only one member was a Privy Councillor, and he became known as the Chancellor of the Exchequer. During the eighteenth century the First Lord of the Treasury Commission acquired responsibilities additional to the Treasury (and with Walpole became recognized as the chief Ministerial office), and the Chancellor of the Exchequer emerged as the senior financial Minister.

Because the Treasury's origins are so distant, there is no statute governing its structure and powers, and in this it is unlike most of the other newer departments. Nominally, the Treasury is still managed by the Board of Commissioners of the Treasury, made up of the Prime Minister, Chancellor of the Exchequer, and the five Lord Commissioners, but this body last met in 1921, and then only for ceremonial purposes. In practice, the First Lord of the Treasury is always Prime Minister today, and the Chancellor of the Exchequer remains the senior Treasury Minister. He is assisted now by another senior Minister, the Chief Secretary to the Treasury, and by the Financial Secretary, who carries higher status than junior Ministers in other departments. In addition, the Parliamentary Secretary, and the five Lord Commissioners of the Treasury, act as Government Whips. The Treasury is a small department with an establishment of about 1,500, only 150 being Administrative Class. It generally receives a rather higher standard of recruit than most other departments, as it tends to be the most popular department among recruits to the Administrative Class, about one-third of them naming it as their first choice. The joint

---

[1] For works on the Treasury see Lord Bridges, *The Treasury*, London 1964; H. Roseveare, *The Treasury*, London 1969; S. H. Beer, *Treasury Control*, London 1957; S. H. Beer, 'Treasury Control: the Coordination of Financial Policy in Great Britain', *APSR* 1955, pp. 144–60; Sir H. Brittain, 'The Treasury's Responsibilities', *Pub. Admin.* 1961, pp. 1–15.

Permanent Secretary to the Treasury receives a higher salary than do officials of equivalent rank in other departments. Promotion is generally slow within the Treasury, and there is less promotion from the Executive Class to the Administrative Class than in most departments. There is, however, a big movement of staff from the Treasury to the other departments, and generally about a quarter of all Permanent Secretaries have had Treasury experience.

The basis of the Treasury's organization is functional, in the sense that it is organized in sections that cover functions common to several departments, rather than in sections that deal with the work of individual departments. Very broadly, its functions today are the raising of revenue and the control o expenditure, while until 1968 it was also responsible for the management of the Civil Service. Treasury Ministers are also responsible, however, for the Board of Inland Revenue, the Customs and Excise Department, the Stationery Office, the Central Office of Information, and a number of other associated matters. The Office of the Parliamentary Counsel, who are responsible for the preparation of Government Bills, is also attached to the Treasury. Before 1919 there were sometimes two, and even three Permanent Secretaries to the Treasury, but from 1919 to 1956 there was only one. In 1956 two Permanent Secretaries were appointed, one as Secretary to the Cabinet and also in charge of the management of the Civil Service, and the other in charge of the Treasury's financial and economic responsibilities.[1] In 1962, following the report of the Plowden Committee on the control of public expenditure,[2] the post of Secretary to the Cabinet was detached from the Treasury, and one Permanent Secretary was put in charge of the sections of the Treasury that dealt with the pay and management of the Civil Service, while the other was in charge of the two sections (Finance and Public Sector) that dealt with the Treasury's

[1] For details of Treasury development in this period see S. Brittan, *The Treasury Under the Tories 1951–64*, London 1964; D. N. Chester, 'The Treasury 1956', *Pub. Admin.* 1957, pp. 15–23.

[2] Report of the Committee on the Control of Public Expenditure, Cmnd. 1432 (1961). See also D. N. Chester, 'The Treasury 1962', *Pub. Admin.* 1962, pp. 419–26; 'Plowden Report on the Treasury', *Pub. Admin.* 1963, pp. 1–50; U. K. Hicks, 'Plowden, Planning and Management in the Public Services', *Pub. Admin.* 1961, pp. 299–312.

financial functions of controlling Government expenditure and raising revenue. Until 1964 this second Permanent Secretary was also responsible for the work of the National Economy Section of the Treasury, in supervising national economic policy, but in 1964 this passed temporarily to the Department of Economic Affairs.[1] Since 1968 the Treasury's responsibility for the management of the Civil Service has been delegated to a new Civil Service Department,[2] so that now the Treasury has only one permanent Secretary. Under consideration here, therefore, are the Treasury's financial responsibilities, within the broader context of Parliamentary and general Government control of national finances.

Treasury and Parliamentary Control of Finance: I. The Estimates

The annual financial process begins in the autumn, when the various departments submit to the Treasury their estimates for expenditure in the next financial year, though this is preceded by Treasury examination of rough departmental estimates at six-monthly intervals over the previous two years. The annual examination of the estimates by the Treasury lasts from November to February, and the estimates are then presented to Parliament, although if it is not possible for the Treasury to consider all the estimates by February, then the Treasury examination has to be continued concurrently with the Parliamentary examination. The Treasury review of the estimates is often a time of conflict between the Chancellor and other Ministers. The Treasury's task is to see that policy is being achieved economically, but also to decide on policy issues by declaring what can be afforded. The Chancellor has therefore to support one policy rather than another, though at the highest level this is achieved through the Cabinet and Cabinet Committees. The previous year's estimates are included as a comparison, and each spring a memorandum is issued by the Treasury to explain the detailed variations from the previous year, and to make general comparisons over several previous years.

The Defence Estimates (which now replace the separate Service Estimates) differ from the Civil Estimates in form and procedure. With the Civil Estimates each item is examined to

[1] See below, p. 301.   [2] See below, Ch. 11.

see if it can be afforded, but with the Defence Estimates a total figure is fixed and the Secretary of State for Defence then apportions this between the services according to priorities. This procedure is adopted with defence spending because the needs and policies of the defence departments are so closely integrated, but this principle perhaps could be usefully extended to other civil departments whose work is closely integrated. The Civil Estimates are divided into Classes, the Classes into Votes, and the Votes into Subheads. Once the estimates are approved, transfers from Subhead to Subhead can be made only with Treasury approval. With the Defence Estimates, however, transfers can be made from one Vote to another (a practice known as virement), but again only with Treasury agreement. The autumn review of the estimates has lost some of its significance, in that throughout the year the departments have to secure prior Treasury approval for any major policies they may propose, and this prior approval is a major aspect of Treasury financial control. There is no clear rule as to what has to be submitted and what has not, and defence projects differ slightly, in that the Treasury merely looks for value for money within a given sum. Nevertheless, the prior approval of projects involves a more detailed check than the autumn review, though the one form of control does not rule out the other, or make it unnecessary.

The estimates are received by Parliament in February, when the Financial Secretary to the Treasury presents the Civil Estimates, and the Defence Minister the Defence Estimates.[1] Supply is granted by Parliament in two Consolidated Fund Bills, one in March and one in July. The Bill structure dates from the reign of Henry VII, and was designed to prevent the House being rushed into consent. The March Consolidated Fund Bill contains four main items covering three financial years. First of all, it contains Votes on Account for the financial year that is

[1] For a brief but good guide to Parliamentary financial procedure see Taylor, *The House of Commons at Work*, Ch. 6. See also P. Bromhead, 'The Commons and Supply', *Parl. Aff.* 1958-9, pp. 337-48; A. Barker, 'Party and Supply', *Parl. Aff.* 1963-4, pp. 207-17; S. A. Walkland, 'The House of Commons and the Estimates 1960, *Parl. Aff.* 1959-60, pp. 477-88; G. Reid, *The Politics of Financial Control*, London 1967; Sir S. Goldman, 'The Presentation of Public Expenditure Proposals to Parliament', *Pub. Admin.* 1970, pp. 247-63.

about to begin (that is, 1970-1 in the case of the March 1970
Bill) to enable the departments to keep going until the main
estimates have been approved by Parliament in July. The
March Bill also contains some Defence Estimates for the financial year about to begin, to allow the service departments to
continue to function. The first item in the Defence Estimates is
always 'pay etc. of the Officers and Men', and this is approved
in the March Bill, and is then used for general purposes by the
defence departments. This is possible because (as explained
above) under the power of virement, sums in the Defence Estimates can be transferred from one Vote to another. The third
item in the March Bill is the Supplementary Estimates needed
to cover any deficits incurred in the financial year that is about
to end (1969-70 in the case of the March 1970 Bill). Supplementary Estimates can involve big sums if a change of policy or
a major miscalculation is involved, and the Treasury will only
agree to Supplementary Estimates if the matter cannot wait
until the next financial year. If deficits are not discovered until
the end of the financial year, they are met by Excess Votes in
the next March Bill, so that Excess Votes for 1968-9 were the
fourth item contained in the March 1970 Bill.

The July Consolidated Fund Bill contains the remainder of
the estimates for the current session. This involves the main
Civil Estimates, the bulk of the Defence Estimates, and any
Supplementary Estimates for the current session that may
already be found to be necessary. The Bill also 'appropriates'
all the estimates (including those contained in the March Bill)
to their specific purposes, and thus it is also known as the Appropriation Bill. The July Bill is usually the last piece of financial
legislation of the session, but an Autumn Appropriation
Bill may be necessary, or a Bill early in the next session, in
order to deal with some major change of policy. The debates on
the March and July Bills are not specifically financial in content, and are mainly an opportunity for backbenchers to raise
topics. The consideration of the estimates in the House is done
partly by the SCE and partly by the Whole House, much of the
work being done before the Bills are introduced.[1]

Until its abolition in 1967, the Committee of Supply (a
Committee of the Whole House) was the traditional means

[1] See B. Chubb, *The Control of Public Expenditure*, London 1952.

through which the House of Commons exercised financial control, and its task was to consider the Government policy that lay behind the estimates. The Committee of Supply originated in the seventeenth century, when the House of Commons chose to sit as a Committee in order to avoid the surveillance of the King's agent, the Speaker. In later years, a more important factor was that the rules of debate and general procedure were much less rigid when the House sat as a Committee. In the nineteenth century there was no limit on the number of days the House could devote to the Committee of Supply, but in this century the practice developed of allocating twenty-six 'Supply Days', spread throughout a session.[1] After 1918, it also became the practice for the Opposition to choose the topics to be debated on Supply Days, with backbenchers being allowed to raise their own topics on one of the days. Generally, however, supply time was used for general debates on the Government policies that lay behind the estimates, rather than for the consideration of the details of the estimates themselves. Normally only about 2% of supply time was devoted to financial details, and such detailed financial debate as did take place was generally regarded as the least useful part of supply time. This was largely because the very extent of Government expenditure made detailed discussion virtually impossible on the floor of the House, but it was also because of the Constitutional practice that prevented MPs from making an increase in the estimates, while the Government's majority made a reduction well nigh impossible. There were frequent demands that there should be an end to the pretence that the Committee of Supply was still fulfilling financial functions. Eventually, in 1967, it was abolished, and the functions it had been performing were transferred to the House as a whole.

The SCE considers the estimates from the point of view of whether Government policy is being achieved economically, and as well as the consideration of general policy, this also involves an examination of the workings and administrative efficiency of the departments. A Select Committee to supplement the work of the Committee of Supply first appeared in 1912, and from time to time since then various committees of

[1] See A. Barker, "'The Most Important and Venerable Function": A Study of Commons Supply Procedure', *PS* 1965, pp. 45–64.

different forms and powers have been set up, the present committee dating from 1946. An Estimates Committee was set up
in 1912, partly because of the big increase in Government
spending in the early years of this century, and partly because
of the success of the earlier established PAC. At the same time,
there was a desire to make economies when the money was
being asked for in the estimates, rather than wait for the
accounting process to discover wastage, while it was also felt
that if less time was spent on the details of the estimates in the
Committee of Supply, more time could be devoted to general
debates on Government policy. Thus to some extent, the
Estimates Committee was set up because the House as a whole
did not wish to concern itself with financial details. The outbreak of war in 1914 interrupted the Estimates Committee's
activities, and for most of the war period there was no attempt
to enquire in detail into the war estimates. In 1917, however,
rumours of financial waste on munitions led to the appointment of a National Expenditure Committee which (unlike the
1912–14 Committee) worked through sub-committees and was
concerned with reviewing the organization and work of the
departments, rather than their detailed estimates. In 1921 the
National Expenditure Committee was replaced by a less
powerful Estimates Committee on the model of the 1912–14
Committee, primarily because the Government was afraid of a
powerful body enquiring into peacetime finances. Although
this Committee had the power to appoint sub-committees, it
very rarely did so. It survived until 1939, but with the outbreak
of war it was replaced by a National Expenditure Committee
similar to the 1917–21 Committee. This body worked through
sub-committees, and was concerned with departmental organization rather than financial detail.

Finally, in 1946, the present SCE was formed. It now has
thirty-three members, and like the two wartime committees, it
appoints sub-committees, and each sub-committee prepares a
report for submission to the House. The SCE does not pretend
to examine the estimates in detail, and it is concerned more with
the organization and methods of the departments than with the
detailed scrutiny of particular estimates. The committee concentrates on different departments each year, and in its concern with departmental administration and organization the

SCE has served as a useful model for the more recent specialist committees that have been introduced into the House of Commons. However, although the existing SCE is generally accepted as being much more effective than its peacetime predecessors, it has a number of limitations as it operates at present. Its reports, for example, are not examined in detail, and there is no means of ensuring that the Government will take heed of its proposals. The House of Commons could perhaps do more to follow up SCE reports. As the SCE is dealing with current proposals, it has no leisure in which to work, and as it is difficult to alter current spending proposals, it can only really warn for the future. The new Conservative Government is considering replacing the SCE by another committee which would work more effectively through a series of sub-committees, specializing in particular subject areas. No doubt, with the assistance of an 'Examiner of Estimates', with a relationship to the committee similar to that of the C and AG to the PAC, the SCE or its successor could function much more effectively.

Once the estimates have been approved by Parliament, departmental spending is supervised by the Treasury and the C and AG. When the departments require the finance that has been estimated for them, they approach the Treasury, which determines whether the money is needed at that time. The C and AG (in his role as Comptroller) then ensures that the money has been approved by Parliament, and the money is then transferred from the Consolidated Fund to the Paymaster-General's account for the departments.

II. The Accounts

The final level of control over expenditure is through the accounting process.[1] Appropriation accounts are prepared by each department, the Permanent Secretary usually being the departmental Accounting Officer. The form of the accounts is based on the estimates, and they show and explain any differences between the estimates and the actual spending. The accounts are examined initially by the C and AG, who receives the accounts of the Civil Departments by September 30th, and those of the defence departments by December 31st (that is,

[1] See S. A. Walkland and I. Hicks, 'Cost Accounting in British Government', *Pub. Admin.* 1960, pp. 49–60.

September 30th or December 31st 1970 for the accounts of the financial year 1969–70). The accounts and the C and AG's reports are sent in January to the Treasury for their perusal, and then to Parliament, where they are examined by the PAC.

The PAC dates from 1861, and the post of C and AG from the Exchequer and Audit Act 1866, both inspired by Gladstone's search for financial economies. The task of the C and AG and the PAC is to examine the accounts to see if the money has been spent as Parliament authorized, but also to see if due economy has been observed throughout, and to censure doubtful practices. Thus the work of the PAC is essentially different from the accounting process in the commercial world. The PAC is composed of fifteen members in proportion to party strength in the House, with the chairman coming from the Opposition. Members are chosen for their financial knowledge, and are generally reappointed to the committee each session, so that the PAC is essentially specialist. The PAC meets normally on some thirty afternoons, from February to July, after receiving the accounts and report from the C and AG. It has the power to summon civil servants, and question them about the work of their departments. It reports to Parliament in July, and though Parliament may not take account of the committee's detailed findings, the Treasury always does. The key figure behind the work of the PAC, however, is the C and AG, who, as well as preparing the accounts for the committee, gives a report to the committee of his own opinions and recommendations. The C and AG is a Parliamentary officer, and his salary is one of the Consolidated Fund Services. He is not necessarily a trained accountant himself, but he has a staff of 500 Executive Grade officers trained in audit work, spread throughout the departments, and as well as the examination of the accounts at the end of the financial year, this staff conducts a continuous audit throughout the year.

As well as the work of the C and AG, the fact that the PAC is a specialized committee, both in composition and in the advice that it gets, and the fact that it acts and votes largely along non-party lines, means that it has considerable prestige and authority. The value of the committee is thus that it acts as a deterrent to inefficiency and extravagance by the departments, but it has the essential weakness of all accounting processes of dealing with past expenditure. Thus if wastage does occur, it can only be revealed and prevented in the future. To some extent the success of the PAC takes some of the responsibility for finance away from the House of Commons as a whole, and this is one of the factors that delayed the emergence of an Estimates Committee, and prevents the present SCE from being more effective. Before the present SCE was formed in 1946, it was recommended to the Select Committee on Procedure that the PAC should be combined with the wartime Committee on Expenditure to form a National Expenditure Committee of thirty or so members, and with six or so sub-committees.[1] This proposal has been revived from time to time since then. It is argued that the PAC and the SCE are inadequate in themselves, and do not co-operate with each other to a sufficient degree, and that one powerful committee dealing with both estimates and accounts would be a more adequate check upon expenditure than is the existing system. This proposal has been resisted, however, largely on the grounds that the two committees cannot readily be combined. The extra work involved for the C and AG could make him less effective overall, and a better reform might be to give the SCE an official of its own. The proposal has also been resisted by successive Governments on the grounds that the existing committees are in fact adequate, and that a too-powerful committee would interfere too much with Ministerial responsibility. Thus no National Expenditure Committee has been formed, and the SCE has not been given a permanent official to aid it in its activities.

* * *

The role of Parliament and the Treasury in the control of expenditure may now be summarized. Parliamentary control is exercised primarily through Select Committees of the House of Commons. The SCE considers the estimates from the point of view of departmental organization and efficiency, and the PAC, aided by the C and AG, examines the annual accounts. In addition, Parliamentary control is exercised through the passage through Parliament of the Consolidated Fund Bills and the Appropriation Bill, and by the approval of the Financial Resolution that accompanies all Bills involving expenditure.

[1] Report of the Select Committee on Procedure, H.C. 189 of 1945–6.

In a much less specific way, Parliamentary control is also exercised through such influence as Parliament is able to exert over Government legislation and policies in general.

Despite the long-established traditions of Parliament's financial rights, despite the complicated nature of Parliamentary procedure in financial matters, and despite the impressive array of financial committees in the Commons, the very real limitations of Parliamentary control over expenditure have to be emphasized. Ultimately, of course, with finances as with other matters, Parliamentary power is limited by the degree of control that the Government is able to exert over Parliament, but given that Parliament cannot 'control' Government expenditure to any greater extent than it can 'control' Government policy in general, Parliament's ability to consider and comment upon Government expenditure is still very limited. In addition to the specific weaknesses of the individual House of Commons committees, the chief general limitation on Parliamentary consideration of expenditure lies in the sheer size of the sum involved, and the limited time available in which to consider it. In 1969–70 expenditure on the Supply Services was more than £12,000,000,000, and on the Consolidated Fund Services just less than £1,000,000,000.[1] As Government spending tends to increase every year, this problem would seem inevitably to be a growing one, while the greater emphasis on long-term projects and long-term planning commitments adds to the difficulty of trying to relate expenditure to an annual procedure. Thus today, Parliament's role with regard to expenditure is primarily to ensure through the accounting process that money is spent as it was appropriated, to publicize Government policies, particularly those that are financially extravagant, and to uncover and publicize any departmental inefficiency that results in financial wastage.

Treasury control of expenditure is achieved most effectively by the examination of the estimates that culminates in the annual autumn review, and by the requirement of prior Treasury approval for all major projects. It is also achieved through the control of virement, through control over actual withdrawals from the Consolidated Fund, and through the examination of the reports of the C and AG. As a more general form of control,

[1] See Table XXVII.

Treasury Ministers must approve the Financial Resolution that accompanies all Bills that involve expenditure, and Treasury Ministers examine all Cabinet memoranda (as do the Law Officers) before they go to the rest of the Cabinet, to ensure that the attention of Cabinet Ministers will be drawn to the financial implications of any proposed policy.

Thus the Treasury's influence is felt at all stages in the financial process, although it must be realized that all Ministers, and not just Treasury Ministers, are concerned with economy to some extent, in that they all share the Government's collective desire to avoid extravagance, or policies that lead to high taxation. Also, as a result of the policy of Warren Fisher, Permanent Secretary to the Treasury 1919–38, each department has its own Permanent Secretary as Accounting Officer, and the effect is to provide a strong force for economy within each department. To avoid possible censure for departmental extravagance, a Permanent Secretary must officially record any disagreements that he has with his Minister over policies which he feels to be financially unwise. Thus the specific and detailed control over expenditure that is exercised by the Treasury, is supplemented by departmental controls, and by the general control that exists through the collective responsibility of all members of the Government for all policies, financial and otherwise.[1]

III. National Revenue

The national revenue to meet expenditure consists of Ordinary Revenue from the Crown Lands, Extraordinary Revenue from taxation, and revenue from borrowing. Annual revenue from the Crown Lands amounts to about £1,500,000, and since 1761 this has accrued to the Exchequer in exchange for an annual Civil List payment to the Monarch. Of the Extraordinary Revenue, direct taxes, such as Income Tax, Surtax, Supertax, Profits Tax, and Death Duties, are administered by the Inland Revenue, while indirect taxes on goods and commodities, in the form of Customs Duties on foreign goods and Excise Duties on home goods, are administered by the Customs

[1] See A. S. Moore, 'Departmental Financial Control', *Pub. Admin.* 1957, pp. 169–78.

and Excise Departments. In addition, there are a number of other miscellaneous taxes, including the motor vehicle tax. In 1969–70 revenue from taxation came to about £15,000,000,000, direct taxes accounting for about 55%, indirect taxes about 40%, and miscellaneous taxes about 5%.[1] The precise distribution of the burden between direct and indirect taxation in any one year is, however, a matter partly of economic and partly of political concern.

The Government's annual Budget proposals for regulating taxation are presented by the Chancellor of the Exchequer to the House of Commons, and are debated before being incorporated in the Finance Bill.[2] The main Budget comes in the spring, although in recent years there has been an increasing tendency also to have an Autumn Budget dealing with interim measures.

In preparing the Budget, the Chancellor of the Exchequer is advised by the Budget Committee of the Treasury.[3] This committee, which meets regularly from July until the Budget is presented at the start of the financial year, includes the Permanent Secretary in charge of the Treasury's financial section, the heads of the Public Sector and Finance Groups of the Treasury, and senior figures from the Inland Revenue and the Customs and Excise Departments. It meets as early as July to consider the effect of the previous Budget, and to see if autumn measures are needed. The Chancellor of the Exchequer is most directly involved in the committee's work from November onwards, when Budget preparations proceed concurrently with the examination of the estimates of departmental expenditure. The utmost secrecy surrounds the preparation of the Budget, and though the Chancellor of the Exchequer consults with the Prime Minister, and perhaps senior colleagues, over taxation proposals, Ministers sometimes complain of being ignored in these matters. Before the Budget proposals are revealed, reviews of the economic situation and the statistical background to the proposals are provided by the publication of economic and statistical data, including the White Paper on the Preliminary

[1] See Table XXVII.

[2] See Sir H. Brittain, *The British Budgetary System*, London 1959; A. Williams, *Public Finance and Budgetary Policy*, London 1963.

[3] See Lord Amory, 'Preparing the Budget', *Parl. Aff.* 1960–1, pp. 451–9.

TABLE XXVII

Exchequer Account 1965–6 and 1969–70

Revenue

	1965–6 Year ending March 31st 1966	1969–70 Year ending March 31st 1970
	£000,000	£000,000
Taxation		
Inland Revenue		
Income Tax	3,678	4,900
Surtax	203	255
Profits Tax, EPT and EPL	437	—
Corporation Tax	—	1,687
Death Duties	292	365
Stamp Duties	75	120
Capital Gains Tax	—	127
Other Inland Revenue Duties	—	22
Total Inland Revenue	4,687	7,476
Customs and Excise	3,401	4,952
Motor Vehicle Duties	234	417
Selective Employment Tax	—	1,888
Total Taxation	8,323	14,733
Miscellaneous Receipts		
Interest and Dividends	512	92
Broadcasting Receiving Licences	68	101
Other	239	340
Total Revenue	9,144	15,266

Expenditure

Supply Services		
Defence Budget	2,055	2,204
Other Supply	5,084	9,812
Total Supply Services	7,139	12,016
Consolidated Fund Standing Services		
Interest on and Management of the		
National Debt	1,136	513
Northern Ireland	148	252
Miscellaneous	30	41
Total Expenditure	8,455	12,822
Surplus	688	2,444

Estimates of National Income and Expenditure, and the Economic Survey.

The Budget itself is presented by the Chancellor of the Exchequer to the House of Commons (sitting as the Committee of Ways and Means) before May 4th, the last day for the annual renewal of Income Tax. Immediately after the Chancellor's Budget speech, the Budget Resolutions are approved by the House in order to legalize the collection of any taxes that are to be operative immediately. There then follows five or six days of debate on the Budget proposals on the floor of the House, after which the Finance Bill, incorporating the Budget proposals, is introduced. The Finance Bill passes through the House during the next three months on a strict timetable, with the various stages taken on different days. In a normal session of about 150 sittings, fifteen or so days are generally devoted to the Finance Bill in the Commons. The Bill must be given a second reading within twenty days of the completion of the Budget debates. Until 1968 the committee stage of the Bill was always taken in Committee of the Whole House, but since 1968 some clauses have been dealt with in a Standing Committee. This avoids spending time on the floor of the House on points of technical detail. Changes in the detailed proposals frequently occur during the Bill's passage through the House, and the influence of industrial and commercial pressure groups is felt particularly at the committee stage, when debates tend to be highly technical and detailed.[1] The Government is loath to use the guillotine procedure too vigorously, and sometimes gives way to criticism in order to save time. Amendments are often made on the Government's own initiative, though fewer changes would be necessary if the Chancellor revealed more to his colleagues during the preparation of the Budget. After passing the Commons, the Bill goes to the Lords where it receives formal approval, generally after only one day or half a day of debate on general financial policy.

Very often, some provisions of the Finance Bill relate purely to administrative changes, and there is perhaps a case for a separate Tax Management Bill to deal with detailed administrative changes, with such a Bill being dealt with in a Standing Committee. On the whole, the problem of tax reform has been

[1] See above, p. 145.

neglected over the years, partly because of the antiquity of the tax system, and the administrative and political problems involved in making fundamental changes, but also because the Treasury's prime concern is with how much money is to be raised rather than with the equity of the method. Since 1962, however, the Public Income and Outlay Division of the Treasury has been concerned with this factor.

For maximum efficiency it is necessary for some taxes to become operative as soon as they are announced, long before the Finance Bill is finally passed. This is achieved today through the terms of the Provisional Collection of Taxes Act 1913, which was passed following a legal battle fought by Gibson Bowles, a Conservative backbench MP. In 1912 he refused to pay certain taxes on the grounds that although the House of Commons had passed resolutions approving the tax proposals, the collection of the taxes was not legal until the Finance Bill had received the Royal Assent. He argued that the practice of collecting some taxes as soon as they were announced, was a circumvention of Parliamentary control of finance, and an imposition on individual rights. The Court upheld Bowles'[1] objection, and ruled that taxes could not become operative until Parliament (and not merely the Commons) had approved them. The Court pointed out that a mere resolution of the House of Commons did not make law. Thus there followed in 1913 the Provisional Collection of Taxes Act, which permits the collection of taxes up to August 5th on the strength of what is proposed in the Budget Resolution, although the Finance Bill must then receive the Royal Assent by August 5th. This applies only to variations in existing taxes and not to new taxes. At first it applied only to Income Tax and Customs and Excise Duties, but it has since been extended to other taxes. Also, the Import Duties Act 1932 established the principle that the level of import duties could be varied without further legislative approval, and this principle has been extended to other taxes, until today most indirect taxes can be varied by up to 10%. This provides the Chancellor of the Exchequer with a flexible means of influencing the economy between Budgets.

Because there are definite economic and political limitations on the amount of money that can be raised by taxation at any

[1] *Bowles* v. *the Bank of England* (1913) 82 L.J. Ch. 124.

one time, some revenue has to be obtained by long-term and short-term borrowing. The amount of money that the Government owes as a result of this borrowing makes up the National Debt. There has been a huge increase in the National Debt this century, largely as a result of the borrowing that was necessary to pay for the vast expenditure during the two world wars. On March 31st 1913 the National Debt stood at just over £650,000,000, but by 1919 it had risen to over £7,400,000,000. This figure was slightly reduced by 1923, but by 1945 it had almost trebled to more than £21,300,000,000. It has increased further since 1945, largely as a result of financing investment in schools, roads, and other tangible projects, and today it stands at about £30,000,000,000.

The Government borrows from various sources, with different rates of interest and dates of redemption, and with repayments spread as evenly as possible over the year. Stock Exchange Securities and Treasury Bills make up more than half of the Debt. Nominally, control over the Debt is in the hands of the National Debt Commissioners, who were first appointed in 1786, and who include the Chancellor of the Exchequer, the Speaker of the House of Commons, and the Master of the Rolls. In fact, however, their responsibilities are performed by the Controller-General of the National Debt Office, who in this matter works with the Treasury and the Bank of England. Since 1945 there has been little attempt to reduce the size of the Debt, largely because peacetime borrowing, more than wartime borrowing, is used to finance progressive investment in the public services. As early as 1716, however, the principle was established that any excess of revenue at the end of the financial year should go to a Sinking Fund to pay off the Debt, and this principle was reinforced in the Exchequer and Audit Act 1866. Also, attempts were made in the past to set aside specific repayment sums each year, and for this purpose a New Sinking Fund was established in 1875. This project failed, however, with the vast increase in the Debt after 1914, though the management costs and interest on the Debt are now a permanent charge on the Consolidated Fund.

In addition to the various long-term borrowings, short-term borrowing is necessary to help to manage the day-to-day finances of the departments. Income and expenditure is not spread evenly over the year, and income from taxation accrues mainly in the last quarter of the financial year, so that daily deficits in the first three quarters of the year have to be met by borrowing. The Bank of England co-operates with the Treasury in this matter, and the Treasury tries to reduce outside borrowing to a minimum by making full use of the public money within the Government's control, like the National Insurance Fund. Ultimately, day-to-day borrowing can be made from the Bank of England, while in the last quarter of the financial year any daily surplus of revenue is absorbed by the Bank.[1]

Thus, with income as with expenditure, real control lies with the Treasury. Nevertheless, despite the obvious limitations that exist on the Commons' ability to influence revenue policy, the Commons' power to amend the details of the Government's taxation proposals is greater than its ability to alter Government expenditure proposals. Budget debates in the Commons, and the debates at the various stages of the Finance Bill, are more 'financial' in content than are proceedings in the SCE, or the debates on the Consolidated Fund and Appropriation Bills. Such control as the House of Commons is able to achieve over national finances today is exerted primarily over the details of the Finance Bill.

The Co-ordination of Economic Policy[2]

Until 1964 the Treasury had the direct responsibility for the co-ordination of national economic planning. In October 1964, however, with the advent of the Labour Government to power, the Department of Economic Affairs was created, with the Deputy Prime Minister, George Brown, as Minister for Economic Affairs. The DEA's life was short, as it was abolished in 1969, but it represents the most direct and ambitious of the many attempts that have been made to remove from the Treasury the direct responsibility for the control of long term economic policy. Before 1914, economic policy as such was the preserve primarily of the Treasury, but with other departments, like the Board of Trade, also involved in economic policy to

[1] For the general role of the Bank in national finances see A. C. L. Day, 'The Bank of England in the Modern State', *Pub. Admin.* 1961, pp. 15–26; 'The Organisation and Status of the Bank of England', *Pub. Admin.* 1960, pp. 67–72.   [2] See J. Mitchell, *Groundwork to Economic Planning*, London 1966.

some extent. In 1925 a Cabinet Committee on economic research was created, and was succeeded in 1930 by the Economic Advisory Council. The Prime Minister was chairman of this body, but as with all such advisory committees, its authority was limited, in that it did not have the backing of a department of state. In 1939 the Central Economic Information Service was set up within the Cabinet Secretariat, and in 1941 this was divided into the Central Statistical Office and the Economic Section. During the war, however, the real control of economic policy lay with the Lord President of the Council, and the Treasury's influence was limited by the emphasis in the wartime economy on physical controls rather than controls through Treasury financial policy. This arrangement was continued by the Labour Government after 1945, but in 1947 Sir Stafford Cripps was made Minister for Economic Affairs, and when later in 1947 he was appointed Chancellor of the Exchequer, he took his responsibility for economic policy to the Treasury with him. This marked a reaction against physical controls as a means of economic planning, and was the beginning of a period of more direct Treasury control of economic policy through monetary and fiscal means.

Churchill, in his Government formed in 1951, tried to limit the Treasury's responsibility for economic planning by means of a committee to supervise the work of R. A. Butler, the Chancellor of the Exchequer, although the Treasury retained ultimate authority. Towards the end of the long Conservative period of office, the 1962 changes in Treasury organization, the creation of the National Economic Development Council and the National Incomes Commission, the appointment in 1963 of Edward Heath as President of the Board of Trade and Secretary of State for Industry, can all be seen as attempts to establish economic planning machinery, and reduce the Treasury's absolute control of economic planning.[1] Nevertheless, throughout the Conservative period of office from 1951 to 1964, the Treasury retained final responsibility for the control of economic planning. Treasury control was achieved first of all through the Central Statistical Office in the Cabinet Secretariat (respon-

[1] See J. Mitchell, 'The Functions of NEDC', *PQ* 1963, pp. 354–65; H. Phelps Brown, 'The National Economic Development Organisation', *Pub. Admin.* 1963, pp. 239–46.

sible for providing factual information about economic growth), secondly through the Economic Section of the Treasury (responsible for the study of economic problems), and thirdly through the two National Economy Groups of the Treasury (responsible for economic forecasting and the development of policies for economic growth). Economic planning was aided by the Treasury's direct responsibility for the Budget, and for the supervision of Government expenditure.

Thus before 1964, various attempts to control economic policy had been made—through advisory committees before 1940; through physical controls under non-departmental Ministers from 1940 to 1947; and through Treasury control after 1947. Various other methods were also canvassed from time to time. It was proposed, for example, that there should be a co-ordinating committee for economic policy, made up of Ministers and officials and presided over by the Prime Minister. It was suggested that there should be an extension of the power and status of NEDC to give it the authority of a full department of state, with more access to the centres of power. It was also suggested that the Treasury should lose its functions with regard to the management of the Civil Service and the control of Government expenditure, leaving it purely as a department for raising revenue and controlling economic policy. In 1964, however, these proposals were all rejected in favour of the creation of a special department for economic planning. The Labour Government claimed that the DEA was desirable because the Treasury was essentially economy-minded, and lacked the necessary approach for an economic planning department.[1] The Government argued that the Treasury approach was too negative, merely telling the departments what they could do rather than what they must do. Attempts to control the economy by fiscal and monetary means were seen as inadequate, and a more positive approach towards economic planning was sought from an entirely new department. It was further argued that the Treasury was overworked, and lacked the staff necessary for long-term planning, while Chancellors of the Exchequer had too many responsibilities and tended to leave too much influence over economic planning in the hands of Treasury

[1] See, for example, 701 H.C. Deb. 5s. 214–48, and 720 H.C. Deb. 5s. 1155–78, for Government and Opposition attitudes.

officials. The big differences in economic prosperity from one region of Britain to another, were also presented as a factor that produced a need for a new department which could include among its functions the development of economic policy from a regional as well as a national standpoint.

For these various reasons an entirely new department was created to take over the control of economic policy from the Treasury and the various subsidiary economic bodies. The DEA was set up as a department with no executive functions, and thus as a department that could concern itself with short-term and long-term policy rather than with administration.[1] With an establishment of some 550 the DEA was the smallest of the departments, and had a very high concentration of econo-mists, statisticians, and industrialists. As originally created, it was divided into five divisions, two for economic co-ordination, one for long-term economic planning, one for industrial policy, and one for regional development. These divisions sought to co-ordinate the activities of the various economic departments, particularly the Treasury, the Board of Trade, and the Min-istries of Labour, Technology, Power, and Transport, in an attempt to secure planned and steady economic expansion without inflation. The DEA sought to persuade employers and the trade unions to co-operate to achieve planned economic expansion. To this end a National Plan was produced in 1965, and a second one in 1969, and the DEA attempted to develop a national incomes and prices policy through the National Board for Prices and Incomes.[2] It also sought to encourage regional development through the creation of Development Councils in the regions.

The creation of the DEA, and its subsequent activities, were criticized by the Opposition, who claimed that Treasury con-trol was the best means of regulating economic policy. They argued that as the Treasury's main concern is with financial policy, and as the Budget is a major economic weapon, the Treasury should have responsibility for economic policy in

[1] See G. Owen, 'The Department of Economic Affairs', *PQ* 1965, pp. 380–9; Sir E. Roll (*et al.*), 'The Machinery for Economic Planning', *Pub. Admin.* 1966, pp. 1–72.

[2] J. Mitchell, 'The National Board For Prices and Incomes', *Pub. Admin.* 1970, pp. 57–68.

general. The Opposition argued that as the Chancellor of the Exchequer raises the revenue for Government expenditure, he should have the central place in the economic planning machinery, and that without Treasury control, irresponsible and financially unwise policies would emerge, which would lead to friction between the Treasury and the DEA. They claimed also that the Treasury's special place in the machinery of government, with its direct influence over all departments, could not be matched by the DEA, even under a dynamic and high-ranking Cabinet Minister. Thus at the 1966 election the Conservatives said that they would abolish the DEA if they were returned to office.

The DEA's critics were proved correct. It failed to achieve the ends for which it was created, partly, perhaps, because it had to operate against a background of almost continuous economic restraint. With the balance of payments and sterling crises of the 1964-8 period, the 1967 devaluation, and the cuts in public expenditure which accompanied it, the Treasury retained its role as the main department controlling economic policy. Given a period in which rapid economic expansion was possible, the DEA might have had a more auspicious history, but as it was, its original powers were gradually reduced, and it was finally abolished in 1969. With successful relations at an individual level, the Treasury, the planning of national economic policy, and the Government machine as a whole, no doubt could benefit from a division of power between the Treasury and a separate economic Ministry like the DEA. At present, however, the Treasury remains as the centre of the Government machine. This is perhaps inevitable with the fundamental importance of finance in the process of government, so that the Chancellor of the Exchequer and the other Treasury Ministers have a special place in the Ministerial hierarchy, and Treasury officials are regarded as the core of the Civil Service. This Treasury position goes some way towards overcoming the difficulty of achieving a central directing force within the British system of government.[1]

[1] See S. Brittan, *Steering the Economy: The Role of the Treasury*, London 1969; A. H. Hanson, *Planning and the Politicians*, London 1969; Political and Economic Planning, *Economic Planning and Policies in Britain, France and Germany*, London 1969.

11

The Central Administration

A CIVIL SERVANT may be formally defined as a servant of the Crown employed in a civil capacity who is paid wholly and directly from money voted by Parliament.[1] This excludes the political and judicial servants of the Crown, and also the armed services, who are employed in a military and not a civil capacity. It also excludes public servants in local government and the public corporations, who are not 'servants of the Crown', and are not paid directly from money voted by Parliament. In all, there are about a million civil servants in Britain, and of these about two-fifths are industrial civil servants (such as employees in naval dockyards and Royal Ordnance factories), and some three-fifths are non-industrial civil servants, who are the main concern of this examination.

Development of the Civil Service

As with so many aspects of British government, the modern structure of the Civil Service is a result of various *ad hoc* developments over the past two centuries.[2] In the eighteenth century, and for much of the nineteenth century, Civil Service organization was chaotic. Recruitment was largely by patronage, or by the purchase of sinecure posts, with the heads of the various departments having almost complete independence in the question of recruitment. There was little suggestion of appointments being made according to ability, and there was no system of

[1] Based on a definition by the Royal Commission on the Civil Service 1929–31 (The Tomlin Commission), Cmd. 3909 (1931).
[2] For a general history of the Civil Service see E. Cohen, *The Growth of the British Civil Service*, London 1965; H. Parris, *Constitutional Bureaucracy*, London 1969.

examinations to test the ability of potential recruits. Civil Service pay consisted partly of regular salaries paid out of departmental receipts, and partly of additional bonuses and perquisites, which varied from department to department. The only overall supervision was provided by the Auditers of Imprest, who exercised a very general and limited control over departmental accounts.

Some attempts at reform were made in the early years of the nineteenth century, in the interests of economy, but it was not until the appearance in 1854 of the Report on the Organization of the Permanent Civil Service[1] by Sir Stafford Northcote (Secretary at the Board of Trade) and Sir Charles Trevelyan (an Assistant Secretary at the Treasury), that fundamental changes were made in Civil Service organization. The report was inspired largely by the earlier introduction of competitive examinations as a basis for recruitment to the Indian Civil Service, and by reforms in the organization of Oxford and Cambridge Universities, with the emphasis on examinations as a test of ability. In 1848, a House of Commons Select Committee enquiry into the costs of the Civil Service, before which Sir Charles Trevelyan gave evidence, led to the appointment of Northcote and Trevelyan to enquire into the whole structure and organization of the Civil Service—just as in 1966 a House of Commons Estimates Committee enquiry into the Civil Service[2] led to the appointment of the Fulton Commission for a full-scale enquiry into the service. The Northcote–Trevelyan Report attacked the existing system of patronage, and recommended that recruitment should be by open-examinations, as with the Indian Civil Service. They advocated the creation of a Civil Service Commission as an independent body to organize recruitment, and they proposed that there should be two classes throughout the service, junior posts recruited between the ages of seventeen and twenty-one, and senior posts recruited from University graduates. They further proposed that within each class there should be a system of promotion by merit in order to stimulate talent and ambition.

[1] H.C.P. 27 (1854).
[2] *Recruitment to the Civil Service*, Sixth Report of the Estimates Committee Session 1964–5. H.C. 308 (1965). See also E. N. Gladden, 'The Estimates Committee Looks at the Civil Service', *Parl. Aff.* 1965–6, pp. 233–40.

These recommendations were naturally criticized by those who benefited from the existing system of patronage and departmental independence, but more significantly the report was attacked by those who argued that academic ability was not the best criterion on which to base recruitment. It was also argued that a Civil Service based on academic talent would become *too* efficient and *too* powerful, and would consequently be a threat to the authority of Ministers. Thus opposition to the proposals was strong, but they were implemented in two main stages. The Crimean War revealed basic inefficiencies in army organization, which also reflected upon the home Civil Service, while in 1855, Palmerston (who favoured Civil Service reform) replaced Aberdeen as Prime Minister. Thus in 1855, by Orders in Council, three Commissioners were appointed and were given the task of organizing (for those departments that requested it) a system of examinations for Civil Service recruits. They were to devise qualifying examinations to test the ability of potential recruits, and also competitive examinations of a limited type, whereby two or three candidates competed for one post. A system of open competition examinations, however, did not emerge until 1870, when, again by Orders in Council, Gladstone introduced a system of open competition for all departments except the Home Office and the Foreign Office (who were particularly opposed to the principle of open competition). All the departments were unified into one 'Civil Service', and certain general rates of pay and pensions were laid down, so that today civil servants belong to an integrated service, with common conditions of employment, standards, and traditions.

Since 1870 the Civil Service has been subjected to a number of enquiries, including, in particular, the 1890 Ridley Commission,[1] the 1914 Macdonnell Commission,[2] the 1918 Gladstone Committee,[3] and the 1931 Tomlin Commission,[4] although none of these enquiries had the impact or significance of the Northcote–Trevelyan report.[5] The Fulton Commission which

[1] Report of the Commission on Civil Establishments.

[2] Report of the Commission on the Civil Service, Cd. 7338 (1914).

[3] Report of the Committee on Problems of Recruitment to the Civil Service.

[4] Report of the Commission on the Civil Service, Cmd. 3909 (1931).

[5] See E. Hughes, 'Postscript to the Civil Service Reforms of 1855', *Pub. Admin.* 1955, pp. 299–306; G. K. Fry, *Statesmen in Disguise*, London 1969.

reported in 1968 on the structure, recruitment, and management of the Civil Service, is thus only the latest of a long line of enquiries. All of these enquiries were concerned with the structure and organization of the service, and by 1931 the basis of the modern structure had emerged.

Modern Structure of the Civil Service

In examining the modern structure of the non-industrial Civil Service,[1] an initial distinction (which cuts across the division into classes outlined below) has to be made between the 80% or so who make up the permanent establishment of the service, and who thereby qualify for full pension rights, and the 20% or so of civil servants who are employed on a temporary or probationary basis. As well as this broad division, however, the non-industrial Civil Service can be divided into three main groups. Firstly, there are the departmental classes, like the Diplomatic Service, the Inland Revenue Officers, and the Ministry of Education Inspectorate, who are restricted to one department, and whose conditions of service are largely controlled by their own department. Secondly, there are the general or 'Treasury classes', who are common to several departments, and whose conditions of service are controlled by the Treasury. Finally, there are the various specialists or technical classes of lawyers, scientists, and medical advisers, who are recruited for their specialist qualifications, but who (unlike the departmental classes) are common to several departments. In particular among the specialist classes there is the Government Legal Service, made up of the barristers and solicitors who act as advisers on matters of legal procedure, and the Scientific Class, which consists of various grades that correspond roughly to the grades within the general classes.

The general or Treasury classes are at present sub-divided into the Administrative, Executive, and Clerical Classes. The Administrative Class consists of some 2,500 civil servants who are concerned with the formulation and administration of policy. The class is sub-divided into the grades of Permanent Secretary,

[1] For a more detailed analysis of structure, see W. J. M. Mackenzie and J. W. Grove, *Central Administration in Britain*, London 1957.

Deputy Secretary, Under Secretary, Assistant Secretary, Principal, and Assistant Principal, the members of the first four grades (who are in regular personal contact with Ministers) making up the 'Higher Civil Service'.[1] In most years about half of the entrants into the Administrative Class are promoted or transferred from other parts of the service, particularly from the executive class, and the other half are recruited from University graduates with good honours degrees, mainly from Oxford and Cambridge Universities. The recruitment of these graduates is either by Method One, which consists of a qualifying test, an interview, and a written competitive examination in academic subjects, or by Method Two, which consists of a preliminary test, Civil Service Selection Board interviews and tests over a two-day period, and a final interview. The CSSB was set up in 1945 with its headquarters originally at the Stoke D'Abernon 'country house' outside London, and it was designed to meet the particular post-war problem of recruiting for a vast number of vacant posts. The principle behind the CSSB, and behind the Method Two form of recruitment, is that entry to the Civil Service should not be based entirely on academic merit, but should be based also on the consideration of 'personal qualities' which cannot be measured by academic examinations. Throughout the Civil Service, recruitment is based on written examinations and interviews, with the importance of the interview increasing towards the top of the Civil Service hierarchy. The emphasis that is put on interviews, particularly in Method Two, is widely criticized, however, as giving an advantage to recruits who have the 'correct' social background of public school and Oxbridge, and it is this aspect of Civil Service recruitment that has received most attention and criticism in recent years.

The Executive Class, with a numerical strength of some 70,000, is made up of the Executive Officers and the several grades of Higher, Senior, Chief, and Principal Executive Officers. The Executive Class is described as being responsible for the execution of policy under the supervision of the Administrative Class. It is recruited partly by an open examination among those who leave school at 18 with good leaving quali-

[1] See H. Dale, *The Higher Civil Service*, London 1941, for an analysis of the features of this body. See also J. S. Harris and T. V. Garcia, 'The Permanent Secretaries: Britain's Top Administrators', *PAR* 1966, pp. 31-44.

fications, partly (and increasingly) from graduates, and partly (about 60% in most years) by promotion from the Clerical Class. The proportion of graduates recruited into the Executive Class is increasing, as many 18-year-olds who in the past might have entered the Executive Class are now continuing their education at the Universities. At the same time, many graduates are choosing to enter the Executive Class and then seek promotion to the Administrative Class, rather than attempt direct entry into the Administrative Class.

The Clerical Class is divided into the grades of Higher Clerical Officer, Clerical Officer, and Clerical Assistant, making a total, including temporary clerks, of about 200,000. Recruitment of Clerical Officers is partly from among 16-year-old school leavers and partly (just over half) by the promotion of Clerical Assistants.

The Diplomatic Service, which consists of less than 20,000 members, has a separate structure and organization from that of the Home Civil Service. It was formed in 1965 through the amalgamation of the Foreign Service, the Commonwealth Service, and the Trade Commissioner Service. This followed the 1964 report of the Plowden Committee on the overseas services, which advocated the merger of the Commonwealth and Colonial Offices, and the formation of a common Diplomatic Service for the Foreign and Commonwealth Offices.[1] The logical merger of the Foreign and Commonwealth Offices, to form just one Ministry for all overseas affairs, has since been completed, and since 1968 there has been one Secretary of State for Foreign and Commonwealth Affairs. Members of the Diplomatic Service are employed in various types of diplomatic, consular or information work in Britain or abroad, and their numbers are supplemented by various advisers who are seconded to the Service from other departments, and from the armed forces. Within the Diplomatic Service the organizational distinctions between the administrative and executive branches are less clear cut than in the Home Civil Service.

The Administrative Class of the Home Civil Service consists very broadly of two groups—those who were recruited into the class directly from University, and those who were promoted or

[1] Report of the Committee on the Overseas Services, Cmnd. 2276 (1964).

transferred from other classes within the Civil Service.[1] The former group tend to have more exclusive middle-class and upper-middle-class backgrounds than the latter, and tend to be drawn predominantly from the public schools and Oxbridge (mainly with degrees in Arts subjects or Classics), while the promotees,[2] in the main, have an educational background of grammar school and provincial University, or no University at all. In 1950, for example, 82% of the direct entrants to the Administrative Class were from Oxbridge, compared with 20% of the promotees, and 70% had attended public schools, again compared with 19% of the promotees.[3] At least in their first few years in the service, the direct entrants lack the practical experience of the promotees, and their general approach tends to be more theoretical and academic, but perhaps more imaginative, than that of the promotees. Thus the direct entrants can perhaps be likened to the often inexperienced and theory-bound Sandhurst-trained officers of the regular army, while the promotees can be likened to the NCOs or the officers who have risen from the ranks.

The presence of a large proportion of promotees within the Administrative Class thus reduces somewhat the social exclusiveness of the Class, and means that the Administrative Class is composed of more diverse social elements, and is less academic and 'amateur', than is often imagined. It has been claimed, for example, that the social background of Administrative Class civil servants is more akin to that of Labour Ministers than of Conservative Ministers.[4] It remains true, however, that in the highest posts of the Administrative Class the direct entrants are much more numerous, and in 1966 40% of the total membership of the Administrative Class were promotees, compared with only 13% of the Permanent Secre-

[1] See F. Dunnill, *The Civil Service: Some Human Aspects*, London 1956, Ch. 1, for a more detailed analysis on these lines.

[2] Here and throughout, 'promotees' refers to those who were promoted or transferred from other classes in the service.

[3] R. K. Kelsall, *Higher Civil Servants in Britain*, London 1955, p. 125. This book remains the most extensive survey of the social structure of the Civil Service. See also K. Robinson, 'Selection and the Social Background of the Administrative Class', *Pub. Admin.* 1955, pp. 383–8; and a rejoinder by R. K. Kelsall, *Pub. Admin.* 1956, pp. 169–74.

[4] Blondel, *Voters, Parties and Leaders*, p. 201.

taries and Deputy Secretaries.[1] In his detailed examination of
the social structure of the Higher Civil Service, R. K. Kelsall
revealed that between 1929 and 1950 the proportion of direct
entrants among the Higher Civil Service declined from 56% to
43%, and that in this period the social exclusiveness of this
group was gradually reduced.[2] In 1965, however, the Estimates
Committee enquiry into the structure of the Administrative
Class revealed that between 1957 and 1963 there was an
increase in Administrative Class entrants drawn from boarding
schools, from Oxbridge, and from families in Class I of social
groupings.[3]

The Foreign Service has always been more socially exclusive
than the Home Civil Service. In 1964 the Plowden Committee
revealed that 78% of the successful applicants to the senior
branch of the Foreign Service came from public schools or
direct grant schools, while 95% were from Oxbridge.[4] The
Plowden Committee pointed out that there was a need for
entrants to the proposed Diplomatic Service to be drawn from
state schools and from provincial Universities—although the
Plowden Committee also advocated the payment of additional
educational allowances to enable members of the Diplomatic
Service to send their children to boarding schools. In fairness to
those responsible for recruitment, however, it must be pointed
out that one of the reasons for the large number of Oxbridge
graduates in the Diplomatic Service, and in the Civil Service
as a whole, is that graduates from other Universities tend not to
apply for entry.

The Problems of Reform

One of the problems involved with the existing structure of
the Civil Service is that recruitment policy is geared to an
educational system that is rapidly changing. It may be questioned, for example, whether it is necessary for the Civil Service
Commission to rely so much on their own series of recruitment
examinations, at all levels, when there exists today such a large
(and growing) range of school and University examinations,

[1] Treasury memorandum to the Fulton Commission, published in *Pub.
Admin.* 1966, pp. 473–9.
[2] Kelsall, *Higher Civil Servants in Britain*, p. 16.
[3] H.C. 308 (1965). [4] Cmd. 2276 (1964).

which provide indications of the academic ability of potential Civil Service recruits. Also, there have been difficulties in recruitment in recent years because many people who in the past might have entered the Clerical Class after leaving school at 15 or 16, are now staying on at school until they are 18, Similarly, many who in the past would have left school at 18 and entered the Executive Class, are now going to University. while many graduates who previously might have entered the Administrative Class are now seeking careers in school or University teaching, or in commerce or industry. In recent years there have been insufficient numbers of recruits into the Administrative Class, and in 1965 the Class was 10% under-staffed at Principal level. Since 1954, the annual number of applicants and appointments has remained constant, despite increases in the number of graduates being produced. Similarly, the Civil Service Commissioners have complained that they have had difficulty in filling Executive Class posts, while recruit-ment to the specialist classes has had to contend with increasing competition from lucrative occupations outside the service.

In 1968 the Fulton Commission, as one of its main proposals, recommended the creation of a single unified grading structure to replace the existing separate departmental classes, and to reduce the number of different grades within the service.[1] Such a reform had long been advocated, and the Treasury itself, in evidence to the Fulton Commission, had proposed the re-placement of the Administrative and Executive classes by a single General Management Group of eight grades. The Fulton Commission's proposal was accepted in principle by the Government in 1968, and once it is fully implemented, a 'comprehensive' grading system should provide a more flexible structure, and should permit a more adaptable recruitment policy than is possible with the existing divisions into Admini-strative and Executive classes. It should also end the present tendency for the higher grades of the Executive class and the lower grades of the Administrative class to be involved in over-

---

[1] Report of the Fulton Commission, Cmnd. 3638 (1968). See also G. K. Fry, 'Some Weaknesses in the Fulton Report on the British Home Civil Service', PS 1969, pp. 484–94; M. J. Fores and J. B. Heath, 'The Fulton Report: Job Evaluation and the Pay Structure', Pub. Admin. 1970, pp. 15–22.

lapping work. The merging of the several classes and grades into a unified structure is likely to be a lengthy process, as the task is being undertaken piecemeal, with the unification of the senior grades being considered initially.

*   *   *

Another Fulton proposal is that the professional and scientific classes within the service should have a much better chance than they have at present of reaching the top levels of the service. At present the technical experts are to be found alongside the general administrators, but the distinction between 'administrators' and 'experts' is clearly preserved throughout the service.[1] In 1964 only 13% of Higher Civil Servants had degrees in science or mathematics,[2] and even though the situation has changed considerably in recent years, the number of Treasury officials with economics degrees, or economic training, is not as great as critics of the Civil Service would wish. The 'amateur tradition' of the British Civil Service is based on the notion that administration is an art which is best learnt by experience, which needs no specifically technical qualifications, and which requires little formal post-entry training. The main requirement is that recruits should have a broad general education, a 'good mind', and the ability to examine all issues, technical or not, from the standpoint of the intelligent amateur. Thus the Permanent Secretary and other leading figures in the Treasury and the Ministry of Trade and Industry do not need to have degrees or training in economics; officials of the Ministry of Technology do not need to have technological qualifications; officials of the Ministry of Agriculture do not need to have degrees in agriculture; the officials of the Ministry of Health do not need to have medical degrees. The theory is that specifically technical information can be supplied by the experts from outside the Civil Service who serve on advisory committees, or by the specialist classes within the Civil Service, who

[1] See V. Subramaniam, 'Specialists in British and Australian Government Services: A Study in Contrast', *Pub. Admin.* 1963, pp. 357–74; Sir James Dunnett, 'The Civil Service Administrator and the Expert', *Pub. Admin.* 1961, pp. 223–38; Z. M. T. Tarkowski and A. V. Turnbull, 'Scientists versus Administrators', *Pub. Admin.* 1959, pp. 213–56.
[2] Lord Bridges in *Whitehall and Beyond*, p. 64.

nevertheless remain distinct from the general administrators who occupy the highest posts in the Service.

The amateur basis of the Civil Service means, however, that civil servants are often at a disadvantage in their dealings with industry at a technical level. This was well illustrated in 1964, when the Ferranti electronics firm had made large profits from a Government contract, while in 1967 the PAC revealed that the costs of some Government defence and civil projects had been unnecessarily high. Thus it is often argued that the amateur tradition is out of date in face of the technical needs of the modern state. It is claimed that there should be more recruitment for specific technical qualifications rather than for general ability; that there should be more post-entry training for all civil servants; and that (as the Treasury has proposed) there should be greater opportunities for members of the specialist classes to reach the top administrative posts. It is also argued that there should be an increase in the number of specialists who are brought into the Civil Service on a temporary basis from the Universities, industry, and the public corporations, and that there should be more secondment of civil servants to industry.

As there is no equivalent in Britain (as yet) to the French École Nationale d'Administration, which gives a broad pre-entry training to recruits to the French Civil Service,[1] and as there is only a limited amount of post-entry training for British civil servants, it is perhaps all the more necessary to recruit more graduates for their specific qualifications in languages, economics, science, and technology, rather than for their general abilities as revealed in academic achievements in Arts subjects and Classics. In 1964 the Plowden Committee emphasized the importance of the commercial work of the overseas departments.[2] The committee urged the recruitment of more people competent in languages and technical subjects, and called for the recruitment of more science graduates. In 1965 the Estimates

[1] For an examination of the Civil Service in France and elsewhere, see Brian Chapman, *The Profession of Government*, London 1959; W. A. Robson, *The Civil Service in Britain and France*, London 1956; E. Strauss, *The Ruling Servants: Bureaucracy in Russia, France and Britain*, London 1961; C. H. Sisson, *The Spirit of Public Administration and some European Comparisons*, London 1966.

[2] Cmd. 2276 (1964).

Committee pointed out (and deplored the fact) that between 1957 and 1963, of the recruits into the Administrative Class as a whole, the proportion who had degrees in Classics actually increased, despite the persistent demands for more science graduates.[1]

Post-entry training does exist within the service. Members of the Inland Revenue Department, for example, have to learn taxation principles after entry, while all entrants to the Civil Service undergo a short post-entry induction course, and a system of day-release classes exists for Clerical Officers. In general, however, little attention has been given in the past to post-entry training, and there has been considerable criticism of this since 1945.[2] Some progress has been made. On the recommendations of the Assheton Committee[3] in 1944 a Director of Training and Education was appointed at the Treasury, and Training Officers were set up in some departments, and in 1963 the Treasury Centre for Administrative Studies was set up to provide courses for Assistant Principals after they had been in the service for two years. These courses last for fourteen weeks, or twenty-one weeks in the case of members of the economic departments, and consist of lectures and tutorials in public administration, the structure of industry, economics, and other related subjects. This development has not satisfied the critics, however, and although the Plowden Committee rejected the idea of a Diplomatic Service Staff College, it recommended that there should be more training in languages for members of the Diplomatic Service.[4] Then, in 1968, Fulton advocated the creation of a Civil Service College to develop post-entry training schemes, and this is being implemented.

With regard to the problems of recruitment policy and of post-entry training of new recruits, it must be realized that just

[1] H.C. 308 (1965).

[2] S. A. Bailey, 'Training the Technician in Administrative Practices', *Pub. Admin.* 1955, pp. 375–82; R. J. S. Baker, 'The Training of Assistant Principals at the Post Office', *Pub. Admin.* 1963, pp. 71–82; K. R. Stowe, 'Staff Training in the National Assistance Board', *Pub. Admin.* 1961, pp. 331–52.

[3] Report of the Committee on the Training of Civil Servants, Cmd. 6525 (1944). See also D. Hubback, 'The Treasury's Role in Civil Service Training', *Pub. Admin.* 1957, pp. 99–110.

[4] Cmd. 2276 (1964).

as the majority of the present Permanent Secretaries, Deputy Secretaries, and Under Secretaries were recruited before, during, or just after the last war, any immediate changes that are made in recruiting policy and post-entry training will not affect the composition of the top ranks of the Civil Service until today's recruits reach these levels in twenty or more years' time. This makes all the more urgent the question of the reform of the whole social and organizational structure of the Civil Service.

Management of the Service

Each department is responsible for its own internal organization, and the departmental Minister is the 'primary' employer for each department, performing this function on behalf of the Crown. There are Establishment and Finance Officers in each department, and they and the Training Officers, who are attached to most departments, help to achieve uniformity throughout the service. Until the creation of the Civil Service Department in 1968, general control of the Civil Service was exercised by the Treasury.[1] The Joint Permanent Secretary to the Treasury was head of the Civil Service, and was chief adviser to the Prime Minister on Civil Service matters. Technically, the Treasury's authority was based on an Order in Council of 1956 (which replaced an Order in Council of 1920), but in practical terms the Treasury's power was based on its financial role within the machinery of government. The Treasury's role was thus somewhat delicate, forming the employer's side of the National Whitley Council negotiating machinery for conditions of service. As well as this, the Treasury controlled the size and structure of the service, determining the total numbers to be employed, and their distribution throughout the departments.[2] In recruitment matters, however, responsibility lay with six Civil Service Commissioners who controlled the arrangements for the recruitment to all grades, and who allocated new entrants to the departments.[3]

In 1968, the Fulton Commission proposed that a special

[1] For details, see Lord Bridges, *The Treasury*, p. 107. See also above, p. 285.
[2] A. J. D. Winnifrith, 'Treasury Control of Establishments', *Pub. Admin.* 1958, pp. 9–18.
[3] Sir George Mallaby, 'The Civil Service Commission: Its Place in the Machinery of Government', *Pub. Admin.* 1964, pp. 1–10.

Civil Service Department be created to take over the management and recruitment functions from the Treasury and the Civil Service Commissioners. The Government accepted the recommendation, and the new department was created with the Prime Minister as its head, but with Lord Shackleton (then Paymaster-General) acting on the Prime Minister's behalf. Sir William Armstrong, who had been responsible for the management of the Civil Service as Joint Permanent Secretary at the Treasury, became Permanent Secretary in the new department. The initial task of the department was to create the Civil Service College, and review the other recommendations of the Fulton Commission, and this was continued in 1970, despite the change of Government.

Within the Clerical and Executive Classes, departmental promotion procedure is based on interview boards and on annual reports that are made about each member of the service, and which over the years form detailed records of the careers of civil servants. In these two classes, promotion is often slow and often necessitates moving from area to area. In the Administrative Class up to the grade of Under Secretary, promotions are made by the departmental Minister on the advice of the Permanent Secretary of the department. After 1920, and until the creation of the new department, promotion to the rank of Deputy Secretary or Permanent Secretary was made by the Prime Minister on the advice of the Permanent Secretary to the Treasury, and this was a vital aspect of the control that the Treasury exerted over the rest of the service. In the past, critics of Treasury control of senior appointments claimed that the Treasury tended to secure the appointment of an excessive number of men with Treasury experience, thereby causing a further permeation of Treasury influence and attitudes throughout the service. Indeed, one of the main arguments used to justify the creation of a special department to take over the Treasury's long-standing responsibility for Civil Service management, was that it was desirable to limit this Treasury influence over top appointments in the service. It remains to be seen how the new department will perform its role. Certainly, it could lead to major changes in the Whitehall machine, and thus could have far-reaching consequences for the British system of government, as since 1920, and especially since 1945, the Treasury's special place within the central administration has been based to a considerable degree on its powers of general management of the Civil Service.

The National Whitley Council consists of representatives of the Treasury, and the Permanent Secretaries of the departments on the employer side, and the representatives of the various Civil Service Unions and Staff Associations on the other. The Association of First Division Civil Servants is the main body for Administrative Class civil servants, while the Society of Civil Servants includes most of the Executive Class, and the Civil Service Clerical Association covers most of the Clerical Class.

TABLE XXVIII

*Some Civil Service Pay Scales, 1970**

Permanent Secretary at the Treasury	£10,400
Other Permanent Secretaries	£9,800
Deputy Secretaries	£7,100
Under Secretaries	£6,000
Assistant Secretaries	£4,045–£5,200
Principals	£2,475–£3,596
Senior Chief Executive Officers	£3,550–£4,200
Chief Executive Officers	£2,860–£3,570
Senior Executive Officers	£2,220–£2,856

* Some scales vary from department to department.

Other smaller and more specialized bodies are the Inland Revenue Staff Federation, and the Institute of Professional Civil Servants. Pay negotiations can be assisted by the Civil Service Arbitration Tribunal, made up of one representative from each side of the Whitley Council, plus a third neutral figure chosen by the Minister of Labour. Following the recommendation in 1956 of the Priestly Commission on Civil Service salaries, the Civil Service Pay Research Unit was created to examine the salary situation in similar occupations outside the service, so as to achieve the principle of comparability.[1]

[1] Report of the Royal Commission on the Civil Service, Cmd. 9613 (1956). See also S. J. Frankel, 'Arbitration in the British Civil Service', *Pub. Admin.* 1960, pp. 197–212; H. R. Kahn, *Salaries in the Public Service in England and Wales*, London 1962.

Nevertheless, with regard to the pay and conditions within the Civil Service, the general impression remains of lower salaries than in private industry, but of regular increments, assured promotion to certain levels, security of tenure, good pension schemes, and (at least in the lower grades) fairly good hours of work and generous holidays. Even in the nineteenth century the Civil Service had good pension schemes, and the Superannuation Act 1857 established a scheme that gave most civil servants pensions of as much as two-thirds of their retirement salary. Today, established civil servants have a non-contributory pension scheme which gives them a lump sum on retirement, plus a pension that can be as much as half of their salary averaged over the last three years of service. The hours of work, however, is one sphere in which Civil Service conditions have deteriorated, in that for most of the nineteenth century a five- or six-hour day was normal, and even up to 1939, most lower-grade civil servants enjoyed a short working day.

The political activities of civil servants are formally restricted. The Trade Disputes Act 1927 forbade strike action by Civil Service Unions, and although this Act was repealed in 1946, the tradition remains. In 1949 the Masterman Committee of enquiry into the political activities of civil servants produced certain guiding principles,[1] which were accepted in modified form. The principles that apply today are, firstly, that there are no restrictions on industrial civil servants, or non-industrial civil servants in the minor grades; secondly, the Clerical Class are free to indulge in political activity short of Parliamentary candidature; and thirdly, the Executive Class and Administrative Class are free to belong to a political party, but should not indulge in any activity beyond this. These principles form part of the Civil Service 'code of behaviour', and civil servants have thus to resign their posts if they wish to pursue a Parliamentary career.

*   *   *

The 'image' of the Civil Service is often presented as one of slowness and caution, contrasted with the enterprise and slick-

[1] Report of the Committee on the Political Activities of Civil Servants, Cmd. 7718 (1949).

ness of private industry. References are made to Civil Service
'red-tape', to a multiplicity of forms and memos written in
triplicate, and to detailed records stored in literally miles of files
in the Registry. The popular picture of the Higher Civil
Servant is that of an aloof and reticent, but extremely authoritative and influential figure at the centre of power, while of the
lower levels of the service the impression is often that of slow
and uninspired handling of routine tasks. At the same time, it
is probably true to say that in Britain the public attitude
towards the Civil Service is more favourable than in most
countries. Civil servants in Britain are generally regarded as
honest and conscientious, and the British Civil Service is not
equated with corruption and the misuse of power in the way
that are many bureaucrats elsewhere.

To a considerable extent, caution and red-tape do char-
acterize Civil Service activities, largely because the principle of
public accountability means that minor Civil Service actions
can be the subject of Parliamentary scrutiny, particularly
through Question Time in the House of Commons.[1] Undoubtedly the Civil Service as a whole tends to be slow in changing
its methods of work, but the popular concept of the Civil
Service contains basic inconsistencies, in that the popular
picture of Civil Service caution is hardly compatible with the
equally popular idea of civil servants 'running the country'
while Ministers merely look on. How much authority do civil
servants actually wield, and where does real power lie as
between the Ministerial and permanent sides of the Government machine? This matter can be looked at from the point of
view of the general relationship between Ministers and civil
servants in the policy-making process, and also in relation to
the question of the powers of the executive through delegated
legislation and administrative adjudication.

Where Does Power Lie?

The general problem of how much power the Civil Service
has and should have within the system of government, is that

[1] W. Hampton, 'Parliament and the Civil Service', *Parl. Aff.* 1963–4,
pp. 430–8; E. N. Gladden, 'Parliament and the Civil Service', *Parl. Aff.*
1956–7, pp. 165–79.

of relating the influence of the permanent administrators to the demands of popular government.[1] The permanent officials who are in touch with the details of their departments' work must be closely involved in the formulation of policy, but the principles of public accountability demand that the responsibility should lie with the Ministers. One solution to the problem is to have a popularly elected or a politically nominated Civil Service. Thus in Britain in the pre-Northcote and Trevelyan era, most civil servants were appointed through a system of patronage, and in the USA today most of the top national and local administrators are political appointees, with a Republican President tending to surround himself with Republican civil servants who vacate their posts if a Democratic President is elected.

The British Civil Service is permanent, in the sense that civil servants remain in power despite changes of Government. The electoral defeat of a Government, and the emergence of a new set of Ministers, does not lead to wholesale changes in the Civil Service. The principle behind a permanent and neutral Civil Service is that it is possible for independent and impartial (in the sense of non-partisan) administrators to serve Governments of differing political complexions. It is claimed that the British experience proves this, and that this system allows the development of continuity in policy, and prevents the nepotism that is often associated with a politically nominated administration. It is often argued, however, that today the role of top civil servants is so significant, and their involvement in the policy-making process is so great, that the tradition of a truly independent and non-partisan Civil Service (at least at the very top of the administrative structure) is almost impossible to achieve. Between the wars, many Socialists argued that the Civil Service was essentially conservative (if not Conservative with a capital 'C'), and that a Socialist Government would meet with obstruction from the Civil Service.[2] Today many who argue that the

[1] L. Blair, 'The Civil Servant: Political Reality and Legal Myth', *PL* 1958, pp. 32–49; J. B. Christoph, 'Political Rights and Administrative Impartiality in the British Civil Service', *APSR* 1957, pp. 67–87; Sir Charles Cunningham, 'Policy and Practice', *Pub. Admin.* 1963, pp. 229–38.

[2] See in particular Harold Laski, *Parliamentary Government in England*, London 1938, Ch. 6. For more recent comments, see P. Shore, *The Right to Know*, London 1965.

Labour Governments have not been truly Socialist Governments still claim that a Government with a red-blooded Socialist programme would need to have a different Civil Service to carry through this programme.

The theoretical 'distribution of power' between Ministers and their civil servants is that the Ministers make the policy decisions, and these decisions are then executed by the Civil Service, but undoubtedly the reality of the situation is very far from this theoretical concept. Inevitably, civil servants are bound up to a considerable extent in the policy-making process. Because of the very extent of Governmental activities today as compared with the pre-1914 period, and because of the technical nature of much of the work of modern government, it is clear that considerable initiative in policy making now rests with civil servants, particularly the Permanent Secretaries, and the Deputy and Under Secretaries. Ministers are frequently moved from department to department, and they cannot hope to obtain a detailed knowledge of the workings of their departments. Most Ministers are also members of the Commons, and they have Parliamentary and constituency duties as well as Ministerial responsibilities. In this respect Ministers who are drawn from the House of Lords have an advantage.[1] Although a Permanent Secretary may try to keep a Minister informed of the most important aspects of the department's activities, there must inevitably be many matters that escape him, and many decisions that are made in the lower levels of the departmental structure can be much more significant than is at first realized. Much legislation is described as 'Civil Service legislation', in that it is concerned with minor technical and administrative matters, or, as with Consolidation Bills, is concerned with gathering existing legislation into one composite statute. Civil Service initiative with such legislation is considerable, while (as is revealed below) civil servants have considerable initiative with regard to delegated legislation.

At a more significant level, civil servants are sometimes accused of misusing their wide discretionary powers. In a submission to the Fulton Committee in 1966, the NEC of the Labour Party attacked the Civil Service for excessive secrecy in its activities, and for withholding information from Ministers

[1] See above, p. 274.

in efforts to persuade them to adopt particular policies.[1] Some
extreme critics have argued that the Civil Service is largely to
blame for Britain's supposed 'lack of purpose' and backward-
ness in economic development in the nineteen-fifties and 'sixties,
claiming that civil servants have misused the wide discretionary
powers that are inevitably theirs in the modern process of
Government.[2]

Despite all of these considerations, however, it is necessary
to avoid the conclusion that civil servants make all the important decisions, and that Ministers are thereby merely
observers. It has often been pointed out that politicians struggle
long and hard to attain Ministerial rank, and that they are
thus unlikely to be prepared to surrender initiative to the Civil
Service when they do gain office. Similarly, a stock-in-trade of
politicians has to be the ability to influence people, and this will
be a considerable advantage to a Minister in his dealings with
the Civil Service. Most Ministerial contact with his department
is through the Permanent Secretary. Some Ministers even
choose to deal solely with the Permanent Secretary (using him
as a funnel for all departmental attitudes), and a strong Minister can presumably impose his will on the Permanent Secretary
to a considerable degree. The fact that policy decisions have
to be acceptable to the Cabinet, the Treasury, the Party, and
Parliament, means that the Minister, through his contact with
these bodies, retains the last word on all policy decisions. The
fact that major Civil Service blunders (such as were revealed,
for example, in the Crichel Down episode)[3] are so rare, may
merely be because mistakes that are made rarely come to light,
or it may be that such examples of maladministration are
indeed rare. The often-heard criticism of the British Civil
Service as being essentially 'amateur' conflicts with the notion
of civil servants dominating their Ministers through their
expert knowledge, and from this point of view it can be argued
that the real limitation on a Minister's power is not the Civil
Service, but is the pressure groups, advisory committees, and

---

[1] *The Times*, 2.1.67.

[2] See for example Brian Chapman, *British Government Observed*, London
1963. For a defence of the Civil Service see D. N. Chester's review of
Chapman's book in *Pub. Admin.* 1963, p. 375.

[3] See below, p. 336.

technical experts outside the Government machine, on whom Ministers and civil servants rely for technical information.[1]

It is extremely difficult, however, to come to any clear conclusion as to how much influence lies with the Civil Service, and where the precise division is to be found between the power of Ministers and that of civil servants.[2] To a considerable extent it must vary from situation to situation. There must be variations from department to department, and from one Minister to another, with some Ministers clearly being stronger than others, and more capable of dominating their departments. It has been said that a Minister will be able to get his way in the department if he is clear in his own mind precisely what he wishes to achieve, but that many Ministers, and many Governments, are not clear as to the policies they wish to adopt. A Government that newly comes to power generally has a number of predetermined policies that it wishes to implement, while a Government that has been in power for a long time is probably more inclined to be conditioned into accepting 'the departmental point of view'. At the same time, there is a clear distinction between major policies which are often incorporated in the party programme, and which will be the concern of the Minister, and minor issues which can be handled by an Under Secretary or Assistant Secretary, and which will only be referred to the Minister if they acquire sudden significance, perhaps through a Parliamentary question. All of these considerations are clearly variables, and make difficult the application of any final and definite rule on this question. It is generally accepted, however, that Civil Service influence is increasing, and it is often urged that it is necessary to halt this trend. One proposal that is often made for increasing the power of the Minister within his department is that the Minister should introduce into his department his own private *cabinet* of advisers drawn from outside the Civil Service. At present, each Minister has his Private Office, consisting of a Private Secretary (generally a Principal or Assistant Secretary) and a few personal assistants within the department. The Private Office and Private Secretary 'network' undoubtedly provides a considerable degree of

[1] For details see Political and Economic Planning, *Advisory Committees in British Government*, London 1960.

[2] See *Pub. Admin.* 1965, pp. 251-87, for further discussions on this theme.

Ministerial control within the departments. Nevertheless, it is often claimed that the Private Office is inadequate as it operates at present, and that, as in France, Ministers should bring with them into the departments experts and political advisers of their own choosing. Such a development has been resisted, however, largely because of the conflict that would almost inevitably arise between the advice a Minister received from the permanent civil servants, and the advice he got from his private *cabinet*.[1]

The Problem of Delegated Legislation

Another and more specific aspect of the authority of the Civil Service is involved in the question of the delegation by Parliament of direct legislative authority to the executive. Many Acts of Parliament merely lay down the broad outline of proposed changes, and include a clause which delegates to the Minister the power to work out the details of the provisions—a process which has been well defined as 'the statutory practice whereby the Parliament empowers the Administration (generally a Minister or the Queen in Council) to make rules and regulations'.[2] The main purposes for which powers are delegated by Parliament in this way are to allow the amendment of existing legislation in order to bring it up-to-date; to create machinery to administer the Act; or, most generally, to allow the departments to decide details within the framework of legislation that consists only of broad principles. This often also involves sub-delegation, whereby the Minister is empowered to delegate these powers to his departmental officials, subject to his confirmation, and two or three tiers of delegation can be involved in the granting of delegated powers.

The justification of the practice is three-fold. In the first place, it is a speedy process which avoids the delay that is frequently involved in the consideration of legislative proposals in Parliament, and there is an ever-increasing need for speed in the governmental process. Secondly, it is a flexible process which

[1] T. D. Kingdom, 'The Confidential Advisers of Ministers', *Pub. Admin.* 1966, pp. 267–74.
[2] J. A. G. Griffith and H. Street, *Principles of Administrative Law*, London 1967, p. 4.

allows regular revision of legislation without involving constant Parliamentary approval of this revision. Thirdly, in many instances Parliament is not competent to deal with aspects of highly technical legislation, and the detail of such legislation is best worked out by the Ministers and the departments, once Parliament has approved the principles. Thus the defence of the principle of delegated legislation is based on the frequently heard criticism that the Parliamentary legislative process is slow, cumbersome, and is essentially government by non-experts, and that the delegation of legislative authority to the executive is justified as a means of combating these limitations.

The growth of the practice of delegated legislation is largely, but not entirely, a twentieth-century problem.[1] It has developed in the main from the increase in the scope of government activities with the beginnings of the Welfare State after 1906, and more particularly since 1945, with the extension of government activities into more and more social, economic, and industrial spheres. These developments have meant that Parliament has not had the time, and has not been technically competent, to deal with many of the details of the consequent legislation. This was particularly the case during and immediately after the two world wars, and the Defence of the Realm Act 1914, and the Emergency Powers Acts of 1939 and 1940, empowered the Government to make such regulations as were necessary to meet the wartime emergencies. Many of the regulations introduced during the second world war were retained for a while after 1945, and wide powers were granted to the Government by the Emergency Laws Act and the Supplies and Services Act of 1945. This, combined with the extension of state activity through the Attlee Government's nationalization and social welfare schemes, involved a further big increase in delegated legislation, while more recent extensions of government responsibilities in the economic sphere have led inevitably to further increases.

Criticisms of the whole principle of delegated legislation are sometimes made, and it is condemned as a practice that offends the principle that legislation should be made in Parliament. It is argued (perhaps somewhat unrealistically) that Parlia-

[1] See J. Eaves, *Parliament and the Executive in Great Britain*, London 1957, for a survey of this development.

mentary procedure should be reformed so as to make unnecessary the delegation of legislative powers. More generally, however, critics acknowledge that delegated legislation is necessary, but claim that the methods of Parliamentary supervision of the process are inadequate. Concern over the problem was most acute during the nineteen-twenties and 'thirties. In 1929 in *The New Despotism*[1] Lord Hewart claimed that the Old Despotism of *Royal* domination of Parliament had been replaced by the New Despotism of *executive* domination of Parliament, which was proving to be just as big a threat to Parliament's authority and to public liberties, with Parliament being used as a cloak for executive despotism. Similarly, W. A. Robson in *Justice and Administrative Law*,[2] stressed the Constitutional problems involved in these developments. Much of the concern was not over the question of the delegation of powers to the Minister, but was over the sub-delegation of these powers to civil servants. The disquiet that was aroused led to the appointment of the Donoughmore Committee to enquire into the question of delegated legislation. The Committee reported in 1932,[3] and declared that the growth of delegated powers was necessary and was not getting out of hand. This assuaged public disquiet somewhat, and during the wartime emergency, the public was prepared to accept the delegation of wide legislative powers to the executive.

When the war situation improved, however, some alarm was expressed about the amount of delegation that was taking place, and about the casualness of Parliamentary supervision,[4] and this led in 1944 to the creation of a Select Committee to scrutinize the process. In 1946, the Select Committee on Procedure,[5] which had been set up as part of the post-war enquiry into the machinery of government, criticized the existing machinery for Parliamentary scrutiny (which was based on the Rules Publication Act 1893), and in 1952 the Select

[1] London 1929.

[2] London 1930. See also Sir C. K. Allen, *Bureaucracy Triumphant*, London 1931; Sir C. Carr, *Delegated Legislation*, London 1921.

[3] Cmd. 4060 (1932).

[4] See for example A. B. Keith, *The Constitution Under Strain*, London 1942; R. Kidd, *British Liberty in Danger*, London 1941; Sir C. K. Allen, *Law and Orders*, London 1945 (latest edition 1965).

[5] Report of the Select Committee on Procedure, H.C. 181 of 1945–6.

Committee on Delegated Legislation made a more detailed analysis of the problem. The main criticisms that emerged from these post-war enquiries were that the executive was assuming the legislative role of Parliament to an extent that endangered liberty, and that many of the powers that were delegated to Ministers were too loosely defined. It was pointed out that prior consultation was not always possible with those affected by delegated legislation, and that the protection of the Courts was denied by many of the regulations, with the prerogative of the Crown often making redress difficult. It was widely argued that there should be closer Parliamentary scrutiny of delegated powers; that there should be more consultation with affected parties; that there should be definite limits on the powers that were delegated; and that fuller publicity should be given to the power that was delegated to Ministers.

The post-war period also saw a further spate of literature, including Christopher Hollis's *Can Parliament Survive?*[1] and G. W. Keeton's *The Passing of Parliament*,[2] which included criticisms of the effect of delegated legislation in increasing Parliament's subservience to the executive. In more recent years, concern over the question of delegated legislation has been less marked, partly because the system of Parliamentary supervision of delegated powers has worked more smoothly than in the nineteen-forties and early 'fifties, but also because concern over Parliament's role has shifted to other aspects of Parliamentary procedure.

The Control of Delegated Powers[3]

Safeguards against the dangers inherent in delegated legislation are to be found in various forms. Some safeguards are provided by the process of consultation that takes place with affected parties before a Bill is introduced into Parliament.[4] Thus some of those who are to be affected by legislative powers

---

[1] London 1949.   [2] London 1952.

[3] For general surveys see Griffith and Street, *Principles of Administrative Law;* J. F. Garner, *Administrative Law*, London 1963; H. W. R. Wade, *Administrative Law*, London 1961; D. Foulks, *Introduction to Administrative Law*, London 1964; W. A. Robson, *The Governors and the Governed*, London 1964.

[4] J. F. Garner, 'Consultation in Subordinate Legislation', *PL* 1964, pp. 105–24.

that are to be delegated to the executive, are able to comment upon, and perhaps influence the contents of the parent statute. At the other end of the process, once the powers are in operation, judicial safeguards exist to ensure that any powers that have been delegated have not been exceeded, and the Courts can be used to question whether executive actions have a legal authority, based either on prerogative powers, or on legislative or delegated legislative authority. In the case of delegated powers, the Courts can check that executive actions have not exceeded the powers granted by the parent statute, and that the correct procedures of consultation and adequate publicity have been observed. Within this judicial control, however, a great limitation has always been that some delegated powers are so wide as to justify almost any action by the executive, as with the wartime emergency powers, and the clause that was contained in some legislation, giving the Minister the power to make any changes necessary to put the legislation into effect.

Thus Parliamentary scrutiny of the actual granting of delegated powers remains as the most important safeguard. The existing means of Parliamentary scrutiny are based primarily on the Statutory Instruments Act 1946 (replacing the Rules Publication Act 1893), which came partly as a result of the Report of the post-war Select Committee on Procedure.[1] The Act clarified and modified the existing methods of control rather than introduced new principles. The term 'Statutory Instrument' was used to describe the documents that grant delegated powers (replacing the multiplicity of Rules and Orders that had existed before), and the Select Committee that had been set up in 1944 to scrutinize the process of delegated legislation, was put on a permanent basis as the Statutory Instruments Committee. Today the methods of Parliamentary supervision rest partly on the activities of the Statutory Instruments Committee, and partly on the initiative of individual MPs, who are often prompted in this by pressure groups.[2]

[1] J. T. Craig, 'The Working of the Statutory Instruments Act 1946', *Pub. Admin.* 1961, pp. 181–92.

[2] J. E. Kersell, 'Parliamentary Ventilation of Grievances Arising out of Delegated Legislation', *PL* 1959, pp. 152–68; E. H. Beet, 'Parliament and Delegated Legislation', 1945–53; *Pub. Admin.* 1955, pp. 325–32; J. E. Kersell, *Parliamentary Supervision of Delegated Legislation*, London 1960.

All Statutory Instruments are published by HMSO and are placed on general sale to the public. They are formally presented to Parliament, with copies being sent to the Speaker of the Commons and the Lord Chancellor, and to all MPs who ask for them. The MP can then take action under the procedures allowed. There are three distinct procedures which can be used for the presentation of Statutory Instruments to Parliament, with the parent statute defining which procedure is to be used. One procedure is for the Statutory Instrument to come into effect merely after having been presented to both Houses of Parliament.[1] This procedure allows for little more than publicity for the Statutory Instrument, as neither House has the power to annul the Instrument, and no positive Parliamentary acceptance of the Instrument is necessary. It thus affords little chance of Parliamentary control, but generally it is used only for minor matters. The second procedure is for the Statutory Instrument to be laid before both Houses for a period of forty days (excluding vacations), in which time the Government has to take the initiative and find time for the approval of an affirmative resolution in both Houses. The third and most used procedure is for the Statutory Instrument to be laid before both Houses for a period of forty days, and the Instrument is operative until, or unless, it is annulled by a Prayer for Annulment in either House in this period. An Instrument can be annulled, but it cannot be amended. Thus with this procedure the Statutory Instrument automatically becomes operative unless there is a successful move to stop it, whereas by the second procedure the Instrument does not become operative unless the Government takes the initiative and secures its positive approval.

Prayers for Annulment can be taken on any day, and the Government has to find time for the consideration of Prayers. Although the Prayers are invariably defeated by the imposition of the Government Whip, the procedure provides a means of publicizing the Statutory Instrument. It also represents a means of harrying the Government, and in the period from 1950 to 1953, when firstly the Attlee Government and then the Churchill Government had small majorities in the Commons,

[1] J. E. Kersell, 'Upper Chamber Scrutiny of Delegated Legislation', *PL* 1959, pp. 46–60.

THE CENTRAL ADMINISTRATION

333

Prayers for Annulment were used extensively to force all-night sittings, as Prayers at that time were taken at the end of the day's business at 10.30 p.m. Since 1953, however, business has been interrupted at 7.30 p.m. in order to deal with Prayers, and as a result, there has been less use of Prayers as a means of obstruction. The Prayers tend to be initiated by the same MPs, perhaps suggesting that the majority are not greatly interested in this form of Parliamentary activity.

*　　*　　*

In addition to this form of scrutiny by individual MPs, supervision of delegated legislation is achieved through the Statutory Instruments Committee. The Committee consists of eleven members based on party composition in the Commons, with the Chairman coming from the Opposition. Its work is aided by the specialist knowledge of most of its members, gained in long service on the Committee. It has the task of examining all Statutory Instruments, and can bring a particular Instrument to the attention of the House on any of six counts—if it imposes a charge; if it cannot be challenged in the Courts; if it has a retrospective effect; if it involves an unjusti; fiable delay in its publication; if it contains obscurities in form- or if it makes 'unusual or unexpected use' of powers conferred by the parent statute. Of these six considerations, three (imposing a charge, excluding the Courts, or retrospective effect) are largely of academic value only, while two others (delay in publication, or obscurities in form) have been largely ignored, in that many of the verbal obscurities contained in Instruments, common in 1946, have now been removed. 'Unusual or unexpected use' of powers is the most frequent reason that is given for bringing an Instrument to Parliament's attention, no doubt largely because it can be controversial and open to comment on policy as well as administrative grounds, and because it is more likely to produce disagreements between the Committee, the Minister and department concerned.[1]

In general, however, the grounds for bringing an Instrument to Parliament's attention are very narrow, and only about 1% of those Instruments that are examined are referred to the

[1] S. A. Walkland, ' "Unusual or Unexpected Use" and the Select Committee on Statutory Instruments', *Parl. Aff.* 1959–60, pp. 61–9.

House. The total number of Instruments involved in any one session is so large that the Committee's examination is necessarily selective. The Committee is also hindered in that it has merely to approve an Instrument or refer it to the House, and it has no power of amendment, and no power to comment on the merits of the policy behind the Instrument. As well as drawing the attention of the House to specific Instruments, however, the Committee issues general reports which have done something to produce greater clarity in the form and language of Statutory Instruments and of legislation in general.

The Problem of Administrative Adjudication

Linked with the question of delegated legislation is that of administrative adjudication, whereby machinery is created, generally in the form of a tribunal, to determine cases of alleged misuse or non-use of executive powers. Disputes between an individual and the state sometimes can be settled by political action through an MP, by judicial action through the Courts, or (where the machinery exists) by action through a tribunal that has been specially created. This last practice has been defined as 'the statutory power of the Administration to decide issues arising between individuals and the Administration, or, occasionally, between two parts of the Administration itself',[1] and the main feature of the process is that the department itself, or more particularly, the machinery that it creates, is the judge of its own case in instances of alleged maladministration.[2] Very often the factors that make it desirable to delegate legislative authority from Parliament (the need for speed, and the technical nature of the issue) also make it necessary to create administrative adjudication machinery to consider aspects of the administration or maladministration of the matter concerned. Public concern over the question of administrative law has thus been closely linked with concern over delegated legislation, and between the wars the writings of Lord Hewart and W. A. Robson, and the enquiry by the Donoughmore Com-

[1] Griffith and Street, *Principles of Administrative Law*, p. 4.
[2] For general surveys, see C. J. Hamson, *Executive Discretion and Judicial Control*, London 1954; H. W. R. Wade, *Towards Administrative Justice*, Ann Arbor, 1963; H. J. Elcock, *Administrative Justice*, London 1969.

mittee, were concerned with administrative law as well as delegated legislation. Similarly, since 1945 the problem has been emphasized by the increase in governmental activity, with the consequent need for speedy means of assessing claims for social benefits, and for judging appeals for compensation in cases of compulsory purchase.[1]

One justification of the use of administrative tribunals as a means of redress is that without tribunals the Law Courts would be grossly overworked, but tribunals have advantages over the Courts for citizen and state alike. Tribunals, are cheap, speedy, less hidebound by formalized legal rules, accessible to the public, and are composed of experts in the matter to be dealt with. Also, any constitutional theory of the rigid separation of judicial and executive powers is irrelevant to the British system, in that there is nothing novel in the notion of the executive assuming judicial powers. Even without the tribunal system, the overlap between the executive and judiciary in Britain is quite considerable, in that judges are appointed on the advice of the Lord Chancellor and the Prime Minister, while the Lord Chancellor, the Attorney-General, and the other law officers are members of the Government as well as being judicial figures. It is also argued (rather idealistically) that ultimately the best control over Ministers, departments, and tribunals, is a political and Parliamentary one, and that within this general safeguard the departments can be trusted not to abuse the tribunal system.

The objections in principle to the system of administrative tribunals, however, are based partly on opposition to the increase in executive authority and the range of executive influence, and partly on the argument that no matter how fair the system may be, it *seems* to be unjust, in that it offends against the principle that no party should judge a case in which it is itself involved. Tribunals are thus objected to on the grounds that justice must not only be done, but must be seen to be done. Nevertheless, even when the need for administrative tribunals is accepted in principle, the practical operation of the existing system is often criticized as not fully achieving the three prin-

[1] See R. S. W. Pollard, *Administrative Tribunals at Work*, London 1950; G. W. Keeton, *Trial by Tribunal*, London 1952; Sir C. K. Allen, *Administrative Jurisdiction*, London 1956.

ciples of 'openness, fairness, and impartiality', which are seen as being essential to the satisfactory operation of the system. Proposals to introduce more uniformity and informality into the rules of operation of the various tribunals are often resisted, however, as being likely to destroy many of their basic advantages of speed, cheapness, and informality. Thus the difficulty is that of balancing administrative effectiveness with judicial fairness, it being impossible to achieve maximum effectiveness and maximum fairness at the same time.

*　　*　　*

Concern over the problem of administrative tribunals reached a head in the mid-nineteen-fifties, following the Crichel Down episode.[1] Crichel Down was an area of land in Dorset that had been requisitioned by the Air Ministry in 1940 as a bombing range. It was agreed when the land was acquired that the previous owner was to have the chance of taking over the land when the Air Ministry released it. After the war, however, when the Air Ministry no longer had use for the land, it was offered to various other departments, and the Ministry of Agriculture decided to take it over and develop it for agricultural purposes. The original owner claimed the land, but the Ministry of Agriculture ignored the original undertaking and would not relinquish its claim. The Minister of Agriculture, Sir Thomas Dugdale, eventually agreed to a public enquiry, and when the report of the enquiry was published in 1954,[2] the Minister resigned. The incident aroused much concern, because it was revealed by the report that there had been a lack of contact between the Minister and his department. It was not clear to what extent the Minister had been informed on the matter, and it was thus quoted as an example of the increased powers of the executive. It was only because of the eventual initiative of the Minister that an enquiry had been held, and the incident revealed the lack of safeguards that there were for the citizen against the administrative machine.

[1] See H. W. R. Wade, 'Are Public Inquiries a Farce?', *Pub. Admin.* 1955, pp. 389–94; R. M. Jackson, 'Tribunals and Inquiries', *Pub. Admin.* 1955, pp. 115–24; G. Marshall, 'The Courts, Ministers and the Parliamentary Process', *Pub. Admin.* 1956, pp. 51–60.

[2] Cmd. 9176 (1954).

As a result of the public concern, a committee was set up in 1955, under the chairmanship of Sir Oliver Franks, to look into the question of administrative adjudication. The Committee reported in 1957,[1] and most of its proposals were implemented in the Tribunals and Enquiries Act 1958. About 70% of the Committee's proposals were accepted in full by the Government, and most of the others were accepted in a modified form. It has thus been praised as a useful report that led to practical achievement, but its critics have argued that the main reason why its recommendations were so readily accepted was that they dealt only with details, and did not tackle the heart of the problem.[2]

It is debatable to what extent the existing system of tribunals (which is based partly on gradual developments over several years, and partly on machinery created by the 1958 Act) achieves a satisfactory balance between the two factors of administrative efficiency and judicial fairness. There are a multiplicity of tribunals, most of them products of social welfare and state planning legislation. The Franks Committee classified the various tribunals into five main groups according to the matters they dealt with—land and property tribunals (like local Valuation Courts and Agricultural Land Tribunals), social service tribunals (National Insurance Tribunals and Industrial Injury Tribunals), health service tribunals (Medical Practices Committees), transport tribunals (Licensing Authorities for Public Service Vehicles), and various miscellaneous bodies, including the Independent Schools Tribunal. Some degree of uniformity of structure and procedure for these various tribunals resulted from the findings of the Franks Committee. The Chairmen of Tribunals are appointed by the Lord Chancellor, though the other members are appointed by the department concerned.[3] Appeals on points of law are allowed to the Court of Appeal. Most significantly of all, perhaps, the 1958 Act created a Council on Tribunals to supervise the working of the

[1] Cmd. 218 (1957).

[2] See W. A. Robson, 'Administrative Justice and Injustice: A Commentary on the Franks Report', *PL* 1958, pp. 12–31; G. Marshall, 'The Franks Report on Administrative Tribunals and Enquiries', *Pub. Admin.* 1957, pp. 347–58.

[3] S. McCorquodale, 'The Composition of Administrative Tribunals', *PL* 1962, pp. 298–326.

whole system, and to advise the tribunals regarding rules of procedure and appointments. The Council, which consists of ten to fifteen members, with a special Scottish Committee of four members, is concerned, however, with the procedure of the tribunals, rather than with the substance of the issues they handle, and the scope of the Council's activities has been criticized as being too narrow.[1] Nevertheless, it generally deals with fifty to a hundred complaints each year.

Considerable secrecy still surrounds the activities of the tribunals, and great variations still exist between the procedures of the different tribunals. Some tribunals allow legal representation at the hearings, keep detailed records of the proceedings, and allow appeals against their decisions. Others have a less formalized procedure. The Rent Tribunal, for example, which determines fair rents for some properties, is appointed by the departmental Minister concerned (the Minister of Housing and Local Government), and it keeps no records. In contrast, the Lands Tribunal (which deals with disputes over the valuation of property) is appointed by the Lord Chancellor, rather than the departmental Minister, and has a legally qualified chairman. It sits in public, travels in circuit around the country, and gives a written decision explaining the reasons for the decision.

The Parliamentary Commissioner

Continued dissatisfaction with the existing structure of the tribunals system has produced various proposals for a wholesale reorganization.[2] A proposal for an amalgamation of the existing multiplicity of tribunals into three broad groups, was rejected by the Franks Committee because of the lack of any marked overlapping of functions between the tribunals. The Committee also rejected proposals for the creation of a single tribunal in

[1] See H. W. R. Wade, 'The Council on Tribunals', *PL* 1960, pp. 351–66; J. A. G. Griffith, 'The Council and the Chalkpit', *Pub. Admin.* 1961, pp. 369–74; J. F. Garner, 'The Council on Tribunals', *PL* 1965, pp. 321–47; S. A. de Smith, 'The Council on Tribunals', *Parl. Aff.* 1958–9, pp. 320–8.

[2] See, for example, Sir John Whyatt, *The Citizen and the Administration*, London 1962. See also G. Marshall, 'Tribunals and Enquiries: Developments Since the Franks Report', *Pub. Admin.* 1958, pp. 261–70; K. C. Wheare, 'The Redress of Grievances', *Pub. Admin.* 1962, pp. 125–8.

each region to deal with all complaints in that region. It was claimed that such a body would lack specialist knowledge of the many matters with which it would have to deal. For a similar reason the Franks Committee rejected a proposal for an overall Administrative Appeals Tribunal to hear appeals from all tribunals on questions of fact or law. Other proposals that have been made are that there should be set up Inspectors of Tribunals, and that legal aid should be available for hearings before tribunals.

Most drastically of all, it has been suggested that there should be created a distinct Administrative Law Division within the legal system. In France, the structure of the Courts is divided into three branches, Criminal, Civil, and Administrative. Within the Administrative Law Branch, a Council of State supervises the various specialist courts for military, financial, or social service administration, and also supervises prefectorial councils in each of a number of regions.[1] In Germany the courts structure is divided into six distinct branches for Civil Law, Criminal Law, Administrative Law, social security questions, labour relations, and financial questions. Each of the six branches has its own Appeals Court.[2] In the USA the Supreme Court has functions of general supervision over the executive, including administrative law questions. Any attempt to model any of these structures would clearly involve a fundamental reorganization of the administrative law system, and of the whole legal structure in Britain, and these proposals have been resisted because of the difficulties involved in transplanting foreign institutions.

One change that has been made, based on foreign example, has been the introduction of an Ombudsman, or Parliamentary Commissioner for Administration, to examine complaints of maladministration. Such an official has existed in Sweden since 1915, and also exists in Finland, Norway, Denmark, and New Zealand. A Parliamentary Commissioner was created in Britain in 1967 after more than a decade of arguments as to the desirability of such a creation, and Sir Edmund Compton, formerly

---

[1] See C. E. Freedeman, *The Conseil D'Etat in Modern France*, New York, 1961.

[2] See A. J. Heidenheimer, *The Governments of Germany*, New York 1966, Ch. 7.

C and AG, became the first holder of the office.[1] One of the arguments used to support the creation was that the existing tribunals system was an inadequate means of dealing with public grievances, and that there were many complaints that were not covered by the tribunals system. At the same time, redress through Parliament was becoming increasingly difficult as government activities continued to expand, and thus it was claimed that there was a need for some supplementary means of dealing with grievances. It was argued that the Ombudsman worked satisfactorily in Scandinavia and New Zealand, and that a similar official could usefully be introduced in Britain.

The proposal met with considerable opposition, however, particularly among MPs who felt that it would lead to a diminution of their authority. It was argued that what worked well in a country like Sweden, with only seven million population, would not necessarily work in Britain with a population of fifty-five million, and that much of the Parliamentary Commissioner's activities would be inevitably superficial. The form in which the Parliamentary Commissioner finally appeared in 1967 also aroused much criticism.[2] He is an officer of Parliament and can only act on complaints he receives through an MP. He has no executive authority of his own, and can only enquire into, and report to Parliament, on any complaint that is referred to him, while Ministers retain the right to veto the disclosure of any official document. The Commissioner's activities do not extend to local government or the nationalized industries, but are confined to the departments of state. In 1969, however, his area of enquiry was extended to include Northern Ireland. He has a staff of some fifty investigators, and there is a Select Committee of the House of Commons which is in much the same relationship to him as is the PAC to the C and AG. The departments of state which give rise to most complaints are, perhaps

[1] See D. C. Rowat, *The Ombudsman*, London 1965; G. Sawer, *Ombudsmen*, London 1964; T. E. Utley, *Occasion for Ombudsman*, London 1961; B. Chapman, 'The Ombudsman', *Pub. Admin.* 1960, pp. 303–10; L. J. Blom-Cooper, 'An Ombudsman in Britain', *PL* 1960, pp. 145–51; J. D. B. Mitchell, 'The Ombudsman Fallacy', *PL* 1962, pp. 24–33; S. A. de Smith, 'Anglo-Saxon Ombudsman?', *PQ* 1962, pp. 9–19.

[2] For more details see the *Parliamentary Commissioner for Administration*, Cmnd. 2767 (1965).

inevitably, the Inland Revenue and the Ministry of Social Security.

Thus while the creation of the Parliamentary Commissioner was welcomed in many quarters, the limitations of the powers that were given to him caused much disappointment, as leaving untouched many of the general criticisms of the existing machinery dealing with questions of alleged maladministration. As with so many aspects of the reform of the governmental process in Britain, reform proposals were diluted almost beyond recognition, not so much as a result of the conservatism of the Government, but because of the conservatism of Parliament.

12

The Public Corporations

THE STATE ownership of industry has long been a major point of dispute between the Labour and Conservative Parties, and this factor alone makes the issue an important one in British politics. In addition to the party political considerations, however, the question of the nationalized industries is significant in the context of this section of the book because of the particular relationship between Parliament, Ministers, and the public corporations that run the bulk of the nationalized industries, and also because of the important place of the nationalized industries in the general sphere of Government control of the economy.

State Intervention in Industry

Over the last century and a half there has been in Britain a gradual increase in state intervention in industry. In the early nineteenth century the functions of government were seen as being little more than to maintain internal order, guard against external attack and regulate currency, while in the economic sphere it was assumed that maximum prosperity would be best achieved by the free play of market forces—a principle epitomized by the nineteenth-century free-trade movement. This principle was discredited to some extent during the nineteenth century, however, by many of the social consequences of the industrial revolution. It came to be accepted that state activity in the form of Factory Acts, Mines Acts, and Public Health Acts, was necessary in order to counter some of the worst effects of industrialization, while it was also recognized that state intervention in industry was necessary at times for the good of industry itself, as for example through trade union legislation to

342

achieve a balance of power between employer and employee, so that 'healthy competition' could develop between these opposing forces.

State intervention in the economic life of the nation increased during the two world wars, and was further boosted by the growing acceptance of the Keynesian concept of general economic planning, and then by the early post-war attempts to achieve planned economic progress. In more recent years, there has been a further upsurge of confidence in the principle of national economic planning, and while there is still a tendency to regard *laissez faire* as 'normal', and state intervention as exceptional, there has long been a growing acceptance of the principle that the free market mechanism alone cannot satisfy the desired ends of full employment, economic equality, and steady national economic growth. Precisely how much state intervention is desirable, and how much freedom from control should be allowed to industry, remain, however, highly controversial economic and political issues.

State intervention in industry today can take various forms.[1] In some directions the state intervenes in the free market system, as it did in the nineteenth century, not so much in an attempt to replace the system by some other, but rather to aid and improve the system so that it can work more effectively. Thus the Government provides statistical information on which industry can base its future plans, it provides Employment Exchanges to help the redeployment of labour, it creates arbitration machinery to help settle industrial disputes. The Government also intervenes to protect one party in the free market process against another. Protection for workers through Factory Acts, and more recently through Wages Councils, protection for shareholders through Company Acts, protection for consumers through anti-monopoly legislation, all represent aspects of state activity that are designed to reform and improve the system of free competition between economic forces.

A rather different form of state activity is represented by attempts to establish an overall economic plan for industry,

[1] See J. W. Grove, *Government and Industry in Britain*, London 1962; P. S. Florence, *Industry and the State*, London 1957; Sir R. Streat, 'Government Consultation with Industry', *Pub. Admin.* 1959, pp. 1–8; M. Stewart, 'Planning and Persuasion in a Mixed Economy', *PQ* 1964, pp. 148–60.

where it is felt that the free play of market forces will not fully satisfy national needs (as opposed to purely private needs). This form of state activity is exemplified by Government attempts to encourage production in certain industries in order to stimulate exports and curb imports, and thereby achieve a favourable balance of trade for the nation. Overall economic planning by the Government can be implemented by fiscal controls and incentives, as with financial burdens on industry through profits tax or purchase tax, or by financial aid to industry as with grants, tax concessions, and protective tariffs. Alternatively, direct physical controls can be used, perhaps by placing statutory limits on incomes, prices, production, or investment. These different methods of seeking to control industry have all been used with varying degrees of success by British Governments since 1945.[1]

Most directly of all, however, state intervention in industry can take the form of direct industrial participation by the state, either by the acquisition of private industries, or by the creation of new state enterprises where previously there was no activity. Thus rather than attempting to modify and improve the private enterprise sector of the economy, private enterprise is replaced by public enterprise. This can involve state ownership of the whole of the economy in a full Socialist system, or, as in Britain, it can involve state ownership of only sections of industry in a mixed economy. The justification of this form of state activity, the details of how it can be achieved, and the problems that it involves, are considered in the rest of this chapter.[2]

The Public Enterprise Debate

The arguments advanced over the years to justify the public ownership of industry in Britain have been based partly on ideo-

---

[1] See above, p. 301.

[2] See W. A. Robson, *Nationalized Industry and Public Ownership*, London 1962; A. H. Hanson, *Nationalization: a Book of Readings*, London 1963; K. Katzarov, *The Theory of Nationalization*, The Hague 1965; R. Kelf-Cohen, *Twenty Years of Nationalization*, London 1969; M. Shanks, *The Lessons of Public Enterprise*, London 1963; G. L. Reid and K. Allen, *Nationalized Industries*, London 1970; W. Thornhill, *The Nationalized Industries*, London 1968.

logical principles, and partly on pragmatic considerations.[1] Socialists have long advocated public ownership as a means of achieving basic Socialist ideals, and have seen public ownership as a means towards a fairer distribution of wealth throughout the community, by eradicating unearned private income from profits and dividends. Public ownership can also achieve production for use rather than for profit, thereby making the best use of available resources, while it can be argued that it is in the public interest that the essential industries (or 'the commanding heights of the economy') should be publicly owned, with this being particularly true for public utilities such as water, gas, and electricity. As well as these largely Socialist arguments, other arguments of principle can be advanced in support of public ownership, and it can be argued that where a monopoly situation exists, it is best controlled by the state, in that a public monopoly is ultimately answerable to democratic controls through the political process. Large-scale organizations have certain advantages, such as large-scale planning, rationalization, and economies of size, which can apply equally well to large publicly owned organizations as to large private enterprise organizations such as ICI, Unilever, or Shell. Also, in some situations only the state is in a position to act, perhaps because of the size and scope of the concern, or because vast capital sums are required for development, without there being any immediately apparent commercial returns. Similarly, the state may have to take over and run at a financial loss some essential sector of industry where private enterprise can no longer produce profits. Public ownership of large sections of industry can also be a vital means of influencing national economic policy, while public ownership of a highly profitable concern can be used as a means of securing public revenue, in the way that some municipal enterprises are used to supplement local authority income. Although this last argument is not one that has been widely used to justify public ownership in Britain in recent years, it nevertheless remains a very valid consideration.

These various arguments, of course, are not universally accep-

[1] For pre-1945 works on public ownership see H. Morrison, *Socialization and Transport*, London 1933; P. Snowden, *If Labour Rules*, London 1923; W. A. Robson, *Public Enterprise*, 1937; T. E. O'Brien, *British Experiments in Public Ownership and Control*, London 1937.

ted, and the opponents of public ownership claim that there are a number of illogicalities in Socialist thinking and practice, and that many of the supposed advantages of public ownership apply only when the whole of industry is publicly owned. The champions of private enterprise claim that supply and demand, and the free play of market forces, form a better basis for economic progress than state control through public ownership, and that Socialist condemnation of the basic principles of private enterprise is inconsistent with the acceptance of the mixed economy. They further claim that public bodies are not fitted to run commercial concerns, and (as is discussed below[1]) that the economic performance of the nationalized industries in Britain demonstrates this. Although these theoretical and doctrinal arguments form the background to the public enterprise debate, in practice such public ownership of industry as exists in Britain today was introduced in the main for practical reasons that bore only an incidental relationship to ideological principles. In 1908 the Liberal Government created the Port of London Authority in order to establish unified public control over the vast complex of London docks. In 1926 the Conservative Government established the Central Electricity Generating Board to bring standardization and overall national control to electricity generation. Also in 1926, the British Broadcasting Corporation was set up as a public body (though free from direct Ministerial control) because of the fundamental importance of broadcasting as a means of communication. In 1933 the National Government set up the London Passenger Transport Board to achieve the integration of road and rail passenger transport within the London area. In 1939 the Chamberlain Government established the British Overseas Airways Corporation as a publicly owned body, partly because of the importance of the airlines for international prestige, and partly because of the vast subsidies that were required for the effective development of the airlines.

Thus before 1945 there was already established by non-Socialist Governments some tradition of public ownership based on pragmatic motives, and in the extension of public ownership that was undertaken by the 1945–51 Labour Governments, largely pragmatic arguments were used to justify the various

[1] See p. 367.

measures.[1] The nationalization of the Bank of England in 1946 was accepted with little dissent because it was generally recognized that the Bank had a special place in the finances of the nation, and because there had long been a close link between the Bank and the Treasury. The Coal Nationalization Act embodied the oldest of the Labour Movement's public ownership proposals, but in fact the main justifications for the Act in 1946 lay in the findings of the Technical Advisory Committee on Coal Mining (the Reid Committee) which reported in 1945.[2] The Committee claimed that the British mines were in need of large-scale modernization, and public ownership was widely seen as the best practical means of implementing the Committee's recommendations. Also in 1946, the Civil Aviation Act created British European Airways and British South American Airways (later merged with BOAC) as public corporations, for much the same reasons as the creation of BOAC in 1939. In the case of road and rail transport, the Report of the Royal Commission on Transport in 1930[3] had advocated the modernization (though not the nationalization) of the railways in order to allow them to meet road competition. The Commission had argued for the co-ordination of road and rail transport, and in 1947 there was already a big overlap in the ownership of private enterprise road and rail concerns. After the war, there was a big need for capital investment in the railways, and public ownership was seen by the Labour Government as an essential part of transport reconstruction and integration, although the inclusion of road transport in the public ownership proposals led to strong opposition from the industry and from the Conservative Party.

The public utilities of gas and electricity were brought under full public ownership in 1947 and 1948. The Central Electricity Generating Board had been created in 1926 to standardize electricity generation, and in 1936 the McGowan Committee[4] reported on the need for changes in the organization of electricity (about two-thirds of which was municipally owned). The McGowan Committee had favoured privately owned regional

---

[1] See A. A. Rogow, *The Labour Government and British Industry*, London 1955.
[2] Cmd. 6610 (1945).   [3] Cmd. 3751 (1930).
[4] Report of the Committee on Electricity Distribution.

organizations to work with the local authorities, but in 1947 electricity distribution was brought under national control, because, it was argued, national control of electricity generation, and the operation of the grid system, logically called for national control of distribution, and because national control was the best means of achieving a big capital expansion in the electricity industry. In the case of the gas industry (about one-third of which was municipally owned), the Heyworth Committee[1] of enquiry in 1945 found that the industry was reasonably efficient, but was in need of much larger units to make the best use of its resources, and the Government used the report to justify complete public ownership of the industry.

In the case of iron and steel, however, the background to the Government's proposals was very different in numerous respects from the background to the earlier public ownership measures.[2] No impartial technical committee had enquired into the industry, and although the industry had been in difficulty during the depression years, various factors, including the creation of the Iron and Steel Federation as a control body within the industry, had served to re-establish the industry's profitability. Private enterprise was prepared to make a test case out of the steel industry in order to fight the principle of public ownership, and the industry's resistance was strengthened by the fact that by 1948 a general election was drawing near, and the Conservative Party had pledged itself to return the industry to private ownership if it came to power.[3]

Despite opposition in and out of Parliament, the Labour Government proceeded with the Iron and Steel Bill, claiming that the industry should be publicly owned because it was basic to the economy, and because it was one in which cartels and restrictive practices were rife. The Bill duly became law, and was brought into operation after the 1950 general election, but after the Conservatives' victory at the 1951 general election the bulk of the iron and steel industry was returned to private hands. Thus the controversy over the desirability of public ownership of iron and steel continued, and to a considerable extent the

[1] Report of the Committee of Inquiry into the Gas Industry, Cmd. 6699 (1945).

[2] See G. W. Ross, *The Nationalization of Steel*, London 1965.

[3] See above, p. 271.

whole public ownership debate in the nineteen-fifties centred on
the steel industry issue. With the return of a Labour Government to power in 1964, fresh public ownership proposals were
introduced, and in 1967 the 13 major steel firms were brought
under public ownership, these 13 firms accounting for 70% of
the industry's manpower, and 90% of the basic steel production
in Britain.

Despite the long controversy over iron and steel, and despite
the bitter party feelings that it aroused, the Conservative Party
was clearly not altogether opposed to the *principle* of public
ownership, in that Conservative Governments before 1945
established public corporations, and in 1954 the Conservative
Government created the Atomic Energy Authority to control
the development of the peaceful uses of atomic energy.[1] It is
interesting to speculate whether a Conservative Government,
had it been elected in 1945, would also have adopted a similar
public ownership policy towards the Bank of England, the
mines, the railways, air transport, electricity and gas, and
whether, as a result, public ownership would still be associated
today with bitter party political strife.[2]

Forms of Public Enterprise

Public enterprise can take many forms, and various media
can be used to administer publicly owned or publicly controlled
concerns. Municipal control of commercial concerns was widely
advocated by the early Socialists, and even in the nineteenth
century 'Gas and Water Socialism' envisaged local authorities
as the best means of controlling public utilities. Before 1939
more than two-thirds of electricity distribution, and about one-
third of the gas industry was under municipal control, and today
water supplies remain under local control. A high proportion
of municipal authorities provide their own passenger transport
services, and some local authorities have experimented with
civic restaurants, but on the whole, local authority enterprise

[1] See R. Darcy Best, 'The United Kingdom Atomic Energy Authority',
Pub. Admin. 1956, pp. 1–16.

[2] See D. Abel, 'British Conservatives and State Ownership', *J of P* 1957,
pp. 227–39.

would seem to be on the decline. The extension of nationalization has to some extent been at the expense of municipal undertakings, and within the party politics of local government,
private enterprise interests have been quick to condemn local
authority enterprise as 'gambling with the rates'. There are,
however, many instances of joint trading by groups of local authorities, and joint ownership of airports and joint water boards
provide examples. Joint water undertakings have increased in
number in recent years, with the growth of problems over water
supplies, although plans are at present afoot for the nationalization of water distribution. With the growth in popularity of
regional planning, it is conceivable that regional trading concerns could be developed between the national and local levels.
This, however, must await the establishment of an effective
system of regional government, or a thorough reform of the
local government system on the lines of the Maud and Wheatley
Commissions.[1]

For the administration of nationalized concerns, the chief
media used in the past have been departments of state, under a
Minister's direct control, or else public corporations, which provide a degree of independence from direct Ministerial control.
In general, administrative control by a department of state
means that the Minister is directly responsible for all aspects of
policy and administration, and that the employees of the concern are civil servants (industrial or non-industrial as the case
may be). It also generally means that the Treasury has direct
control over the finances of the concern, all income and expenditure being paid into and out of the Exchequer. The State
Management Schemes for the control of the licensed trade in
parts of Cumberland and parts of Scotland are run directly by
the Home Office and the Scottish Office.[2] Until 1969 the Post
Office was run by a department of state, although between
1956 and 1969 a series of steps were taken towards greater
financial and administrative autonomy, culminating in the
creation in 1969 of a public corporation to run the Post Office.[3]

[1] See below, p. 400.
[2] See R. M. Punnett, 'State Management of the Liquor Trade', *Pub.
Admin.* 1966, pp. 193–212.
[3] See R. Nottage, 'The Post Office: A Pioneer of Big Business', *Pub.
Admin.* 1959, pp. 55–64; 'New Status of the Post Office', *Pub. Admin.* 1962,
pp. 94–6.

Until 1956 all Post Office financial surpluses were paid into the Exchequer, and thus represented a form of national revenue. In 1956 a requirement was introduced whereby the Post Office paid £5,000,000 per year to the Treasury, but retained any additional surplus for its own uses. A system of completely self-contained Post Office finances was introduced by the Post Office Act 1961, which created a Post Office Fund, into which all income was to be paid, and from which all expenditure was to be drawn. The Post Office was thus freed from the obligation to pay its annual surpluses to the Exchequer, but it was required to pay off its £800,000,000 capital debt to the Treasury over the subsequent twenty-five years. As a result of the 1961 Act, the Post Office gained a self-contained financial structure. Administrative control of the Post Office, however, remained directly with the Postmaster-General, while Post Office employees remained civil servants and were thus still subject to the Treasury's control of Civil Service personnel. In 1966, however, it was announced that Post Office freedom from Ministerial control was to be taken a stage further by the creation of a public corporation to administer the Post Office,[1] and this was achieved through the Post Office Act 1969.

A public corporation is characterized by the fact that it is run by an administrative Board rather than directly by the Minister, with the Minister being responsible to Parliament for overall policy, but not for day-to-day administration. The employees of a public corporation are not civil servants, and thus can be recruited on terms of employment determined by the corporation itself. A public corporation also has a self-contained financial structure, in that annual surpluses are used for the corporation's own purposes, and are not transferred to the Exchequer as national revenue. There are also some public bodies, like the Arts Council and the British Council, whose administrative and financial arrangements lie midway between those of a department of state and a public corporation. These bodies are not staffed by civil servants, and Ministerial control over their affairs extends only to general control of policy, but unlike public corporations, they are not self-financing and are financed entirely, or almost entirely, from the Exchequer.

The theory behind the public corporation concept is that

[1] Re-organization of the Post Office, Cmnd. 3233 (1967).

this form of structure combines the commercial freedom that is enjoyed by a private concern, with the public account- ability that is desired for a publicly owned concern—the basic assumption being that commercial freedom is restricted by an excessive degree of detailed Ministerial control. The question of precisely where the line is to be drawn between Ministerial control of policy, but not of administration, is, however, a matter of some controversy, and this and some of the other problems involved in the public corporation form of structure are considered later in this chapter.

There are other forms of public enterprise which provide even more commercial freedom, and less Ministerial control, than is the case with the public corporation. Government purchase of shares in private concerns can achieve public control, or even full public ownership, without altering the basic administrative structure by which the concern is operated, and thus without destroying the private enterprise facade of the concern. Share purchase as a method of public enterprise can involve the pur- chase of all the shares by the Government, and can extend to the appointment of all the directors, as with Cable and Wire- less Ltd. To this end a holding company can be created to manage the Government's interests, as is the case with Thomas Cook and Son, and Dean and Dawson. Alternatively, state holdings can take the form of only part ownership, with Govern- ment control of a concern being secured by the ownership of 51% of the stock. The Suez Finance Co., in which the Gov- ernment secured a controlling interest during the nineteenth century, is a long-established example of this type of mixed enterprise. Over the years, the state has acquired interests in various assorted concerns, and in general, such Government share purchase has been motivated by a desire to protect essential British interest, or to save an industry from financial difficulties. Largely for these reasons in 1965 the Plowden Committee, reporting on the British aircraft industry,[1] advocated Govern- ment acquisition of a controlling interest in the British Aircraft Corporation and Hawker Siddeley.

Share purchases enable the Government to partake of the profits of a concern in a way that is not always the case with other forms of public enterprise, and also enable the state to

[1] Report of the Committee on the Aircraft Industry, Cmnd. 2853 (1965).

influence policy without having sole and direct responsibility (although the Government may not choose to use its power in this direction). The major public utilities in Britain have now been brought under full public control through public corporations, but it can be argued that public corporations and departments of state are less suitable as a means of exerting control over the more directly commercial industries. Share purchase is advocated as a much simpler and more subtle form of public control than full-scale nationalization through a public corporation, and because of this, it has proved attractive to a large section of the Labour Party, where there has been some disillusionment with the public corporation, and where there has been some concern over the seeming rigidity of the party's attitude towards public enterprise.[1] Also, share purchase is less likely to arouse political opposition, in that in the public mind anti-nationalization propaganda is not generally associated with this form of public enterprise. Similarly, international commercial prejudice, which may operate against an openly nationalized concern, is less likely to operate against a concern in which the state merely owns shares. For these reasons, the Labour Party has attempted in recent years to indicate that there are many ways of furthering public enterprise, and that share purchase can be recognized as well as full-scale public ownership through a public corporation or department of state.

This view, however, is not universally accepted within the Labour Party, and many members of the party argue that a Labour Government should seek to destroy as much as possible of the capitalist, competitive, private profit-seeking element of the economy, and that share purchase does not achieve this. They point out that share purchase merely links the state with the sins of private enterprise, and that because of this the Government is in fact strengthening rather than undermining the capitalist system. They also claim that there is no adequate Parliamentary supervision of industries in which the Government acquires shares, and that even with acceptance of the

[1] See in particular Hugh Gaitskell, *Socialism and Nationalization* (Fabian Tract 300), London 1956. See also J. Dugdale, 'The Labour Party and Nationalization', *PQ* 1957, pp. 254–9; H. E. Weiner, *British Labour and Public Ownership*, London 1960; E. Eldon Barry, *Nationalization in British Politics*, London 1966.

mixed economy, there is still room for more direct public ownership of whole firms and industries. At the same time, share purchase by the state is condemned by private enterprise as representing a subversive and hidden form of Government interference in the private sector, giving the Government power without responsibility.

*   *   *

From this survey of the principles involved in public enterprise, and the theories behind the various forms of public control and public ownership, it can be seen that many of the general assumptions that are often made about public enterprise are not necessarily valid. In the first place, public ownership is not exclusively a Socialist doctrine, in that Labour, Conservative, Liberal, and Coalition Governments have all been responsible for extending public ownership in Britain, while the nationalization measures of the Labour Governments were introduced for pragmatic as much as doctrinal reasons. Secondly, public enterprise can be furthered by means other than by full-scale nationalization, in that municipal or regional enterprises represent alternatives to nationalization, while share purchase represents a means of achieving public control of private industry that does not involve direct management through a public corporation or department of state. Also, full public ownership of a firm or an industry is not essential in order to achieve public control, and ownership of part of a firm or part of an industry, through mixed enterprise, can be enough to give the state a large or overwhelming measure of control. Finally, public enterprise is not necessarily to be equated with unprofitability (despite the financial problems of many of the concerns nationalized by the 1945 Labour Government), in that there is a strong case to be made out for the public ownership of highly profitable concerns as a form of public investment.

Problems of the Public Corporations: I. Administrative Structure[1]

The administrative boards of the public corporations generally have ten or so members, appointed by the Minister. They are

[1] See Acton Society Trust, *Nationalized Industry* (parts 1 to 12), London 1950–2.

drawn from industry or from the public service, and in the main they are recruited for their general business qualifications. They are not recruited as direct representatives of interests, so that the Socialist principle of workers' control, widely canvassed between the wars, does not form the basis of Board membership.[1] It has often proved difficult to recruit suitable members for the Boards, to some extent because many of the industries involved, particularly the mines and the railways, have unattractive images, but also because the salaries and terms of appointment have been considerably less attractive than those applying in private industry. In face of these limitations, the role of the chairmen of the Boards is especially vital, with the relationship between the Chairman of the Board and the Minister being in many ways the key to the question of the degree of commercial freedom that is allowed to the Corporation.

In most nationalized industries, and particularly with those nationalized since 1945, it was assumed in the creation of their administrative structures that most of the advantages claimed for public ownership could be achieved only through a high degree of centralized national control. Centralized control was seen as essential for large-scale planning and nationalization, and for the elimination of the wastage involved in unnecessary duplication and competition. At the same time, such a structure was seen as creating a number of top management posts which would attract the best available talent. Co-ordination and co-operation between industries was regarded as being best achieved through concentrated authority within each industry, and the involvement of the nationalized industries in national economic planning was thought to be possible only through a high degree of centralization within each industry. Centralized Ministerial control was also seen as the best means of achieving public accountability through the Minister and Parliament.

This concept of large centralized concerns had many critics, however,[2] and it was argued that centralization led to remote and bureaucratic control; that centralization involved too much

---

[1] See, however, R. D. V. Roberts and H. Sallis, 'Joint Consultation in the Electricity Supply Industry 1949–59', *Pub. Admin.* 1959, pp. 115–34; C. G. Richards and H. Sallis, 'The Joint Consultative Committee and the Working Group', *Pub. Admin.* 1961, pp. 361–8.

[2] See, for example, H. A. Clegg and T. E. Chester, *The Future of Nationalization*, London 1955.

middle management; and that at the top of a centralized structure there was inevitably much duplication of functions between
the Boards and the departments of state. It was also argued that
'supermen' would be needed to administer concerns as big as
the original nationalized transport undertaking. In more recent
years, many of the advantages claimed for regional government
have been used to support the case for regional administrative
structures for the public corporations.

Thus a strong case was made out for the introduction of
federal structures to replace the centralized unitary structures
that were originally created for most of the nationalized industries. The strength of these decentralization arguments appealed
particularly to the 1951–64 Conservative Governments, and in
this period there was in some nationalized industries a movement away from rigid centralization. In the case of transport,
the 1947 Act gave centralized control over the nationalized
transport undertakings to the British Transport Commission,
with the object of creating an integrated road, rail, and waterways transport system. Such decentralization as did exist was
functional, in that the management of the BTC's responsibilities
lay with six Executives (for Hotels, Railways, Road Haulage,
Docks and Inland Waterways, Road Passenger Transport, and
London Transport). In 1953, a reduction was made in the
overall responsibilities of the BTC by the denationalization of
the bulk of road transport, and this was followed in 1955 by a
decentralization of railway organization through the introduction of six Area Boards. In 1960 a White Paper on Transport
Reorganization was published,[1] and was implemented by the
Transport Act 1962.[2] The BTC was abolished, and its responsibilities were shared among a British Railway Board, a London
Transport Board, and smaller undertakings for Docks and
Waterways. Thus there has been a gradual movement away
from a centralized and integrated transport system, and this
will make difficult any future attempts to achieve a fully inte-

[1] Reorganization of Nationalised Transport Undertakings, Cmnd. 1248
(1960).
[2] See J. R. Sargent, *British Transport Policy*, London 1958; C. D. Foster,
The Transport Problem, London 1963; K. M. Gwilliam, *Transport and Public
Policy*, London 1964; A. J. Pearson, *The Railways and the Nation*, London
1964; 'Reorganization of Nationalized Transport', *Pub. Admin.* 1962,
pp. 436–40.

grated national system. An alternative form of decentralized control, however, would be through geographical rather than functional decentralization, with Area Transport Boards responsible for all road, rail, and waterway transport services in their area, on the same principle as London Transport.

The structure of the electricity industry also underwent a process of decentralization during the nineteen-fifties. The Electricity Act 1947 set up the Central Electricity Authority with control over electricity generation, and twelve Area Boards with control over distribution. In 1956, the Herbert Committee of enquiry into the electricity industry reported in favour of greater decentralization,[1] and this led to a revision of the industry's structure in 1957.[2] The Central Electricity Authority was abolished, and was replaced by a central Generating Board to control electricity generation, and by an Electricity Council, made up some of the members of the Generating Board and the chairmen of the twelve Area Boards, to supervise the whole industry. The Area Boards retained control over distribution, and in addition were made financially independent from the central body. The administrative structure designed for the gas industry was the most decentralized of all the post-1945 creations, but it remains to be seen whether greater control will be needed to allow for the full development of the potential of the North Sea natural gas deposits, which have recently provided a boost for the industry.

Not all of the public corporations have shown a tendency towards greater regional autonomy, however. The structure of the NCB was based in 1946 on eight coal-producing Divisions, with these eight Divisions being sub-divided into fifty or so Areas, and these into sub-Areas. There was some criticism that this was an overcentralized structure, and numerous proposals were made for an increase in local autonomy. In 1955, however, the Fleck Committee of enquiry into the coal industry reported that in fact NCB structure was, if anything, too decentralized,[3] and the committee's findings led to an increase in central

[1] Report of the Committee of Inquiry into the Electricity Supply Industry, Cmd. 8672 (1956).
[2] See A. H. Hanson, 'Electricity Reviewed: the Herbert Report', *Pub. Admin.* 1956, pp. 211–14.
[3] NCB: Report of the Advisory Committee on Organization, 1955.

control over the local areas.[1] Similarly in the case of the air corporations, structure has become more unified over the years, as BOAC absorbed Imperial Airways and British Airways in 1940, and British South American Airways in 1949.[2] Thus the degree of centralization within the administrative structures of the nationalized industries varies considerably from one industry to another, and in most industries has varied to some extent over the years with no clear and universal pattern emerging. In many ways this typifies one of the fundamental limitations of the public corporations, in that in this, as in so many other respects, there has been a lack of guidance and long-term overall planning by successive Governments in their dealings with the nationalized industries.

II. Ministerial Control

The Ministers chiefly involved with the affairs of the nationalized industries are the Ministers of Transport, Technology, and Posts and Telecommunications. The creation of a special post of Minister for the Nationalized Industries has been advocated from time to time, but no such post has yet been created (although the Minister of Technology is responsible now for most of the state-owned industries). As part of his Overlords scheme in 1951, Churchill experimented with a Minister for the Co-ordination of Transport, Fuel and Power, but with little success.[3] In the case of the public corporations created before 1945, there was a tenuous level of Ministerial control. The Corporations were in the main financially self-supporting, and this was reflected in their degree of administrative independence, but in general the post-1945 Acts gave greater statutory powers to the Ministers than did the pre-1945 legislation. The statutory powers given to the Minister are generally the power to appoint and dismiss the members of the Board, the power to give general directives on policy matters, particularly on mat-

[1] See H. A. Clegg, 'The Fleck Report', *Pub. Admin.* 1955, pp. 269–76; C. A. Roberts, 'The NCB and the Fleck Report', *Pub. Admin.* 1957, pp. 1–14; C. A. Roberts, 'The Reorganization of the NCB's Management Structure', *Pub. Admin.* 1966, pp. 283–95.

[2] See D. Corbett, *Politics and the Airlines*, London 1965.

[3] See above, p. 209.

ters affecting the national interest, and specific powers with regard to accounts, training, and research policy, which vary from one corporation to another. The Minister and the Treasury also have power over the needs of the corporations for capital investment. Much Ministerial intervention in the affairs of a public corporation is by means of informal 'backstairs' pressure at a personal level between Ministers and Board members, and this can be seen as perhaps the least desirable form of control, in that it enables the Minister to wield power without having direct responsibility.

Resistance to excessive Ministerial control of public corporations is based on the view that the industries will prosper commercially only when they are given something approaching the degree of freedom of activity that is enjoyed by a private enterprise concern, and this view greatly influenced the attitude of Labour Ministers (particularly Herbert Morrison) in the creation of the public corporations after 1945. As well as this consideration, however, close Ministerial supervision leads inevitably to centralization, which, as has been discussed above, is not necessarily desirable for all the nationalized industries, and the consequent overloading of Ministers and their departments with responsibility for the detailed administration of the nationalized industries inevitably contributes to the problems of an overworked central government machine. The case for independence from Ministerial control is not universally accepted, however, and a greater degree of Ministerial control than exists at present is often demanded because of the vital economic nature and monopolistic position of the industries nationalized since 1945, and because of the extent of the public interest bound up in them. It is also claimed that co-ordination and rationalization (often quoted as major justifications for public ownership) are only possible through strict Ministerial control. The fuel and power industries, for example, are widely quoted as examples of the need for more Ministerial control in order to achieve a co-ordinated service, while it is argued that the role of the nationalized industries in national economic planning demands a growing degree of Ministerial control.[1] Thus it has been

[1] See W. G. Shepherd, *Economic Performance under Public Ownership*, London 1965. See also W. A. Robson, 'Ministerial Control of the Nationalized Industries', *PQ* 1969, pp. 103–12 *and* 494–6.

suggested that the Minister should in fact be Chairman of the Board of a public corporation, thereby reviving the proposal of some of the earliest advocates of public corporations.[1]

Despite the numerous arguments in favour of close Ministerial control, however, and despite the fact that the post-1945 public corporations have been subject to a greater degree of Ministerial intervention than those created before 1945, the general trend today is towards less rather than more Ministerial control. This is perhaps indicated by the recent developments in Post Office administration, by the attempts to place the nationalized industries, and particularly the railways, on a more self-sufficient commercial footing, and by the growth in the popularity of share purchase as a medium for public enterprise which affords even less scope for Ministerial control than is achieved through a public corporation. Thus the Morrisonian dictum of commercial freedom for publicly owned concerns is still widely accepted today.

III. Parliamentary Supervision

Whatever the merits or demerits of close Parliamentary scrutiny of the affairs of the public corporations, there are several factors that limit the effectiveness of Parliament for this purpose.[2] The overcrowded Parliamentary timetable, the technical nature of many of the issues, and the limitations that exist today on Parliamentary control of any Minister, all restrict Parliament's ability to scrutinize the nationalized industries.[3] The problem is increased by the difficulty of distinguishing between policy

[1] See in particular A. H. Hanson, *Parliament and Public Ownership*, London 1962. See also Lord Reith, 'Public Corporations: Need to Examine Control and Structure', *Pub. Admin.* 1956, pp. 351–4.

[2] See Hanson, *Parliament and Public Ownership*; E. P. Pritchard, 'The Responsibility of the Nationalized Industries to Parliament', *Parl. Aff.* 1963–4, pp. 439–49; D. N. Chester, 'Boards and Parliament', *Pub. Admin.* 1958, pp. 87–92 and pp. 285–7; A. H. Hanson, 'Parliamentary Control of Nationalized Industries', *Parl. Aff.* 1957–8, pp. 328–40; R. Nottage, 'Reporting to Parliament on the Nationalized Industries', *Pub. Admin.* 1957, pp. 143–68; G. H. Daniel, 'Public Accountability of the Nationalized Industries', *Pub. Admin.* 1960, pp. 27–34.

[3] See above, Ch. 8.

and day-to-day administration in the affairs of the nationalized industries, and thus of distinguishing those matters for which the Minister is directly responsible to Parliament. This is reflected particularly in the case of Parliamentary questions to Ministers. Early in the 1945–50 Parliament the principle was established, and has been adhered to ever since, that questions on policy matters were permissible while questions on day-to-day administration were not, but the problem remains of determining where the dividing line is to be drawn between policy and administration. Ultimately, responsibility for determining what questions are permissible rests with the Speaker, but even when the Speaker permits a question the Minister can deny responsibility. Thus in the immediate post-war years, and to a lesser extent since then, Ministers often refused to answer questions because they regarded the matter as one of day-to-day administration, or else answered the question for information while denying actual responsibility. In 1960 the Government announced that there was to be no relaxation in the rules governing the admissibility of questions, despite previous hints that there might be a change in the practice. In some ways it is ironic that the most persistent questioners are often those critics of the nationalized industries who wish to see them being more commercially successful, and yet any increase in MPs' powers to question Ministers would presumably lead to more Ministerial control over the industries, and thus to a lessening of their commercial freedom.

MPs can also raise matters connected with the nationalized industries during debates in the normal Parliamentary timetable, and in addition, the Government allocates three days of its time each session to the discussion of the Annual Reports of the various industries. Debates on the Annual Reports, however, are often devoted to raising minor constituency grievances rather than big general issues. All the public corporations, except the BBC, were created by statute (the BBC being created by Royal Charter), and any legislation amending these original statutes, or any legislation creating further public corporations, provides additional opportunities for debating the principles and general issues involved in public enterprise. Further, the normal methods of Parliamentary control over delegated legislation can give an opportunity for comment on any Statutory Instruments that apply to the corporations. Parliamentary control over the financial affairs of the public corporations is limited basically by the principle that the aim of a public corporation is to have a self-contained financial structure, free from Treasury control, and thus free from direct Parliamentary supervision. The SCE, the PAC, and the C and AG do not examine the estimates or accounts of most of the public corporations, although before the creation of the Select Committee on Nationalized Industries, the PAC did look in general terms at the Nationalized Industries' Annual Reports and Accounts, and still retains the power to do so. Nevertheless, in so far as a nationalized industry depends on the Treasury for capital for investment, the Treasury, Parliament, and the C and AG do have direct control over financial affairs of the corporation.

The most useful medium for Parliamentary supervision of the public corporations is probably the Select Committee on Nationalized Industries.[1] The proposal for the creation of a permanent Select Committee originated in the 1945–50 Parliament, and although the Labour Government took no action (on the basis that such a committee would represent too great a limitation on the commercial freedom of the public corporations), the Conservative Government elected in 1951 set up a Select Committee to examine the various aspects of Parliamentary control of nationalized industries. Very broadly, two views emerged, a majority favouring the creation of a permanent Select Committee with an officer and staff to aid it in its work, and a minority favouring a committee that would operate only at seven- or ten-yearly intervals. In 1955 a permanent committee was set up, but it reported that its terms of reference were too narrow for it to be effective, and it was consequently dissolved. A second committee was set up in 1956 with broader powers, and this committee has remained ever since.

This committee has eighteen members, and it examines the

[1] See D. Coombes, *The MP and the Administration*, London 1966; Sir Toby Low, 'The Select Committee on Nationalized Industries', *Pub. Admin.* 1962, pp. 1–16; E. Davies, 'The Select Committee on Nationalized Industries', *PQ* 1958, pp. 378–88; D. Coombes, 'The Scrutiny of Ministers' Powers by the Select Committee on Nationalized Industries', *PL* 1965, pp. 9–29; D. N. Chester, 'The Select Committee on the Nationalized Industries', *Pub. Admin.* 1956, pp. 93–5.

Reports and Accounts of nationalized industries, generally dealing with one industry each year, although sometimes looking at general problems such as the 1968 enquiry into Ministerial control. It works very closely with the Boards of the industries, the Treasury, and the departments concerned, and relies a great deal on their co-operation. The committee has led to an increase in Parliamentary and public knowledge about the nationalized industries, and it has probably helped towards a lessening of bitter party feeling on the floor of the House about the nationalization issue. The Committee could perhaps achieve more if it had an official on the lines of the C and AG to aid it in its work, but the committee itself has rejected this suggestion as being likely to destroy much of the co-operation and confidence that exists at present between the committee and the corporations.

As well as proposals to strengthen the Select Committee, numerous other proposals have been made to increase the efficiency and extent of Ministerial control and Parliamentary supervision. As has been noted above, it has been proposed that the Minister should be chairman of the Board of a public corporation, and that there should be a special Minister of (or for) the Nationalized Industries. It has been proposed that, as in France, a special Commission should be appointed to examine the efficiency of the nationalized industries, although the proposals vary as to the form that this body should take. To secure greater consideration of the annual capital investment plans of the industries, it has been suggested that a Nationalized Industries Investment Bill should be introduced each year, while as an alternative to this, a National Advisory Council for capital plans has been suggested. These various proposals have all been resisted, however, largely because it was said by the Government of the day that they would be too great a limitation on the commercial freedom of the industries.

It is very difficult to compare the accountability of a public corporation with that of a private firm. On the one hand, Parliament is much more in touch with the affairs of the public corporations than are the shareholders of a private concern, but on the other hand the size, importance, and monopoly basis of the public corporations means that they are much more powerful than private concerns, and there is much greater need for detailed control. Consumer Councils exist for all the nationalized industries, as a supplement to public accountability through Parliament. These Councils act as advisory bodies as well as complaints bodies, and the principle behind their activities is that there should be better consumer relations in a publicly owned concern than is the case with private concerns.[1] On the whole, however, the consumer is not noticeably more satisfied with the service from nationalized concerns than with the service from private enterprise, and as means of improving consumer relations, it has been suggested that Joint Consumer Councils should be set up to deal with complaints about all nationalized industries in a locality, or that the activities of the Parliamentary Commissioner[2] should extend to complaints about the nationalized industries. As yet, however, little headway has been made in this direction.

IV. Financial Structure

A basic requirement that follows from the principle of a self-contained financial structure for public corporations is that a corporation should pay its way, taking an average of good and bad years. There has been much confusion as to precisely what is meant by 'taking an average of good and bad years', although the 1961 White Paper on the Financial and Economic Obligations of the Nationalized Industries defined this as being over a five-year period.[3] A second basic requirement is that any financial surplus that a corporation produces should be used for its own purposes (that is, to form a reserve, finance capital investment, repay loans, or reduce future prices), thus benefiting consumers and employees, rather than being transferred to the Exchequer as a form of national revenue. This vision of a public corporation as a self-contained financial unit was largely achieved in the case of the public corporations created before 1945, but the financial difficulties of the post-1945 public corporations has meant that it has not been achieved in their case. The vast sums needed for compensation payments and for capital

[1] See M. Howe, 'The Transport Act 1962 and the Consumers Consultative Committees', *Pub. Admin.* 1964, pp. 45–56; G. Mills and M. Howe, 'Consumer Representation and the Withdrawal of Railway Services', *Pub. Admin.* 1960, pp. 253–62.
[2] See above, p. 339.   [3] Cmnd. 1337 (1961).

investment programmes, combined with the inability of some of the corporations to avoid trading losses, have meant that the actual financial arrangements for these corporations have been very different from the theoretical ideal of financial self-sufficiency.

The payment of compensation to shareholders in the event of nationalization is necessary on the grounds of equity and political expediency, but compensation payments load the nationalized industries with a large initial debt. Various methods can be used to determine the level of compensation that is to be paid. One method is to base the figure on Stock Exchange share prices on given dates, as was done with transport, private gas and electricity holdings, and iron and steel in 1951. Alternatively, the average price over a given period can be taken, as with iron and steel in 1966. Yet again, compensation can be based on assessments made by an arbitration tribunal, as with coal, or it can take the form of a token sum determined by the Government, as with payments to local authorities for their gas and electricity undertakings. It is generally accepted, however, that whichever method was used in the post-1945 period, the awards were more than generous, and railway and coal shareholders in particular seemed to benefit as a result of nationalization.

Financial needs for capital investment present a particularly acute problem when an industry is greatly in need of modernization, as was the case with the railways and the coal industry, or when there is a rapidly expanding consumer demand, as with electricity, atomic energy, the airlines, and gas[1] (in face of recent developments with North Sea gas). All the major nationalized industries were faced early in their lives with the problem of how money for capital investment was to be raised.[2] To meet the needs out of trading surpluses was not practical because of the vast sums required, and because of the commercial instability of most of the industries. The compensation payments and capital needs of the NCB came solely from the sale of Government stock backed by the Treasury, but the other nationalized industries raised the bulk of their compensation and investment

---

[1] I. Hicks, 'Finance of the Gas Industry', *Pub. Admin.* 1958, pp. 157–68.
[2] See S. Please, 'Government Control of the Capital Expenditure of the Nationalized Industries', *Pub. Admin.* 1955, pp. 31–42; R. J. S. Baker, *The Management of Capital Projects*, London 1962.

finance through the sale of their own stock. By 1956 the nationalized industries had issued stock to the value of more than
£1,500,000,000, but in 1956 the Government placed a restriction on the market borrowing of these industries, so that since
then all the nationalized industries have been dependent on the
Treasury for their capital projects. In their turn, Treasury loans
to the nationalized industries are raised primarily by Treasury
borrowing rather than by taxation.

The financing of capital investment by loans from the
Treasury has been criticized as providing the nationalized industries with too ready a source of finance. Certainly, the
Treasury has no adequate economic yardstick by which to
measure the capital needs of the nationalized industries, and an
impression emerges of technical experts asking for vast sums for
modernization projects, the true necessity and economic desirability of which the Treasury has no satisfactory means of
judging. The commercial instability of the railways, and perhaps
of the NCB, limits their ability to raise capital on the open
market, but the other nationalized industries, and particularly
the Electricity Boards, could conveniently raise capital on the
open market.

The 1961 White Paper on the Financial and Economic
Obligations of the Nationalized Industries[1] (as well as recommending five years as the period over which a balance should
be achieved between losses and surpluses), recommended that
in future a much bigger share of a nationalized industry's capital
investment should come from its own reserves. The White Paper
recommended that the industries should produce sufficient surpluses to cover costs, build up reserves, and also redeem their
capital. This requirement that the industries should redeem
their capital, and thus become debt-free undertakings, is an
obligation that does not fall upon private enterprise, and can
be condemned as placing further huge financial burdens on the
nationalized industries. The creation of reserves for these purposes has been hindered in the case of some of the post-1945
corporations by the provision of many uneconomic services, and
thus by the lack of adequate surpluses with which to build up
reserves. In face of uneconomic services in a publicly owned
concern, attempts can be made to eradicate these losses by the

[1] Cmnd. 1337 (1961).

normal commercial methods of increasing prices, or reducing costs through improved efficiency. Alternatively, the service can be discontinued, as with the closure of some uneconomic railway lines or coal mines. On the other hand, the principle of cross-subsidization can be applied, with the losses of one service being compensated by the surplus from another service. It is debatable, however, to what extent the principle of cross-subsidization is economically or morally justified, and how far it can be logically extended; whether, for example, rail losses should be subsidized by road profits in an overall transport scheme. As yet another alternative, the loss on a service can be officially accepted and a subsidy paid by the Treasury to cover the cost of un-economic but socially necessary services, as with some rail or air services to remote areas.

The distinction between a 'nationalized' and a 'socialized' concern can be said to be that a nationalized concern seeks to clear its losses like any private concern, whereas a socialized concern is one which, if necessary, provides services at a financial loss to itself, as a form of social service, relying on subsidies to clear any such losses. By this definition, the public corporations were not designed to operate as socialized concerns, in that they are statutorily required to cover their losses, and the 1961 White Paper emphasized this. In fact, however, the majority of the public corporations, and the railways in particular, have continued to provide services that were not commercially viable, as a matter of social responsibility. Much of the confusion surrounding the financial arrangements of the nationalized industries has arisen from the fact that while they were statutorily required to clear their losses, in practice they have been providing many services as social services rather than commercial services. Only recently have Governments recognized the need to subsidize the public corporations for the maintenance of un-economical services, and in the past the railways in particular suffered from the lack of such Treasury assistance. In this respect it may be questioned whether the public corporation, with its requirement to clear losses, is the best medium through which to run concerns that have social as well as commercial obligations.

Public Ownership in Britain: an Assessment

The record of public ownership in Britain, and particularly the record of the industries nationalized by the 1945 Labour Government, and administered by the big public corporations, is attacked from many angles.[1] The nationalized industries are often criticized as being unwieldy, impersonal and bureaucratic, and as being commercially inefficient as a consequence. It is claimed that there is little employee loyalty, and little desire to please the consumer, partly because of the impersonality of the concerns, and partly because of the lack of the 'incentives' that exist in private enterprise. It is argued that the nationalized industries are protected from competition by their monopolistic position, but despite this (or because of it) they have not achieved markedly better consumer services, and have not achieved the 'new millennium' in industrial relations that was expected in many quarters. As far as their financial record is concerned, it is argued that because the industries are so big, and have so many technical problems, there can be no adequate Ministerial or Treasury assessment of the economic viability of capital investment projects. Because of this, and because of a blind faith in large-scale investment as the answer to the industries' problems, it is claimed that there has been much wastage of capital which was acquired too easily. Critics thus advance proposals, if not for wholesale denationalization, at least for more decentralization, for the introduction of greater incentives within the industries, and for greater competition between the industries themselves, and between the industries and private enterprise.

In defence of the record of the nationalized industries, however, it must be pointed out that they have suffered because successive governments failed to produce sufficiently detailed and long-term plans for the industries. In 1945 the Labour Government had only *ad hoc* plans for nationalization, with no overall strategy, and certainly no twenty-year plan, while the Conservative Governments after 1951 were largely unsympathetic towards the public corporations. The main industries nationalized in the 1945–50 period were financially derelict before nationalization, and were greatly in need of capital development. The financial difficulties of the nationalized in-

[1] See, for example, Kelf-Cohen, *Twenty Years of Nationalization.*

dustries were accentuated by the more than generous compensation paid on nationalization; by the requirement that the public corporations should redeem their capital; and by the lack of any clear definition as to whether they were to provide commercial or social services. They have been expected to produce cheap and sometimes unprofitable services, and yet clear their losses, and they have incurred losses as a result of being used by the Government as a means of influencing the economy. Largely because of this, the nationalized industries have suffered from a bad public image, which they themselves have failed to counter with adequate public relations. It is also the case that many of the criticisms of the nationalized industries become irrelevant when it is realized that the purpose and policies of a public concern are basically different from those of a private enterprise concern, so that the criteria that are used to judge the success of a private firm cannot necessarily be applied to a public corporation. The fundamental differences that exist between a private firm, a department of state, and a public corporation in matters like financial policy, management structure, accountability, and general objectives, are not always appreciated, and this leads to much confusion over the evaluation of the success of public corporations.

With regard to their trading position, they have not always benefited from their monopolistic position because social and political pressure has been applied to prevent this, and in many respects they have less freedom to operate than private concerns. Far from the nationalized industries being protected from competition, there has been intense competition in the fuel and power field, with gas, electricity and coal facing fierce competition from oil[1] (with coal in particular being in a poor position to deal with this competition), while the airlines are subject to considerable competition at an international level, and to some competition within the United Kingdom. Many transport problems stem not from nationalization in 1947, but from the 1953 denationalization of the profitable road transport services. Examples are often quoted of the industries being encouraged to 'buy British', even when this was not economic; of them 'selling cheap and buying dear' in their dealings with private enterprise;

[1] See G. L. McVey, 'Policy for Fuel', *PQ* 1964, pp. 46–57; 'Co-operation between Electricity and Gas Boards', *Pub. Admin.* 1959, pp. 179–81.

and of limits being placed on their manufacturing and export policies in order to prevent damage to private enterprise interests. Thus the nationalized industries have been used to give general help to private industry and to the community at large, which may be a legitimate use of the public sector of industry, but which should be acknowledged as being incompatible with the maintenance of economic services.

Any attempt to draw up a final 'balance sheet' as to the overall failure or success of the nationalized industries is, of course, hindered by the close party political involvement in the public enterprise issue, and by the consequent difficulty of distinguishing between the legitimate arguments and the propaganda. What is clear, however, is that the opponents of nationalization have presented such a case against the post-1945 nationalized industries, and against the public corporation type of structure, that despite all the factors that can be advanced in their defence, future extensions of public control or ownership are likely to see share purchase and mixed enterprise as more desirable than the nationalization of the whole of an industry, and the creation of a public corporation to administer it.

13

Local Government

In Britain the system of government is unitary, in that sovereignty lies solely with one central government. It has been noted above,[1] however, that within this broad principle, certain areas enjoy a degree of legislative and administrative independence. The Scottish Education, Development, Agriculture and Fisheries, Home and Health Departments are centred in Edinburgh rather than Whitehall. The Channel Islands and the Isle of Man have their own Parliaments, and are largely self-governing in internal matters. Most significantly of all, Northern Ireland enjoys administrative and legislative independence in most respects, although the United Kingdom Parliament retains the power to withdraw this degree of self-rule. Also, throughout the United Kingdom a long-established system of local government operates, although again, this does not represent a breach in the principle of unitary government, in that all the powers enjoyed by the local government authorities in England, Wales, Scotland, and Northern Ireland are powers which have been conferred (and which can be withdrawn) by the central government.[2]

Local and Central Government

A system of local government such as operates in Britain can be regarded as valuable in a number of respects. It can serve

---

[1] See p. 162.

[2] For general descriptions of local government in Britain see J. J. Clarke, *The Local Government of the United Kingdom*, London 1955; R. M. Jackson, *The Machinery of Local Government*, London 1958. See also H. Benham, *Two Cheers for the Town Hall*, London 1964; D. M. Hill, *Participating in Local Affairs*, London 1970.

to protect interests within the broader framework of a national system of government, and local government authorities can concern themselves with the details of the particular problems of a locality in a way that is difficult for the central government. This can produce a more effective handling of local affairs, while at the same time, an efficient system of local government can relieve the work burden of the central government. This is perhaps especially important at a time when government activity is extending into more and more spheres. In this respect, some services can be administered more efficiently at a local level than at a national level. Local government can be a political and administrative training ground for central government, although in Britain, while some MPs serve a political 'apprenticeship' on local authority councils, there is little movement of personnel between central and local government officials. Local government can also bring the citizen into closer contact with the details of government, and this can perhaps increase the political consciousness of the public, although the extent to which the local authorities are subordinate to the central government inevitably reduces public interest in local affairs. Local government can thus play a valuable role in a political system, although fundamental to its role is the relationship between the local and central governments. While the local government seeks to preserve local interests, the central government safeguards national interests, and brings standardization to the whole system. Although both of these functions are important, they are often irreconcilable, so that a balance has to be sought between the two.

In Britain, local government is entirely subordinate to the central government. The local authorities can only engage in activities for which they have statutory authority, and they must perform the tasks that are demanded of them. Their powers are conferred by statute—either general Acts which apply to all local authorities, or private Acts which are promoted by local authorities themselves, and which apply only to individual authorities or groups of authorities. Some statutes demand that local authorities provide and administer certain services, while others merely permit the local authorities to provide certain services if they so desire. Legislative control is thus the most fundamental form of central control over local government, in that the whole basis of the system can be altered by Act of Parliament. In addition, however, central control is exerted by administrative and judicial means.

In Great Britain, the Minister for the Environment, the Secretary of State for Wales, and the Secretary of State for Scotland are the Ministers primarily responsible for local government, although the Ministers of Education,[1] and Social Security, and the Home Secretary, are also involved. As is revealed in more detail below,[2] the central government is able to exert influence over local government through the control of grants and loans to local authorities, and through the examination of local authorities' accounts. In addition, Ministerial consent is required for certain actions by local authorities, including the making of by-laws, and the appointment of some officials. Building plans require Ministerial approval, and the administration of some services, particularly the police, fire brigade, and education, is subject to examination by Ministry inspectors.[3] Some legislation that gives powers to local authorities, particularly with regard to planning and land development, allows for appeals to the appropriate Minister. Ultimately, the central government can remove a local authority's powers if it has neglected its duties.

Judicial control can be exerted over local authorities, in that like any citizen, they are subject to the jurisdiction of the law courts, and local authorities must not be guilty of non-feasance (neglecting their duties) or misfeasance (improper use of powers).[4] The judicial remedy for non-feasance lies in the application to the High Court for a writ of Mandamus, ordering the authority to do its duty, or in an Indictment for the neglect of duty. Ordinary civil action against a local authority is also

[1] J. A. G. Griffith, *Central Departments and Local Authorities*, London 1966; N. Boaden, 'Central Departments and Local Authorities', *PS* 1970, pp. 175–86.

[2] See p. 390.

[3] J. S. Harris, 'Central Government Inspection of Local Services in Britain', *PAR* 1955, pp. 26–34; Sir James Dunnett, 'The Relationship Between Central and Local Government in the Planning of Road Schemes', *Pub. Admin.* 1962, pp. 253–66.

[4] See W. O. Hart, *Introduction to the Law of Local Government and Administration*, London 1957; Sir I. Jennings, *Principles of Local Government Law*, London 1960.

allowed for in some legislation. In the case of misfeasance, a remedy lies in the application for a writ of Certiorari if the local authority is abusing its powers, or for a writ of Prohibition if it is about to abuse its powers. Local authorities can also be restrained by an injunction, although the determination of which of these legal procedures is to be used in a particular case is a matter for legal experts.

Central government control, whether by legislative, administrative, or judicial means, is to be welcomed if it maintains the efficiency of the local government system, achieves the standardization of local government services throughout the country, protects the citizen from the abuse of power by the local authorities, reduces the chances of corruption in the system, and helps towards the attainment of national financial, economic, and general planning policies. It is clearly undesirable, however, if it reduces efficiency through needless controls and red-tape, destroys local initiative, and leads to over-centralization and remoteness.[1]

The History and Structure of Local Government

In England the origins of local government can be traced back to the Saxon period, when within the Kingdom of England, local administrative independence was enjoyed by the shires (similar in size to the modern counties), and by the hundreds (combination of townships), both of which were under the authority of members of the nobility.[2] In addition, there were some townships or boroughs which had some independence from noble domination. After 1066 some towns were granted royal charters, and were allowed to administer their own affairs, while in the counties powerful nobles were given the title of Justice of the Peace, with the power to administer affairs in parts of the county. These developments formed the basis of the distinction between counties and boroughs in the modern local government structure. By the sixteenth century,

[1] See West Midland Group, *Local Government and Central Control*, London 1956.

[2] For general histories see J. J. Clarke, *A History of Local Government in the United Kingdom*, London 1955; K. B. Smellie, *A History of Local Government*, London 1957; B. Keith Lucas, *The History of Local Government in England: Josef Redlich and Francis W. Hirst*, London 1970.

parishes had emerged as the main local administrative units in the counties outside the independent boroughs. In the middle ages the functions of the local administrators were primarily the upkeep of roads, bridges, and jails, but in 1601 the Poor Relief Act called upon parishes to provide for the poor and destitute, for which purpose they were given the power to levy rates.

The modern shape of local government dates only from the nineteenth century, however, and is largely a product of the need to deal with conditions created by the industrial and agrarian revolutions.[1] The social and economic distress at the beginning of the nineteenth century led to the Poor Law Amendment Act 1834, which provided for poor relief to be administered at a local level, supervised by the Poor Law Commissioners in London. The Police Act 1829 created the Metropolitan police force, and the Municipal Corporations Act 1835 reformed the local government system in a number of boroughs, extending the franchise, introducing a borough audit, and ending a number of corrupt practices. The responsibilities of local authorities in the spheres of public health and housing were developed during the nineteenth century, particularly by the Public Health Acts of 1848 and 1878, while in 1870 the Education Act allowed for the creation of School Boards with the power to levy rates to build schools. Towards the end of the century there emerged a new structure for local government to allow for the more effective management of these local services. The Local Government Act 1888 (which established the structure and powers of county and county borough councils), and that of 1894 (establishing urban districts, rural districts, and parishes) created the basis of the modern structure of local government in England and Wales, and the Local Government Act 1933 gathered various existing statutes into one comprehensive measure.

Very broadly, the services that local authorities provide today can be classed either as environmental, protective, or personal services. The environmental services are those that are concerned with the citizens' immediate physical surroundings, and they include road construction and maintenance, the provision of street lighting, water supplies, recreation grounds, street

[1] See V. D. Lipman, *Local Government Areas, 1834–1945*, London 1949.

cleansing, and refuse disposal. The protective services are concerned with the safety of the citizen, and are primarily the
provision of police and fire services. The personal services, concerned with the individual well-being of citizens, include the
provision of housing, education (including school meals, further
education grants, libraries and museums, as well as schools),
and health services (including child welfare clinics, day
nurseries, and health visitors). Local authorities also provide
trading services, such as passenger transport services in some
areas, but local authority trading is today much less widespread
than before 1945.[1] In the first forty years of this century, there
was an expansion of the public health and sanitation services
provided by local authorities, and since 1945 they have acquired
new responsibilities for town and country planning, child care,
welfare services, and health services. It is sometimes claimed
that the health and welfare services could be developed further,
and that in addition, local government could be used to provide
more artistic, recreational, and sporting facilities in the provinces.[2] On the other hand, since 1945 the local authorities
have lost their responsibility for hospitals, and for gas and
electricity services, and at present there is much pressure for
the nationalization of other services, especially education, police
and water distribution.

*   *   *

In England and Wales (outside London), the main units
through which these services are administered are the county
boroughs and the administrative counties. The county boroughs
are all-purpose authorities, in that they are responsible for all
the local government services in their area. Boroughs are
created by Royal Charter, and some have acquired the title of
'city', either as a result of long usage, or as a result of the
conferment of the title in its charter or by a special Order in
Council. In the counties some services are provided by the
counties and others by various subordinate but autonomous
units within the counties. The counties are divided into non-

[1] See above, p. 349.
[2] Dame Evelyn Sharp, 'The Future of Local Government', *Pub. Admin.*
1962, pp. 375–87; H. Carleton Greene, 'Local Broadcasting and the Local
Authority', *Pub. Admin.* 1961, pp. 323–31.

county boroughs, urban districts, and rural districts, and the rural districts are subdivided into parishes, some with a parish council and other smaller parishes with provision for parish meetings.[1] The division of power between the counties and the district authorities is based on the principle that the county provides services like education and police, which require uniformity of action throughout the county, while the districts provide those services which can best be managed locally, like refuse disposal, and street lighting.

A similar structure and distribution of power operates in London, in that the Greater London Council provides some services for the whole of the Greater London area, while other services are provided by the Corporation of the City of London, the individual London Boroughs, and the Inner London Education Authority. This structure of local government in London was created by the London Government Act 1963, the main provisions of which were in turn based on the proposals of the Royal Commission on Local Government in Greater London, which reported in 1960.[2] The GLC, responsible for some eight million people, replaced the old London County Council, and also encompassed the whole of Middlesex and parts of Surrey, Kent, and Hertfordshire. The main arguments used to justify the 1963 changes in London's local government were that the area of the GLC more closely corresponds to the real geographical, economic, and social boundaries of London than did the LCC, and that the GLC and the London boroughs (which replaced the smaller metropolitan boroughs) would be able to provide better services as a result of their greater size and wealth. The change was resisted by many of the metropolitan boroughs, and by the counties who were losing population and status to the GLC, and the change was attacked in some quarters as a party political move, designed to destroy the Labour Party stronghold of the LCC. The distribution of

[1] See P. G. Richards, 'Rural Boroughs', *PS* 1966, pp. 87–9; D. Senior, 'The City Region as an Administrative Unit', *PQ* 1965, pp. 82–91.

[2] Cmmd. 1164 (1960). For comments see J. F. Garner, 'London Government and its Reform', *PL* 1961, pp. 256–70; P. Self, 'The Herbert Report and the Values of Local Government', *PS* 1962, pp. 146–62; W. A. Robson, 'The Reform of London Government', *Pub. Admin.* 1961, pp. 59–72. See also S. K. Ruck and G. Rhodes, *The Government of Greater London*, London 1970.

power between the GLC and the London boroughs was also criticized as giving too much power to the boroughs at the expense of the overall authority of the GLC.

Outside London the local government divisions are based on the long-established administrative counties, which today are not always convenient local government units. There are considerable variations in size, population, and wealth among the various counties and county boroughs, while within the counties many of the non-county boroughs, and even some of the urban districts, have populations greater than some county boroughs. From 1945 to 1949 a Local Government Boundary Commission considered a revision of local authority structure, but without concrete results, and in 1958 two new Local Government Commissions were created (one for England and one for Wales).[1] Some of the Commissions' proposals were implemented, but in 1965 the English Commission was replaced by a full-scale Royal Commission (the Redcliffe-Maud Commission) with a separate Royal Commission (under Lord Wheatley) for Scotland.[2] The Redcliffe-Maud Report appeared in 1969, and advocated the complete overhaul of local government boundaries and functions.[3] It proposed the division of England into eight 'provinces'. Within these broad regional divisions it proposed the formation of fifty-eight large 'unitary' local government areas, plus three special metropolitan authorities of the GLC type, for the Birmingham, Liverpool and Manchester conurbations. The Labour Government accepted the main Redcliffe-Maud recommendations, although the change of Government in 1970 may delay or prevent their implementation.

In Scotland the local government system evolved in a different pattern from England and Wales, and it remains a distinct system today, although the basic principles of structure, and of composition, organization, and central control, are similar to those that apply in England and Wales.[4] The present structure

[1] J. G. Thomas, 'Local Government Areas in Wales', *PL* 1962, pp. 160–74. See 'Areas and Status of Local Authorities in England and Wales', Cmd. 9831 (1956).

[2] J. P. Mackintosh, 'The Royal Commission on Local Government in Scotland', *Pub. Admin.* 1970, pp. 49–56.   [3] Cmnd. 4039 and 4040.

[4] See HMSO, *Local Government in Scotland*, Edinburgh 1958.

in Scotland is based on the Local Government (Scotland) Act 1929, and the main units are the counties of cities (Glasgow, Edinburgh, Aberdeen, and Dundee), and the counties. Within the counties there are the large burghs (generally with a population of 20,000 or more), the small burghs, and the districts. The counties of cities are all-purpose authorities, but a division of functions applies in the counties. The large burghs provide all their own services except education, valuation, and the registration of electors, but in the case of the small burghs and the districts, the county councils provide the bulk of the services. Outside Glasgow, fire services are provided on a regional basis. In 1969 the Wheatley Commission advocated the complete rationalization of the system through the formation of a two-tier system throughout Scotland, with seven regional and thirty-seven district authorities to replace the four hundred or so existing bodies. As with Redcliffe-Maud, it remains to be seen how much of this will be implemented. In Northern Ireland the structure of local government is more akin to that of England than Scotland. There are six county councils, and two county borough councils, and within the counties there are a number of borough, urban district, and rural district councils which provide some services within the counties.

The Personnel of Local Government

The Council. In boroughs (non-county boroughs and London boroughs as well as the county boroughs) the council is composed of councillors, aldermen, and a Mayor. Councillors serve for three years, one-third retiring annually. Generally, a borough is divided into wards, with three councillors representing each ward. Aldermen, who number one-third of the councillors, are elected by the councillors, usually from among their own number, any vacancies thereby created among the councillors being filled through by-elections. Aldermen are elected for six years, half of them retiring, or seeking re-election, every three years. The Mayor is elected by the aldermen and councillors, usually (but not necessarily) from among their own number. The Mayor holds office for a year, though he may be re-elected. He acts as chairman of the council, and is the official representative of the borough. He also has a number of judicial duties, in some boroughs acting as Returning Officer at Parliamentary elections.

In the counties, and in the GLC, the provision for councillors and aldermen is the same as in the boroughs, except that the election of councillors takes place only once in three years, when all councillors retire together. The county is split into divisions, with one councillor representing each division. A chairman of the council is elected, normally from among the members of the council. He is elected on an annual basis, but generally he is re-elected over several years. In the urban districts, rural districts, and parishes, the council consists of a chairman, who is elected annually, and councillors, who are elected for three years, normally with a third retiring annually. In parishes that are too small for a council (that is, if they have a population of less than 200), a parish meeting must be held at least four times a year, at which all adult members of the parish can attend and vote. The system of annual elections in the county boroughs means that changes in party composition on the councils come more gradually than in the counties, where the elections are triennial. Annual elections involve greater expense and administrative upheaval, however, and it can be argued that the more infrequent the elections, the more stable is the system. Also, annual elections are hardly practical for county councils, as only one councillor serves each division of the county.

In Scotland the burgh councils, and the councils of the counties of cities, are composed of councillors (elected, as in England, for three years, one-third retiring annually), and bailies, who are elected by the councillors from among their own numbers. Bailies serve until their term of office as councillors expires. A Provost is elected from among the councillors to serve as leader of the council for three years. A Dean of Guild is appointed to preside over the council committee that supervises plans for the erection of public buildings. In the large and small burghs, the Dean of Guild is appointed by the members of the council from their own ranks, but in the counties of cities someone from outside the council is appointed by local commercial corporations. In the counties, the council consists of councillors elected for three years (all of them retiring together), and representatives of the burghs, chosen by the burgh councils, who participate only in matters that affect their burgh. A convener, chosen by the councillors from their own number, presides over the council for a three-year period. The district council consists of county councillors for that district, plus district councillors elected in wards within the district. In Northern Ireland the composition of the various councils is the same as for the equivalent councils in England and Wales, except that in the boroughs and county boroughs in Northern Ireland, elections are held only once in three years, with all the councillors retiring together.

To be eligible to serve as a councillor, a person must be registered as a local government elector in the local authority area in which he seeks to serve. Anyone who holds a paid office with the local authority is disqualified, as are undischarged bankrupts, and anyone who has been sentenced to more than three months' imprisonment (without the option of a fine) over the previous five years. Councillors can be removed from office if they have failed to attend council meetings over the previous six months, or if they have been surcharged by the District Auditor within the previous five years, for sums of more than £500.[1] Unlike Parliamentary elections, no financial deposit is required from candidates, although there are restrictions on the amount of money that can be spent by each candidate on his election campaign.[2] To qualify for the vote in local elections, a person must be a British subject, aged 18 or over, and resident in the area. Until 1969 non-residents were also eligible to vote in an area if they held property there. In this way some people could vote in more than one local authority, through a residential qualification in one and a property qualification in another. This property qualification was ended, however, by the Representation of the People Act 1969.

The aldermanic system is often criticized as an undemocratic and self-perpetuating aspect of council composition, in that aldermen are not chosen directly by the electorate. They may be drawn from outside the council, and they serve for six years without requiring reappointment. The method of choosing

---

[1] See below, p. 390.

[2] For details of the law of local government elections see A. N. Schofield, *Local Government Elections*, London 1954. See also B. Keith-Lucas, *The English Local Government Franchise*, London 1952.

aldermen varies from one council to another. In some councils the senior councillors become aldermen, in others the appointments are made in proportion to political party representation among the councillors, and in others, the majority party monopolizes the aldermanic appointments. The first practice is criticized as producing an aldermanic bench composed of the oldest members of the council, who have a deadening influence on the whole of the council. The second practice can be difficult to operate satisfactorily, and the third practice is criticized as enabling a party to maintain control over the council, even though it has lost its majority among the councillors. It is also claimed that aldermen are largely superfluous, in that, apart from acting as Returning Officers in council elections in some areas, they have no functions distinct from those of councillors.

In defence of the aldermanic system, however, it may serve as a means of recruiting on to the council some valuable non-party political figure who does not wish to enter the fray of council elections. It can also be used as a means of preserving a place on the council for some valuable councillor who is in danger of losing his seat at the next elections, or as a means of rewarding good service on the council. The fact that aldermen serve for six years and are not directly dependent upon the whims of the electorate, and the use of aldermen as a means of emphasizing the majority of the controlling party on the council, help to produce greater stability and continuity in council composition—although not all would see this as desirable.

* * *

The quality of council members is often criticized. Some people become councillors out of a desire to serve the local community, and out of a genuine interest in local government affairs. Others regard council service as a means of gaining local prestige, with the ultimate reward of the aldermanic bench or the Mayoralty. Others regard council service as a stage in a party political career, and perhaps as a preliminary to a Parliamentary candidature. Many people are deterred from local council service, however, by the fact that it is unpaid. Loss of earnings allowances are paid, but they are not generous. The payment of council members is sometimes advocated, or the payment of committee chairmen, although these proposals are often accompanied by demands for fewer and larger local authorities, and fewer council members. As well as financial considerations, however, many people are prevented from serving as council members because the nature of their employment would prevent them from attending council and committee meetings, while many others are deterred by the amount of time and work involved in being a council member.

It is dangerous to make generalizations about the social composition of local councils, as there are about 50,000 councillors, aldermen, and bailies in England, Wales, and Scotland, and information about their social background is limited. Nevertheless, one sample survey of the occupations of the members of some 20% of the county and county borough councils in England and Wales in the period 1958-61, revealed that among members of the county councils, on average 47% were drawn from the upper and middle classes (that is, members of Classes I and II of the five social classes used in census returns[1]), 17% were drawn from the working class (social classes III, IV, and V), and the rest were housewives or retired persons.[2] In the county boroughs, on average 48% of council members were from the upper and middle classes, 30% were from the working class, and the rest were housewives or retired persons. The middle-class proportion was higher on Conservative-controlled councils than on Labour-controlled councils, although on all councils the middle class formed a higher proportion of the council members than of the population as a whole. Because of the amount of time at their disposal, housewives and retired persons are often thought of as forming the backbone of many councils. In the county and county borough councils analysed in this particular survey, they formed a sizeable proportion of council members, particularly on the county councils, although they were very far from constituting a majority on any council.

These general findings were supported by the results of a survey of four county and nine borough councils in the Greater London area in 1959.[3] This survey revealed that the upper and middle classes formed 67% of council members in the counties,

[1] See above, p. 68.
[2] L. J. Sharpe, 'Elected Representative in Local Government', *BJS* 1962, pp. 189–208.
[3] L. J. Sharpe, 'The Politics of Local Government in Greater London', *Pub. Admin.* 1960, pp. 157–72.

and 49% in the boroughs, while there were many more retired people on the county councils than on the borough councils. Similarly, an analysis of the social background of the Newcastle-under-Lyme borough council between 1932 and 1962 revealed that nearly two-thirds of council members in this period were non-manual workers, even though this group formed less than a third of the total population of the borough in 1962.[1] In an historical analysis of the social composition of three local authorities in the south-east of England (Kent county, Croydon county borough, and Lewisham metropolitan borough), it was found that the proportion of middle-class members of the councils declined between 1930 and 1958, as did the proportion of retired people on the council.[2] The proportion of working-class members of the council increased from 4% to 11% in Kent, from 8% to 30% in Croydon, and from 6% to 50% in Lewisham. This general trend is probably typical of councils throughout the country, and it forms the basis of the claim that is frequently made (with or without justification) that the 'quality' of council members has declined as compared with pre-war years.

The Officials. The policy decisions that are made by the council are administered by the various local government officials and employees, who range from the Town Clerk and the County Clerk, and the staff in the council offices, to the school teachers, transport staff, managers of municipal enterprises, and manual workers employed in the local government service. Local authorities are statutorily obliged to appoint a clerk, treasurer, and heads of some specified departments, but this requirement varies with the type of authority.

In general, local government officers are appointed and dismissed at the discretion of the council, and although the Minister for the Environment (or the Secretary of State in Scotland) retains the power of veto over some appointments, this is only rarely applied. Those who fill the senior posts in local government administration, and the heads of departments in particular, normally have professional qualifications. In 1968, however, the Mallaby Committee on the staffing of Local Government emphasized the problems encountered by many local

---

[1] Bealey, Blondel, and McCann, *Constituency Politics*, p. 304.
[2] Sharpe, *BJS* 1962.

authorities (and especially the smaller ones) in recruiting suitably qualified officers. The 'trade union' of local government
officers is the National and Local Government Officers Association, catering for all grades. NALGO has only recently become
affiliated to the TUC, and it has a record of co-operation rather
than conflict with the local authorities. Rates of pay and conditions of service are governed by recommendations made by
Whitley Councils, composed of representatives from NALGO
and other unions, and representatives of the local authorities.
Chief of these Councils is the National Joint Council for Local
Authorities' Administrative, Professional, Technical, and Clerical Servants.[1]

Officials cannot stand as candidates at elections of the council
which employs them, and members of the council (and ex-
councillors for a period of at least twelve months after their
retirement) cannot become council employees. The officials are
expected to be politically non-partisan in their attitudes, in the
same tradition as the permanent and neutral Civil Service.[2]
As with the Civil Service, however, the activities of the senior
officials are inevitably bound up with political issues to a considerable extent. The clerk, treasurer, education officer and
other heads of departments attend council and committee
meetings in an advisory capacity. The heads of departments
are concerned primarily with managerial and administrative
matters, but the distinction between administrative and policy
issues can be as blurred in local government as it is in central
government. There is much informal contact between heads
of departments and members of the council, particularly the
chairmen of the various committees of the council, and the
question of where the power of councillors ends (or should end),
and that of officers begins (or should begin) remains one of the
problems of local government.

The clerk of the council is the chief officer within a local
authority.[3] His main responsibility is to ensure that the council

[1] L. Kramer, 'Reflections on Whitleyism in English Local Government',
Pub. Admin. 1958, pp. 47–70; M. McIntosh, 'The Negotiation of Wages and
Conditions of Service for Local Authority Employees in England and
Wales', *Pub. Admin.* 1955, pp. 149–62, *and* 307–24 *and* 401–18.

[2] See above, p. 323, for comments on this.

[3] For the role of the Town Clerk see T. Headrick, 'The Town Clerk: His
Training and Career', *Pub. Admin.* 1958, pp. 231–48 *and* 335–51; C. Barratt,

operates within its legal powers, although he also has the general task of guiding and influencing the activities of the council. It is often argued, however, that the role of the clerk is too passive, and that the local government system would benefit from the introduction of a new official with a more dynamic role to play as 'managing director' of the local authority. In many local authorities in the USA, a City or County Manager fulfils this role. He is appointed by the council or the Mayor, is given wide discretionary powers within a general budget, and is free to appoint his own subordinates. In other local authorities in the USA, considerable administrative power is given to the Mayor, who is elected directly by the people, and who appoints most senior officials.[1] It is often suggested that these systems could be copied to advantage in Britain, although wholesale adoption of the City Manager system would be contrary to the principle of group administration which is the basis of the present local government system. Nevertheless, Newcastle-upon-Tyne employs a form of City Manager, although his powers are nothing like so wide as those of City Managers in the USA.

Local Government in Operation

To a considerable extent, local authorities are free to make their own internal arrangements for the conduct of their affairs, although in practice, basic procedures vary little between authorities of similar types. All local councils must meet at least four times a year. The county councils generally meet more frequently than this minimum, and borough councils usually meet once per month. The public and the press are admitted to council meetings, although they can be excluded, and the council can go into private session if it is felt that this is in the public interest. The Mayor or chairman of the council is in charge of council meetings. He is expected to be neutral,

---

'The Town Clerk in British Local Government', *Pub. Admin.* 1963, pp. 157–72.

[1] See W. A. Robson (editor), *Great Cities of the World: Their Government, Politics and Planning*, London 1957; G. H. Chipperfield, 'The City Manager and Chief Administrative Officer', *Pub. Admin.* 1964, pp. 123–32.

although he can exercise a casting vote. Council meetings take the form of an examination of proposals made by the committees of the council. Questions of principle are decided by the council, but the committees work out the details of policies. The minutes of council meetings are not a record of council debates, but are a record of each committee's proposals. At meetings of the full council, the chairmen of the committees introduce their minutes, which are debated and then accepted, rejected, or referred back to the committee. In most local authorities, however, and certainly in the largest authorities, the work of the council (and its committees) is dominated by party political organizations, with council decisions really being controlled by party group meetings. The importance of party politics in local government is considered in more detail below, however.[1]

The standing committees of local government are functional, in that each committee deals with a particular service provided by the council, such as housing, highways, or education. The most important and busiest committees are divided into subcommittees. There is usually a General Purpose Committee to deal with any matters not covered by the other committees, although sometimes the Finance Committee performs this role. In some authorities a Policy Advisory Committee is appointed, composed of committee chairmen, or of the senior members of the majority party on the council. It acts as a 'Cabinet', supervising and co-ordinating the work of the various committees. On other councils, this supervising and co-ordinating function is performed by the leader of the majority party, acting with his colleagues in group meetings, and on other small councils it is performed by the whole council. Some committees are mandatory, in that they are demanded by statute, but the majority are created at the discretion of the council. The vast majority of the committees are advisory, and merely make proposals which the whole council accepts or rejects, but the council vests its authority in some committees, and gives them executive powers. In addition to the standing committees there are various specialist committees appointed to deal with particular problems, and there are also joint committees or boards, such as joint water boards, which are made up of representa-

[1] See p. 395.

tives from more than one authority, and which deal with services such as an airport, area planning, or water supplies, in which more than one authority is involved.

In the larger authorities, committee membership is generally in proportion to party strength on the council, with the majority party taking all or most of the committee chairmanships. Sometimes an attempt is made to put a councillor from each ward on the most important committees, but this is not really practical in the very large councils. The membership of most committees is confined to council members, but non-council members can be co-opted on to some committees, and have to be co-opted on to others. Although co-option is often criticized as being undemocratic, it serves to introduce well-informed outsiders on to the committees, and it makes use of people who do not have the time or inclination to serve as full-time members. The co-opted members can also break up a too-rigid political party division on a committee, and they often hold the balance between the political party groups on the committees.

As well as the general principle that the smaller the decision-making body the more effective it will be, the chief merit of the committee system is that it brings individual members of the council into closer contact with the details of administration than would otherwise be possible. The committee system enables councillors to become specialized in particular subjects, and this is perhaps increasingly desirable as the work of government in general becomes more detailed and specialized. Councillors are only part-timers, and cannot afford a great deal of time for council work, so that the committee system enables the council's responsibilities to be shared out among groups of councillors, with the full council meeting only occasionally to consider committee recommendations. This is perhaps especially important in the case of the county councils, where geographical considerations can mean that council meetings are held less frequently than in the boroughs. The commitee system is often criticized, however, as taking authority away from the council as a whole, and placing it in the hands of small groups of councillors, and local government officials often criticize the committee system as giving councillors too much power over the details of administration. Also, specialization in itself need not be a virtue, and can merely produce narrowness in outlook. In 1967, the Maud Committee on the Management of Local Government condemned the committee system as being outdated. In general, however, it can be said that the value of the committee system depends to a large degree on the type of council involved, with the larger the council, and the greater its responsibilities, the greater the need for committees to deal with detailed matters.

*   *   *

The control of local authority expenditure is partly an internal responsibility of the council and its officials, and partly an external matter in the hands of the District Auditor. The internal control is exercised by the whole council, and all expenditure requires council authorization, but more specifically, control is exercised by the Finance Committee and the treasurer. General financial policy is determined by the full council and the Finance Committee, and is applied throughout the year through the approval or rejection of all plans that involve expenditure. In addition to this main general control, there is the annual process of preparing and securing approval for the council's 'Budget' of proposed expenditure, and planned income for meeting the expenditure. This begins with the preparation of departmental estimates by the officials of the departments. This process usually takes place in the autumn, to fit in with the financial year beginning on April 1st, and the chairmen of the committees generally work in close co-operation with the heads of the departments in this matter.

It is generally recognized that the preparation of the estimates is a skilled job, and as a general rule the committees do not interfere with the details of the estimates. The estimating process can be very accurate, as the sums dealt with are not as big as those dealt with in national finance, nor are the variations as great from year to year. The system is flexible, however, and once the estimates have been approved, adjustments can be made from one head to another. When necessary, supplementary estimates can be sought. All the estimates are examined in detail by the Finance Committee, which is in many ways the most important of the committees in local government. It is usually made up of the senior or most important

members of the council, or of the chairmen of all the committees, although in some local authorities all the members of
the council serve on the Finance Committee. After the Finance
Committee's scrutiny, the approval of the full council is generally a formality, although disputes between the Finance
Committee and a particular committee may have to be settled
by the full council.

At the end of the financial year, the examination of the
accounts is undertaken by the District Auditor, or in some cases
by auditors appointed by the council. The District Auditors,
who are appointed by the central government, examine the
accounts of all counties, urban districts, rural districts, and
some boroughs (about 15% of the county boroughs and about
50% of the non-county boroughs). The other boroughs employ
a professional firm of auditors, or else arrange for three borough
auditors, two of whom are elected by the local government
electors, and a third appointed by the Mayor from among the
councillors. This latter practice is rarely adopted today, however. Some borough accounts, particularly education and police
accounts, have to be examined by the District Auditor. As with
the examination of central government accounts by the C and
AG,[1] the District Auditor is concerned not only with examining
the general financial state of the department, and pointing
out any irregularities, but also with ensuring that all expenditure has been authorized, and with censuring any seeming
extravagance. The District Auditor also provides the central
government with a check on the accuracy of grant claims. If
the District Auditor uncovers any wastage of public money
caused by neglect or malpractice, he must surcharge the councillors or officials who are responsible.

Local Government Income[2]

Local authority expenditure now accounts for some 10% of
the gross national product, and the main sources of income to

---

[1] See above, p. 291.
[2] See A. H. Marshall, *Financial Administration in Local Government*, London
1960; N. P. Hepworth, *Finance of Local Government*, London 1970; W. S.
Steer, 'The Financing of Local Government', *PQ* 1957, pp. 423–33.

meet this are the rates, government grants, and loans. In addition, some authorities gain revenue from trading enterprises, although in this context a distinction has to be made between those trading services, like municipal transport services, which may produce a trading profit, and other services for which a charge is made, as with library fines and cemetries, but which are not run on commercial lines.

Loans. Local authorities borrow money mainly in order to pay for capital investments that cannot readily be financed from current income from rates or grants, but also on the principle that the cost of investments with long-term benefits should be met by loans which can be repaid gradually over the life of the asset, as the benefits of the investment materialize. As with private concerns, local authorities can raise loans by issuing stock on the Stock Exchange, by internal borrowing from the authorities' own funds, by private mortgages, or by a bank overdraft in the case of small sums. Some large authorities also borrow abroad. In addition, local authorities' can borrow from the central government through the Public Works Loan Board, while a small authority can borrow from a larger one. Loans from the Public Works Loan Board are repaid in instalments, with the rates of interest fixed by the Treasury. The larger authorities tend to rely mainly on the open market, while the smaller authorities rely more on the Loans Board. Whichever source is used, however, the vast majority of loans require Ministerial consent. This is designed to ensure that the authorities only borrow what they can afford to repay, and thereby maintain the reputation of local authorities as good financial investments. Control over local authority borrowing is also a valuable form of government influence over the economy.

Rates. The basic principle behind the rates is that of the taxation of property in proportion to the benefit that accrues to the occupier, and it represents the main form of local authority income from local sources. The annual value of a property, be it a house, factory, business premises, or an area of land, is assessed in terms of a gross annual rental value. Until 1950, local authorities were themselves responsible for making the assessments, but the Local Government Act 1948 transferred this task to the Board of Inland Revenue as from 1950, in an attempt to achieve a national standard of assessments. A reassessment of values is normally made every five years. Deductions are made from the gross annual rental value of the property, to cover the cost of repairs and maintenance, and this produces a net annual rental value, which represents the rateable value of the property. This rateable value is then used as the basis for calculating the annual rates to be paid by the property owner. The council fixes a rate poundage according to its financial needs for that year. If the rate poundage is fixed at 10s. in the £, someone who owns property with a rateable value of £50 will pay 50 × 10s., or £25. If the rate poundage is 30s. in the £, he will pay 50 × 30s., or £75.

Thus the determination of the amount of rates to be paid by each property owner each year depends first of all on the rateable value of the property, and secondly on the rate poundage fixed by the council each year. In the counties, the urban district, rural district, and borough councils are the rating authorities, and they receive notice from the county councils and parish councils of the rates that they require. In Scotland, all authorities are rating authorities except the district councils, and the county councils also issue an annual requisition to the burghs for the cost of services within the burgh that are provided by the county council.[1] In Northern Ireland, all authorities except urban districts are rating authorities. About £1,000,000,000 is raised in rates each year, about half of it coming from domestic property. Before 1963, commercial premises were given a 20% concession on their rateable value, and industrial premises had a 50% concession (compared with a 75% concession between 1925 and 1958). These concessions were removed in 1963, but agricultural land remains exempt from rates. In rented property the landlord often pays the rates, and allows for this in the rent that he charges to his tenants. In so far as the payment of rates stimulates interest in local government, this distinction between paying rates directly, and paying them through a rent, can be significant, and in 1957 in a nation-wide survey by NALGO, of public attitudes to local government, it was revealed that of those householders

[1] A. Currie, 'Valuation and Rating in Scotland', *Pub. Admin.* 1957, pp. 187–91.

who paid their rates directly, 92% knew how much they paid when interviewed, compared with only 55% of those who paid their rates through a rent.[1]

The rating system is a convenient form of taxation, in that it is cheap to run and easy to administer. In some ways land and buildings form a good basis for taxation, as unlike some forms of income, they cannot be concealed from the assessors. At the same time, size of house is not necessarily a good indication of wealth, or of the ability to pay, and extremely profitable commercial or industrial concerns can be housed in small premises. The rating system also tends to discourage improvements to property, in that the better the property the higher the rates. The bigger the family, and thus the bigger the house that is required, the higher the rates are likely to be, and this is the reverse of the principle that applies with income tax, where tax allowances increase as the size of the family increases. Since 1965, however, there has been in operation a system of rate rebates for low income groups.

The rates tend to be more unpopular than most other forms of taxation, to some extent because rates involve an actual cash payment, while most other forms of taxation are deducted at source. Since 1965, all local authorities have been required to allow for the payment of rates in monthly instalments (although many local authorities had systems of instalment payments before this), and this has removed some of the objections to the payment of rates in a lump sum. Opposition to the rates, however, is also based partly on the tarnished image of local government, with local authorities often being thought of by the public as being guilty of much wasteful expenditure. Numerous proposals have been made over the years for alternative forms of local revenue to supplement or even replace the rates. Local income tax, purchase tax, entertainments tax, and betting levy have all been advocated, and it has been suggested that part of National Insurance contributions could go to local authorities. At present, the local authorities collect on behalf of the central government the licence duty on motor vehicles, and it has been suggested that this is a form of revenue that could readily be transferred from the central to the local

[1] 'NALGO Survey: Interest in Local Government', *Pub. Admin.* 1957, pp. 305-9.

exchequer. Levies on restaurant meals, hotel accommodation, and advertising displays have also been proposed. In general, however, the most frequently repeated proposals for relieving the rate burden are for more local government services (particularly education) to be transferred directly to the central government, or for central government grants to local authorities to be increased.

Grants. A small proportion (about 10%) of the grants that are paid by the central government to local authorities are in the form of particular service grants, paid to most local authorities towards the cost of specific services. Some of these, like the police grant, are calculated on a percentage basis, and the size of the grant is in direct proportion to the local authority's expenditure on that service. Other particular service grants are calculated on a unit basis, with payments being made for each unit of a particular service, as in the case of housing. The main central government grants to local authorities, however, are the rate support grants, which were established in 1966, and which account for some 90% of the total grants figure. These grants are not tied to specific services, but are distributed as a general form of revenue. The size of the grant is assessed by a formula based on factors such as the size of the authority, its population, and the number of children of school age. Prior to 1966 the grant system was based on the Local Government Act 1958, and the Local Government Miscellaneous Financial Provisions (Scotland) Act 1958, which established general grants for county and county borough councils, and also rate deficiency grants (exchequer equalization grants in Scotland) which were paid to local authorities whose income from rates fell below the national average. The Local Government Act 1966, however, replaced the general grants and the rate deficiency grants by the rate support grants, although the 1966 changes were seen as interim arrangements until a full-scale reform of local government finance could be achieved.

The various grants that are paid to local authorities serve to ease the rate burden, and enable the local authorities to undertake services that they could not afford if they were dependent solely on local revenue. They enable the central government to exert control over local government, although the degree of control varies with the type of grant. Unit and

LOCAL GOVERNMENT   395

percentage grants allow the central government to encourage
the development of certain services, but the rate support grants
provide local authorities with revenue 'without strings'. Before
1958 there were a greater number of specific grants paid for
education, health and welfare services, fire services, town planning, and various other services. The Local Government Act
1958 reduced the number of particular services grants and replaced them by the general grant, thereby giving the local
authorities greater freedom over the way in which they decided
priorities for expenditure among the different services,[1] and the
Local Government Act 1966 preserved this policy.

Over the years there has been an increase in local authority
revenue from both rates and government grants, but the
revenue from grants has increased to a greater extent than that
from rates. Until the second world war, on the national average,
income from rates exceeded that from grants, but since 1945
the reverse has been the case. The 1966 Act sought to achieve
a regular annual increase of 1% in the proportion of grant
revenue as opposed to rate revenue, and the Act also established
machinery to ensure that the effect of transferring more of the
financial burden from rates to grants would be to ease particularly the rate burden of householders, as opposed to industrial
and commercial property owners. In general it may be said
that the greater the dependence of local authorities on central
government grants, the greater will be the degree of central
government control over local government (for good or ill).
As central control tends to produce uniformity, the greater the
dependence on government grants, the greater will be the
degree of uniformity of standards and practices throughout
the local government system. The more the local authorities
depend upon local sources of income, the more aware the public
is likely to be of the financial implications of local government
activities, and as a result, the more interest they are likely to
take in local government affairs. Because of the particular
unpopularity of the rates as a form of taxation, however, the
more dependent local authorities are on the rates, the more
cautious they are likely to have to be in their policies. Thus the
balance that is achieved between local authority revenue from

[1] J. Vaizey, 'Block Grants and the Control of Education', *PQ* 1958,
pp. 155–65.

rates and from government grants is of fundamental importance for the nature of the local government system.

Party Politics and Public Attitudes

Throughout this chapter passing references have been made to political parties on councils, and it is necessary to consider now the precise place of party politics in local government. Not all councils are run on party lines, and as with so many aspects of local government, it is difficult to make generalizations about this matter, as the nature and extent of party political activity varies considerably between the different types of local authority, and even between authorities of the same type.[1] At one extreme, 'party' organization can merely involve a group of council members organizing themselves for the purpose of handling council affairs, while at the other extreme it can involve all the facets of political party organization. On some councils one party has a monopoly of all the seats. On others an opposition party exists, but it may be small and destined to be permanently in opposition. In some authorities, control of the council alternates from one party to another, and in others the council seats are shared fairly equally among three or more parties. Party control of the council can involve one party monopolizing the Mayoralty, aldermanic seats, the committee chairmanships, and perhaps even all the committee places. On the other hand, the controlling party may allocate some offices to the other parties.

The attitudes of the main political parties vary over the question of party politics in local government, with the Labour Party being much more conscious of its value. In a survey in Newcastle-under-Lyme in 1958,[2] Conservative voters were found to be two to one in favour of leaving party politics out of local government, compared with only a small minority of Labour voters, and these tendencies were supported by survey

---

[1] J. G. Bulpitt, *Party Politics in English Local Government*, London 1967; W. Thornhill, 'Agreements Between Local Political Parties in Local Government Matters', *PS* 1957, pp. 83–8; J. Stanyer, 'Electoral Behaviour in Local Government', *PS* 1970, pp. 187–204.

[2] F. Bealey and J. D. Bartholomew, 'The Local Elections in Newcastle-under-Lyme, May 1958', *BJS* 1962, pp. 273–85 and 350–68.

findings in Glasgow in 1964.[1] The Labour Party usually retains
its name in local government politics, and such studies as have
been made of voting behaviour at local government elections,
suggest that it draws its support from much the same social and
demographic groups as in national politics. The main opposition to the Labour Party, however, may be provided by Anti-
Socialists, Progressives, Municipal Party, or Independents,
although these generally correspond more or less to the national
Conservative Party in their policies and attitudes, and in the
sources of their electoral support.

Party politics in local government is not a new development,
and although party labels have appeared on ballot papers
only since 1969, there were parties or groups in local politics
even in the nineteenth century. It is probably true to say that
the political differences between the Labour and Conservative
parties in local government are less now than before 1945, but
the extent of party politics on local councils is still widely
criticized today. It is argued that doctrinal party attitudes are
irrelevant in most of the issues dealt with in local government,
and that party domination of local council elections can exclude non-party men from council service. While the party that
is in power in national politics may change every few years,
some local councils have permanent majorities for one party,
producing permanent single-party government. In such cases,
council meetings and council elections tend to be mere formalities, and there is less public interest in local government as a
result. It was found, for example, in an analysis of London
borough elections between 1945 and 1958, that there was a
direct correlation between voting turnout and the strength of
party control on the council, with the turnout declining from
one borough to another as the strength of the opposition party
declined.[2]

The value of party politics in local government, however, is
that opinion has to be organized if it is to be effective, and party
organization helps to provide the stability and consistency that
is essential in any form of government. The alternative to
control by parties is government by personalities, which is

[1] I. Budge, 'Electors' Attitudes towards Local Government: A Survey in
a Glasgow Constituency', *PS* 1965, pp. 386–92.
[2] Sharpe, *Pub. Admin.* 1960.

perhaps an undesirable alternative. On the larger councils, party politics is in many ways inevitable, in that some local government issues are matters which reflect national political party issues. Similarly, on every council a broad distinction tends to emerge between those who wish to develop services, and those who wish to keep expenditure (and thus the rates) at the lowest possible level, and this distinction corresponds very roughly to the respective attitudes of Labour and Conservative politicians.

*   *   *

It is generally assumed that there is a great deal of public apathy towards local government, and there is much evidence to support this assumption. Voting turnout tends to be much lower at local elections than at general elections, and surveys have suggested that few people attend council meetings, or can even name their councillors. Table XXIX shows how much lower was the turnout of voters in the municipal elections in Glasgow in 1964, 1965, and 1966, than in the general elections of 1964 and 1966. An analysis of local elections in Newcastle-under-Lyme and surrounding districts between 1932 and 1962[1] showed that turnout in county council elections was much lower than in borough or rural district elections. This analysis also suggested that working-class electors and young electors were more likely to abstain than were middle-class electors and the older electors. In Newcastle-under-Lyme in 1958, a quarter of those interviewed had not heard of the impending local elections one week before polling day, and few could name a candidate.[2] In one survey conducted in Glasgow soon after the municipal elections of 1964, only about a third of those interviewed could name the newly-elected councillor for their ward.[3] In another survey in Glasgow, conducted two months before the 1965 municipal elections, 80% of those interviewed were unable to name any of the three councillors for their ward, while 14% could name one only.[4] In NALGO's nationwide survey of public attitudes to local government, 81% of those interviewed claimed to have read about council affairs in

[1] Bealey, Blondel, and McCann, *Constituency Politics*, p. 226.
[2] Bealey, *BJS* 1962.   [3] Budge, *PS* 1965.
[4] J. Brand, *Glasgow Herald*, 3. and 4.6.65.

TABLE XXIX
Voting Turnout at General and Municipal Elections in Glasgow 1964–6

Parliamentary Constituencies	October 1964	March 1966	Municipal Wards	May 1964	May 1965	May 1966
Maryhill	70·5	68·5	Maryhill	37·9	35·8	36·0
			Ruchill	31·6	25·5	24·8
Provan	75·7	70·8	Provan	35·7	30·1	27·9
			Dennistoun	49·5	51·9	52·1
Springburn	69·2	66·6	Springburn	33·3	30·4	30·9
			Cowlairs	27·2	25·2	26·5
Woodside	78·9	73·0	Woodside	38·4	37·4	38·6
			North Kelvin	33·9	34·3	32·9
			Partick East	39·6	37·1	38·3
Bridgeton	63·6	58·8	Calton	24·1	21·4	21·2
			Dalmarnock	26·4	22·9	19·4
			Mile End	26·4	20·1	20·2
Shettleston	71·4	68·6	Parkhead	39·8	36·1	39·4
			Shettleston and Tollcross	33·9	32·4	29·3
Central	62·4	58·7	Cowcaddens	25·6	24·8	26·0
			Townhead	29·1	29·6	25·1
			Exchange	29·6	28·7	24·2
Kelvingrove	67·4	66·3	Anderston	36·1	29·2	32·0
			Park	34·2	34·7	32·6
Hillhead	74·7	73·5	Kelvinside	43·2	45·7	46·9
			Partick West	38·9	38·6	38·1
			Whiteinch	41·4	38·8	40·9
Scotstoun	77·2	74·3	Knightswood	38·5	32·0	34·1
			Yoker	45·5	42·5	41·4
Cathcart	79·3	79·7	Cathcart	45·2	46·1	41·3
			Langside	43·7	43·8	45·2
			Govanhill	43·4	43·1	39·3
Gorbals	64·5	61·7	Gorbals	25·6	19·9	19·2
			Hutchesontown	31·7	26·2	27·7
Govan	70·3	67·5	Kingston	27·2	26·3	24·4
			Kinning Park	40·5	36·6	35·9
			Govan	34·3	33·3	29·2
Craigton	80·1	80·4	Fairfield	37·3	37·5	40·3
			Craigton	47·8	48·4	47·2
			Pollokshields	46·5	44·1	42·1
Pollok	77·8	79·0	Pollokshaws	41·0	35·8	35·6
			Camphill	46·8	47·2	47·5
Average	72·2	69·8		36·5	34·4	33·6

Source: Glasgow Herald

the press, and 17% said that they belonged to ratepayers' associations, but only 6% said that they attended council meetings.[1]

The general lack of public interest in local government is often attributed to the supposedly poor quality of local councillors, or to the prevalence of party political attitudes in local government, which are often regarded as being irrelevant in local issues. Most people also see local government as being concerned primarily with minor and somewhat boring questions which do not arouse a great deal of interest, despite the fact that they affect people's daily lives. The fact that local government is subordinate to the central government also contributes to the general image of local government as being of relatively minor importance. For most people, such interest as they do have is bound up with the payment of rates, and in this context the ratepayer's prime concern tends to be with the limiting of local government expenditure in order to keep rate payments low. Here, however, there is often an inconsistency in public attitudes. The survey in Newcastle-under-Lyme in 1958, for example, revealed that the majority of people felt that the rates were too high, but at the same time the majority wished to see more local government services provided, and also wanted local government to be subject to less central control. To satisfy all of these demands, increased services would presumably have to be financed by increased central government grants, with the central government at the same time seeking less control over the spending of its grants.

Public concern over various local government services varies from one area to another, and from one section of the community to another. For example, in the urban areas covered by the Newcastle-under-Lyme survey in 1958, most people gave roads the greatest priority for improvement, followed by education, parks, and playgrounds. In the rural areas, on the other hand, sewerage was given by the far the greatest priority. In most large towns, housing and education are probably the services that arouse most concern, and in Glasgow in 1964 it was found that there were marked differences between age groups, and between supporters of the two main parties, in their attitudes to expenditure on these two services. A clear majority of Labour voters, and voters aged under 45, favoured more

[1] NALGO Survey, *Pub. Admin.* 1957.

expenditure on housing and education, while a big majority of Conservative voters, and of voters aged over 45, called for less.

Regionalism and Devolution

One of the fundamental criticisms levelled against the existing system of local government is that its structure is out of date, consisting of too many small authorities which bear little relation to modern economic and social units. It is often argued that it is not enough to seek to adapt the existing pattern of local authorities, but that a fundamental recasting of the system is required, with larger units being created on a regional basis.[1] It is claimed that a system of regional government would lead to a fuller recognition of regional problems, and that with an effective system of regional administration the central government machine could be relieved of some of its responsibilities, and thereby made more efficient. Numerous proposals have been made for the creation of regional units within Britain (the Redcliffe-Maud and Wheatley Reports being the latest of these), with considerable variations as to the size of the regional units, their organization and powers, and their relationship with the central government and with the existing local authorities. During the second world war, Great Britain was divided into twelve regions (ten for England, one for Wales, and one for Scotland), and in the event of a breakdown of communications each region was to have been under the control of a regional commissioner. Since 1945 the most ambitious proposals have been for the creation of regional authorities to replace entirely the existing local authorities. Others have sought the creation of regional bodies as a third tier of government between central and local government, responsible for providing on a regional basis some services such as water supplies, airports, police, and ambulance services.

[1] See H. V. Wiseman, 'Regional Government in the United Kingdom', *Parl. Aff.* 1965–6, pp. 56–82; Sir Keith Joseph, 'Local Authorities and Regions', *Pub. Admin.* 1964, pp. 215–26; P. Self, 'Regional Planning and the Machinery of Government', *Pub. Admin.* 1964, pp. 227–40; Dudley Lofts, 'The Future Pattern of Local Government in England and Wales', *Pub. Admin.* 1959, pp. 275–92.

When the Labour Party came to power in 1964, they announced plans for the creation of regional bodies to work alongside the local authorities, and deal with economic, transport, and housing problems on a regional basis. In England, six Economic Planning Boards (originally called Regional Planning Boards) were set up in 1964 (and were later increased to eight), with separate Boards for Wales and Scotland. The Boards were composed of members of the central government departments concerned with regional problems, and they were accompanied by Economic Planning Councils, made up of members drawn from the local authorities, industry, trade unions, the universities, and other similar bodies in the regions. The members of the Planning Councils are nominated, and are not directly elected by the electorate in the region. These bodies have not satisfied most advocates of regional government, in that they have been concerned almost entirely with economic matters. They have in no way become a third tier of government between local and central government, and they have merely produced an extension of central government control in the regions.

In Scotland and Wales particularly, regional planning as it has operated since 1964 has not represented an answer to the demands for regional government. In Scotland and Wales, the question of regionalism is associated very closely with the question of nationalism,[1] and the Scottish National Party and Plaid Cymru have advocated complete independence for Scotland and Wales. As an alternative, the Liberal Party has advocated the creation of separate Parliaments for Scotland and Wales to deal with these countries' domestic affairs, on the lines of the system of devolution that operates in Northern Ireland. Thus in 1967 Scottish and Welsh Liberal MPs, with their party's backing, introduced Private Members' Bills in the House of

[1] See H. J. Hanham, *Scottish Nationalism*, London, 1969; N. McCormick (ed), *The Scottish Debate*, London 1970; G. McCrone, *Scotland's Future: the Economics of Nationalism*, London 1969; J. N. Wolfe (ed), *Government and Nationalism in Scotland*, London 1969. See also J. P. Mackintosh, 'Devolution, Regionalism and the Reform of Local Government: The Scottish Case', *PL* 1964, pp. 19–32; J. P. Mackintosh, 'Regional Administration: Has it Worked in Scotland?', *Pub. Admin.* 1964, pp. 253–76; J. P. Mackintosh, 'Scottish Nationalism', *PQ* 1967, pp. 389–402; G. H. Jones, B. Smith and H. V. Wiseman, 'Regionalism and Parliament', *PQ* 1967, pp. 403–10.

Commons seeking to secure a limited degree of home rule for Wales and Scotland. The extension of the Northern Ireland system of devolution to Scotland and Wales would carry with it the various advantages that are claimed for regional government, and it would have the additional merit of placating national feelings in Wales and Scotland.[1] It would involve the creation of Scottish and Welsh Parliaments (whether of a single house, or of two houses as in Northern Ireland), the appointment of Governors to act as representatives of the Crown and perform certain constitutional roles, the introduction of special Scottish and Welsh taxes to pay for local services, and in the case of Wales, the creation of Welsh-based administrative departments. Such changes clearly go much further than any system of regional government that seems possible in the foreseeable future. Nevertheless, following the success of the Scottish National Party and Plaid Cymru in by-elections and local government elections in 1967 and 1968, the Government set up in 1968 a Royal Commission on the Constitution, to examine in detail the implications of the various devolution proposals. It remains to be seen what recommendations and actions will result from this.

[1] See, however, R. J. Lawrence, 'Devolution Reconsidered', *PS* 1956, pp. 1–17; A. H. Birch, 'A Note on Devolution', *PS* 1956, pp. 310–11.

part five

Conclusion

14

The Nature of the
British Political System

Democracy in Britain

Modern concepts of western democracy are based largely on
the principles of free and regular elections, a broad suffrage,
and the existence of a party (or coalition of parties) capable
of forming an alternative government. Also implied is the view
that all sections of society should participate in the political
process, at least to the extent of voting at elections, while many
(but not all) would claim that, for a true democracy, it is necessary that the political leaders, as well as being representative
of the views of the electorate, should be drawn from all social,
economic, religious, and ethnic groups within the community,
and should not be drawn merely from an exclusive section of
society. It is further implied that in a democracy, between
elections, pressure groups and the mass media should give expression to electoral opinions, although attitudes vary as to the
extent to which the Government should, or in practical terms,
could be expected to respond to electoral opinions between
elections.

In Britain the effective working of the two-party system
means that there exists an alternative government, and the
electorate is given the opportunity, at regular intervals, to elect
this alternative government to power. Her Majesty's Loyal
Opposition is formally recognized within Parliament, and the
official post of Leader of the Opposition carries with it a salary
paid as one of the Consolidated Fund Services. The Government and Opposition parties present themselves to the

electorate at least every five years (other than in wartime emergencies), and in practice general elections are held every three to four years. The voters are then able to examine the record and proposals of the Government and of the Opposition, and also the general images of the parties and their leaders, and vote for the party that they find most acceptable (or least objectionable). The party favoured by the majority becomes the Government, and (apart from exceptional circumstances) remains in power for four or so years, conscious that at the end of that period it will have to submit itself to the electorate once again. All adults (with a few exceptions) are eligible to vote, and although voting is not compulsory, some 70% to 80% of the electorate normally do vote at general elections. The parties pay for the cost of their candidates' election campaigns, and salaries are paid to MPs and Ministers of the Crown, so that in this respect financial consideration need not form a barrier to political participation. For those people who do not choose to be active through the political parties, a multiplicity of pressure groups exist that provide an opportunity for political influence. The system of local government (although subordinate to the central government in the British unitary system) provides another means of political participation that is available to all members of the community.

These various considerations represent the main institutional features of British democracy, but while accepting the undoubtedly democratic basis of the system, it is necessary to realize that many of these features operate in a manner that is very different from the way that is suggested by idealized democratic theory. The electoral system, for example, has a number of deficiencies when looked at from the point of view of achieving in the House of Commons a true reflection of the views of the electorate. A candidate can be elected without receiving an absolute majority of the votes cast in his constituency, as happened in about a quarter of the constituencies in 1970. The proportion of seats that the respective parties win can be very different from the proportion of votes that they get, and in 1970 the Conservatives received 46% of the votes but won 52% of the seats. A party can gain a majority of seats without getting even a *simple* majority of votes, as happened in the 1929 and 1951 elections. These aspects of the electoral system were considered in more detail in Chapter 2, and it was pointed out that the system could not be adapted to achieve a greater degree of proportional representation without endangering the electoral system's great merit—the tendency to produce Governments with stable majorities in the House of Commons. As well as these criticisms of the detailed working of the electoral system, however, other and more fundamental criticisms are often levelled at British democracy. In order to examine the chief of these criticisms, it is necessary to consider, first of all, the credibility of the notion of an alternative government; secondly, the extent to which the people of Britain actually do participate in the political process; and thirdly, the extent to which, between elections, Governments take note of, and respond to public wishes.

An Alternative Government

The existence of an opposition party is a safeguard for democracy only if it is a real and genuine alternative, and is not merely a pale shadow of the existing government party, and also if it has a real chance of gaining power, and is not doomed to permanent opposition. One frequently repeated criticism of the British party system is that there is so little difference between the two main parties, that the electorate is faced merely with a choice between Tweedledum and Tweedledee. From one point of view it is argued that the Labour and Conservative Parties do not reflect very real differences in attitude that exist among the electorate in Britain, while from another point of view it is argued that the extent of the political consensus in Britain is such that British society, and thus the British parties, are divided only over political details. These views have been discussed in earlier chapters, and rejected in favour of the view that very real and significant differences do exist between the parties, particularly with regard to their basic attitudes and social structures.

The differences between the parties are sufficient to maintain the basic solidarity of party electoral loyalties, and are strong enough to make each party deplore the prospect of their opponents being in office. At the same time, the electoral support of the parties is sufficiently evenly balanced, and there is a large enough pool of potential floating voters, to keep Governments aware of the possibilities of electoral defeat. The danger of unpopularity leading to electoral defeat is thus a vital factor limiting what a Government can do, but the immense advantages that the electoral system gives to a Government, counters this factor to some extent. This is reflected particularly in the question of the Government's initiative in the timing of general elections—a factor which (despite Labour's defeat in 1970) gives to the Government of the day a considerable advantage over the Opposition party. This is no new feature of the electoral system, and Governments have also long been able to produce vote-catching measures to coincide with the timing of the election. In addition, however, the Government's increased ability since 1945 to influence the state of the national economy, and the more widespread acceptance of the Government's responsibilities in this direction, have meant that the election can be timed to coincide with an economic boom, or a boom to coincide with the election. The greater attention that has been paid to the opinion polls in recent years has also provided Governments with a guide (additional to by-election results, press attitudes, and other factors) to the extent of their unpopularity among the electorate, and thus to the wisdom of holding a general election, although the credibility of the polls was clearly undermined in June 1970.

For much of the nineteenth century there was a regular swing of the electoral pendulum from Government to Opposition, with the parties alternating in office at regular intervals. In part this seemed to be because a Government acquired a certain amount of unpopularity merely because it was the Government, thereby causing its electoral defeat, perhaps after it had been in power for only one Parliament. This regular swing of the pendulum was particularly marked in the period from 1868 to 1895, when Conservative (or Unionist) and Liberal Governments alternated in power. From 1895 to 1905 there was a continuous period of Unionist rule, followed by a decade of Liberal rule which was interrupted by the first world war and the split in the Liberal Party during the war. Between the wars the upheavals in the party system produced by the decline of the Liberal Party and the rise of the Labour Party, followed by the emergence of the National Government out of the traumatic events of 1931, meant that Conservative Governments, or Conservative-dominated Coalitions, held office for practically the whole of the inter-war period. The Labour election victory of 1945, and then the Conservative win in 1951, suggested that there had been a return to a regular alternation in office by two main parties, but at both the 1955 and 1959 elections the Conservative Government secured an increase in its majority in the Commons.

Thus it seemed in the nineteen-fifties and early nineteen-sixties that in effect the two-party system had developed into one-party dominance, with a permanent Government party and a permanent Opposition party, and that the electoral pendulum had ceased to swing. In fact, however, by-election results and the public opinion polls suggest that during every Parliament since 1945 the Government passed through at least one period of considerable unpopularity (see Table XXX), and that the pendulum of electoral popularity continued to swing—at times quite markedly. Undoubtedly the extent of a Government's mid-term unpopularity is easily exaggerated, and can be attributed in part to the fact that the electors at by-elections are well aware that they are not choosing a Government, and are thus more likely than at a general election to record a 'protest' vote, while public opinion polls can be misleading, in that the pollsters are posing a hypothetical question when, in the middle of a Parliament, they ask people how they would vote *if* there was an election the next day. Nevertheless, even allowing for distortions that may occur because of these factors, it is normally the case that there is a mid-term swing of opinion against the Government. It is clear that the pendulum of electoral opinion continues to swing today, and despite the fact that a Government has considerable power to combat or avoid the worst effects of a trend of opinion that develops against it, four of the eight elections since 1945 have produced a change of government.

The defeat of the Conservative Government in 1964 (with the 1966 election being the second part of this process), and of the Labour Government in 1970, revealed that there are limits to the amount of mid-term unpopularity that a Government can overcome. In 1964 particularly, the Government defeat was widely attributed to the fact that the electorate felt

TABLE XXX

Voting Intention—Gallup Poll

1945–50 Parliament (Labour Government)		Lab. % lead over Con.
1946	Jan.	19
	May	3
1947	Jan.	3
	June	0
	Sept.	−4
1948	Jan.	−1
	May	−3
	Sept.	−5
1949	Jan.	−3
	May	−4
	Sept.	−6
1950	Jan.	0

1951–5 Parliament (Conservative Government)		Con. % lead over Lab.
1952	Jan.	−3
	May	−4
	Sept.	−7
1953	Jan.	−3
	May	2
	Sept.	−3
1954	Jan.	−1
	May	−1
	Sept.	−5
1955	Jan.	1
	May	3

1950–1 Parliament (Labour Government)		Lab. % lead over Con.
1950	May	2
	Sept.	3
1951	Jan.	−11
	May	−8
	Sept.	−11

1955–9 Parliament (Conservative Government)		Con. % lead over Lab.
1955	Sept.	3
1956	Jan.	−1
	May	−3
	Sept.	−2
1957	Jan.	−5
	May	−7
	Sept.	−13
1958	Jan.	−6
	May	−10
	Sept.	2
1959	Jan.	0
	May	1
	Sept.	5

TABLE XXX—*contd.*

1959–64 Parliament (Conservative Government)		1964–6 Parliament (Labour Government)	
	Con. % lead over Lab.		Lab. % lead over Con.
1960 Jan.	4	1965 Jan.	7
May	2	May	−2
Sept.	6	Sept.	6
1961 Jan.	3	1966 Jan.	6
May	3	Mar.	8
Sept.	−2		
1962 Jan.	0		
May	−4		
Sept.	−7	For the 1966–70 Parliament	
1963 Jan.	−11	(Labour Government)	
May	−9	See Table XII, p. 50.	
Sept.	−13		
1964 Jan.	−9		
May	−17		
Sept.	−2		

Source: Figures for 1945–60 are taken from Butler and Freeman, *British Political Facts*, pp. 133–5; figures for 1960–6 are taken from *Gallup Political Index*, issued monthly by Social Surveys (Gallup Poll) Ltd

that it was 'time for a change', and that the Conservative Party was tired and lacking in inspiration after an excessively long period in office. This explanation of the Conservative defeat suggests that as well as temporary swings of opinion for and against a Government, sooner or later a more permanent swing of opinion develops, based to a large extent on the feeling that it is time 'the other side' was given a chance. Thus a Government can slow down a swing that may develop against it, and can remain in power for long periods by a judicious manipulation of its policies, the national economic situation, and the election date, but the 1959–64 and 1966–70 Parliaments illustrate that despite all the factors that are working for it, a Government cannot entirely halt a trend of opinion that develops against it, and therefore is not guaranteed permanent electoral success.

Government of the People?

To what extent do the British people participate in the political processes? In general the vast majority of people in Britain play little or no direct part in the activities of the political parties, and most people's involvement extends no further than voting at elections, while some people do not participate even to this extent. While the membership of the British political parties is high in comparison with parties in other countries, active party members form only a very small proportion of the total membership. Further, at this level, but more particularly at a Parliamentary and Ministerial level, some social groups are over-represented in proportion to their numbers in the community as a whole. There exists in Britain an undoubted social elite, based in particular on the exclusive educational background of a limited section of the community, and this social elite holds a degree of political influence that is out of all proportion to its numerical strength. In the case of the Conservative Party in Parliament, and especially in Conservative Governments when they are in power, a dominant position is occupied by the upper- and upper-middle-class element, whose educational background is that of public school, Oxbridge, and the law or big business. In the long periods this century when the Conservative Party has been in power (29 years alone, and a further 16 years in Coalition), this exclusive social element has thus enjoyed a preponderant share of Ministerial power. Even when the Labour Party (or earlier the Liberal Party) has been in office, this exclusive social element has not been excluded entirely from Ministerial power, in that Liberal and Labour Governments have also included a number of Ministers with that type of social background. Also, this social elite predominates among the top levels of the civil service, so that whichever political party is in power, the social elite retains considerable influence throughout the executive machine.

The existence of a small group who at any given time have a dominant share of political and economic power, is to be found in any political system, be it democratic or totalitarian, but in Britain this group is characterized by its *social* exclusiveness, and by its ability to perpetuate itself through the educational and social system. Marxists claim that this group constitutes a distinct Ruling Class, which has pronounced boundaries, which enjoys almost exclusive power, and which is dedicated to the maintenance of the existing social and capitalist system. Most people, however, would reject the notion that there is in Britain today a 'conspiracy' by a completely dominant and totally exclusive Ruling Class, and a more accurate picture is probably that of a predominant (although not exclusive) share of political power being held by the upper-middle-class–public school–Oxbridge-based elite. This section of society does not have rigid boundaries, and in many ways its very strength is that it is flexible and fluid, and does accept newcomers into its ranks, thereby placating and encompassing potential opposition. It does not have an exclusive share of power. Not all Conservative Ministers and MPs, and not all top civil servants have an exclusive social background, while within the Labour Party the social elite, though influential, is very far from dominant. In fact the powerful position of the working-class trade union element within the Labour Party represents a very clear limitation on any notion that the upper-middle-class element has an exclusive share of political influence in Britain. In the Labour Party, political activity through a trade union leading to Parliament has represented an alternative means to Ministerial power for those members of society whose schooling was restricted to an elementary or secondary school, who attended no University, and who were manual workers or 'white collar' union officials before entering Parliament. The part played by the trade unions in the affairs of the Labour Party, and particularly their role in the selection of the party's Parliamentary candidates, means that in at least some respects the trade unionists form a power elite within the Labour Party. The place of the trade unionists within the Labour Party, however, is not as dominant as that of the upper-middle-class element within the Conservative Party, and the trade unionists have nothing like a monopoly of Ministerial power when the Labour Party is in office. Indeed, to a great extent the trade unions have been content to use their power and influence within the Labour Party to support party leaders who were drawn from the ranks of the party's intelligentsia.

Nevertheless, both the main parties have their respective elites, which in the case of the Conservative Party overlaps with the social elements that dominate the Civil Service, the business world, and other centres of power. Although the basis of recruitment to the Civil Service is by open competition, and although membership of the political parties, and thus ultimately Parliamentary candidature, is open to all, access to these centres of power is dominated by limited sections of society. Political activity through a pressure group is open to most people, and the leaders of the various pressure groups in Britain are drawn from various sections of society, and not merely from the trade union and social elites. Some of the most powerful groups, however, are those that represent trade union and business interests, so that in this respect also, the influence of the elites that dominate the two main parties extends to the most powerful pressure groups.

Governments and Public Opinion

Whether or not Governments in Britain are drawn from only limited sections of society, they are ultimately answerable to all members of the community at general elections. Apart from the ultimate possibility of unpopularity leading to electoral defeat, however, are there any other considerations that cause Governments to take note of public wishes between general elections? The doctrine of the mandate is sometimes advanced as one such consideration. This doctrine states that a Government is only constitutionally justified in introducing policies for which it has an electoral mandate. The doctrine implies that a Government can only introduce measures that have previously been submitted for approval to the electorate at a general election, and any policies that have been presented to, and approved by the electorate, must be carried to fruition. The Government has, of course, to deal with unexpected events and crises that develop between elections, but such crises apart, Government policies must have electoral approval. Thus in the past there have been instances of Parliament being dissolved in order that the Government might secure an electoral mandate for a specific issue. In the two elections of 1910, the Liberal Government sought electoral approval for the specific issues of the 1909 Finance Bill and the reform of the powers of the House of Lords. In 1923 Baldwin secured an early dis-

solution of Parliament and sought a mandate for specific proposals for tariff reform. In 1961, and again in 1967, it was
argued in some quarters that Britain should not seek entry into
the European Common Market until the electorate had 'pronounced' on the issue in a general election or in a referendum.
One of the arguments quoted to justify a delaying power for
the House of Lords is that the Lords should be able to delay
legislation until such time as the electorate has had time to
consider it.

In general, however, theoretical support for the mandate
doctrine has come primarily from the Labour and Liberal
Parties. Their view of the Constitution sees Constitutional
authority as stemming from the people, with the electorate
having the right to pronounce on specific policies as well as
choose the Government. Thus the proud boast of the Labour
Party at the 1950 general election was that it had achieved all
the policies (and only those policies) for which it had received a
mandate in 1945. Again in the 1966 election campaign, the
Labour Party claimed that given a full Parliament the Government would fulfil all the pledges made in 1964, and renewed
and extended in 1966, and to a considerable extent the 1970
general election was fought over the question of whether
Labour had 'kept its promises.' The 'Tory view of the Constitution', on the other hand, is that Constitutional authority
stems from the Crown, and the role of the electorate is to
choose the Government but not Government policies. Thus at
an election the Government is seen as securing a general mandate to rule as it thinks fit, without being committed to specific
policies.

Despite this theoretical distinction between the parties' Constitutional attitudes over the mandate, in practice the clearest
distinction in attitudes towards the doctrine tends to be between
the Government and the Opposition. Opposition parties tend
to support the doctrine, criticizing the Government for introducing measures for which it has no mandate, while Governments tend to ignore the doctrine, regarding it as an undesirable limitation on their ability to deal with issues in a pragmatic fashion. Certainly the practicality of the doctrine can be
questioned, in that while the parties may submit detailed policy
proposals to the electorate in their election manifestos, election

campaigns tend to be fought on general issues rather than on detailed policy items, and electoral loyalties are determined in the main by party images and personalities rather than by individual policy items. The elections of 1910 and 1923, when specific mandates were sought, illustrated the difficulty, in an election campaign, of isolating specific items of policy for electoral approval. Although a Government may strive to complete in one Parliament all the measures proposed in its election programme (whether or not the electorate had been aware of the details), in practice the mandate doctrine does not prevent a Government from adapting its policies to changing circumstances, nor does it prevent a Government from introducing entirely new measures to deal with particular situations, without submitting these measures for electoral approval. In practice, therefore, the mandate doctrine does not greatly hamper a Government's freedom of action between elections, and does not represent a major electoral limitation on a Government's activities.

In the early and middle years of a Parliament a Government is in a position to ignore to a large extent public attitudes as expressed in the press, on TV and radio, through opinion polls or by-elections, or through pressure groups or constituency contacts with MPs. It can pursue its policies in the knowledge that it has three or four years in which to build up its popularity before the next general election is due. A Government's position is helped by the fact that the strength of party loyalties in Britain is such that no matter how unpopular the Government might be with the majority of the electorate (made up of the Opposition parties' supporters, and all or most of the normally uncommitted voters), there is always a substantial minority among the electorate (consisting of the Government party's die-hard supporters) on whose support the Government can rely in virtually all circumstances. The Government's position is further strengthened by the widespread lack of political enthusiasm among the electorate. As well as the deference of many voters towards the Conservative Party, there is in Britain a more general deference among all sections of the community towards the political leaders, which manifests itself particularly in a willingness to 'leave it to the Government'. Political demonstrations and rallies, and other such forcible expressions of political attitudes, involve in the main only a small percentage of the population, and for the vast majority of the people in Britain political activity extends only to voting at general elections (and perhaps not even to that). At times of major political crisis, as with the Suez furore in 1956, there is increased public interest and participation in pressure group activities connected with the crisis, but even at such times there remains an underlying willingness to leave matters to the Government's initiative, or at least to the Government and Opposition leaders and MPs to fight out among themselves. The vast majority of people in Britain, though perhaps firm in their views, remain reticent in the expression of their views.

Nevertheless, there are limits to the extent to which the electorate is happy to 'leave it to the Government', and there are limits to the extent to which the Government can ignore public attitudes. Just as the majority of people are prepared to trust the Government, so Governments are anxious not to betray this trust. The British system of government is based to a large extent upon the existence of some degree of consensus, and on the achievement of a considerable amount of trust between government and governed. Governments rely greatly on the goodwill of the various interests with which they deal, and prefer discussion, agreement, and compromise to the imposition of Government wishes on unwilling interests. Thus Governments are loath to adopt statutory powers of coercion until informal persuasion and goodwill have failed to achieve the desired ends. In recent years governments have often seemed disinclined to take a 'firm' line on issues as diverse as Parliamentary reform, regional government, taxation policy, economic planning, or the control of trade unions, despite 'declarations of intent' when new Governments come to power. One reason for this is a general desire to avoid major clashes with interested parties, which might lead to a rupture in the generally happy relations that exist in Britain between Government and people. The desire to maintain government by mutual consent is something that affects all British Governments, and tends to produce considerable modifications in Government intentions in the process of translating party ideals and policies into legislative and executive realities.

The Art of the Possible

So far in this chapter the emphasis has been placed on the limitations of British democracy. The cataloguing of deficiencies, however, should not be allowed to distract attention from the basic qualities of the system. The overriding feature of the British system is that of government by mutual consent, and this alone justifies the claim that the system is fundamentally democratic. Indeed, in many ways the British system is democratic to a fault, in that too often Governments resist desirable changes that are not acceptable to the overwhelming majority of the people of Britain, thereby producing a tendency towards stagnation. The need to preserve a high degree of trust between rulers and ruled is, however, only one of numerous factors that limits what Governments can achieve. The formal concentration of authority in the hands of the Cabinet, and particularly in the hands of the Prime Minister, suggests that Governments in Britain have virtually unlimited powers. This formal concentration of authority is based on a number of constitutional and political considerations which were discussed in Chapters 6 and 7. In practical terms, however, there is a marked distinction between what the formal concentration of authority permits a Government to do, and what practical considerations allow it to do. The dependence of Governments upon pressure groups for information and administrative co-operation has been examined in earlier chapters, as has the complexity of the administrative machine, and the dependence of Ministers upon civil servants. As well as this, a Government's power is diffused among several elements within the community. In addition to the importance of the Civil Service in the formulation and administration of Government policies, the co-operation of affected parties is also crucial. For the development of a transport policy the Government depends upon the co-operation of the nationalized industries, private enterprise transport concerns, and the various trade unions of transport employees. For the administration of education policy the Government depends upon the local authorities, and the co-operation of the various teachers' organizations, while for the achievement of national economic plans the Government relies particularly upon the trade unions and business interests. Thus Governments frequently declare that the extension of national prosperity depends upon a partnership between the Government and the various elements and interests within the state, thereby acknowledging the extent to which all Governments need the voluntary co-operation of the community as a whole.

A Government's annual legislative programme gives ample evidence of the amount of legislation that stems from Civil Service and pressure group sources. Governments are faced each year with legislation that must be enacted annually (as with the annual financial legislation); with numerous routine but essential administrative measures; with legislation that unexpectedly has been made necessary by previous measures; with legislation to deal with sudden crises. Also, the complexity of the process of preparing and passing through Parliament a major piece of legislation limits the number of measures that a Government can produce in any one session, and this is particularly true of major and controversial measures. Thus a Government that comes to power with a big legislative programme, as did Labour in 1945 and 1964, often finds that legislative priorities have to be established, with inevitable disagreements as to the order of the priorities. In this respect the Government is also limited in what it can achieve by the numerous different elements that exist within the British parties, and by the consequent difficulty of producing policies that will be acceptable to moderate and extremist elements alike. In the 1964–6 Parliament, for example, the Labour Government's plans for iron and steel nationalization were delayed, partly because of the difficulties of producing proposals that would satisfy all elements within the Labour Party.

All Government activities that have international effects are inevitably limited by Britain's standing in the world, and by Britain's international obligations. Thus MPs who call upon Governments to impose military solutions on all of Britain's overseas problems (whether in Suez or in Rhodesia) overestimate the extent to which Britain is able to impose her will upon other powers (and particularly the USA) in these matters. Similarly, demands for British Governments to pursue an independent foreign policy under-estimate Britain's dependence upon her allies in economic as well as political terms. All Governments since 1945 have faced recurring economic crises

over the strength of sterling and Britain's trading position, and
inevitably this has limited what Governments can achieve in
terms of foreign and domestic affairs. Ambitious social welfare
schemes, public building plans, and other forms of public enterprise, cannot be financed unless a healthy and expanding
economy can provide the Government with adequate revenue,
and at the same time maintain a healthy balance of trade.
Consequently, all post-war Governments have emphasized the
need for a healthy economy, and particularly increased exports,
as an essential basis for their policies. Demands for greater
governmental control over the economy are in large part
stimulated by the desire to achieve sure and steady economic
prosperity, and end the recurrent economic crises that limit
what a Government can achieve in its domestic and foreign
policies.

The Conservative Government elected in 1970 is committed
to a policy of 'less government', with reduced interference in
the private sector, and a reduction in public expenditure. It is
thus seeking to reverse, or at least to halt, the post-1945 trend
towards the extension of Government activities into more and
more spheres. Today, Labour and Conservative Governments
alike assume responsibilities in the spheres of social welfare and
the control of the economy to an extent that even in 1945 or
1950 would have aroused considerable inter-party and intra-
party conflict. As well as this (and to some extent because of it),
other vital developments have been the growth in the size of the
administrative machine (with consequent problems in Minister-
Civil Service relationships), and the increased Government contact with, and dependence upon, pressure groups for information, policy formulation, and administrative co-operation. These
factors, combined with the increased limitations on Britain's
ability to 'go it alone' in international political and economic
affairs, have greatly restricted the ability of British Governments to act decisively and independently in domestic and
external matters. Over the years the British political system has
been characterized by its durability, evolving as it has over
several centuries without the dramatic political upheavals that
have occurred in most other nations of the world. In the
nineteen-seventies, the durability of the system is likely to be
severely tested, as means are sought of dealing with the problem

of maintaining the democratic bases of the system, while at the same time overcoming the practical factors that limit the ability of British Governments to take the speedy and decisive actions that are required in the modern world.

Bibliography

This bibliography is divided into four sections. The first section contains a selection of general books that have been written about British government and politics, and which contain sections dealing with some or most of the themes covered in this book. Section two contains more detailed texts that relate to topics dealt with in specific chapters, arranged according to chapter topics. Section three is a bibliography of articles again arranged in order of chapter topics. The final section contains a selection of political biographies, autobiographies and memoirs.

The abbreviations used for the titles of the journals referred to in the bibliography (and in the footnotes in the text) are as follows:

AJPH	*Australian Journal of Politics and History*
APSR	*American Political Science Review*
ASR	*American Sociological Review*
BJS	*British Journal of Sociology*
CBR	*Canadian Bar Review*
CP	*Comparative Politics*
CPA	*Canadian Public Administration*
CJEPS	*Canadian Journal of Economics and Political Science*
G and O	*Government and Opposition*
ISSJ	*International Social Science Journal*
JAS	*Journal of American Studies*
JBS	*Journal of British Studies*
J of P	*Journal of Politics*
JRSS	*Journal of the Royal Statistical Society*
Man. Sch.	*Manchester School of Economic and Social Studies*
MJPS	*Midwest Journal of Political Science*
PAR	*Public Administration Review*
Parl.	*The Parliamentarian*
Parl. Aff.	*Parliamentary Affairs*
PL	*Public Law*
Pol.	*Politics*
Poli. Sci.	*Political Science*
POQ	*Public Opinion Quarterly*
PQ	*Political Quarterly*

PS   *Political Studies*
PSQ   *Political Science Quarterly*
Pub. Admin.   *Public Administration*
R of P   *Review of Politics*
Soc.   *Sociology*
SR   *Sociological Review*
Table   *The Table*
UTLJ   *University of Toronto Law Journal*
WP   *World Politics*
WPQ   *Western Political Quarterly*
YB   *Yorkshire Bulletin of Economic and Social Research*

SECTION ONE: GENERAL TEXTS

S. D. Bailey, *British Parliamentary Democracy,* rev. ed., 3rd ed., Houghton Mifflin, Boston, 1970.

R. Bassett, *The Essentials of Parliamentary Democracy,* Barnes & Noble, New York, 1965.

S. H. Beer and A. B. Ulam, *Patterns of Government,* Random House, New York, 1962.

R. Benewick and R. E. Dowse (eds.), *Readings on British Politics and Government,* International Publications Service, New York, 1968.

A. H. Birch, *The British System of Government,* Praeger, New York, 1967.

A. H. Birch, *Representative and Responsible Government,* U. of Toronto, 1964.

F. Boyd, *British Politics in Transition 1945–63,* Praeger, New York, 1964.

F. H. Brasher, *Studies in British Government,* Macmillan, London, 1965.

D. E. Butler and J. Freeman, *British Political Facts 1900–68,* St. Martin's, New York, 1968.

C. R. Coote, *The Government We Deserve,* Eyre & Spottiswoode, London, 1969.

H. Fairlie, *The Life of Politics,* Basic Books, New York, 1968.

H. Finer, *The Major Governments of Modern Europe,* Harper, New York, 1960.

I. Gilmour, *The Body Politic,* Hutchinson, London, 1969.

J. Gollan, *The British Political System,* Lawrence & Wishart, London, 1954.

J. H. Grainger, *Character and Style in English Politics,* CUP, London, 1969.

H. R. G. Greaves, *The British Constitution,* Allen & Unwin, London, 1955.

J. and A. M. Hackett, *British Economy: Problems and Prospects,* Humanities Press, New York, 1968.

A. H. Hanson and M. Walles, *Governing Britain,* Fontana, London, 1970.

W. Harrison, *The Government of Britain,* Hutchinson, London, 1966.

J. Harvey and L. Bather, *The British Constitution,* Macmillan, London, 1963.

J. Harvey and K. Hood, *The British State,* Lawrence & Wishart, London, 1958.

Sir I. Jennings, *The British Constitution,* CUP, London, 1966.

A. King, *British Politics,* Heath, Boston, 1966.

H. J. Laski, *Parliamentary Government in England,* Augustus M. Kelley, New York, 1970.

G. H. Le May, *British Government 1914–53: Select Documents,* Barnes and Noble, New York, 1955.

E. Liggett, *British Political Issues* (2 vols.), Pergamon Press, Elmsford, N.Y., 1965.

S. Low, *The Governance of England,* Unwin, London, 1904.

L. J. Macfarlane, *British Politics 1918–64,* Pergamon, London, 1965.

J. P. Mackintosh, *The Government and Politics of Britain,* Hutchinson, London, 1970.

P. J. Madgwick, *Introduction to British Politics,* Hutchinson, London, 1970.

A. Mathiot, *The British Political System,* Stanford U.P., Stanford, Calif., 1958.

A. Maude, *The Common Problem,* Constable, London, 1969.

W. N. Medlicott, *Contemporary England 1914–64,* David McKay, New York, 1967.

G. C. Moodie, *The Government of Great Britain,* 2nd ed., Thomas Y. Crowell, New York, 1964.

C. L. Mowat, *Britain Between the Wars,* U. of Chicago, 1955.

P. Myers, *Introduction to Public Administration,* Butterworth, London, 1970.

M. Nicholson, *The System: The Misgovernment of Modern Britain,* McGraw-Hill, New York, 1969.

H. Pelling, *Modern Britain 1885–1955,* Norton, New York, 1966.

W. A. Robson, *Politics and Government at Home and Abroad,* Allen & Unwin, London, 1968.

R. Rose, *Politics in England,* Little Brown, Boston, 1964.

A. Sampson, *The Anatomy of Britain Today,* rev. ed., Harper and Row, New York, 1965.

K. B. Smellie, *A Hundred Years of English Government,* Duckworth, London, 1950.

Diana Spearman, *Democracy in England,* Collier, New York, 1962.

F. Stacey, *The Government of Modern Britain,* OUP, London, 1968.

W. J. Stankiewicz, *Crisis in British Government,* Macmillan, New York, 1967.

M. Stewart, *The British Approach to Politics,* 6th rev. ed., Humanities Press, New York, 1967.

H. B. Stout, *British Government,* OUP, London, 1953.

A. J. B. Taylor, *English History 1914–45,* OUP, New York, 1970.

C. W. White and W. D. Hussey, *Government in Great Britain,* CUP, London, 1961.

N. Wilson, *The British System of Government,* International Publications Service, New York, 1964.

SECTION TWO: SPECIALIZED TEXTS

Chapters 1 and 3

M. Abrams and R. Rose, *Must Labour Lose?,* Penguin, London, 1960.

R. R. Alford, *Party and Society,* Murray, London, 1964.

A. J. Allen, *The English Voter,* Lawrence Verry, Mystic, Conn., 1964.

G. Almond and S. Verba, *The Civic Culture,* Little, Brown, Boston, 1965.

Walter Bagehot, *The English Constitution,* Cornell U.P., Ithaca, N.Y., 1966.

M. Banton, *Race Relations,* Basic Books, New York, 1968.

F. Bealey (ed.), *The Social and Political Thought of the British Labour Party,* Weidenfeld & Nicolson, London, 1970.

F. Bealey, J. Blondel, & W. P. McCann, *Constituency Politics,* Free Press, New York, 1966.

M. Benney, A. P. Gray, & R. H. Pear, *How People Vote,* Routledge, London, 1956.

D. R. Berry, *The Sociology of Grass Roots Politics: A Study of Party Membership,* St. Martin's Press, New York, 1970.

A. H. Birch, *Small Town Politics,* OUP, London, 1959.

R. M. Blackburn, *Union Character and Social Class,* Batsford, London, 1968.

R. Blackburn and A. Cockburn, *The Incompatibles: Trade Union Militancy and the Consensus,* Penguin Special, London, 1968.

J. Blondel, *Voters, Parties and Leaders,* Pelican, London, 1963.

J. G. Blumler and D. McQuail, *Television in Politics: Its Uses and Influence,* U. of Chicago, 1969.

V. Bogdanor and R. Skidelsky (eds.), *The Age of Affluence 1951–64,* St. Martin's Press, New York, 1970.

J. Bonham, *The Middle Class Vote,* Faber, London, 1954.

A. Briggs, *History of Broadcasting in the United Kingdom* (2 vols.), OUP, London, 1961–5.

S. Brittan, *Left or Right: The Bogus Dilemma,* Secker & Warburg, London, 1969.

I. Budge & D. W. Urwin, *Scottish Political Behaviour,* Fernhill House, New York, 1966.

D. E. Butler and D. Stokes, *Political Change in Britain,* St. Martin's Press, New York, 1969.

A. M. Carr Saunders, D. Caradog-Jones, & C. Moser, *Social Conditions in England and Wales,* OUP, London, 1958.

R. Caves *(et al.), Britain's Economic Prospects,* Brookings Institution, Washington, D.C., 1968.

Central Office of Information, *Britain: An Official Handbook,* HMSO, London (published annually).

G. D. H. Cole, *The Post-war Condition of Britain,* Routledge, London, 1956.

G. D. H. Cole, *Studies in Class Structure,* rev. ed., Humanities Press, New York, 1964.

L. Coser (ed.), *Political Sociology,* Harper Torchbooks, New York.

H. Daudt, *Floating Voters and the Floating Vote,* Stenfert Kroese, Leiden, 1961.

P. Deane & W. A. Cole, *British Economic Growth,* 2nd ed., CUP, London, 1969.

H. J. Eysenck, *The Psychology of Politics,* Humanities Press, New York, 1963.

J. E. Floud, A. H. Halsey, & F. M. Martin, *Social Class and Educational Opportunities,* Heinemann, London, 1957.

D. V. Glass (editor), *Social Mobility in Britain,* Humanities Press, New York, 1963.

J. Goldthorpe *(et al.), The Affluent Worker: Political Attitudes and Behaviour,* CUP, London, 1968.

J. H. Grainger, *Character and Style In English Politics,* CUP, London, 1969.

W. L. Guttsman, *The British Political Elite,* Basic Books, New York, 1964.

W. L. Guttsman (ed.), *The English Ruling Class,* Weidenfeld & Nicolson, London, 1969.

C. Hill, *Immigration and Integration,* Pergamon, London, 1970.

H. Hopkins, *The New Look: A Social History of the Forties and Fifties in Britain,* Houghton Mifflin, Boston, 1964.

T. W. Hutchison, *Economics and Economic Policy in Britain 1946–66*, Augustus M. Kelley, New York, 1968.

Institute of Race Relations, *Colour and the British Electorate*, Pall Mall, London, 1965.

B. Jackson & D. Marsden, *Education and the Working Class*, Routledge, London, 1962.

W. Kendall, *The Revolutionary Movement in Britain 1900–21*, Humanities Press, 1969.

M. Kinnear, *The British Voter. An Atlas and Survey since 1885*, Cornell U.P., Ithaca, N.Y., 1968.

R. Lewis & A. Maude, *The English Middle Classes*, Howard Fertig, New York, 1953.

R. Lewis & A. Maude, *Professional People*, Phoenix House, London, 1952.

I. Macdonald, *Race Relations and Immigration Law*, Butterworth, London 1968.

R. T. McKenzie and A. Silver, *Angels in Marble*, U. of Chicago, 1968.

D. C. Marsh, *The Changing Social Structure of England and Wales*, Humanities Press, New York, 1965.

D. Marvick (ed.), *Policy Decision Makers*, Free Press, New York, 1961.

D. R. Matthews, *The Social Background of Political Decision Makers*, Random House, New York, 1964.

R. Millar, *The New Classes*, Longmans, London, 1966.

R. S. Milne & H. C. Mackenzie, *Marginal Seat*, Hansard Society, London, 1958.

R. S. Milne & H. C. Mackenzie, *Straight Fight*, Hansard Society, London, 1954.

K. Newton, *The Sociology of British Communism*, Fernhill House, New York, 1970.

D. Nicholls, *The Church and State in Britain Since 1820*, Routledge, London, 1969.

E. A. Nordlinger, *The Working Class Tories*, U. of California, Berkeley, 1967.

F. Parkin, *Middle Class Radicalism*, Praeger, New York, 1968.

T. H. Pear, *English Social Differences*, Fernhill House, New York, 1956.

H. Pelling, *Popular Politics and Society in Late Victorian Britain*, Macmillan, London, 1969.

H. Pelling, *Social Geography of British Elections 1885–1910*, St. Martin's Press, New York, 1967.

S. Pollard, *The Development of the British Economy, 1914–67*, 2nd ed., St. Martin's Press, New York, 1969.

S. Pollard and D. W. Crossley, *The Wealth of Britain 1085–1966*, Schocken Books, New York, 1969.

R. Rose (ed.), *Studies in British Politics,* St. Martin's Press, New York, 1966.

J. F. S. Ross, *Parliamentary Representation,* Eyre & Spottiswoode, London, 1948.

E. A. Rowe, *Modern Politics,* Humanities Press, New York, 1970.

C. Seymour-Ure, *The Press, Politics and the Public,* Methuen, London, 1968.

M. Stacey, *Tradition and Change,* OUP, London, 1960.

H. Thomas, *The Establishment,* Blond, London, 1959.

E. P. Thompson, *Out of Apathy,* Stevens, London, 1960.

D. Thomson, *England in the Twentieth Century,* Pelican, London, 1965.

Graham Wallas, *Human Nature in Politics,* Constable, London, 1908.

K. Waltz, *Foreign Policy and Democratic Politics: the American and British Experience,* Little Brown, Boston, 1967.

E. G. Wedell, *Broadcasting and Public Policy,* International Publications Service, New York, 1968.

John Whale, *The Half-Shut Eye,* St. Martin's Press, New York, 1969.

R. Wilkinson, *The Prefects,* OUP, London, 1964.

J. Wilson, *Public Schools and Private Practice,* Allen & Unwin, London, 1962.

A. J. Youngson, *Britain's Economic Growth 1920–67,* Allen & Unwin, London, 1968.

Chapter 2

D. E. Butler, *The British Electoral System Since 1918,* OUP, London, 1963.

D. E. Butler, *The British General Election of 1951,* Macmillan, London, 1952.

D. E. Butler, *The British General Election of 1955,* Humanities Press, New York, 1970.

D. E. Butler & A. King, *The British General Election of 1964,* St. Martin's Press, New York, 1965.

D. E. Butler & A. King, *The British General Election of 1966,* Macmillan, London, 1966.

D. E. Butler & R. Rose, *The British General Election of 1959,* Humanities Press, New York, 1971.

T. Cauter & J. S. Downham, *The Communication of Ideas,* Chatto & Windus, London, 1954.

F. W. S. Craig, *British Parliamentary Election Results 1918–49,* International Publications Service, New York, 1970.

Daily Telegraph, *Election '66,* Daily Telegraph, London, 1966.

C. S. Emden, *The People and the Constitution*, OUP, London, 1962.

R. Fulford, *Votes for Women*, Faber, London, 1957.

W. B. Gwyn, *Democracy and the Cost of Politics in Britain*, OUP, New York, 1962.

L. M. Helmore, *Corrupt and Illegal Practices*, Humanities Press, New York, 1967.

R. Hodder-Williams, *Public Opinion Polls and British Politics*, Routledge & Kegan Paul, London, 1970.

J. H. Humphreys, *Proportional Representation*, Methuen, London, 1911.

Institute of Electoral Research, *Parliaments and Electoral Systems*, Scorpion Press, London, 1962.

E. Lakeman, *How Democracies Vote: A Study of Majority and Proportional Electoral Systems*, Humanities Press, New York, 1970.

E. Lakeman & J. D. Lambert, *Voting in Democracies*, Faber, London, 1959.

B. Lapping, *The Labour Government 1964–70*, Penguin, London, 1970.

R. L. Leonard, *Elections in Britain*, Van Nostrand Reinhold, New York, 1968.

S. M. Lipset, *Political Man*, Doubleday, New York, 1960.

T. Lloyd Humberstone, *University Representation*, Hutchinson, London, 1951.

R. B. McCallum & A. Readman, *The British General Election of 1945*, Humanities Press, New York, 1964.

W. J. M. Mackenzie, *Free Elections*, Humanities Press, New York, 1958.

B. R. Mitchell & K. Boehm, *British Parliamentary Election Results, 1951–64*, CUP, London, 1966.

H. G. Nicholas, *The British General Election of 1950*, Macmillan, London, 1951.

R. Oakley and P. Rose (eds.), *The Political Year 1970*, British Book Centre, Elmsford, N.Y., 1971.

P. Paterson, *The Selectorate*, MacGibbon, London, 1967.

P. G. J. Pulzer, *Political Representation and Elections*, Praeger, New York, 1968.

D. W. Rae, *The Political Consequences of Electoral Laws*, Yale University Press, 1967.

A. Ranney, *Pathways to Parliament*, Macmillan, London, 1965.

R. Rose, *Influencing Voters*, St. Martin's Press, New York, 1967.

J. F. S. Ross, *Elections and Electors*, Eyre & Spottiswoode, London, 1955.

M. Rush, *The Selection of Parliamentary Candidates*, Nelson, London, 1969.

A. N. Schofield, *Parliamentary Elections,* Shaw, London, 1959.

The Times, *House of Commons 1970,* The Times, London, 1970 (published after each general election).

J. Trenaman & D. McQuail, *Television and the Political Image,* Methuen, London, 1961.

J. Vincent, *Pollbooks: How Victorians Voted,* CUP, London, 1967.

Chapter 4

C. R. Attlee, *The Labour Party in Perspective: and Twelve Years Later,* Gollancz, London, 1949.

S. D. Bailey, *The British Party System,* Hansard Society, London, 1953.

A. Beattie (ed.), *English Party Politics* (2 vols.), British Book Centre, Elmsford, N.Y., 1971.

S. H. Beer, *Modern British Politics,* Faber, London, 1965.

M. Beloff, *The Party System,* Phoenix House, London, 1958.

R. Benewick, *Political Violence and Public Order,* Allen Lane, London, 1969.

R. Blake, *The Conservative Party from Peel to Churchill,* St. Martin's Press, New York, 1971.

J. Boyd-Carpenter, *The Conservative Case,* Wingate, London, 1950.

C. F. Brand, *The British Labour Party,* OUP, London, 1965.

A. Briggs & J. Saville, *Essays in Labour History,* Macmillan, London, 1960.

I. Bulmer Thomas, *The Growth of the British Party System* (2 vols.) 2nd ed., Humanities Press, New York, 1967–68.

I. Bulmer Thomas, *The Party System in Great Britain,* Phoenix House, London, 1953.

D. Carlton, *Macdonald Versus Henderson: The Foreign Policy of the Second Labour Government,* Humanities Press, New York, 1970.

R. S. Churchill, *The Fight for the Tory Leadership,* Houghton Mifflin, Boston, 1964.

G. D. H. Cole, *A Short History of the British Working Class Movement, 1789–1947,* rev. ed., Humanities Press, New York, 1960.

G. O. Comfort, *Professional Politicians, a Study of the British Party Agents,* Public Affairs Press, Washington, 1958.

C. Cross, *The Fascists in Britain,* Barrie & Rockliff, London, 1961.

R. E. Dowse, *Left in the Centre,* Northwestern U.P., Evanston, Ill., 1966.

M. Duverger, *Political Parties,* 2nd ed., Barnes & Noble, New York, 1964.

S. J. Eldersveld, *Political Parties,* Rand McNally, Chicago, 1964.

L. Epstein, *British Politics in the Suez Crisis,* U. of Illinois, Urbana, 1964.

E. J. Feuchtwanger, *Disraeli, Democracy and the Tory Party,* OUP, London, 1968.

R. Fulford, *The Liberal Case,* Pelican, London, 1959.

M. R. Gordon, *Conflict and Consensus in Labour's Foreign Policy 1914–65,* Stanford U.P., Stanford, Calif., 1969.

J. Grimond, *The Liberal Challenge,* Hollis & Carter, London, 1963.

Lord Hailsham, *The Conservative Case,* Pelican, London, 1959.

M. Harrison, *Trade Unions and the Labour Party Since 1945,* Allen & Unwin, London, 1960.

S. Haseler, *The Gaitskellites: Revisionism in the British Labour Party 1951–64,* Fernhill House, New York, 1969.

J. D. Hoffman, *The Conservative Party in Opposition, 1945–51,* Humanities Press, New York, 1964.

R. T. Holt and J. E. Turner, *Political Parties in Action,* Collier-Macmillan, London, 1969.

C. Irving, *Scandal '63,* Heinemann, London, 1963.

E. G. Janosik, *Constituency Labour Parties in Britain,* Praeger, New York, 1968.

R. Jenkins, *The Labour Case,* Pelican, London, 1959.

Sir I. Jennings, *Party Politics* (3 vols.), CUP, London, 1960–2.

G. Kaufman (ed.), *The Left,* International Publications Service, New York, 1966.

J. Klugmann, *History of the Communist Party of Great Britain: Formation and Early Years,* Lawrence & Wishart, London, 1969.

A. Leiserson, *Parties and Politics,* Knopf, New York, 1958.

N. A. McDonald, *The Study of Political Parties,* Random House, New York, 1955.

L. J. Macfarlane, *The British Communist Party,* Dufour Editions, Chester Springs, Pa., 1966.

R. T. McKenzie, *British Political Parties,* rev. ed., Praeger, New York, 1964.

W. F. Mandle, *Anti-Semitism and the British Union of Fascists,* Fernhill House, New York, 1968.

C. Mayhew, *Party Games,* Hutchinson, London, 1969.

R. Michels, *Political Parties,* Dover Books, New York.

R. Miliband, *Parliamentary Socialism: A Study in the Politics of Labour,* Merlin Press, London, 1961.

S. Neumann, *Modern Political Parties,* CUP, London, 1956.

J. Northcott, *Why Labour?,* Pelican, London, 1964.

G. N. Ostergaard & A. H. Halsey, *Power in Cooperatives,* International Publications Service, New York, 1965.

M. I. Ostrogorski, *Democracy and the Organisation of Political Parties* (2 vols.), Haskell House, New York, 1970.

H. Pelling, *The British Communist Party*, Black, London, 1958.

H. Pelling, *A History of British Trade Unionism*, St. Martin's Press, New York, 1963.

H. Pelling, *A Short History of the Labour Party*, 3rd ed., St. Martin's Press, New York, 1968.

D. N. Pritt, *The Labour Government 1945–51*, International Publishers, New York, 1964.

T. Raison, *Why Conservative?*, Pelican, London, 1964.

J. Rasmusson, *The Liberal Party: A Study of Retrenchment and Revival*, Constable, London, 1965.

G. K. Roberts, *Political Parties and Pressure Groups in Britain*, Weidenfeld & Nicolson, London, 1970.

E. Shinwell, *The Labour Story*, Macdonald, London, 1963.

R. Skidelsky, *Politicians and the Slump: the Labour Government of 1929–31*, Macmillan, London, 1968.

B. Smith & G. N. Ostergaard, *Constitutional Relations Between the Labour and Cooperative Parties*, Hansard Society, London, 1960.

G. Thayer, *The British Political Fringe*, International Publications Service, New York, 1965.

J. Vincent, *The Formation of the Liberal Party 1857–68*, Charles Scribner's Sons, New York, 1967.

A. Watkins, *The Liberal Dilemma*, MacGibbon, London, 1961.

G. Watson (ed.), *The Radical Alternative*, Eyre & Spottiswoode, London, 1962.

F. Williams, *Fifty Years March: the Rise of the Labour Party*, Odhams, London, 1949.

T. Wilson, *The Downfall of the Liberal Party 1914–35*, Cornell U.P., Ithaca, N.Y., 1966.

W. Young, *The Profumo Affair: Aspects of Conservatism*, Penguin, London, 1963.

Chapter 5

V. L. Allen, *Power in the Trade Unions*, Longmans, London, 1954.

V. L. Allen, *Trade Union Leadership*, Longmans, London, 1957.

V. L. Allen, *Trade Unions and the Government*, Longmans, London, 1960.

C. Arnold-Baker, *The 5,000 and the Power Tangle*, Murray, London, 1967.

M. J. Barnett, *The Politics of Legislation: the Rent Act 1957*, Weidenfeld & Nicolson, London, 1969.

E. C. Black, *The Association,* Harvard U.P., Cambridge, Mass., 1963.

T. F. Carbery, *Consumers in Politics,* Augustus M. Kelley, New York, 1969.

J. B. Christoph, *Capital Punishment and British Politics,* U. of Chicago, 1962.

H. A. Clegg, A. J. Killick, & R. Adams, *Trade Union Officers,* Harvard U.P., Cambridge, Mass., 1961.

C. H. Copeman, *Leaders of British Industry,* MacGibbon, London, 1955.

C. Driver, *The Disarmers,* Hodder & Stoughton, London, 1964.

H. Eckstein, *Pressure Group Politics,* Stanford U.P., Stanford, Calif., 1967.

H. W. Ehrmann, *Interest Groups on Four Continents,* University Press, Pittsburgh, 1958.

S. E. Finer, *Anonymous Empire,* 2nd ed., Humanities Press, New York, 1966.

S. E. Finer, *Private Industry and Political Power,* Pall Mall, London, 1958.

A. Flanders & H. A. Clegg, *The System of Industrial Relations in Great Britain,* Blackwell, London, 1956.

R. Gregory, *The Miners and British Politics 1906–14,* OUP, London, 1968.

R. A. Manzer, *Teachers and Politics in England and Wales,* U. of Toronto, 1970.

R. Martin, *Communism and the British Trade Unions,* OUP, London, 1969.

G. C. Moodie and G. Studdert-Kennedy, *Publics, Opinions and Pressure Groups,* Allen & Unwin, London, 1970.

F. Parkin, *Middle Class Radicalism: The Social Bases of the British Campaign for Nuclear Disarmament,* Praeger, New York, 1968.

M. Parkinson, *The Labour Party and the Organization of Secondary Education 1918–65,* Humanities Press, New York, 1970.

Political and Economic Planning, *Advisory Committees in British Government,* Allen & Unwin, London, 1960.

A. M. Potter, *Organised Groups in British National Politics,* Faber, London, 1961.

J. J. Richardson, *The Policy-making Process,* Humanities Press, New York, 1970.

B. C. Roberts, *Trade Union Government and Administration in Great Britain,* Bell, London, 1957.

G. Rose, *The Struggle for Penal Reform,* Stevens, London, 1962.

A. Roth, *Business Background of MPs*, Parliamentary Profiles, London, 1967.

C. Rover, *Women's Suffrage and Party Politics in Britain 1866–1914*, U. of Toronto, 1967.

P. Self & H. Storing, *The State and the Farmer*, U. of California, Berkeley, 1963.

D. Steel, *No Entry: The Background and Implications of the Commonwealth Immigrants Act, 1968*, Humanities Press, New York, 1970.

J. D. Stewart, *British Pressure Groups*, OUP, London, 1958.

E. O. Tuttle, *The Crusade Against Capital Punishment in Great Britain*, Stevens, London, 1962.

K. C. Wheare, *Government by Committee*, OUP, London, 1955.

E. L. Wigham, *Trade Unions*, OUP, London, 1969.

H. H. Wilson, *Pressure Group*, Rutgers U.P., New Brunswick, N.J., 1961.

N. Wood, *Communism and British Intellectuals*, Columbia University Press, New York, 1959.

G. Wootton, *Workers, Unions and the State*, Schocken Books, New York, 1967.

J. Wootton, *The Politics of Influence*, Harvard U.P., Cambridge 1963.

Chapters 6 and 7

G. B. Adams, *Constitutional History of England*, Cape, London, 1956.

R. K. Alderman & J. A. Cross, *The Tactics of Resignation*, Humanities Press, New York, 1968.

L. S. Amery, *Thoughts on the Constitution*, OUP, London, 1964.

Sir J. Anderson (editor), *British Government Since 1918*, Allen & Unwin, London, 1950.

Sir W. R. Anson, *The Law and Custom of the Constitution* (2 vols.), OUP, London, 1922–35.

BBC, *Whitehall and Beyond*, BBC Publications, London, 1964.

H. Berkeley, *The Power of the Prime Minister*, Allen & Unwin, London, 1967.

J. Bray, *Decision in Government*, International Publications Service, New York, 1971.

H. Calvert, *Constitutional Law in Northern Ireland*, Stevens, London, 1968.

B. E. Carter, *The Office of Prime Minister*, Faber, London, 1956.

D. N. Chester (ed.), *Lessons of the British War Economy*, CUP, London, 1951.

S. B. Chrimes, *English Constitutional History*, 4th ed., OUP, London, 1967.

J. J. Clarke, *Outlines of Central Government,* Pitman, London, 1961.

W. C. Costin & J. S. Watson, *The Law and Working of the Constitution: Documents 1660–1914* (2 vols.), 2nd ed., Fernhill House, New York, 1961–4.

J. A. Cross, *Whitehall and the Commonwealth,* Humanities Press, New York, 1967.

H. Daalder, *Cabinet Reform in Britain 1914–63,* OUP, London, 1964.

A. V. Dicey, *Introduction to the Study of the Law of the Constitution,* 10th ed., St. Martin's Press, New York, 1959.

J. Ehrman, *Cabinet Government and War 1890–1940,* Archon Books, Hamden, Conn., 1969.

P. Gordon Walker, *The Cabinet,* Cape, London, 1970.

H. J. Hanham (ed.), *The Nineteenth Century Constitution 1815–1914,* CUP, London, 1969.

Lord Hankey, *Diplomacy by Conference,* Benn, London, 1946.

Lord Hankey, *Government Control in War,* CUP, London, 1945.

R. F. V. Heuston, *Essays in Constitutional Law,* Stevens, London, 1964.

O. Hood Phillips, *Constitutional and Administrative Law,* Sweet & Maxwell, London, 1962.

O. Hood Phillips, *Leading Cases in Constitutional and Administrative Law,* Sweet & Maxwell, London, 1967.

O. Hood Phillips, *Reform of the Constitution,* Chatto & Windus, London, 1970.

A. Howard & R. West, *The Making of a Prime Minister,* Cape, London, 1965.

Sir I. Jennings, *Cabinet Government,* 3rd ed., CUP, London, 1969.

Sir I. Jennings, *The Law and the Constitution,* 5th ed., Lawrence Verry, Mystic, Conn., 1963.

Sir. I. Jennings, *The Queen's Government,* Pelican, London, 1954.

F. A. Johnson, *Defence by Committee,* OUP, London, 1960.

J. E. A. Jolliffe, *The Constitutional History of Medieval England,* W. W. Norton, New York, 1967.

D. L. Keir, *The Constitutional History of Modern Britain,* W. W. Norton, New York, 1967.

D. L. Keir and F. H. Lawson, *Cases in Constitutional Law,* OUP, London, 1967.

A. B. Keith, *The British Cabinet System,* Stevens, London, 1952.

A. B. Keith, *The Constitution of England from Queen Victoria to George VI* (2 vols.), Macmillan, London, 1940.

A. King (ed.), *The British Prime Minister,* Humanities Press, New York, 1970.

H. J. Laski, *Reflections on the Constitution,* Manchester University Press, London, 1962.

R. J. Lawrence, *The Government of Northern Ireland,* OUP, London, 1965.

K. Loewenstein, *British Cabinet Government,* OUP, London, 1967.

A. L. Lowell, *The Government of England* (2 vols.), Macmillan, New York, 1912.

J. P. Mackintosh, *The British Cabinet,* 2nd ed., Barnes and Noble, New York, 1968.

F. W. Maitland, *Constitutional History of England,* CUP, London, 1961.

G. Marshall & G. C. Moodie, *Some Problems of the Constitution,* Hutchinson, London, 1961.

Lord Morrison, *Government and Parliament,* OUP, London, 1964.

R. K. Mosley, *The Story of the Cabinet Office,* Humanities Press, New York, 1970.

M. Ogilvy Webb, *The Government Explains,* Allen & Unwin, London, 1965.

G. S. Pryde, *Scotland,* Benn, London, 1956.

R. S. Rait, *The Parliaments of Scotland,* Maclehose, Jackson, Glasgow, 1924.

P. G. Richards, *Patronage in British Government,* U. of Toronto, 1963.

Royal Institute of Public Administration, *The New Whitehall Series* (studies of individual Ministries), Allen & Unwin, London.

B. Smith, *Advising Ministers,* Humanities Press, New York, 1969.

Zara S. Steiner, *The Foreign Office and Foreign Policy,* CUP, London, 1970.

N. J. Vig, *Science and Technology in British Politics,* Pergamon, London, 1968.

M. J. C. Vile, *Constitutionalism and the Separation of Powers,* OUP, London, 1967.

E. C. S. Wade & G. G. Phillips, *Constitutional Law,* 7th ed., Lawrence Verry, Mystic, Conn., 1965.

F. M. G. Willson & D. N. Chester, *The Organization of British Central Government,* Allen & Unwin, London, 1957.

G. Wilson, *Cases and Materials on Constitutional and Administrative Law,* CUP, London, 1966.

H. V. Wiseman, *Parliament and the Executive,* Humanities Press, New York, 1966.

D. C. M. Yardley, *Introduction to British Constitutional Law,* Butterworth, London, 1969.

Chapter 8

L. Abraham & S. C. A. Hawtrey, *A Parliamentary Dictionary*, Butterworth, London, 1970.

A. Barker and M. Rush, *The Member of Parliament and His Information*, U. of Toronto, 1970.

H. Boardman, *The Glory of Parliament*, Allen & Unwin, London, 1960.

P. A. Bromhead, *Private Members' Bills*, Routledge, London, 1956.

P. Brookes, *Women at Westminster*, Davies, London, 1967.

P. W. Buck, *Amateurs and Professionals in British Politics 1918–59*, U. of Chicago, 1963.

R. Butt, *The Power of Parliament*, John Weatherhill, New York, 1968.

Lord Campion, *Introduction to the Procedure of the House of Commons*, Macmillan, London, 1958.

Lord Campion, *Parliament: a Survey*, Allen & Unwin, London, 1963.

D. N. Chester & N. Bowring, *Questions in Parliament*, OUP, London, 1962.

B. Crick, *The Reform of Parliament*, Weidenfeld & Nicolson, London, 1964.

R. Day, *The Case for Televising Parliament*, Hansard Society, London, 1966.

Sir H. Dunnico, *Mother of Parliaments*, Macdonald, London, 1951.

S. E. Finer, H. B. Berrington, and D. J. Bartholomew, *Backbench Opinion in the House of Commons, 1955–9*, Pergamon Press, London, 1961.

M. Foot, *Parliament in Danger!*, Pall Mall, London, 1965.

R. Fulford, *The Member and his Constituency*, Ramsay Muir Trust, London, 1957.

S. Gordon, *Our Parliament*, 6th ed., OUP, 1964.

Hansard Society, *Parliamentary Reform 1933–60*, Hansard Society, London, 1961.

A. H. Hanson and B. Crick (eds.), *The Commons in Transition*, Fontana, London, 1970.

A. H. Hanson & H. V. Wiseman, *Parliament at Work*, Stevens, London, 1962.

Sir A. P. Herbert, *The Ayes Have It*, Methuen, London, 1937.

A. Hill & A. Whichelow, *What's Wrong with Parliament?*, Penguin, London, 1964.

P. Howarth, *Questions in the House,* Lane, London, 1956.

E. Hughes, *Parliament and Mumbo Jumbo,* Fernhill House, New York, 1966.

Sir C. Ilbert, *Parliament,* OUP, London, 1960.

Inter-Parliamentary Union, *Parliaments,* Praeger, New York, 1963.

R. J. Jackson, *Rebels and Whips,* St. Martin's Press, New York, 1968.

Sir I. Jennings, *Parliament,* CUP, London, 1969.

Sir I. Jennings, *Parliamentary Reform,* Gollancz, London, 1934.

Lord Kilmuir, *The Law of Parliamentary Privilege,* Athlone Press, London, 1959.

H. King, *Parliament and Freedom,* Murray, London, 1962.

P. Laundy, *The Office of Speaker,* OUP, London, 1964.

K. R. Mackenzie, *The English Parliament,* Pelican, London, 1959.

Sir T. E. May, *The Law, Privileges, Proceedings and Usage of Parliament,* Butterworth, London, 1964.

D. Menhennet and J. Palmer, *Parliament in Perspective,* Dufour Editions, Chester Springs, Pa., 1967.

N. Nicolson, *People and Parliament,* Weidenfeld & Nicolson, London, 1958.

A. F. Pollard, *The Evolution of Parliament,* 2nd ed., Russell and Russell, New York, 1964.

E. Porritt & A. G. Porritt, *The Unreformed House of Commons* (2 vols.), Augustus M. Kelley, New York, 1903.

J. Redlich, *The Procedure of the House of Commons* (3 vols.), AMS Press, New York, 1969.

P. G. Richards, *Honourable Members,* 2nd ed., Hillary House, New York, 1964.

P. G. Richards, *Parliament and Conscience,* Allen & Unwin, London, 1970.

P. G. Richards, *Parliament and Foreign Affairs,* Allen & Unwin, London, 1968.

E. Taylor, *The House of Commons at Work,* Pelican, London, 1965.

B. S. Trinder, *The Victorian MP and His Constituents,* Banbury Historical Society, 1969.

J. Tunstall, *The Westminster Lobby Correspondents,* Fernhill House, New York, 1970.

S. A. Walkland, *The Legislative Process in Great Britain,* Praeger, New York, 1968.

K. C. Wheare, *Legislatures,* 2nd ed., OUP, London, 1968.

N. Wilding & P. Laundy, *An Encyclopaedia of Parliament,* 3rd ed., Humanities Press, New York, 1968.

Chapter 9

S. D. Bailey (editor), *The Future of the House of Lords,* Hansard
    Society, London, 1954.
R. Bassett, *1931 Political Crisis,* Macmillan, London, 1958.
F. W. G. Benemy, *The Queen Reigns: She Does Not Rule,* Har-
    rap, London, 1963.
P. A. Bromhead, *The House of Lords and Contemporary Politics,*
    Routledge, London, 1958.
Lord Chorley, B. Crick, & B. Chapman, *Reform of the Lords,*
    Fabian Society (Research Series, 169), London, 1954.
Dod's Parliamentary Companion, Business Dictionaries Ltd., Lon-
    don (published annually).
John Grigg, *Is the Monarchy Perfect?,* Calder, London, 1958.
F. Hardie, *The Political Influence of the British Monarchy 1868–
    1952,* Harper and Row, New York, 1970.
R. Jenkins, *Mr.Balfour's Poodle,* Chilmark Press, New York, 1968.
W. K. Jordan (ed.), *The Chronicle and Political Papers of King
    Edward VI,* Cornell U.P., Ithaca, N.Y., 1966.
A. B. Keith, *The King and the Imperial Crown,* Longmans, Lon-
    don, 1936.
K. Martin, *The Crown and the Establishment,* Pelican, London,
    1963.
J. Murray-Brown (ed.), *The Monarchy and Its Future,* Allen &
    Unwin, London, 1969.
Sir C. Petrie, *The Modern British Monarchy,* Eyre & Spottis-
    woode, London, 1961.
L. O. Pike, *Constitutional History of the House of Lords from
    Original Sources,* Burt Franklin, New York, 1964.
Vachar's Parliamentary Companion, Vachar, London (published
    quarterly).
A. Wedgwood Benn, *The Privy Council as a Second Chamber,*
    Fabian Society (Tract No. 305), London, 1957.
C. C. Weston, *English Constitutional Theory and the House of
    Lords,* AMS Press, New York, 1965.

Chapter 10

S. H. Beer, *Treasury Control,* OUP, London, 1957.
Lord Bridges, *The Treasury,* Allen & Unwin, London, 1967.
Lord Bridges, *Treasury Control,* Athlone Press, London, 1950.
British Association for the Advancement of Science, A. R. Prest
    (ed.), *Public Sector Economics,* Augustus M. Kelley, 1968.

Sir H. Brittain, *The British Budgetary System,* Allen & Unwin, London, 1959.

S. Brittan, *Steering the Economy: The Role of the Treasury,* Secker & Warburg, London, 1969.

S. Brittan, *The Treasury under the Tories 1951–64,* Pelican, London, 1964.

B. Chubb, *The Control of Public Expenditure,* OUP, London, 1952.

H. Dalton, *The Principles of Public Finance,* 4th ed., Augustus M. Kelley, New York, 1968.

J. C. R. Dow, *The Management of the British Economy,* CUP, London, 1970.

H. C. Edey & A. T. Peacock, *National Income and Social Accounting,* Hutchinson, London, 1960.

P. Einzig, *The Control of the Purse,* Secker & Warburg, London, 1959.

A. H. Hanson, *Planning and the Politicians,* Augustus M. Kelley, New York, 1970.

P. D. Henderson (ed.), *Economic Growth in Britain,* Fernhill House, New York, 1966.

U. K. Hicks, *Public Finance,* Nisbet, London, 1955.

N. Johnson, *Parliament and Administration,* Augustus M. Kelley, New York, 1966.

J. Mitchell, *Groundwork to Economic Planning,* Secker & Warburg, London, 1966.

E. L. Normanton, *The Accountability and Audit of Governments,* Manchester University Press, London, 1967.

A. T. Peacock and D. J. Robertson, *Public Expenditure: Appraisal and Control,* Oliver & Boyd, London, 1963.

A. T. Peacock & J. Wiseman, *The Growth of Public Expenditure in the United Kingdom,* OUP, London, 1961.

Political and Economic Planning, *Economic Planning and Policies in Britain, France and Germany,* Allen & Unwin, London, 1969.

A. R. Prest, *Public Finance in Theory and Practice,* Weidenfeld & Nicolson, London, 1960.

A. R. Prest, *Public Sector Economics,* Manchester University Press, 1968.

G. Reid, *The Politics of Financial Control,* Hutchinson, London, 1967.

H. Roseveare, *The Treasury,* Columbia U.P., New York, 1970.

Royal Institute of Public Administration, *Budgeting in Public Authorities,* Allen & Unwin, London, 1959.

A. Shonfield, *British Economic Policy Since the War*, Penguin, London, 1958.

S. Strange, *Sterling and British Policy*, OUP, London, 1971.

A. Williams, *Public Finance and Budgetary Policy*, Fernhill House, New York, 1963.

M. Wright, *Treasury Control of the Civil Service 1854–74*, OUP, London, 1969.

Chapter 11

M. Abramovitz & V. F. Eliasberg, *The Growth of Public Employment in Great Britain*, OUP, London, 1957.

Sir C. K. Allen, *Administrative Jurisdiction*, Stevens, London, 1956.

Sir C. K. Allen, *Bureaucracy Triumphant*, OUP, London, 1931.

Sir C. K. Allen, *Law and Orders*, Stevens, London, 1965.

Sir C. K. Allen, *Law in the Making*, 7th ed., OUP, London, 1964.

Lord Bridges, *Portrait of a Profession*, CUP, London, 1950.

R. D. Brown, *The Battle of Crichel Down*, Bodley Head, London, 1955.

R. G. S. Brown, *The Administrative Process in Britain*, Barnes & Noble, New York, 1970.

G. A. Campbell, *The Civil Service in Britain*, Duckworth, London, 1965.

Sir C. Carr, *Concerning English Administrative Law*, AMS Press, New York, 1941.

B. Chapman, *British Government Observed*, Allen & Unwin, London, 1963.

B. Chapman, *The Profession of Government*, Humanities Press, New York, 1959.

E. W. Cohen, *The Growth of the Civil Service*, Allen & Unwin, London, 1965.

Sir John Craig, *A History of Red Tape*, Macdonald, London, 1955.

T. A. Critchley, *The Civil Service Today*, Gollancz, London, 1951.

H. E. Dale, *The Higher Civil Service*, OUP, London, 1941.

S. A. de Smith, *Judicial Review of Administrative Action*, Stevens, London, 1959.

F. Dunnill, *The Civil Service: Some Human Aspects*, Allen & Unwin, London, 1956.

J. Eaves, *Parliament and the Executive in Great Britain 1939 –51,* Hansard Society, London, 1957.

H. J. Elcock, *Administrative Justice,* Fernhill House, New York, 1970.

D. Foulks, *Introduction to Administrative Law,* Butterworth, London, 1964.

G. K. Fry, *Statesmen in Disguise: The Changing Role of the Administrative Class of the British Home Civil Service 1853–1966,* Humanities Press, New York, 1970.

J. F. Garner, *Administrative Law,* Butterworth, London, 1963.

W. Gellhorn, *Ombudsmen and Others,* Harvard U.P., 1968.

E. N. Gladden, *British Public Service Administration,* Staples Press, London, 1961.

E. N. Gladden, *Civil Service or Bureaucracy?,* Staples Press, London, 1956.

E. N. Gladden, *Civil Services of the United Kingdom,* Augustus M. Kelley, New York, 1967.

E. N. Gladden, *An Introduction to Public Administration,* Staples Press, London, 1966.

H. R. G. Greaves, *The Civil Service in the Changing State,* Allen & Unwin, London, 1948.

J. A. G. Griffith & H. Street, *A Casebook of Administrative Law,* Pitman, London, 1965.

J. A. G. Griffith & H. Street, *Principles of Administrative Law,* Pitman, London, 1967.

C. J. Hamson, *Executive Discretion and Judicial Control,* Stevens, London, 1954.

E. G. Henderson, *Foundations of English Administrative Law,* Harvard U.P., Cambridge, Mass., 1963.

Sir A. P. Herbert, *Anything But Action?,* Transatlantic Arts, Levittown, N.Y., 1961.

Lord Hewart, *The New Despotism,* Benn, London, 1929.

C. Hollis, *Can Parliament Survive?,* Kennikat Press, Port Washington, N.Y.

R. M. Jackson, *Machinery of Justice,* CUP, London, 1960.

H. R. Kahn, *Salaries in the Public Services in England and Wales,* Fernhill House, New York, 1962.

G. W. Keeton, *The Passing of Parliament,* Benn, London, 1952.

R. K. Kelsall, *Higher Civil Servants in Britain,* Humanities Press, New York, 1955.

J. E. Kersell, *Parliamentary Supervision of Delegated Legislation,* Stevens, London, 1960.

W. J. M. Mackenzie & J. W. Grove, *Central Administration in Britain,* Longmans, London, 1957.

H. Parris, *Constitutional Bureaucracy*, Allen & Unwin, London, 1969.

G. Rhodes, *Administrators in Action*, U. of Toronto, 1965.

F. F. Ridley (ed.), *Specialists and Generalists*, Barnes & Noble, New York, 1968.

W. A. Robson, *The Civil Service in Britain and France*, Hogarth, London, 1956.

W. A. Robson, *The Governors and the Governed*, Louisiana State U.P., Baton Rouge, 1964.

W. A. Robson, *Justice and Administrative Law*, Greenwood Press, Westport, Conn., 1951.

D. C. Rowat, *The Ombudsman*, 2nd ed., U. of Toronto, 1968.

G. Sawer, *Ombudsmen*, CUP, London, 1964.

B. Schwartz, *Law and the Executive in Britain*, CUP, London, 1949.

C. H. Sisson, *The Spirit of Public Administration and some European Comparisons*, Faber, London, 1966.

E. Strauss, *The Ruling Servants: Bureaucracy in Russia, France and Britain*, Allen & Unwin, London, 1961.

H. Thomas (ed.), *Crisis in the Civil Service*, Blond, London, 1968.

T. E. Utley, *Occasion for Ombudsman*, Johnson, London, 1961.

Sir G. Vickers, *The Art of Judgement: A Study of Policy Making*, Basic Books, New York, 1965.

H. W. R. Wade, *Administrative Law*, 3rd ed., OUP, London, 1971.

H. W. R. Wade, *Towards Administrative Justice*, University of Michigan Press, Ann Arbor, 1963.

Sir J. Whyatt, *The Citizen and the Administration*, Stevens, London, 1962.

F. M. G. Willson, *Administrators in Action: British Case Studies*, U. of Toronto, 1961.

T. Wilson, *Policies for Regional Development*, Lawrence Verry, Mystic, Conn., 1966.

Chapter 12

Acton Society Trust, *Nationalized Industry* (twelve parts), Acton Society, London 1950–2.

R. J. S. Baker, *The Management of Capital Projects*, Bell, London, 1962.

G. B. Baldwin, *Beyond Nationalization*, Harvard U.P., Cambridge, 1955.

E. E. Barry, *Nationalization in British Politics,* Cape, London, 1966.

H. A. Clegg, *Industrial Democracy and Nationalization,* Blackwell, London, 1953.

H. A. Clegg & T. E. Chester, *The Future of Nationalization,* Blackwell, London, 1955.

K. Coates and A. Topham, *Industrial Democracy in Great Britain,* MacGibbon & Kee, London, 1968.

D. Coombes, *The MP and the Administration,* Allen & Unwin, London, 1966.

D. Corbett, *Politics and the Airlines,* U. of Toronto, 1965.

Fabian Group, *The Future of Public Ownership,* Fabian Society (Tract No. 344), London, 1963.

P. S. Florence, *Industry and the State,* Hutchinson, London, 1957.

C. D. Foster, *The Transport Problem,* Blackie, London, 1963.

W. G. Friedmann (editor), *The Public Corporation,* Stevens, London, 1954.

Hugh Gaitskell, *Socialism and Nationalization,* Fabian Society (Tract No. 300), London, 1956.

J. W. Grove, *Government and Industry in Britain,* Fernhill House, New York, 1962.

K. M. Gwilliam, *Transport and Public Policy,* Lawrence Verry, Mystic, Conn., 1964.

A. H. Hanson, *Managerial Problems in Public Enterprise,* Asia, London, 1962.

A. H. Hanson (editor), *Nationalization: A Book of Readings,* U. of Toronto, 1963.

A. H. Hanson, *Parliament and Public Ownership,* Cassell, London, 1962.

A. H. Hanson, *Public Enterprise and Economic Development,* Routledge, London, 1959.

W. W. Haynes, *Nationalization in Practice,* Maxwell Reprint, Elmsford, N.Y., 1953.

C. Jenkins, *Power at the Top,* MacGibbon, London, 1959.

J. Jewkes, *Public and Private Enterprise,* U. of Chicago, 1966.

K. Katzarov, *The Theory of Nationalization,* Nijhoff, The Hague, 1965.

R. Kelf-Cohen, *Twenty Years of Nationalization,* St. Martin's Press, New York, 1969.

H. Morrison, *Socialization and Transport,* Constable, London, 1933.

T. H. O'Brien, *British Experiments in Public Ownership and Control,* Allen & Unwin, London, 1937.

A. J. Pearson, *The Railways and the Nation*, Allen & Unwin, London, 1964.

G. L. Reid and K. Allen, *Nationalized Industries*, Penguin, London, 1970.

W. A. Robson, *Nationalized Industry and Public Ownership*, Allen & Unwin, London, 1962.

W. A. Robson (editor), *Problems of Nationalized Industries*, Allen & Unwin, London, 1952.

W. A. Robson (editor), *Public Ownership*, Allen & Unwin, London, 1937.

A. A. Rogow, *The Labour Government and British Industry*, Blackwell, London, 1955.

G. W. Ross, *The Nationalization of Steel*, International Publications Service, New York, 1965.

J. R. Sargent, *British Transport Policy*, OUP, London, 1958.

M. Shanks (editor), *The Lessons of Public Enterprise*, Cape, London, 1963.

W. Thornhill, *The Nationalized Industries*, Nelson, London, 1968.

L. J. Tivey, *Nationalization in British Industry*, Cape, London, 1966.

W. E. Weiner, *British Labour and Public Ownership*, Stevens, London, 1960.

Chapter 13

Acton Society Trust, *Regionalism in England* (3 vols.), Acton Society, London, 1966.

H. Benham, *Two Cheers for the Town Hall*, Hutchinson, London, 1964.

H. J. Boyden, *Councils and their Public*, Fabian Society (Research Series 221), London, 1961.

J. G. Bulpitt, *Party Politics in English Local Government*, Fernhill House, New York, 1967.

E. Burney, *Housing on Trial: A Study of Immigrants in Local Government*, OUP, London, 1967.

R. H. Campbell, *Scotland Since 1707*, Blackwell, London, 1968.

Central Office of Information, *Local Government in Scotland*, HMSO, Edinburgh, 1958.

D. N. Chester, *Central and Local Government*, Macmillan, London, 1951.

J. J. Clarke, *A History of Local Government in the United Kingdom,* Fernhill House, New York, 1955.

J. J. Clarke, *The Local Government of the United Kingdom,* Pitman, London, 1955.

J. J. Clarke, *Outlines of the Local Government of the United Kingdom,* Pitman, London, 1960.

R. V. Clements, *Local Notables and the City Council,* Macmillan, London, 1969.

M. Cole, *Servant of the County,* Dobson, London, 1956.

C. A. Cross, *Principles of Local Government Law,* Sweet & Maxwell, London, 1966.

J. B. Cullingworth, *Housing and Local Government,* Allen & Unwin, London, 1967.

J. B. Cullingworth, *Town and Country Planning in England and Wales,* Allen & Unwin, London, 1970.

J. B. Cullingworth and S. C. Orr (eds.), *Regional and Urban Studies,* Sage Publications, Beverly Hills, Calif., 1969.

L. de Paor, *Divided Ulster,* Penguin, London, 1970.

G. Drain, *The Organization and Practice of Local Government,* Lawrence Verry, Mystic, Conn., 1966.

J. M. Drummond, *The Finance of Local Government,* rev. ed., Lawrence Verry, Mystic, Conn., 1962.

O. D. Edwards, G. Evans, I. Rhys and H. MacDiarmid, *Celtic Nationalism,* Barnes and Noble, New York, 1968.

H. Finer, *English Local Government,* Methuen, London, 1950.

Louis Golding, *Dictionary of Local Government in England and Wales,* Lawrence Verry, Mystic, Conn., 1962.

L. P. Green, *Provincial Metropolis: The Future of Local Government,* Fernhill House, New York, 1959.

J. A. G. Griffith, *Central Departments and Local Authorities,* U. of Toronto, 1966.

H. J. Hanham, *Scottish Nationalism,* Harvard U.P., Cambridge, 1969.

J. S. Harris, *British Government Inspection: The Local Services and the Central Departments,* Stevens, London, 1955.

W. O. Hart, *Introduction to the Law of Local Government and Administration,* Butterworth, London, 1962.

Max Hastings, *Ulster 1969: The Fight For Civil Rights in Northern Ireland,* Gollancz, London, 1970.

T. E. Headrick, *The Town Clerk in English Local Government,* U. of Toronto, 1962.

N. P. Hepworth, *Finance of Local Government,* Lawrence Verry, Mystic, Conn., 1970.

D. M. Hill, *Participating in Local Affairs*, Pelican, London, 1970.

R. M. Jackson, *The Machinery of Local Government*, Macmillan, London, 1958.

W. E. Jackson, *Local Government in England and Wales*, Pelican, London, 1959.

W. E. Jackson, *The Structure of Local Government in England and Wales*, Longmans, London, 1966.

Sir I. Jennings, *Principles of Local Government Law*, 4th ed., Lawrence Verry, Mystic, Conn., 1960.

R. E. C. Jewell, *Central and Local Government*, Charles Knight, London, 1968.

G. W. Jones, *Borough Politics*, Macmillan, London, 1969.

B. Keith-Lucas, *The English Local Government Franchise*, Blackwell, London, 1952.

B. Keith-Lucas (ed.), *The History of Local Government in England: Josef Redlich and Francis W. Hirst*, Macmillan, London, 1970.

J. G. Kellas, *Modern Scotland: The Nation since 1870*, Praeger, New York, 1968.

E. Layton, *Building by Local Authorities*, U. of Toronto, 1961.

J. M. Lee, *Social Leaders and Public Persons*, OUP, London, 1963.

V. D. Lipman, *Local Government Areas, 1834–1945*, Blackwell, London, 1949.

D. Lofts (editor), *Local Government Today and Tomorrow*, Municipal Journal, London, 1963.

N. MacCormick (ed.), *The Scottish Debate*, OUP, London, 1970.

G. McCrone, *Regional Policy in Britain*, Lawrence Verry, Mystic, Conn., 1969.

G. McCrone, *Scotland's Future: The Economics of Nationalism*, Augustus M. Kelley, New York, 1969.

J. P. Mackintosh, *The Devolution of Power*, Penguin Special, London, 1968.

B. J. McLoughlin, *Urban and Regional Planning: A Systems Approach*, Praeger, New York, 1969.

A. H. Marshall, *Financial Administration in Local Government*, U. of Toronto, 1961.

G. Marshall, *Police and Government*, Methuen, London, 1968.

Sir J. Maud & S. E. Finer, *Local Government in England and Wales*, OUP, London, 1953.

J. H. Morris, *Local Government Areas*, Shaw, London, 1960.

H. J. Paton, *The Claim of Scotland*, Humanities Press, New York, 1968.

J. Redlich & F. W. Hirst, *The History of Local Government in England*, Augustus M. Kelley, New York, 1970.

A. M. Rees & T. Smith, *Town Councillors*, Acton Society, London, 1964.

E. Rhodes, *Public Administration in Northern Ireland*, Magee University College, Londonderry, 1967.

G. R. Rhodes and S. K. Ruck, *The Government of Greater London*, Lawrence Verry, Mystic, Conn., 1970.

P. G. Richards, *Delegation in Local Government*, Allen & Unwin, London, 1956.

P. G. Richards, *The New Local Government System*, Lawrence Verry, Mystic, Conn., 1968.

P. Riddell, *Fire Over Ulster*, Hamish Hamilton, London, 1970.

B. J. Ripley, *Administration in Local Authorities*, Butterworth, London, 1970.

W. A. Robson, *The Development of Local Government*, Allen & Unwin, London, 1954.

W. A. Robson, *The Government and Mis-Government of London*, Allen & Unwin, London, 1948.

W. A. Robson, *Local Government in Crisis*, Allen & Unwin, London, 1968.

W. A. Robson (editor), *Great Cities of the World*, Allen & Unwin, London, 1957.

Royal Institute of Public Administration, *New Sources of Local Revenue*, Allen & Unwin, London, 1956.

S. K. Ruck, *London Government and the Welfare Services*, Fernhill House, New York, 1963.

S. K. Ruck, *Municipal Entertainment and the Arts in Greater London*, Allen & Unwin, London, 1968.

A. N. Schofield, *Local Government Elections*, Shaw, London, 1954.

W. H. Shape, *How To Find Out About Local Government*, Pergamon, London, 1969.

L. J. Sharpe, *A Metropolis Votes*, LSE, London, 1962.

L. J. Sharpe (ed.), *Voting in Cities: The 1964 Borough Elections*, Lawrence Verry, Mystic, Conn., 1967.

F. Smallwood, *Greater London: the Politics of Metropolitan Reform*, Bobbs-Merrill, Indianapolis, 1965.

K. B. Smellie, *A History of Local Government*, 3rd ed., Fernhill House, New York, 1969.

B. C. Smith, *Regional Institutions*, Acton Society, London, 1964.

J. Stanyer, *County Government in England and Wales*, Humanities Press, New York, 1968.

J. H. Warren, *The English Local Government System*, 8th ed., Lawrence Verry, Mystic, Conn., 1965.

J. H. Warren, *The Local Government Service*, Lawrence Verry, Mystic, Conn., 1952.

West Midland Group, *Local Government and Central Control*, Fernhill House, New York, 1956.

H. V. Wiseman, *Local Government at Work*, Humanities Press, New York, 1967.

J. N. Wolfe (ed.), *Government and Nationalism in Scotland*, Aldine Publishing, Chicago, 1969.

SECTION THREE: ARTICLES

Chapters 1 and 3

M. Abrams, 'Social Change in Modern Britain', *PQ* 1959, pp. 149–56.

M. Abrams, 'Social Class and British Politics', *POQ* 1961, pp. 342–51.

M. Abrams, 'Social Trends and Electoral Behaviour', *BJS* 1962, pp. 228–42.

M. Abrams, 'British Elite Attitudes and the European Common Market', *POQ* 1965, pp. 236–46.

M. Abrams, 'Press, Polls and Votes in Britain Since the 1955 General Election', *POQ* 1957, pp. 543–7.

P. Abrams & A. Little, 'The Young Activist in British Politics', *BJS* 1965, pp. 315–32.

P. Abrams & A. Little, 'The Young Voter in British Politics', *BJS* 1965, pp. 95–109.

A. J. Allen, 'Voting Recollections and Intentions in Reading: an Opinion Poll Experiment', *Parl. Aff.* 1967, pp. 170–7.

V. L. Allen, 'The Ethics of Trade Union Leaders', *BJS* 1956, pp. 314–36.

C. Bagley, 'Racial Prejudice and the "Conservative" Personality: A British Sample', *PS* 1970, pp. 134–41.

F. Bealey & D. J. Bartholomew, 'The Local Elections in Newcastle-under-Lyme, May 1958', *BJS* 1962, pp. 278–85 and 350–368.

S. H. Beer, 'The Comparative Method and the Study of British Politics', *CP* 1968–9, pp. 19–36.

R. J. Benewick (*et al.*), 'The Floating Voter and the Liberal View of Representation', *PS* 1969, pp. 177–95.

M. Benney & P. Geiss, 'Social Class and Politics in Greenwich', *BJS* 1950, pp. 310–27.

D. Berry, 'Party Membership and Social Participation', *PS* 1969, pp. 196–207.

A. H. Birch, 'Citizen Participation in Political Life: England and Wales', *ISSJ* 1960, pp. 15–26.

A. H. Birch & P. W. Campbell, 'Voting Behaviour in a Lancashire Constituency', *BJS* 1950, pp. 197–208.

J. M. Bochel and D. J. Denver, 'Religion and Voting: A Critical Review and a New Analysis', *PS* 1970, pp. 205–19.

J. Bonham, 'The Middle Class Elector', *BJS* 1952, pp. 222–30.

J. Bonnor, 'The Four Labour Cabinets', *SR* 1958, pp. 37–47.

A. P. Brainard, 'The Law of Elections and Business Interest Groups in Britain', *WPQ* 1960, pp. 670–7.

A. P. Brier and R. E. Dowse, 'The Politics of the A-political', *PS* 1969, pp. 334–8.

D. E. Butler, 'Voting Behaviour and its Study in Britain', *BJS* 1955, pp. 93–103.

J. Carson, 'Defining and Protecting Civil Liberties', *PQ* 1970, pp. 316–27.

J. B. Christoph, 'Consensus and Cleavage in British Political Ideology', *APSR* 1965, pp. 629–42.

E. J. Cleary & H. Pollins, 'Liberal Voting at the General Election of 1951', *SR* 1953, pp. 27–41.

B. Crick, 'Some Reflections on the Late Election', *PL* 1960, pp. 36–49.

H. J. Eysenck, 'Primary Social Attitudes as Related to Social Class and Political Party', *BJS* 1951, pp. 198–209.

R. Fletcher, 'Social Change in Britain', *PQ* 1963, pp. 399–410.

W. George, 'Social Conditions and the Labour Vote in the County Boroughs of England and Wales', *BJS* 1951, pp. 255–9.

J. H. Goldthorpe & D. Lockwood, 'Affluence and the British Class Structure', *SR* 1963, pp. 133–63.

H. Grisewood, 'The BBC and Political Broadcasting in Britain', *Parl. Aff.* 1962–3, pp. 42–5.

D. W. Harding, 'Political Scepticism in Britain', *PQ* 1959, pp. 18–28.

E. C. Hargrove, 'Values and Change: A Comparison of Young Elites in England and America', *PS* 1969, pp. 339–44.

J. S. Harris, 'Television as a Political Issue in Britain', *CJEPS* 1955, pp. 328–38.

L. H. Harrison & F. E. Crossland, 'The British Labour Party in General Elections 1906–45', *J of P* 1950, pp. 383–404.

E. J. Heubel, 'Church and State in England: the Price of Establishment', *WPQ* 1965, pp. 646–55.

C. O. Jones, 'Inter-Party Competition in Britain 1950–9', *Parl. Aff.* 1963, pp. 50–6.

M. Kahan, D. E. Butler and D. E. Stokes, 'On the Analytical Division of Social Class', *BJS* 1966, pp. 122–32.

D. Kavanagh, 'The Orientations of Community Leaders to Parliamentary Candidates', *PS* 1967, pp. 351–6.

M. P. Kochman, 'Liberal Party Activists and Extremism', *PS* 1968, pp. 253–6.

G. K. Lewis, 'Protest Among the Immigrants: The Dilemma of Minority Culture', *PQ* 1969, pp. 426–35.

T. Lupton and C. Shirley Wilson, 'The Social Background and Connections of "Top Decision Makers"', *Man. Sch.* 1959, pp. 30–52.

R. B. McCallum, 'The Study of Psephology', *Parl. Aff.* 1955, pp. 508–13.

J. E. MacColl, 'Public Attitudes to Politics', *PQ* 1959, pp. 6–17.

R. T. McKenzie, 'Laski and the Social Bases of the Constitution', *BJS* 1952, pp. 260–3.

D. McQuail, L. O'Sullivan and W. G. Quine, 'Elite Education and Political Values', *PS* 1968, pp. 257–66.

D. G. Macrae, 'The Social Science Press: United Kingdom', *ISSJ* 1967, pp. 236–44.

T. H. Marshall (*et al.*), 'The Role of the Social Services', *PQ* 1969, pp. 1–102.

F. M. Martin, 'Social Status and Electoral Choice in Two Constituencies', *BJS* 1952, pp. 231–41.

R. S. Milne & H. C. Mackenzie, 'The Floating Vote', *PS* 1955, pp. 65–8.

W. H. Morris Jones, 'In Defence of Apathy', *PS* 1954, pp. 25–37.

J. P. Nettl, 'Consensus or Elite Domination: the Case of Business', *PS* 1965, pp. 22–44.

T. Nossiter, 'Voting Behaviour 1832–72', *PS* 1970, pp. 380–9.

J. Owen, 'The Polls and Newspaper Appraisal of the Suez Crisis', *POQ* 1957, pp. 350–4.

K. Panther-Brick, 'Social Class and Political Institutions', *PS* 1956, pp. 88–9.

F. Parkin, 'Working Class Conservatives', *BJS* 1967, pp. 278–90.

R. H. Pear, 'The Liberal Vote', *PQ* 1962, pp. 247–54.

J. R. Pennock, 'The Political Power of British Agriculture', *PS* 1959, pp. 291–6.

D. E. G. Plowman, W. E. Minchinton & M. Stacey, 'Local Social Status in England and Wales', *SR* 1962, pp. 161–202.

J. Rasmussen, 'Problems of Democratic Development in Britain: an American View', *PQ* 1964, pp. 386–96.

W. A. Robson, 'Education and Democracy', *PQ* 1959, pp. 67–78.

R. Rose and H. Mossawir, 'Voting and Elections: A Functional Analysis', *PS* 1967, pp. 173–201.

R. Rose, 'Class and Party Divisions: Britain as a Test Case', *Soc.* 1968, pp. 129–62.

W. G. Runciman, ' "Embourgeoisement", Self-Rated Class and Party Preference', *SR* 1964, pp. 137–54.

W. G. Runciman, 'A Method for Cross National Comparison of Political Consensus', *BJS* 1962, pp. 151–5.

P. Self & H. Storing, 'The Birch in the Cupboard', *PL* 1960, pp. 367–95.

C. Seymour-Ure, 'Editorial Policy Making in the Press', *G and O* 1969, pp. 426–525.

R. Stark, 'Class, Radicalism and Religious Involvement in Britain', *ASR* 1964, pp. 698–706.

E. R. Tapper and R. A. Butler, 'Continuity and Change In Adolescent Political Party Preferences', *PS* 1970, pp. 390–4.

R. Turner, 'Sponsored and Contest Mobility and the School System', *ASR* 1960, pp. 855–67.

R. Wilkinson, 'Political Leadership and the Late Victorian Public School', *BJS* 1960, pp. 320–30.

B. Williams, 'Science and Technology as Development Factors: United Kingdom', *ISSJ* 1966, pp. 408–26.

B. Wooton, 'Is there a Welfare State? A Review of Recent Social Change in Britain', *PSQ* 1963, pp. 179–97.

M. Young & P. Willmott, 'Social Grading by Manual Workers', *BJS* 1956, pp. 337–45.

Chapter 2

M. Abrams, 'Opinion Polls and Party Propaganda', *POQ* 1964, pp. 13–19.

M. Abrams, 'Public Opinion Polls and Political Parties', *POQ* 1963, pp. 9–18.

A. Albu, R. Prentice and J. Bray, 'Lessons of the Labour Government', *PQ* 1970, pp. 141–55.

R. K. Alderman, 'Contested Elections in the Constituency of Mr Speaker', *Parl.* 1966, pp. 132–4.

C. R. Bagley, 'Does Candidates' Position on the Ballot Paper Influence Voters' Choice?', *Parl. Aff.* 1965–6, pp. 162–74.

A. Barker, 'Disqualification from the House—the "Reverse System" ', *Parl. Aff.* 1958–9, pp. 469–74.

A. A. Barrett, 'Service Candidates at Parliamentary Elections 1962–3', *Table* 1963, pp. 39–43.

M. Beloff, 'Reflections on the British General Election of 1966', *G and O* 1965–6, pp. 529–34.

H. Berrington, 'The General Election of 1964', *JRSS* 1965, pp. 17–66.

A. H. Birch, P. W. Campbell, & P. G. Lucas, 'The Popular Press in the British General Election of 1955', *PS* 1956, pp. 297–306.

P. Bromhead, 'The General Election of 1966', *Parl. Aff.* 1965–6, pp. 332–45.

J. C. Brown, 'Local Party Efficiency as a Factor in the Outcome of British Elections', *PS* 1958, pp. 174–8.

P. W. Buck, 'Election Experience of Candidates for the House of Commons 1918–55', *WPQ* 1959, pp. 485–91.

P. W. Buck, 'By-Elections in Parliamentary Careers, 1918–59', *WPQ* 1961, pp. 432–5.

P. W. Buck, 'First Time Winners in the British House of Commons Since 1918', *APSR* 1964, pp. 662–7.

D. E. Butler, 'The Redistribution of Seats', *Pub. Admin.* 1955, pp. 125–47.

D. E. Butler, A. Stevens and D. Stokes, 'The Strength of the Liberals Under Different Electoral Systems', *Parl. Aff.* 1969, pp. 10–15.

J. B. Christoph, 'The Press and Politics in Britain and America', *PQ* 1963, pp. 137–50.

J. T. Craig, 'Parliament and the Boundary Commissions', *PL* 1959, pp. 23–45.

P. Crane, 'What's in a Party Image?', *PQ* 1959, pp. 230–43.

N. Deakin and J. Bourne, 'Powell, the Minorities and the 1970 Election', *PQ* 1970, pp. 399–415.

T. Driberg, 'Speaker's Conference on Electoral Law', *Parl.* 1967, pp. 213–16.

H. Durant, 'Public Opinion Polls and Foreign Policy', *BJS* 1955, pp. 149–58.

L. Epstein, 'The Nuclear Deterrent and the British Election of 1964', *JBS* 1966, pp. 139–63.

C. A. E. Goodhart and R. J. Bhansali, 'Political Economy', *PS* 1970, pp. 43–106.

W. Hampton, 'The Electoral Response to a Multi-Vote Ballot', *PS* 1968, pp. 266–72.

M. Harrison, 'Comparative Party Finance: Britain', *J of P* 1963, pp. 664–85.

A. G. Hawkes, 'An Approach to the Analysis of Electoral Swing', *JRSS* 1969, pp. 68–79.

J. Huddleston, 'The Disenchanted Electorate', *Parl. Aff.* 1967–8, pp. 216–25.

N. Johnson, 'Servicemen and Parliamentary Elections', *Parl. Aff.* 1962–3, pp. 207–12 *and* 440–4.

C. O. Jones, 'Inter Party Competition in Britain 1950–9', *Par. Aff.* 1963–4, pp. 50–6.

B. Keith Lucas, 'Three Questions on Electoral Procedure', *Parl. Aff.* 1963–4, pp. 195–9.

M. G. Kendall & A. Stuart, 'The Law of the Cubic Proportion in Election Results', *BJS* 1950, pp. 183–96.

J. D. Lees, 'Aspects of Third Party Campaigning in the 1964 General Election', *Parl. Aff.* 1965–6, pp. 83–90.

W. S. Livingston, 'British General Elections and the Two Party System 1945–55', *MJPS* 1959, pp. 168–88.

W. S. Livingston, 'Minor Parties and Minority MPs 1945–55', *WPQ* 1959, pp. 1017–38.

W. J. M. Mackenzie, 'The Export of Electoral Systems', *PS* 1957, pp. 240–57.

D. McLachlan, 'The Press and Public Opinion', *BJS* 1955, pp. 159–68.

J. C. March, 'Party Legislative Representation as a Function of Election Results', *POQ* 1958, pp. 521–43.

F. C. Newman, 'Money and the Election Law in Britain—Guide for America', *WPQ* 1957, pp. 582–602.

W. Pickles, 'Political Attitudes in the Television Age', *PQ* 1959, pp. 54–66.

W. Pickles, 'Psephology Reconsidered', *PQ* 1965, pp. 460–70.

D. E. G. Plowman, 'Public Opinion and the Polls', *BJS* 1962, pp. 331–49.

H. Pollins, 'The Significance of the Campaign in British Elections', *PS* 1953, pp. 207–15.

A. Ranney, 'Inter-Constituency Movement of British Parliamentary Candidates 1951–9', *APSR* 1964, pp. 36–45.

J. Rasmussen, 'The Implications of Safe Seats for British Democracy', *WPQ* 1966, pp. 517–29.

J. Rasmussen, 'The Disutility of the Swing Concept in British Psephology', *Parl. Aff.* 1964–5, pp. 443–54.

M. Rees, 'Defects in the System of Electoral Registration', *PQ* 1970, pp. 220–3.

W. Rees-Mogg, T. E. M. McKitterick & P. Skelsey, 'The Selection of Parliamentary Candidates', *PQ* 1959, pp. 215–29.

P. G. Richards, 'A Study in Political Apprenticeship', *Parl. Aff.* 1955–6, pp. 353–7.

R. Rose, 'Money and the Election Law', *PS* 1961, pp. 1–15.

R. Rose, 'Political Decision Making and the Polls', *Parl. Aff.* 1962–3, pp. 188–202.

J. F. S. Ross, 'The Incidence of Election Expenses', *PQ* 1952, pp. 175–81.

K. A. F. Sainsbury, 'Democracy and Electoral Methods', *Parl. Aff.* 1958–9, pp. 429–36.

G. N. Sanderson, 'The "Swing of the Pendulum" in British General Elections', *PS* 1966, pp. 349–60.

R. M. Scammon, 'British By-elections 1951–5', *J of P* 1956, pp. 83–94.

B. B. Shaffer, 'The British General Election, 1964: A Retrospect', *AJPH* 1965, pp. 7–22.

W. Thornhill, 'Parliament, The People and Party', *YB* 1964, pp. 42–51.

V. Vale, 'The Computer as Boundary Commissioner?', *Parl Aff.* 1968–9, pp. 240–9.

D. C. Watt, 'Foreign Affairs, the Public Interest, and the Right to Know', *PQ* 1963, pp. 121–36.

P. M. Williams, 'The Politics of Redistribution', *PQ* 1968, pp. 239–254.

P. M. Williams, 'Two Notes on the British Electoral System', *Parl. Aff.* 1966–7, pp. 13–30.

Lord Windlesham, 'Television as an Influence on Public Opinion', *PQ* 1964, pp. 375–85.

K. Younger, 'Public Opinion and Foreign Policy', *BJS* 1955, pp. 169–75.

Chapter 4

R. K. Alderman, 'The Conscience Clause of the PLP', *Parl. Aff.* 1965–6, pp. 224–32.

R. K. Alderman, 'Discipline in the PLP 1945–51', *Parl. Aff.* 1964–5, pp. 293–305.

Lord Attlee, 'The Attitudes of MPs and Active Peers', *PQ* 1959, pp. 29–32.

F. Bealey, 'Keir Hardie and the Labour Groups', *Parl. Aff.* 1956–7, pp. 81–93 *and* 220–33.

R. Bean, 'Militancy, Policy Formation and Membership Opposition in the ETU 1945–61', *PQ* 1965, pp. 181–90.

S. H. Beer, 'Democratic One-Party Government for Britain', *PQ* 1961, pp 114–23.

S. H. Beer, 'Party Government in Britain Today', *WP* 1957–8, pp. 154–60.

S. H. Beer, 'The Conservative Party of Great Britain', *J of P* 1952 pp. 41–71.

S. H. Beer, 'The Future of British Politics', *PQ* 1955, pp. 33–43.

H. Berrington, 'The Conservative Party: Revolts and Pressures', *PQ* 1961, pp. 363–73.

J. Blondel, 'The Conservative Association and the Labour Party in Reading', *PS* 1958, pp. 101–19.

A. Brady, 'The British Two Party System', *Poli. Sci.* 1956, pp. 3–18.

J. M. Burns, 'The Parliamentary Labour Party in Great Britain', *APSR* 1950, pp. 855–72.

A. Butler, '1951–9 The Conservatives in Power', *PQ* 1959, pp. 325–35.

T. W. Casstevens, 'Party Theories and British Parties', *MJPS* 1961, pp. 391–9.

M. G. Clarke, 'National Organisation and the Constituency Association in the Conservative Party', *PS* 1969, pp. 345–7.

D. I. Davies, 'The Politics of the TUC's Colonial Policy', *PQ* 1964, pp. 23–34.

M. Davis & S. Verba, 'Party Affiliation and International Opinions in Britain and France', *POQ* 1960, pp. 590–604.

D. Donnison & D. E. G. Plowman, 'The Functions of Local Labour Parties', *PS* 1954, pp. 154–67.

R. E. Dowse, 'The Entry of the Liberals into the Labour Party 1914–20', *YB* 1961, pp. 78–87.

R. E. Dowse, 'The PLP in Opposition', *Parl. Aff.* 1959–60, pp. 520–9.

R. E. Dowse, 'The Left Wing Opposition During the First Two Labour Governments', *Parl. Aff.* 1960–1, pp. 80–93 *and* 229–43.

R. E. Dowse & T. Smith, 'Party Discipline in the House of Commons —a Comment', *Parl. Aff.* 1962–3, pp. 159–64.

L. Epstein, 'Who Makes Party Policy?', *MJPS* 1962, pp. 165–82.

L. Epstein, 'British Class Consciousness and the Labour Party', *JBS* 1962, pp. 136–50.

L. Epstein, 'British Mass Parties in Comparison with American Parties', *PSQ* 1956, pp. 97–125.

L. Epstein, 'Cohesion of British Parliamentary Parties', *APSR* 1956, pp. 360–78.

L. Epstein, 'Politics of British Conservatism', *APSR* 1954, pp. 27–49.

L. Epstein, 'New MPs and the Politics of the PLP', *PS* 1962, pp. 121–9.

M. A. Fitzsimons, 'Midlothian: the Triumph and Frustration of the British Liberal Party', *R of P* 1960, pp. 187–201.

S. C. Ghosh, 'Decision Making and Power in the British Conservative Party', *PS* 1965, pp. 198–212.

G. W. Grainger, 'Oligarchy in the British Communist Party', *BJS* 1958, pp. 143–58.

H. R. G. Greaves, 'Left and Right in Politics', *PQ* 1955, pp. 229–35.

J. A. W. Gunn, 'Party Before Burke', *G and O* 1968, pp. 223–40.

H. J. Hanham, 'The First Constituency Party?', *PS* 1961, pp. 188–9.

H. J. Hanham, 'The Local Organisation of the British Labour Party', *WPQ* 1956, pp. 376–88.

A. H. Hanson, 'The Future of the Labour Party', *PQ* 1970, pp. 375–86.

N. Harman, 'Minor Political Parties in Britain', *PQ* 1962, pp. 268–81.

M. Harrison, 'Political Finance in Britain', *J of P* 1963, pp. 664–85.

B. Hennessy, 'Trade Unions and the British Labour Party', *APSR* 1955, pp. 1050–67.

K. Hindell & P. Williams, 'Scarborough and Blackpool: An Analysis of Some Votes at the Labour Party Conferences of 1960 and 1961', *PQ* 1962, pp. 306–20.

C. Hollis (*et al.*), 'The Conservative Party', *PQ* 1961, pp. 209–83.

R. Hornby, 'Parties in Parliament 1959–63: the Labour Party', *PQ* 1963, pp. 140–8.

S. J. Ingle, 'The Recent Revival of the British Liberal Party: Some Geographical Social and Political Aspects', *Poli. Sci.* 1966 (II), pp. 39–48.

J. Jupp, 'Socialist "Rethinking" in Britain and Australia', *AJPH* 1958, pp. 193–207.

W. A. Lewis, 'Recent Controversies over Economic Policy in the British Labour Party', *WP* 1957–8, pp. 171–81.

C. Leys, 'Models, Theories and the Theory of Political Parties', *PS* 1959, pp. 127–46.

L. Lipson, 'The Two Party System in British Politics', *APSR* 1953, pp. 337–59.

L. Lipson, 'Party System in the United Kingdom and Older Commonwealth', *PS* 1959, pp. 12–31.

G. Loewenburg, 'The British Constitution and the Structure of the Labour Party', *APSR* 1958, pp. 771–91.

G. Loewenburg, 'The Transformation of British Labor Party Policy since 1945', *J of P* 1959, pp. 234–57.

W. J. M. Mackenzie, 'Mr McKenzie on the British Parties', *PS* 1955, pp. 157–9.

R. T. McKenzie, 'Policy Decision in Opposition: a Rejoinder', *PS* 1957, pp. 176–82.

R. T. McKenzie, 'The Wilson Report and the Future of Labour Party Organization', *PS* 1956, pp. 93–7.

R. T. McKenzie, 'Power in British Parties', *BJS* 1955, pp. 123–32.

T. E. M. McKitterick, 'The Membership of the Labour Party', *PQ* 1960, pp. 312–23.

T. E. M. McKitterick, 'Radicalism after 1964', *PQ* 1965, pp. 52–8.

W. F. Mandle, 'The Leadership of the British Union of Fascists', *AJPH* 1966, pp. 360–83.

J. D. May, 'Democracy, Organization, Michels', *APSR* 1965, pp. 417–29.

J. F. Milburn, 'The Fabian Society and the British Labour Party', *WPQ* 1958, pp. 319–39.

R. Miliband, 'Party Democracy and Parliamentary Government', *PS* 1958, pp. 170–4.

J. P. Nettl, 'Are Two Party Systems Symmetrical?', *Parl. Aff.* 1965–6, pp. 218–23.

F. Newman, 'Reflections on Money and Party Politics in Britain', *Parl. Aff.* 1956–7, pp. 308–32.

L. G. Noonan, 'The Decline of the Liberal Party in British Politics', *J of P* 1954, pp. 24–39.

F. S. Northedge, 'British Foreign Policy and the Party System', *APSR* 1960, pp. 635–46.

F. S. Northedge, 'The Parties and Foreign Policy', *PS* 1960, pp. 183–6.

G. N. Ostergaard, 'Parties in Cooperative Government', *PS* 1958, pp. 197–219.

L. Overacker, 'The British and New Zealand Labour Parties: A Comparison', *Poli. Sci.* 1957 (I), pp. 23–35, *and* (II), pp. 15–32.

D. E. G. Plowman, 'Allegiance to Political Parties', *PS* 1955, pp. 222–34.

A. Potter, 'The English Conservative Constituency Association', *WPQ* 1956, pp. 363–75.

J. E. Powell, '1951–9 Labour in Opposition', *PQ* 1959, pp. 336–43.

R. M. Punnett, 'The Labour Shadow Cabinet 1955–64', *Parl. Aff.* 1964–5, pp. 61–70.

J. Rasmussen, 'Party Responsibility in Britain and the United States', *JAS* 1967, pp. 233–56.

J. Rasmussen, 'The Implications of the Potential Strength of the Liberal Party for the Future of British Politics', *Parl. Aff.* 1961, pp. 378–90.

D. W. Rawson, 'The Life-span of Labour Parties', *PS* 1969, pp. 313–33.

C. Robbins, ' "Discordant Parties": A Study of the Acceptance of Party by Englishmen', *PSQ* 1958, pp. 505–29.

W. A. Robson, 'Freedom, Equality and Socialism', *PQ* 1956, pp. 378–91.

R. Rose, 'The Bow Group's Role in British Politics', *WPQ* 1961, pp. 865–78.

R. Rose, 'The Policy Ideas of English Party Activists', *APSR* 1962, pp. 360–71.

R. Rose, 'Complexities of Party Leadership', *Parl. Aff.* 1962–3, pp. 257–73.

R. Rose, 'Parties, Factions and Tendencies in Britain', *PS* 1964, pp. 33–46.

R. Rose, 'Tensions in Conservative Philosophy', *PQ* 1961, pp. 275–283.

R. Rose, 'The Variability of Party Government', *PS* 1969, pp. 413–445.

S. Rose, 'The Labour Party and German Rearmament', *PS* 1966, pp. 133–43.

S. Rose, 'Policy Decision in Opposition', *PS* 1956, pp. 128–38.

S. Rothman, 'British Labor's "New Left"', *PSQ* 1962, pp. 393–401.

C. Rowland, 'Labour Publicity', *PQ* 1961, pp. 348–60.

G. F. Rutan, 'The Labour Party in Ulster', *R of P* 1967, pp. 526–35.

K. J. Scott, 'The Distribution of Power Within British Parties', *Poli. Sci.* 1956, pp. 139–44.

M. Shanks, 'Politics and the Trade Unionist', *PQ* 1959, pp. 44–53.

M. Shanks (*et al.*) 'The Labour Party', *PQ* 1960, pp. 229–384.

M. Shaw, 'An American Looks at the Party Conferences', *Parl. Aff.* 1961–2, pp. 203–12.

K. L. Shell, 'Industrial Democracy and the British Labor Movement', *PSQ* 1957, pp. 515–39.

J. Stanyer, 'Local Support For National Political Parties: A Theoretical Analysis', *PS* 1970, pp. 395–9.

H. J. Steck, 'The Re-emergence of Ideological Politics in Great Britain', *WPQ* 1965, pp. 87–103.

T. E. Stephenson, 'The Changing Role of Local Democracy', *SR* 1957, pp. 27–42.

T. E. Stephenson, 'The Role of Principles in a Democratic Organization', *PS* 1964, pp. 327–40.

G. Thomson, 'Parties in Parliament: the Conservatives', *PQ* 1963, pp. 249–55.

J. F. Tierney, 'Britain and the Commonwealth: Attitudes in Parliament and Press in the United Kingdom since 1951', *PS* 1958, pp. 220–33.

D. W. Urwin, 'Scottish Conservatism: a Party Organization in Transition', *PS* 1966, pp. 144–62.

M. S. Venhataramani, 'Ramsay MacDonald and Britain's Domestic Politics and Foreign Relations', *PS* 1960, pp. 231–49.

R. W. J. Wilcox, 'Probables and Possibles 1963', *PQ* 1963, pp. 300–5.

N. Wood, 'The Empirical Proletarians: A Note on British Communism', *PSQ* 1959, pp. 256–72.

G. Wootton, 'Parties in Union Government', *PS* 1961, pp. 141–56.

E. Wright, 'The Future of the Conservative Party', *PQ* 1970, pp. 387–98.

Chapter 5

S. H. Beer, 'Representation of Interests in British Government', *APSR* 1957, pp. 613–51.

S. H. Beer, 'Pressure Groups and Parties in Britain', *APSR* 1956, pp. 1–23.

E. C. Black, 'The Tumultuous Petitioners', *R of P* 1963, pp. 183–211.

M. J. Brenner, 'Functional Representation and Interest Group Theory: Some Notes on British Practice', *CP* 1969–70, pp. 111–34.

F. G. Castles, 'Towards a Theoretical Analysis of Pressure Politics', *PS* 1966, pp. 339–48.

F. G. Castles, 'Business and Government: A Typology of Pressure Group Activity', *PS* 1969, pp. 160–76.

J. B. Christoph, 'Capital Punishment and British Party Responsibility', *PSQ* 1962, pp. 19–35.

M. Davis, 'Some Neglected Aspects of British Pressure Groups', *MJPS* 1963, pp. 42–53.

M. Davis, 'British Public Relations: A Political Case-Study', *J of P* 1962, pp. 50–72.

N. Deakin, 'The Politics of the Commonwealth Immigrants Bill', *PQ* 1968, pp. 24–45.

N. Deakin, 'Racial Integration and Whitehall', *PQ* 1968, pp. 415–426.

R. E. Dowse & J. Peel, 'The Politics of Birth Control', *PS* 1965, pp. 179–97.

H. Eckstein, 'The Politics of the BMA', *PQ* 1955, pp. 345–59.

S. E. Finer, 'The Political Power of Private Capital', *SR* 1955, pp. 279–94, *and* 1956, pp. 5–30.

S. E. Finer, 'The FBI', *PS* 1956, pp. 61–85.

S. E. Finer, 'The Anonymous Empire', *PS* 1958, pp. 16–37.

S. E. Finer, 'Transport Interest and the Roads Lobby', *PQ* 1958, pp. 47–58.

S. C. Ghosh, 'Pressure and Privilege: the Manchester Chamber of Commerce and the Indian Problem 1930–4', *Parl. Aff.* 1964–5, pp. 201–15.

R. Gregory, 'The Minister's Line: or, the M4 Comes to Berkshire', *Pub. Admin.* 1967, pp. 113–28.

B. W. Headey, 'Trade Unions and National Wages Policy', *J of P* 1970, pp. 407–39.

K. Hindell, 'The Genesis of the Race Relations Bill', *PQ* 1965, pp. 390–405.

K. Hindell and M. Simms, 'How the Abortion Lobby Worked', *PQ* 1966, pp. 269–82.

R. W. Howarth, 'The Political Strength of British Agriculture', *PS* 1969, pp. 458–69.

R. Kilroy-Silk, 'Contemporary Theories of Industrial Democracy', *PQ* 1970. pp. 169–81.

R. Kilroy-Silk, 'Legislating on Industrial Relations', *Parl. Aff.* 1968–9, pp. 250–7.

J. M. Lee, 'The Political Significance of Licensing Legislation', *Parl. Aff.* 1960–1, pp. 211–48.

C. Leys, 'Petitioning in the Nineteenth and Twentieth Centuries', *PS* 1955, pp. 45–64.

W. J. M. Mackenzie, 'Pressure Groups: the Conceptual Framework', *PS* 1955, pp. 247–55.

W. J. M. Mackenzie, 'Pressure Groups in British Government', *BJS* 1955, pp. 133–48.

R. T. McKenzie, 'Parties, Pressure Groups and the British Political Process', *PQ* 1958, pp. 5–16.

R. Marshall, 'The Law and Race Relations', *PQ* 1968, pp. 70–82.

J. H. Millett, 'British Interest Group Tactics', *PSQ* 1957, pp. 71–82.

J. H. Millett, 'The Role of an Interest Group Leader in the House of Commons', *WPQ* 1956, pp. 915–26.

F. Noel-Baker, 'The Grey Zone—the Problems of Business Affiliations of MP's', *Parl. Aff.* 1961–2, pp. 87–93.

W. Paynter, 'Trade Unions and Government', *PQ* 1970, pp. 444–454.

J. R. Pennock, 'Agricultural Subsidies in England and America', *APSR* 1962, pp. 621–33.

W. A. P. Phillips, 'The Price of Respectability: Reflections on Current Trends in British Trade Union Studies', *AJPH* 1956–7, pp. 204–17.

D. C. M. Platt, 'The Commercial and Industrial Interests of Ministers of the Crown', *PS* 1961, pp. 267–90.

A. M. Potter, 'Attitude Groups', *PQ* 1958, pp. 72–82.

A. M. Potter, 'The Equal Pay Campaign Committee', *PS* 1957, pp. 49–64.

J. J. Richardson, 'The Making of the Restrictive Trade Practices Act 1956', *Parl. Aff.* 1967, pp. 350–74.

G. Rose, 'Some Influences on English Penal Reform 1895–1921', *SR* 1955, pp. 25–43.

J. B. Sanderson, 'The National Smoke Abatement Society and the Clean Air Act', *PS* 1961, pp. 236–53.

P. Self & H. Storing, 'The Farmers and the State', *PQ* 1958, pp. 17–27.

L. Tivvy & E. Wohlgemuth, 'Trade Associations as Interest Groups', *PQ* 1958, pp. 59–71.

D. C. Watt, 'America and the British Foreign Policy Making Elite 1895–1956', *R of P* 1963, pp. 3–34.

H. H. Wilson, 'Techniques of Pressure: Anti-Nationalization Propaganda in Britain', *POQ* 1951, pp. 225–43.

G. Wootton, 'Ex-servicemen in Politics', *PQ* 1958, pp. 28–39.

D. C. M. Yardley, 'The Work and Status of the Parliamentary Agent', *Parl. Aff.* 1964–5, pp. 162–6.

Chapters 6 and 7

R. K. Alderman & J. A. Cross, 'The Parliamentary Private Secretary', *PS* 1966, pp. 199–207.

R. K. Alderman and J. A. Cross, 'The Parliamentary Private Secretary', *Parl.* 1967, pp. 70–5.

A. Alexander, 'British Politics and the Royal Prerogative of Appointments Since 1945', *Parl. Aff.* 1969–70, pp. 248–57.

W. G. Andrews, 'Some Thoughts on the Power of Dissolution', *Parl. Aff.* 1959–60, pp. 286–96.

W. G. Andrews, 'Three Electoral Colleges', *Parl. Aff.* 1960–1, pp. 178–88.

A. Beattie, 'Coalition Government in Britain', *G and O* 1966, pp. 3–34.

M. Beloff, 'The Foreign and Commonwealth Services', *Pub. Admin.* 1964, pp. 415–22.

C. F. Behrman, 'The Parliamentary Crisis of 1873: A Comment on the Victorian Constitution', *Parl. Aff.* 1969–70, pp. 184–96.

Lord Bridges, 'Haldane and the Machinery of Government', *Pub. Admin.* 1957, pp. 254–66.

A. H. Brown, 'Prime Ministerial Power', *PL* 1968, pp. 28–51 and 96–118.

P. W. Buck, 'MPs In Ministerial Office 1918–55 and 1955–9', *PS* 1961, pp. 300–6.

P. W. Buck, 'The Early Start Towards Cabinet Office 1918–55', *WPQ* 1963, pp. 624–32.

G. E. G. Catlin, 'Septecentenarian Parliament', *PS* 1966, pp. 191–8.

G. Catlin, 'Considerations on the British Constitution', *PSQ* 1955, pp. 481–97.

D. N. Chester, 'The Development of the Cabinet', *Parl. Aff.* 1955–6, pp. 43–7.

D. N. Chester, 'Who Governs Britain?', *Parl. Aff.* 1961–2, pp. 519–527.

R. V. Clements, 'The Cabinet', *PS* 1965, pp. 231–4.

K. E. Couzens, 'A Minister's Correspondence', *Pub. Admin.* 1956, pp. 237–44.

B. Crick, ' "Them and U": Public Impotence and Government Power', *PL* 1968, pp. 8–27.

H. Daalder, 'The Haldane Committee and the Cabinet', *Pub. Admin.* 1963, pp. 117–36.

S. E. Finer, 'The Individual Responsibility of Ministers', *Pub. Admin.* 1956, pp. 377–96.

S. E. Finer, 'Les Silences de Sir Frank Newson', *PS* 1955, pp. 17–27.

G. K. Fry, 'Thoughts on the Present State of the Convention of Ministerial Responsibility', *Parl. Aff.* 1969–70, pp. 10–20.

H. R. G. Greaves, 'British Central Government 1914–56', *PQ* 1957, pp. 383–9.

A. J. Groth, 'Britain and America: Some Requisites of Executive Leadership Compared', *PSQ* 1970, pp. 217–39.

J. S. Harris, 'Decision-Makers in Government Programs of Arts: The Arts Council of Great Britain', *WPQ* 1969, pp. 253–64.

M. Harrison, 'Constitutional Adaptation since 1945', *Parl. Aff.* 1956–7, pp. 132–9.

D. J. Heasman, 'Parliamentary Paths to High Office', *Parl. Aff.* 1962–3, pp. 315–30.

D. J. Heasman, 'The Ministerial Hierarchy', *Parl. Aff.* 1961–2, pp. 307–30.

D. J. Heasman, 'The Prime Minister and the Cabinet', *Parl. Aff.* 1961–2, pp. 461–84.

D. J. Heasman, 'The Emergence and Evolution of the Office of Parliamentary Secretary', *Parl. Aff.* 1969–70, pp. 345–65.

R. W. K. Hinton, 'The Prime Minister as an Elected Monarch', *Parl. Aff.* 1959–60, pp. 297–303.

F. A. Johnson, 'The British Committee of Imperial Defence', *J of P* 1961, pp. 231–61.

G. W. Jones, 'The Prime Minister's Power', *Parl. Aff.* 1964–5, pp. 167–85.

S. King Hall, 'What is Parliamentary Democracy?', *Parl. Aff.* 1962–3, pp. 13–21.

F. H. Lawson, 'Dicey Revisited', *PS* 1959, pp. 109–26 *and* 207–21.

P. J. Madgwick, 'Resignations', *Parl. Aff.*, 1966–7, pp. 59–76.

J. P. Mackintosh, 'The Prime Minister and the Cabinet', *Parl. Aff.* 1967–8, pp. 53–68.

G. Marshall, 'The Constitutional Status of "The People" ', *Parl. Aff.* 1956–7, pp. 148–54.

G. Marshall, 'Parliament and the Constitution', *PQ* 1965, pp. 266–76.

G. Marshall, 'Ministerial Responsibility', *PQ* 1963, pp. 256–68.

R. Middleton, 'The Problems and Consequences of Parliamentary Government', *Parl. Aff.* 1969–70, pp. 55–60.

B. Miller, 'The Colonial Office and the Estimates Committee', *Pub. Admin.* 1961, pp. 173–80.

R. S. Milne, 'The Experiment with "Coordinating Ministers" in the British Cabinet 1951–3', *CJEPS* 1955, pp. 365–9.

J. D. B. Mitchell, 'The Flexible Constitution', *PL* 1960, pp. 332–50.

J. S. Rasmussen, 'Party Discipline in War-Time: The Downfall of the Chamberlain Government', *J of P* 1970, pp. 379–406.

P. G. Richards, 'The Selection of Justices of the Peace', *PL* 1961, pp. 134–49.

W. A. Robson, 'The Reform of Government', *PQ* 1964, pp. 193–211.

K. Sainsbury, 'Patronage, Honours and Parliament', *Parl. Aff.* 1965–6, pp. 346–50.

B. B. Shaffer, 'The Idea of the Ministerial Department: Bentham, Mill and Bagehot', *AJPH* 1957–8, pp. 60–78.

M. Spiers, 'The Computer and the Machinery of Government', *Pub. Admin.* 1968, pp. 411–25.

L. Tivey, 'The System of Democracy in Britain', *SR* 1958, pp. 109–24.

F. Williams, 'The Office of Public Relations Advisor to the Prime Minister', *Parl. Aff.* 1955–6, pp. 260–7.

F. M. G. Willson, 'Routes of Entry of New Members of the British Cabinet 1868–1958', *PS* 1959, pp. 222–32.

F. M. G. Willson, 'The Organization of British Central Government 1955–61', *Pub. Admin.* 1962, pp. 159–206.

F. M. G. Willson, 'The Organization of British Central Government 1962–4', *Pub. Admin.* 1966, pp. 73–101.

F. M. G. Willson, 'Ministries and Boards: Some Aspects of Administrative Development since 1832', *Pub. Admin.* 1955, pp. 43–58.

F. M. G. Willson, 'Defence Organisation—1958 Style', *Pub. Admin.* 1958, pp. 385–90.

F. M. G. Willson, 'Entry to the Cabinet 1959–68', *PS* 1970, pp. 236–8.

D. C. M. Yardley, 'The Primacy of the Executive in Britain', *Parl. Aff.* 1967–8, pp. 155–65.

'Ministers' and Members' Remuneration', *Table* 1964, pp. 48–56.

Chapter 8

R. K. Alderman, 'Parliamentary Party Discipline in Opposition: the PLP 1951–64', *Parl. Aff.* 1967–8, pp. 124–36.

R. K. Alderman and J. A. Cross, 'The Choosing of Mr Speaker', *Parl.* 1966, pp. 77–80.

R. S. Arora, 'Parliamentary Scrutiny: The Select Committee Device', *PL* 1967, pp. 30–41.

A. Barker, 'Parliament and Patience', *PS* 1967, pp. 74–80.

M. J. Barnett, 'Backbench Behaviour in the House of Commons', *Parl. Aff.* 1968–9, pp. 16–37.

M. Beloff, 'The Leader of the Opposition', *Parl. Aff.* 1957–8, pp. 155–62.

H. B. Berrington and S. E. Finer, 'The British House of Commons', *ISSJ* 1961, pp. 600–19.

H. B. Berrington, 'Partisanship and Dissidence in the Nineteenth-Century House of Commons', *Parl. Aff.* 1967–8, pp. 338–374.

R. Body, 'Unofficial Committees in the House of Commons', *Parl. Aff.* 1957–8, pp. 295–302.

M. F. Bond, 'The Office of Clerk of the Parliaments', *Parl. Aff.* 1958–9, pp. 297–310.

R. L. Borthwick, 'The Welsh Grand Committee', *Parl. Aff.* 1967–8, pp. 264–76.

C. J. Boulton, 'Recent Developments in House of Commons Procedure', *Parl. Aff.* 1969–70, pp. 61–71.

P. Bromhead, 'How Should Parliament Be Reformed?', *PQ* 1959, pp. 272–82.

P. Bromhead, 'The Guillotine in the House of Commons', *Parl. Aff.* 1957–8, pp. 443–54.

P. Bromhead, 'Parliament and the Press', *Parl. Aff.* 1962–3, pp. 279–92.

J. H. Burns, 'The Scottish Committees of the House of Commons 1948–59', *PS* 1960, pp. 272–96.

I. F. Burton and G. Drewry, 'Public Legislation: A Survey of the Session 1968–69', *Parl. Aff.* 1969–70, pp. 154–83.

I. F. Burton and G. Drewry, 'Public Legislation: A Survey of the Session 1969–70', *Parl. Aff.* 1969–70, pp. 308–44.

A. Butler, 'The History and Practice of Lobby Journalism', *Parl. Aff.* 1959–60, pp. 54–60.

R. A. Chapman, 'The Significance of Parliamentary Procedure', *Parl. Aff.* 1962–3, pp. 179–87.

D. N. Chester, 'The British Parliament 1939–66', *Parl. Aff.* 1965–6, pp. 417–45.

Lord Chorley, 'Bringing the Legislative Process into Contempt', *PL* 1968, pp. 52–61.

J. B. Christoph, 'The Study of Voting Behaviour in the British House of Commons', *WPQ* 1958, pp. 301–18.

B. Crick, 'The Prospects for Parliamentary Reform', *PQ* 1965, pp. 333–46.

D. G. Crockett, 'The MP and his Constituents', *Parl. Aff.* 1966–7, pp. 281–4.

J. A. Cross, 'Reviewing the Pay of Members of Parliament', *Parl.* 1966, pp. 273–6.

J. A. Cross, 'Withdrawal of the Conservative Party Whip', *Parl. Aff.* 1967–8, pp. 166–75.

J. A. Cross, 'Deputy Speakers and Party Politics', *Parl. Aff.* 1964–5, pp. 361–7.

R. Crossman, 'The Decline of Parliament', *PQ* 1963, pp. 233–9.

E. Davies, 'The Role of Private Members' Bills', *PQ* 1957, pp. 32–9.

R. E. Dowse, 'The MP and his Surgery', *PS* 1963, pp. 333–41.

L. Epstein, 'British MPs and their Local Parties: the Suez Cases', *APSR* 1960, pp. 374–91.

L. Epstein, 'Partisan Foreign Policy: Britain in the Suez Crisis', *WP* 1959–60, pp. 201–26.

H. R. M. Farmer, 'The Select Committee on Procedure', *Table* 1963, pp. 35–8, *and* 1964, pp. 161–3.

Sir E. Fellowes, 'Changes in Parliamentary Life 1918–61', *PQ* 1965, pp. 256–65.

D. Goldsworthy, 'The Debate on a Parliamentary Committee for Colonial Affairs', *Parl. Aff.* 1965–6, pp. 191–207.

D. Goldsworthy, 'Parliamentary Questions on Colonial Affairs: A Retrospective Analysis', *Parl. Aff.* 1969–70, pp. 141–53.

W. H. Greenleaf, 'Urgency Motions in the Commons', *PL* 1960, pp. 270–84.

L. Hale, 'The Backbencher', *Parl.* 1966, pp. 191–8.

A. H. Hanson, 'The Purpose of Parliament', *Parl. Aff.* 1963–4, pp. 279–95.

A. H. Hanson, 'The Labour Party and House of Commons Reform', *Parl. Aff.* 1956–7, pp. 454–68.

A. H. Hanson and H. V. Wiseman, 'The Use of Committees by the House of Commons', *PL* 1959, pp. 277–92.

D. Houghton, 'The Labour Back-Bencher', *PQ* 1969, pp. 454–63.

L. M. Jeger, 'The Politics of the Non-political', *PQ* 1959, pp. 367–78.

N. Johnson, 'Parliamentary Questions and the Conduct of Administration', *Pub. Admin.* 1961, pp. 131–49.

G. W. Jones, 'A Forgotten Right Discovered', *Parl. Aff.* 1965–6, pp. 363–72.

A. Junz, 'Accommodation at Westminster', *Parl. Aff.* 1959–60, pp. 100–13.

R. Kimber and J. J. Richardson, 'Specialization and Parliamentary Standing Committees', *PS* 1968, pp. 97–101.

H. King, 'The Impartiality of the Speaker', *Parl.* 1966, pp. 125–31.

P. Laundy, 'The Speaker of the House of Commons', *Parl. Aff.* 1960–1, pp. 72–9.

J. M. Lee, 'Select Committees and the Constitution', *PQ* 1970, pp. 182–94.

J. M. Lee, 'Parliament and the Appointment of Magistrates', *Parl. Aff.* 1959–60, pp. 85–94.

W. S. Livingston, 'The Security of Tenure of the Speaker of the House of Commons', *Parl. Aff.* 1957–8, pp. 484–504.

G. Marshall, 'Privilege and "Proceedings in Parliament"', *Parl. Aff.* 1957–8, pp. 396–404.

G. Marshall, 'Parliament and the Prerogative of Mercy', *PL* 1961, pp. 8–25.

L. W. Martin, 'The Bournemouth Affair: Britain's First Primary Election', *J of P* 1960, pp. 654–81.

D. Menhennet, 'The Library of the House of Commons', *PQ* 1965, pp. 323–32.

G. C. Moodie, 'Parliamentary Privilege in 1957', *Parl. Aff.* 1957–8, pp. 211–19.

W. D. Muller, 'Trade Union Sponsored Members of Parliament in the Defence Dispute of 1960–61', *Parl. Aff.* 1969–70, pp. 258–76.

A. E. Musson, 'Parliament and the Press', *Parl. Aff.* 1955–6, pp. 277–88.

J. Palmer, 'Allocation of Time: The Guillotine and Voluntary Timetabling', *Parl. Aff.* 1969–70, pp. 232–47.

M. Partington, 'Parliamentary Committees: Recent Developments', *Parl. Aff.* 1969–70, pp. 366–79.

J. B. Poole, 'Information Services for the Commons: a Computer Experiment', *Parl. Aff.* 1968–9, pp. 161–9.

G. T. Popham and D. Greengrass, 'The Role and Functions of the Select Committee on Agriculture', *Pub. Admin.* 1970, pp. 137–152.

J. E. Powell, 'A Speaker Before "The First"', *Parl. Aff.* 1964–5, pp. 20–2.

D. Pring, 'Standing Committees in the House of Commons', *Parl. Aff.* 1957–8, pp. 303–17.

M. R. Robinton, 'Parliamentary Privilege and Political Morality in Britain 1939–1957', *PSQ* 1958, pp. 179–205.

M. Ryle, 'Committees in the House of Commons', *PQ* 1965, pp. 295–308.

C. Seymour-Ure, 'An Examination of the Proposal to Televise Parliament', *Parl. Aff.* 1963–4, pp. 172–81.

C. Seymour-Ure, 'Parliamentary Privilege and Broadcasting', *Parl. Aff.* 1962–3, pp. 411–18.

C. Seymour-Ure, 'The Misuse of the Question of Privilege in the 1964–5 Session of Parliament', *Parl. Aff.* 1964–5, pp. 380–8.

C. Seymour-Ure, 'Proposed Reforms of Parliamentary Privilege', *Parl. Aff.* 1969–70, pp. 221–31.

D. R. Shell, 'Specialist Select Committees', *Parl. Aff.* 1969–70, pp. 380–404.

G. R. Strauss, 'The Influence of the Backbencher', *PQ* 1965, pp. 277–94.

Study of Parliament Group, 'Parliament and Legislation', *Parl. Aff.* 1968–9, pp. 210–15.

K. Swinhoe, 'Lines of Division Among Members of Parliament Over Procedural Reform in the House of Commons', *PS* 1970, pp. 400–2.

N. J. Vig and S. A. Walkland, 'Science Policy, Science Administration and Parliamentary Reform', *Parl. Aff.* 1965–6, pp. 281–94.

M. Wade Labarge, 'Simon de Montfort's Parliament', *Parl. Aff.* 1964–5, pp. 13–19.

S. A. Walkland, 'Parliament and Science', *Parl. Aff.* 1963–4, pp. 308–20 *and* 389–402, *and* 1964–5, pp. 266–78.

S. A. Walkland, 'A Liberal Comment on Recent Proposals for Parliamentary Reform', *Parl. Aff.* 1962–3, pp. 338–42.

R. Williams, 'The Select Committee on Science and Technology', *Pub. Admin.* 1968, pp. 299–314.

H. V. Wiseman, 'The Leeds Private Bill of 1956', *Pub. Admin.* 1957, pp. 25–44.

H. V. Wiseman, 'Procedure: the House of Commons and the Select Committee', *Parl. Aff.* 1959–60, pp. 236–47.

H. V. Wiseman, 'Parliamentary Reform', *Parl. Aff.* 1958–9, pp. 240–54.

H. V. Wiseman, 'Private Members' Opportunities and Standing Order No. 9', *Parl. Aff.* 1958–9, pp. 377–91.

L. Wolf Phillips, 'Parliamentary Divisions and Proxy Voting', *Parl. Aff.* 1964–5, pp. 416–21.

D Wood, 'The Parliamentary Lobby', *PQ* 1965, pp. 309–22.

D. C. M. Yardley, 'The House of Commons and its Privileges Since the Strauss Affair', *Parl. Aff.* 1961–2, pp. 500–10.

'Promotion of Private Bills by Local Authorities', *Pub. Admin.* 1960, pp. 72–3.

Chapter 9

G. Borrie, 'The Wedgwood Benn Case', *PL* 1961, pp. 349–61.

N. Birnbaum, 'Monarchs and Sociologists', *SR* 1955, pp. 5–23.

P. Bromhead, 'Mr Wedgwood Benn, the Peerage and the Constitution', *Parl. Aff.* 1960–1, pp. 493–506.

P. Bromhead, 'The Peerage Act and the New Prime Minister', *Parl. Aff.* 1963–4, pp. 57–64.

H. Burrows, 'House of Lords—Change or Decay?', *Parl. Aff.* 1963–4, pp. 403–17.

Lord Chorley, 'The House of Lords Controversy', *PL* 1958, pp. 216–35.

B. Crick, 'The Life Peerages Act', *Parl. Aff.* 1957–8, pp. 455–65.

B. Crick, 'What Should the Lords Be Doing?', *PQ* 1963, pp. 174–84.

H. Dalton, '1931', *PQ* 1958, pp. 356–65.

G. Drewry and J. Morgan, 'Law Lords as Legislators', *Parl. Aff.* 1968–9, pp. 226–39.

D. J. Heasman, 'The Monarch, the Prime Minister and the Dissolution of Parliament', *Parl. Aff.* 1960–1, pp. 94–107.

P. G. Henderson, 'Legislation in the House of Lords', *Parl. Aff.* 1967–8, pp. 176–7.

G. C. Moodie, 'The Crown and the Commonwealth', *Parl Aff.* 1957–8, pp. 180–203.

G. C. Moodie, 'The Crown and Parliament', *Parl. Aff.* 1956–7, pp. 256–64.

G. C. Moodie, 'The Monarch and the Selection of the Prime Minister', *PS* 1957, pp. 1–20.

C. O'Leary, 'The Wedgwood Benn Case and the Doctrine of Wilful Perversity', *PS* 1965, pp. 65–79.

R. M. Punnett, 'Ministerial Representation in the House of Lords', *Table* 1961, pp. 67–71, *and* 1964, pp. 69–80.

R. M. Punnett, 'The House of Lords and Conservative Governments 1951–64', *PS* 1965, pp. 85–8.

K. Sainsbury, 'The Constitution—Some Disputed Points', *Parl. Aff.* 1961–2, pp. 213–43.

E. A. Shils & M. Young, 'The Meaning of the Coronation', *SR* 1953, pp. 63–81.

J. R. Vincent, 'The House of Lords', *Parl. Aff.* 1965–6, pp. 475–85.

V. Weare, 'House of Lords—Prophecy and Fulfilment', *Parl. Aff.* 1964–5, pp. 422–33.

D. Weitzman, 'Crown Privilege', *Parl. Aff.* 1956–7, pp. 405–11.

M. A. J. Wheeler-Booth, 'The Stansgate Case', *Table* 1961, pp. 23–56.

Chapter 10

Sir D. Allen, 'The Department of Economic Affairs', *PQ* 1967, pp. 351–9.

Lord Amory, 'Preparing the Budget', *Parl. Aff.* 1960–1, pp. 451–9.

J. N. Archer, 'Development in Treasury Management Services', *Pub. Admin.* 1966, pp. 347–52.

A. Barker, 'The Most Important and Venerable Function: A Study of Commons Supply Procedure', *PS* 1965, pp. 45–64.

A. Barker, 'Party and Supply', *Parl. Aff.* 1963–4, pp. 207–17.

S. H. Beer, 'Treasury Control: The Coordination of Financial Policy in Great Britain', *APSR* 1955, pp. 144–60.

Sir H. Brittain, 'The Treasury's Responsibilities', *Pub. Admin.* 1961, pp. 1–15.

P. Bromhead, 'The Commons and Supply', *Parl. Aff.* 1958–9, pp. 337–48.

Sir Alex Cairncross, 'The Work of an Economic Adviser', *Pub. Admin.* 1968, pp. 1–12.

T. H. Caulcott, 'The Control of Public Expenditure', *Pub. Admin.* 1962, pp. 267–88.

R. A. Chapman, 'The Bank Rate Decision of the 19th September 1957', *Pub. Admin.* 1965, pp. 199–213.

D. N. Chester, 'The Treasury 1962', *Pub. Admin.* 1962, pp. 419–26.

T. G. B. Cocks, 'Control by the Commons of Overseas Expenditure', *Parl. Aff.* 1955–6, pp. 88–95.

E. A. Collins, 'The Price of Financial Control', *Pub. Admin.* 1962, pp. 289–310.

E. A. Collins, 'The Functional Approach to Public Expenditure', *Pub. Admin.* 1966, pp. 295–314.

E. A. Collins, 'Inflation and Public Expenditure', *Pub. Admin.* 1968, pp. 393–410.

A. C. L. Day, 'The Bank of England in the Modern State', *Pub. Admin.* 1961, pp. 15–26.

E. Devons, 'An Economist's View of the Bank Rate Tribunal Evidence', *Man. Sch.* 1959, pp. 1–16.

H. Eckstein, 'Planning: a Case Study', *PS* 1956, pp. 46–60.

E. Fellows, 'Control of Expenditure by the Commons', *Parl. Aff.* 1967–8, pp. 16–18.

Sir S. Goldman, 'The Presentation of Public Expenditure Proposals to Parliament', *Pub. Admin.* 1970, pp. 247–63.

J. P. Harris, 'Legislative Control of Expenditure: The Public Accounts Committee of the British House of Commons', *CPA* 1959, pp. 113–31.

K. M. Hettlage, 'The Problems of Medium Term Financial Planning', *Pub. Admin.* 1970, pp. 263–72.

U. K. Hicks, 'Plowden, Planning and Management in the Public Services', *Pub. Admin.* 1961, pp. 299–312.

A. E. Holmes, 'The Growth of Public Expenditure in the United Kingdom Since 1950', *Man. Sch.* 1968, pp. 313–28.

P. Jay, 'Public Expenditure and Administration', *PQ* 1970, pp. 195–206.

A. S. Moore, 'Departmental Financial Control', *Pub. Admin.* 1957, pp. 169–78.

J. Mitchell, 'The National Board For Prices and Incomes', *Pub. Admin.* 1970, pp. 57–68.

J. Mitchell, 'The Functions of the NEDC', *PQ* 1963, pp. 354–65.

G. Owen, 'The Department of Economic Affairs', *PQ* 1965, pp. 380–9.

H. Phelps Brown, 'The National Economic Development Organisation', *Pub. Admin.* 1963, pp. 239–46.

Lord Plowden (*et al.*), 'Plowden Report on the Treasury', *Pub. Admin.* 1963, pp. 1–50.

Sir E. Roll, (*et al.*), 'The Machinery for Economic Planning', *Pub. Admin.* 1966, pp. 1–72.

M. Ryle, 'Parliamentary Control of Expenditure and Taxation', *PQ* 1967, pp. 435–46.

S. A. Walkland, 'The Form of the Parliamentary Estimates', *YB* 1962, pp. 90–9.

S. A. Walkland, 'The House of Commons and the Estimates 1960', *Parl. Aff.* 1959–60, pp. 477–88.

S. A. Walkland & I Hicks, 'Cost Accounting in British Government', *Pub. Admin.* 1960, pp. 49–60.

S. A. Walkland, 'The Public Accounts Committee: the UGC and the Universities', *Parl. Aff.* 1968–9, pp. 349–60.

H. V. Wiseman, 'Supply and Ways and Means: Procedural Changes in 1966', *Parl. Aff.* 1967–8, pp. 10–15.

'The Organisation and Status of the Bank of England', *Pub. Admin.* 1960, pp. 67–72.

Chapter 11

H. J. Abraham, 'People's Watchdog Against Abuse of Power', *PAR* 1960, pp. 152–7.

S. A. Bailey, 'Training the Technician in Administrative Practices', *Pub. Admin.* 1955, pp. 375–82.

R. J. S. Baker, 'The Art of Delegation', *Pub. Admin.* 1965, pp. 155–72.

R. J. S. Baker, 'Discussion and Decision Making in the Civil Service', *Pub. Admin.* 1963, pp. 345–56.

R. J. S. Baker, 'The Training of Assistant Principals at the Post Office', *Pub. Admin.* 1963, pp. 71–82.

R. J. S. Baker, 'The Written Word in the Civil Service', *Pub. Admin.* 1964, pp. 337–50.

E. H. Beet, 'Parliament and Delegated Legislation 1945–53', *Pub. Admin.* 1955, pp. 325–32.

L. Blair, 'The Civil Servant: Political Reality and Legal Myth', *PL* 1958, pp. 32–49.

L. J. Blom-Cooper, 'An Ombudsman in Britain', *PL* 1960, pp. 145–51.

Sir E. Boyle (*et al.*), 'Who are the Policy Makers?', *Pub. Admin.* 1965, pp. 251–88.

R. G. S. Brown, 'Organization Theory and Civil Service Reform', *Pub. Admin.* 1965, pp. 313–30.

R. A. Chapman, 'The Fulton Report: a Summary', *Pub. Admin.* 1968, pp. 443–52.

B. Chapman, 'The Ombudsman', *Pub. Admin.* 1960, pp. 303–10.

D. N. Chester, 'The Crichel Down Case', *Pub. Admin.* 1954, pp. 389–401.

D. N. Chester, 'The Plowden Report: Nature and Significance', *Pub. Admin.* 1963, pp. 3–15.

D. N. Chester, 'The Treasury 1956', *Pub. Admin.* 1957, pp. 15–24.

J. B. Christoph, 'Political Rights and Administrative Impartiality in the British Civil Service', *APSR* 1957, pp. 67–87.

Sir E. Compton, 'The Administrative Performance of Government', *Pub. Admin.* 1970, pp. 3–14.

J. T. Craig, 'The Working of the Statutory Instruments Act 1946', *Pub. Admin.* 1961, pp. 181–92.

J. T. Craig, 'The Reluctant Executive', *PL* 1961, pp. 45–74.

Sir C. Cunningham, 'Policy and Practice', *Pub. Admin.* 1963, pp. 229–38.

K. C. Davis, 'English Administrative Law: An American View', *PL* 1962, pp. 139–59.

M. E. Dimock, 'The Administrative Staff College', *APSR* 1956, pp. 166–76.

C. H. Dodd, 'Recruitment to the Administrative Class 1960–64', *Pub. Admin.* 1967, pp. 58–80.

Sir J. Dunnett, 'The Civil Service Administrator and the Expert', *Pub. Admin.* 1961, pp. 223–38.

M. J. Fores and J. B. Heath, 'The Fulton Report: Job Evaluation and the Pay Structures', *Pub. Admin.* 1970, pp. 15–22.

M. J. Fores and J. B. Heath, 'Specialists and Generalists', *PQ* 1969, pp. 328–63.

S. J. Frankel, 'Arbitration in the British Civil Service', *Pub. Admin.* 1960, pp. 197–212.

K. A. Friedmann, 'Commons, Complaints and the Ombudsman', *Parl. Aff.* 1967–8, pp. 38–47.

G. K. Fry, 'Some Weaknesses in the Fulton Report on the British Home Civil Service', *PS* 1969, pp. 484–94.

G. Ganz, 'Estoppel and Res Judicata in Administrative Law', *PL* 1965, pp. 237–55.

G. Ganz, 'Administration by Consent', *PL* 1966, pp. 161–73.

J. F. Garner, 'Consultation in Subordinate Legislation', *PL* 1964, pp. 105–24.

J. F. Garner, 'The British Ombudsman', *UTLJ* 1968, pp. 158–63.

A. Gelinas, 'Judicial Control of Administrative Action in Great Britain and Canada', *PL* 1963, pp. 140–71.

E. N. Gladden, 'Parliament and the Civil Service', *Parl. Aff.* 1956–7, pp. 165–79.

E. N. Gladden, 'The Estimates Committee Looks at the Civil Service', *Parl. Aff.* 1965–6, pp. 233–40.

J. V. Greenlaw, 'Training and Education in the Post Office', *Pub. Admin.* 1957, pp. 111–24.

J. A. G. Griffith, 'The Council and the Chalkpit', *Pub. Admin.* 1961, pp. 369–74.

J. A. G. Griffith, 'Judges in Politics: England', *G and O* 1968, pp. 485–98.

W. Hampton, 'Parliament and the Civil Service', *Parl. Aff.* 1963–4, pp. 430–8.

J. S. Harris & T. V. Garcia, 'The Permanent Secretary: Britain's Top Administrators', *PAR* 1966, pp. 31–44.

J. S. Harris, 'Regional Decentralization of Government Departments in Britain', *CJEPS* 1958, pp. 57–63.

D. Hubback, 'The Treasury's Role in Civil Service Training', *Pub. Admin.* 1957, pp. 99–110.

E. Hughes, 'Postscript to the Civil Service Reforms of 1855', *Pub. Admin.* 1955, pp. 299–306.

H. D. Hughes, 'The Settlement of Disputes in the Public Service', *Pub. Admin.* 1968, pp. 45–62.

B. Humphreys-Davies, 'Internal Administrative Services in the Air Ministry', *Pub. Admin.* 1955, pp. 359–74.

R. G. Huxtable, 'Training for Administration: The Senior Officers' Responsibility', *Pub. Admin.* 1968, pp. 281–6.

R. M. Jackson, 'Tribunals and Inquiries', *Pub. Admin.* 1955, pp. 115–24.

L. L. Jaffe, 'English Administrative Law: A Reply to Professor Davis', *PL* 1962, pp. 407–16.

M. R. Joelson, 'The Dismissal of Civil Servants in the Interests of National Security', *PL* 1963, pp. 51–75.

C. D. E. Keeling, 'Treasury Centre for Administrative Studies', *Pub. Admin.* 1965, pp. 191–8.

R. K. Kelsall, 'Selection and the Social Background of the Administrative Class', *Pub. Admin.* 1956, pp. 169–74.

J. E. Kersell, 'Parliamentary Ventilation of Grievances Arising out of Delegated Legislation', *PL* 1959, pp. 152–68.

J. E. Kersell, 'Upper Chamber Scrutiny of Delegated Legislation', *PL* 1959, pp. 46–60.

T. D. Kingdom, 'The Confidential Advisers of Ministers', *Pub. Admin.* 1966, pp. 267–74.

F. H. Lawson, 'An Inspector General of Administration', *PL* 1957, pp. 92–5.

S. McCorquodale, 'The Composition of Administrative Tribunals', *PL* 1962, pp. 298–326.

W. J. M. Mackenzie, 'The Royal Commission on the Civil Service', *PQ* 1956, pp. 129–40.

Sir G. Mallaby, 'The Civil Service Commission: Its Place in the Machinery of Government', *Pub. Admin.* 1964, pp. 1–10.

G. Marshall, 'Pluralist Principles and Judicial Policies', *PS* 1960, pp. 1–15.

G. Marshall, 'The Courts, Ministers and the Parliamentary Process', *Pub. Admin.* 1956, pp. 51–60.

G. Marshall, 'The Franks Report on Administrative Tribunals and Enquiries', *Pub. Admin.* 1957, pp. 347–58.

G. Marshall, 'Tribunals and Enquiries: Developments Since the Franks Report', *Pub. Admin.* 1958, pp. 261–70.

J. D. B. Mitchell, 'The Ombudsman Fallacy', *PL* 1962, pp. 24–33.

J. D. B. Mitchell, 'The Real Argument about Administrative Law', *Pub. Admin.* 1968, pp. 167–70.

J. D. B. Mitchell, 'Administrative Law and Parliamentary Control', *PQ* 1967, pp 360–74.

D. Munby, 'The Procedure of Public Inquiry', *Pub. Admin.* 1956, pp. 175–86.

P. G. Nairne, 'Management and the Administrative Class', *Pub. Admin.* 1964, pp. 113–22.

Sir G. Nicolson, 'The Colonial Office and the Estimates Committee', *Pub. Admin.* 1962, pp. 151–8.

E. J. Norman, 'Relations Between Headquarters and Local Offices', *Pub. Admin.* 1956, pp. 397–404.

H. Parris, 'The Origins of the Permanent Civil Service 1780–1830', *Pub. Admin.* 1968, pp. 143–66.

I. M. Pederson, 'The Parliamentary Commissioner—A Danish View', *PL* 1962, pp. 15–23.

J. F. Pickering, 'Recruitment to the Administrative Class 1960–64', *Pub. Admin.* 1967, pp. 169–99.

D. E. Reagan, 'The Expert and the Administrator', *Pub. Admin.* 1960, pp. 149–68.

K. Robinson, 'Selection and the Social Background of the Administrative Class', *Pub. Admin.* 1955, pp. 383–8.

W. A. Robson, 'The Fulton Report on the Civil Service', *PQ* 1968, pp. 397–414.

W. A. Robson, 'Administrative Justice and Injustice: A Commentary on the Franks Report', *PL* 1958, pp. 12–31.

J. P. Roche and S. Sachs, 'The Bureaucrat and the Enthusiast', *WPQ* 1955, pp. 248–61.

S. A. de Smith, 'The Council on Tribunals', *Parl. Aff.* 1958–9, pp. 320–8.

S. A. de Smith, 'Anglo-Saxon Ombudsman?', *PQ* 1962, pp. 9–19.

F. Stack, 'Civil Service Associations and the Whitley Report of 1917', *PQ* 1969, pp. 283–95.

K. R. Stowe, 'Staff Training in the National Assistance Board', *Pub. Admin.* 1961, pp. 331–52.

H. Street, 'Recent Cases in Administrative Law', *Pub. Admin.* 1956, pp. 215–16.

V. Subramaniam, 'Representative Bureaucracy: a Reassessment', *APSR* 1967, pp. 1010–19.

V. Subramaniam, 'The Relative Status of Specialists and Generalists', *Pub. Admin.* 1968, pp. 331–40.

V. Subramaniam, 'Specialists in British and Australian Government Services: A Study in Contrast', *Pub. Admin.* 1963, pp. 357–74.

Z. M. T. Tarkowski & A. V. Turnbull, 'Scientists versus Administrators', *Pub. Admin.* 1959, pp. 213–56.

F. J. Tickner, 'Public Service Training in the Past Decade', *Pub. Admin.* 1956, pp. 27–38.

A. Turnbull, 'The Use of Case Study in the British Civil Service', *Pub. Admin.* 1957, pp. 125–42.

H. W. R. Wade, 'Are Public Inquiries a Farce?', *Pub. Admin.* 1955, pp. 389–94.

H. W. R. Wade, 'The Council on Tribunals', *PL* 1960, pp. 351–366.

S. A. Walkland, 'Parliamentary Control of Delegated Legislation in Northern Ireland', *Pub. Admin.* 1959, pp. 257–66.

S. A. Walkland, ' "Unusual or Unexpected Use" and the Select Committee on Statutory Instruments', *Parl. Aff.* 1959–60, pp. 61–9.

Sir P. Waterfield, 'Civil Service Recruitment', *Pub. Admin.* 1958, pp. 3–8.

K. C. Wheare, 'The Redress of Grievances', *Pub. Admin.* 1962, pp. 125–8.

R. Williams, 'Administrative Modernization in British Government', *ISSJ* 1969, pp. 100–15.

A. J. D. Winnifrith, 'Treasury Control of Establishments', *Pub. Admin.* 1958, pp. 9–18.

H. T. Woolston, 'The Joint Local Office Experiment', *Pub. Admin.* 1955, pp. 197–205.

D. C. M. Yardley, 'Parliament and Law Reform', *Parl. Aff.* 1964–5, pp. 40–52.

D. C. M. Yardley, 'Rent Tribunals and Rent Assessment Committees', *PL* 1968, pp. 135–53.

'A New Look at the British Civil Service: the Estimates Committee and the Fulton Committee', *Pub. Admin.* 1966, pp. 227–32.

'Civil Service Pay: Further Developments in the Fair Comparison Procedure', *Pub. Admin.* 1961, pp. 197–8.

'Recruitment to the British Civil Service 1958–9', *Pub. Admin.* 1959, pp. 408–9.

'Report of the Royal Commission on the Civil Service', *Pub. Admin.* 1956, pp. 187–98 *and* 321–8.

'Security Precautions in the British Civil Service', *Pub. Admin.* 1957, pp. 297–304.

'The Future Structure of the Civil Service', *Pub. Admin.* 1966, pp. 473–9.

'The Priestly Commission and Afterwards', *Pub. Admin.* 1958, pp. 173–84.

'Training Centre for Administrative Studies', *Pub. Admin.* 1963, pp. 388–92.

Chapter 12

D. Abel, 'British Conservatives and State Ownership', *J of P* 1957, pp. 227–39.

R. J. S. Baker, 'Post Office Building Programmes', *Pub. Admin.* 1958, pp. 125–44.

D. N. Chester, 'Boards and Parliament', *Pub. Admin.* 1958, pp. 87–92 *and* 285–7.

D. N. Chester, 'The Select Committee on the Nationalised Industries', *Pub. Admin.* 1956, pp. 93–5.

T. E. Chester, 'The Guillebaud Report', *Pub. Admin.* 1956, pp. 199–210.

H. A. Clegg, 'The Fleck Report', *Pub. Admin.* 1955, pp. 269–76.

D. Coombes, 'The Scrutiny of Ministers' Powers by the Select Committee on Nationalised Industries', *PL* 1965, pp. 9–29.

G. H. Daniel, 'Public Accountability of the Nationalized Industries', *Pub. Admin.* 1960, pp. 27–34.

R. Darcy Best, 'The United Kingdom Atomic Energy Authority', *Pub. Admin.* 1956, pp. 1–16.

E. Davies, 'The Select Committee on Nationalised Industries', *PQ* 1958, pp. 378–88.

E. Davies, 'Government Policy and the Public Corporation', *PQ* 1955, pp. 104–16.

J. Dugdale, 'The Labour Party and Nationalization', *PQ* 1957, pp. 254–9.

R. S. Edwards, 'The Influence of the Nationalized Industries', *Pub. Admin.* 1961, pp. 45–58.

J. G. L. Francis, 'Costing in the BBC', *Pub. Admin.* 1958, pp. 37–46.

Sir R. Fraser, 'Independent Television in Britain', *Pub. Admin.* 1958, pp. 115–24.

C. A. French, 'Public Board and Local Authority', *Pub. Admin.* 1962, pp. 245–52.

K. H. B. Frere, 'Select Committee on the Nationalised Industries Reports for 1959', *Pub. Admin.* 1959, pp. 403–9.

J. F. Garner, 'New Public Corporations', *PL* 1966, pp. 324–9.

A. H. Hanson, 'Parliamentary Control of the Nationalized Industries', *Parl. Aff.* 1957–8, pp. 328–40.

A. H. Hanson, 'Electricity Reviewed: The Herbert Report', *Pub. Admin.* 1956, pp. 211–14.

I. Hicks, 'Finance of the Gas Industry', *Pub. Admin.* 1958, pp. 157–68.

M. Howe and P. K. Else, 'Railway Closures: Recent Changes in Machinery and Policy', *Pub. Admin.* 1968, pp. 127–42.

M. Howe, 'The Transport Act 1962 and the Consumers Consultative Committees', *Pub. Admin.* 1964, pp. 45–56

Sir I. Jacob, 'Television in the Public Service', *Pub. Admin.* 1958, pp. 311–18.

Sir T. Low, 'The Select Committee on Nationalised Industries', *Pub. Admin.* 1962, pp. 1–16.

G. L. McVey, 'Policy for Fuel', *PQ* 1964, pp. 46–57.

A. J. Merrett, 'A Reconsideration of Investment and Pricing Criteria in the Nationalized Industries', *Man. Sch.* 1964, pp. 261–89.

G. Mills & M. Howe, 'Consumer Representation and the Withdrawal of Railway Services', *Pub. Admin.* 1960, pp. 253–62.

J. R. Nelson, 'The Fleck Report and Area Organisation of the National Coal Board', *Pub. Admin.* 1965, pp. 41–58.

R. Nottage, 'The Post Office: A Pioneer of Big Business', *Pub. Admin.* 1959, pp. 55–64.

R. Nottage, 'Reporting to Parliament on the Nationalised Industries', *Pub. Admin.* 1957, pp. 143–68.

S. Please, 'Government Control of the Capital Expenditure of the Nationalised Industries', *Pub. Admin.* 1955, pp. 31–42.

E. P. Pritchard, 'The Responsibility of the Nationalised Industries to Parliament', *Parl. Aff.* 1963–4, pp. 439–49.

D. F. Prusmann, 'The Finance of Public Utility Companies in the Water Supply Industry', *Pub. Admin.* 1968, pp. 63–80.

R. M. Punnett, 'State Management of the Liquor Trade', *Pub. Admin.* 1966, pp. 193–212.

Lord Reith, 'Public Corporations: Need to Examine Control and Structure', *Pub. Admin.* 1956, pp. 351–4.

C. G. Richards & H. Sallis, 'The Joint Consultative Committee and the Working Group', *Pub. Admin.* 1961, pp. 361–8.

C. A. Roberts, 'The Reorganization of the NCB's Management Structure', *Pub. Admin.* 1966, pp. 283–95.

C. A. Roberts, 'The NCB and the Fleck Report', *Pub. Admin.* 1957, pp. 1–14.

R. D. V. Roberts & H. Sallis, 'Joint Consultation in the Electricity Supply Industry 1949–59', *Pub. Admin.* 1959, pp. 115–34.

W. A. Robson, 'Ministerial Control of Nationalized Industries', *PQ* 1969, pp. 103–12.

W. A. Robson, Ministerial Control of the Nationalized Industries, *PQ* 1969, pp. 103–12 and 494–6.

W. P. Shepherd, 'Public Corporations and Public Action', *PQ* 1964, pp. 58–68.

M. Stewart, 'Planning and Persuasion in a Mixed Economy', *PQ* 1964, pp. 148–60.

Sir R. Streat, 'Government Consultation with Industry', *Pub. Admin.* 1959, pp. 1–8.

L. Tivey, 'The Reform of the Firm', *PQ* 1963, pp. 151–61.

R. L. Wettenhall, 'The Recoup Concept in Public Enterprise', *Pub. Admin.* 1966, pp. 391–414.

J. V. Wood, 'Coal—a Labour Intensive Industry in a Competitive World', *Pub. Admin.* 1965, pp. 289–98.

'A New Report from the Nationalised Industries Committee', *Parl. Aff.* 1959–60, pp. 95–9.

'Cooperation Between Electricity and Gas Boards', *Pub. Admin.* 1959, pp. 179–81.

'New Status of the Post Office', *Pub. Admin.* 1962, pp. 94–6.

'Reorganization of Nationalized Transport', *Pub. Admin.* 1962, pp. 436–40.

'Report from the Select Committee on Nationalised Industries: British Railways', *Pub. Admin.* 1960, pp. 387–9.
'The Financial and Economic Obligations of the Nationalised Industries', *Pub. Admin.* 1961, pp. 263–9.

Chapter 13

Sir H. Banwell, 'The Machinery of Local Government', *Pub. Admin.* 1963, pp. 335–44.
Sir H. Banwell, 'The New Relations Between Central and Local Government', *Pub. Admin.* 1959, pp. 201–12.
C. Barratt, 'The Town Clerk in British Local Government', *Pub. Admin.* 1963, pp. 157–72.
R. Bayliss, 'Tell the People', *Pub. Admin.* 1958, pp. 83–6.
F. Bealey & J. D. Bartholomew, 'The Local Elections in Newcastle-under-Lyme, May 1958', *BJS* 1962, pp. 273–85 *and* 350–68.
A. H. Birch, 'A Note on Devolution', *PS* 1956, pp. 310–11.
N. T. Boaden, 'Central Departments and Local Authorities: The Relationship Examined', *PS* 1970, pp. 175–86.
N. T. Boaden and R. T. Alford, 'Sources of Diversity in English Local Government Decisions', *Pub. Admin.* 1969, pp. 203–24.
J. M. Bochel, 'The Recruitment of Local Councillors', *PS* 1966, pp. 360–4.
J. A. Brand, 'Ministry Control and Local Autonomy in Education', *PQ* 1965, pp. 154–63.
C. E. B. Brett, 'The Lessons of Devolution In Northern Ireland', *PQ* 1970, pp. 261–80.
A. P. Brier, 'The Decision Process in Local Government', *Pub. Admin.* 1970, pp. 153–68.
I. Budge, 'Electors' Attitudes Towards Local Government: A Survey in a Glasgow Constituency', *PS* 1965, pp. 386–35.
J. G. Bulpitt, 'Party Systems in Local Government', *PS* 1963, pp. 11–35.
S. A. Burrell, 'The Scottish Separatist Movement: A Present Assessment', *PSQ* 1955, pp. 358–67.
R. Butterworth, 'Islington Borough Council: Some Characteristics of Party Rule', *Pol.* 1966, pp. 21–31.
H. Carleton Green, 'Local Broadcasting and the Local Authority', *Pub. Admin.* 1961, pp. 323–31.
D. N. Chester, 'Local Democracy and the Internal Organization of Local Authorities', *Pub. Admin.* 1968, pp. 287–98.
J. A. Chetterton, 'Delegation in Local Government', *Pub. Admin.* 1957, pp. 77–81.

G. H. Chipperfield, 'The City Manager and Chief Administrative Officer', *Pub. Admin.* 1964, pp. 123–32.

A. Currie, 'Valuation and Rating in Scotland', *Pub. Admin.* 1957, pp. 187–91.

A. G. Donaldson, 'The Constitution of Northern Ireland: Its Origins and Development', *UTLJ* 1955–6, pp. 1–42.

A. G. Donaldson, 'Fundamental Rights in the Constitution of Northern Ireland', *CBR* 1959, pp. 189–216.

A. G. Donaldson, 'The Senate of Northern Ireland', *PL*, 1958, pp. 135–54.

C. D. Drake, 'Ombudsmen For Local Government', *Pub. Admin.* 1970, pp. 179–80.

Sir J. Dunnett, 'The Relationship Between Central and Local Government in the Planning of Road Schemes', *Pub. Admin.* 1962, pp. 253–66.

P. Fletcher, 'An Explanation of Variations in "Turnout" In Local Elections', *PS* 1969, pp. 495–502.

J. F. Garner, 'London Government and its Reform', *PL* 1961, pp. 256–70.

J. F. Garner, 'Administration in a Small Authority', *Pub. Admin.* 1960, pp. 227–34.

R. G. Gregory, 'Local Elections and the "Rule of Anticipated Reactions"', *PS* 1969, pp. 31–47.

G. H. Gibson, 'What I Expect from O and M', *Pub. Admin.* 1958, pp. 169–72.

I. Gowan and L. Gibson, 'The Royal Commission on Local Government in England', *Pub. Admin.* 1968, pp. 13–24.

N. W. Graham, 'The Administration of Education in Scotland', *Pub. Admin.* 1965, pp. 299–312.

W. P. Grant and R. J. C. Preece, 'Welsh and Scottish Nationalism', *Parl. Aff.* 1967–8, pp. 255–63.

F. H. W. Green, 'Community of Interest and Local Government Areas', *Pub. Admin.* 1956, pp. 39–50.

L. P. Green, 'Municipal Co-ordination', *Pub. Admin.* 1955, pp. 333–44.

T. D. Haddow, 'The Administration of Redevelopment', *Pub. Admin.* 1964, pp. 241–52.

W. Hampton, 'The County as a Political Unit', *Parl. Aff.* 1965–6, pp. 462–74.

W. Hampton, 'Local Government and Community', *PQ* 1969, pp. 151–62.

J. S. Harris, 'Central Government Inspection of Local Services in Britain', *PAR* 1955, pp. 26–34.

J. Hart, 'Some Reflections on the Report of the Royal Commission on the Police', *PL* 1963, pp. 283–304.

T. Headrick, 'The Town Clerk: His Training and Career', *Pub. Admin.* 1958, pp. 231–48 *and* 335–51.

H. H. Heclo, 'The Councillor's Job', *Pub. Admin.* 1969, pp. 185–202.

B. Hindess, 'Local Elections and the Labour Vote in Liverpool', *Soc.* 1967, pp. 187–95.

M. Hobson and J. D. Stewart, 'The Legal Profession in Local Government', *PL* 1969, pp. 199–218.

E. Hudson Davies, 'Welsh Nationalism', *PQ* 1966, pp. 322–32.

P. Hutchison, 'Committee System in East Suffolk', *Pub. Admin.* 1959, pp. 393–402.

E. James & N. Timms, 'Charging for Local Social Services', *Pub. Admin.* 1962, pp. 407–18.

G. H. Jones, B. Smith & H. V. Wiseman, 'Regionalism and Parliament', *PQ* 1967, pp. 403–10.

G. Jones, 'The Local Government Commission and County Borough Extensions', *Pub. Admin.* 1963, pp. 173–88.

G. W. Jones, 'Mr Crossman and the Reform of Local Government', *Parl. Aff.* 1966–7, pp. 77–89.

G. W. Jones, 'County Borough Expansion: the Local Government Commission's View', *Pub. Admin.* 1964, pp. 277–90.

Sir K. Joseph, 'Local Authorities and Regions', *Pub. Admin.* 1964, pp. 215–26.

B. Keith Lucas, 'Local Government in Parliament', *Pub. Admin.* 1955, pp. 207–10.

B. Keith Lucas, 'Three White Papers on Local Government', *PQ* 1957, pp. 20–31.

B. Keith Lucas, 'The Independence of Chief Constables', *Pub. Admin.* 1960, pp. 1–16.

D. G. Kermode, 'Legislative–Executive Relationships in the Isle of Man', *PS* 1968, pp. 18–42.

M. B. Kinch, 'Qualified Administrative Staff in the Local Government Service', *Pub. Admin.* 1965, pp. 173–90.

L. Kramer, 'Reflections on Whitleyism in English Local Government', *Pub. Admin.* 1958, pp. 47–70.

R. J. Lawrence, 'Devolution Reconsidered', *PS* 1956, pp. 1–17.

D. S. Lees, 'The Place of Local Authorities in the National Economy', *Pub. Admin.* 1961, pp. 27–44.

D. Lofts, 'The Future Pattern of Local Government in England and Wales', *Pub. Admin.* 1959, pp. 275–92.

J. P. Mackintosh, 'Scottish Nationalism', *PQ* 1967, pp. 389–402.

J. P. Mackintosh, 'Devolution, Regionalism, and the Reform of Local Government: the Scottish Case', *PL* 1964, pp. 19–32.

J. P. Mackintosh, 'Regional Administration: Has it Worked in Scotland?', *Pub. Admin.* 1964, pp. 253–76.

J. P. Mackintosh, 'The Royal Commission on Local Government In Scotland', *Pub. Admin.* 1970, pp. 49–56.

M. McIntosh, 'The Negotiation of Wages and Conditions of Service for Local Authority Employees in England and Wales', *Pub. Admin.* 1955, pp. 149–62, 307–24, *and* 401–18.

M. McIntosh, 'The Report of the Royal Commission on Local Government in Greater London', *BJS* 1961, pp. 236–48.

I. McLean, 'The Rise and Fall of the Scottish National Party', *PS* 1970, pp. 357–72.

H. Maddick & E. P. Pritchard, 'The Conventions of Local Authorities in the West Midlands', *Pub. Admin.* 1958, pp. 145–56, *and* 1959, pp. 135–44.

G. Marshall, 'Police Responsibility', *Pub. Admin.* 1960, pp. 213–27.

J. V. Miller, 'The Organisation of Internal Audit in Local Government in England and Wales', *Pub. Admin.* 1960, pp. 137–56.

R. Morgan, 'Is Wales a Region?', *Parl. Aff.* 1965, pp. 456–82.

A. J. A. Morris, 'Local Authority Relations With the Local Press', *PL* 1969, pp. 280–99.

K. Newton, 'City Politics in Britain and the United States', *PS* 1969, pp. 208–17.

F. R. Oliver and J. Stanyer, 'Some Aspects of the Financial Behaviour of County Boroughs', *Pub. Admin.* 1969, pp. 169–84.

C. O'Leary, 'Northern Ireland: The Politics of Illusion', *PQ* 1969, pp. 307–15.

K. Ollerenshaw, 'Sharing Responsibility', *Pub. Admin.* 1962, pp. 43–52.

D. E. Regan and A. J. A. Morris, 'Local Government Corruption and Public Confidence', *PL* 1969, pp. 132–52.

P. G. Richards, 'Delegation in Local Government: Recent Developments', *Pub. Admin.* 1958, pp. 271–8.

P. G. Richards, 'Rural Boroughs', *PS* 1966, pp. 87–9.

P. Robshaw, 'Another View of the London Government Royal Commission', *Pub. Admin.* 1961, pp. 247–50.

W. A. Robson, 'The Reform of London Government', *Pub. Admin.* 1961, pp. 59–72.

P. Self, 'The Herbert Report and the Values of Local Government', *PS* 1962, pp. 146–62.

P. Self, 'New Prospects for Local Government', *PQ* 1957, pp. 20–31.

P. Self, 'Regional Planning and the Machinery of Government', *Pub. Admin.* 1964, pp. 227–40.

D. Senior, 'The City Region as an Administrative Unit', *PQ* 1965, pp. 82–91.

Dame Evelyn Sharp, 'The Future of Local Government', *Pub. Admin.* 1962, pp. 375–87.

L. J. Sharpe, 'Elected Representatives in Local Government', *BJS* 1962, pp. 189–208.

L. J. Sharpe, 'The Report of the Royal Commission on Local Government in Greater London', *Pub. Admin.* 1961, pp. 73–110.

L. J. Sharpe, 'The Politics of Local Government in Greater London', *Pub. Admin.* 1960, pp. 157–72.

L. J. Sharpe, 'Theories and Values of Local Government', *PS* 1970, pp. 153–74.

F. Smallwood, 'Reshaping Local Government Abroad: Anglo-Canadian Experiments', *PAR* 1970, pp. 521–30.

T. D. Smith, 'Local Government in Newcastle-on-Tyne', *Pub. Admin.* 1965, pp. 413–18.

M. Spiers & M. J. Le Lohe, 'Pakistanis in the Bradford Municipal Election of 1963', *PS* 1964, pp. 85–92.

J. Stanyer, 'Electoral Behaviour in Local Government', *PS* 1970, pp. 187–204.

W. S. Steer, 'The Financing of Local Government', *PQ* 1957, pp. 423–33.

H. Stein, 'British Administrators' World', *PAR* 1962, pp. 221–230.

J. C. Swaffield, 'Green Fingers in the Council Chamber', *Pub. Admin.* 1960, pp. 131–6.

J. C. Swaffield, 'Local Government in the National Setting', *Pub. Admin.* 1970, pp. 307–16.

J. G. Thomas, 'Local Government Areas in Wales', *PL* 1962, pp. 160–74.

W. Thornhill, 'Agreements Between Local Political Parties in Local Government Matters', *PS* 1957, pp. 83–8.

J. E. Trice, 'Welsh Local Government Reform: An Assessment of Ad Hoc Administrative Reform', *PL* 1970, pp. 277–97.

J. Vaizey, 'Block Grants and the Control of Education', *PQ* 1958, pp. 155–65.

H. V. Wiseman, 'Regional Government in the United Kingdom', *Parl. Aff.* 1965–6, pp. 56–82.

H. V. Wiseman, 'The Working of Local Government in Leeds', *Pub. Admin.* 1963, pp. 51–70 *and* 137–56.

'Local Government Commission Proposals', *Pub. Admin.* 1960, pp. 174–5, *and* 1961, pp. 273–6, 382–5, *and* 1962, pp. 217–19, 432–6, 91–4.

'NALGO Survey: Interest in Local Government', *Pub. Admin.* 1957, pp. 305–9.

'The Basildon Experiment', *Pub. Admin.* 1966, pp. 213–26.
'1956 White Paper on Local Government Areas and Status', *Pub. Admin.* 1956, pp. 309–19.

SECTION FOUR: POLITICAL BIOGRAPHIES, AUTOBIOGRAPHIES AND MEMOIRS

Christopher Addison, *Four and a Half Years: A Personal Diary 1914–19* (2 vols.), Hutchinson, London, 1934.
Christopher Addison, *Politics From Within 1911–18*, Jenkins, London, 1924.
W. G. Allen, *The Reluctant Politician: Derrick Heathcoat Amory*, Johnson, London, 1958.
L. S. Amery, *My Political Life* (3 vols.), Hutchinson, London, 1953–5.
Lady Cynthia Asquith, *Diaries 1915–18*, Alfred A. Knopf, New York, 1969.
C. R. Attlee, *As It Happened*, Heinemann, London, 1954.
Lord Avon, *Memoirs* (2 vols.), Cassell, London, 1960–2.
A. W. Baldwin, *My Father: The True Story*, Allen & Unwin, London, 1955.
A. J. Balfour, *Chapters of Autobiography*, Cassell, London, 1930.
Lord Beaverbrook, *The Decline and Fall of Lloyd George*, Collins, London, 1963.
Lord Beaverbrook, *Men and Power 1917–18*, Arcon Books, Hamden, Conn., 1956.
Lord Beaverbrook, *Politicians and the War* (2 vols.), Arcon Books, Hamden, Conn., 1968.
Lord Beveridge, *Power and Influence*, Hodder & Stoughton, London, 1953.
R. Bevins, *The Greasy Pole*, Hodder & Stoughton, London, 1965.
Lord Birkenhead, *The Life of F. E. Smith, First Earl of Birkenhead*, Eyre & Spottiswoode, London, 1959.
Lord Birkenhead, *Walter Monckton*, Weidenfeld & Nicolson, London, 1969.
Lord Birkenhead, *Halifax*, Hamish Hamilton, London, 1965.
R. Blake, *The Unknown Prime Minister: The Life and Times of Andrew Bonar Law, 1858–1923*, Eyre & Spottiswoode, London, 1955.

R. Blake, *Disraeli*, Methuen, London, 1969.

G. Blaxland, *J. H. Thomas: A Life For Unity*, Muller, London, 1964.

Margaret Bondfield, *A Life's Work*, Hutchinson, London, 1950.

Lord Boothby, *My Yesterday, Your Tomorrow*, Hutchinson, London, 1962.

Lord Boothby, *I Fight to Live*, Gollancz, London, 1947.

J. Bowle, *Viscount Samuel: A Biography*, Gollancz, London, 1957.

F. Boyd, *Richard Austen Butler*, Rockliff, London, 1956.

A. Boyle, *Montagu Norman*, Weybright and Talley, New York, 1968.

Jack and Bessie Braddock, *The Braddocks*, Macdonald, London, 1963.

Vera Brittain, *Pethwick-Lawrence*, Lawrence Verry, Mystic, Conn., 1963.

Lewis Broad, *Winston Churchill 1874–1955*, Hutchinson, London, 1956.

Lewis Broad, *Anthony Eden*, Hutchinson, London, 1955.

Fenner Brockway, *Inside the Left*, Allen & Unwin, London, 1942.

Fenner Brockway, *Outside the Right*, Fernhill House, New York, 1963.

Fenner Brockway, *Socialism Over Sixty Years: The Life of Jowett of Bradford*, Allen & Unwin, London, 1946.

A. Bullock, *The Life and Times of Ernest Bevin*, Vols. 1 and 2, Heinemann, London, 1960–7.

W. Camp, *The Glittering Prizes: A Biographical Study of F. E. Smith, First Earl of Birkenhead*, MacGibbon & Kee, London, 1960.

Sir A. Chamberlain, *Politics From the Inside: An Epistolary Chronicle, 1906–14*, Cassell, London, 1936.

Lord Chandos, *Memoirs*, Bodley Head, London, 1962.

R. S. Churchill, *The Rise and Fall of Sir Anthony Eden*, MacGibbon & Kee, London, 1959.

R. S. Churchill, *Winston S. Churchill* (2 vols.), Houghton Mifflin, Boston, 1968.

Sir W. S. Churchill, *The World Crisis* (6 vols.), Charles Scribner's Sons, New York, 1923–31.

Sir W. S. Churchill, *The Second World War* (6 vols.), Cassell, London, 1948–54.

Lord Citrine, *Three Careers*, Hutchinson, London, 1967.

J. R. Clynes, *Memoirs 1869–1924*, Hutchinson, London, 1937.

Margaret Cole, *Beatrice Webb*, Longmans, London, 1945.

I. Colvin, *Vansittart in Office,* Gollancz, London, 1965.

Colin Cooke, *The Life of Richard Stafford Cripps,* Hodder & Stoughton, London, 1957.

Duff Cooper, *Old Men Forget,* Hart-Davis, London, 1953.

E. Crankshaw, *The Forsaken Idea: A Study of Viscount Milner,* Longmans, London, 1952.

Colin Cross, *Philip Snowden,* Barrie & Rockliff, London, 1966.

Hugh Dalton, *Memoirs* (3 vols.), Muller, London, 1953–62.

D. Dilks, *Curzon In India: Vol 1, Achievement,* Taplinger, New York, 1970.

T. Driberg, *Beaverbrook,* Weidenfeld & Nicolson, London, 1956.

T. Driberg, *Best of Both Worlds,* Phoenix House, London, 1953.

Blanche E. C. Dugdale, *Arthur James Balfour,* Greenwood Press, Westport, Conn., 1936.

G. G. Eastwood, *George Isaacs,* Odhams, London, 1952.

D. H. Elletson, *The Chamberlains,* Murray, London, 1966.

Lord Elton, *The Life of James Ramsay MacDonald,* Collins, London, 1939.

E. Estorick, *Stafford Cripps,* Heinemann, London, 1949.

K. Feling, *The Life of Neville Chamberlain,* Archon Books, Hamden, Conn., 1970.

M. Foot, *Aneurin Bevan. Biography* (2 vols.), MacGibbon & Kee, London, 1962–4.

W. Gallacher, *Last Memoirs,* Lawrence & Wishart, London, 1966.

D. Lloyd George, *War Memoirs* (6 vols.), Nicholson & Watson, London, 1933–6.

R. Lloyd George, *Lloyd George,* Muller, London, 1960.

M. Gilbert (ed.), *Lloyd George,* Prentice Hall, Englewood Cliffs, N.J., 1969.

A. M. Gollin, *Proconsul in Politics: A Study of Lord Milner In Opposition and In Power, 1905–25,* Blond, London, 1963.

Lord Grey, *Twenty-five Years 1892–1916* (2 vols.), Hodder & Stoughton, London, 1925.

Lord Haldane, *Autobiography,* Hodder & Stoughton, London, 1929.

Lord Halifax, *Fulness of Days,* Collins, London, 1957.

Mary A. Hamilton, *Arthur Henderson,* Heinemann, London, 1938.

R. Harris, *Politics Without Prejudice: A Political Appreciation of R. A. Butler,* Staples, London, 1956.

Sir R. F. Harrod, *The Life of John Maynard Keynes,* Discus Books, New York, 1971.

Sir A. P. Herbert, *I Object!,* Bodley Head, London, 1958.

Sir A. P. Herbert, *Independent Member,* Methuen, London, 1950.

C. Hollis, *Along the Road to Frome,* Harrap, London, 1958.

Emrys Hughes, *Keir Hardie,* Allen & Unwin, London, 1956.

H. Montgomery Hyde, *Carson,* Heinemann, London, 1956.

R. R. James (ed.), *Memoirs of a Conservative: J. C. C. Davidson's Memoirs and Papers 1910–37,* Macmillan, New York, 1970.

R. Jenkins, *Asquith,* Dutton, New York, 1964.

D. Johnson, *Doctor in Parliament,* Johnson, London, 1958.

D. Johnson, *On Being an Independent MP,* Johnson, London, 1964.

Thomas Johnston, *Memories,* Collins, London, 1952.

Thomas Jones, *Lloyd George,* OUP, London, 1951.

Thomas Jones, *Diary With Letters, 1931–50,* OUP, London, 1954.

Thomas Jones, *Whitehall Diary Vol. I, 1916–25* (edited by K. Middlemas), OUP, London, 1969.

W. Kent, *John Burns: Labour's Lost Leader,* Williams & Norgate, London, 1950.

Earl of Kilmuir, *Political Adventure,* Weidenfeld & Nicolson, London, 1964.

Sir Ivone Kirkpatrick, *The Inner Circle,* Macmillan, London, 1959.

D. Kirkwood, *My Life in Revolt,* Harrap, London, 1935.

M. M. Krug, *Aneurin Bevan: Cautious Rebel,* Yoseloff, New York, 1961.

Jennie Lee, *This Great Journey,* MacGibbon & Kee, London, 1963.

Sir S. Lee, *King Edward VII: A Biography* (2 vols.), Macmillan, London, 1925–7.

Lord Longford, *Born to Believe,* Cape, London, 1953.

Lord Longford, *Five Lives,* Hutchinson, London, 1964.

G. McAllister, *James Maxton,* Murray, London, 1935.

R. B. McCallum, *Asquith,* Duckworth, London, 1936.

John McGovern, *Neither Fear Nor Favour,* Blandford, London, 1960.

S. McKenna, *Reginald McKenna, 1863–1943,* Eyre & Spottiswoode, London, 1948.

Iain Macleod, *Neville Chamberlain,* Muller, London, 1961.

H. Macmillan, *Memoirs* (Vols. I, II and III), Macmillan, London, 1966–9.

J. McNair, *James Maxton: The Beloved Rebel,* Allen & Unwin, London, 1955.

L. MacNeill Weir, *The Tragedy of Ramsay Macdonald,* Secker & Warburg, London, 1935.

Sir P. Magnus, *King Edward the Seventh,* E. P. Dutton, New York, 1964.

George Mallaby, *From My Level,* Hutchinson, London, 1968.

Jean Mann, *Woman in Parliament,* Odhams, London, 1962.

E. Marjoribanks and I. Colvin, *The Life of Lord Carson* (3 vols.), Macmillan, London, 1932–6.

Lucy Masterman, *C. F. G. Masterman,* Augustus M. Kelley, New York, 1939.

Sir F. Maurice, *Haldane* (2 vols.), Greenwood Press, Westport, Conn., 1939.

K. Middlemas and J. Barnes, *Life of Baldwin,* Macmillan, New York, 1970.

R. J. Minney, *Viscount Addison: Leader of the Lords,* Odhams, London, 1958.

R. J. Minney, *The Private Papers of Hore-Belisha,* Collins, London, 1960.

W. Rees Mogg, *Sir Anthony Eden,* Rockliff, London, 1956.

Lord Moran, *Winston Churchill: The Struggle for Survival 1940–65,* Constable, London, 1966.

Herbert Morrison, *An Autobiography,* Odhams, London, 1960.

L. Mosley, *Curzon: The End of an Epoch,* Longmans, London, 1960.

Oswald Mosley, *My Life,* Nelson, London, 1968.

Sir Gerald Nabarro, *NAB 1: Portrait of a Politician,* Maxwell, London, 1969.

Lord Newton, *Lord Lansdowne: A Biography,* Macmillan, London, 1929.

Sir H. Nicolson, *Curzon: The Last Phase, 1919–25,* Howard Fertig, New York.

Sir H. Nicolson, *King George V: His Life and Reign,* Constable, London, 1952.

N. Nicolson (ed.), *Diaries and Letters of Harold Nicolson, vol. 2: War Years 1939–45,* Atheneum, New York, 1967.

Frank Owen, *Tempestuous Journey: Lloyd George, His Life and Times,* Hutchinson, London, 1954.

Lord Oxford and Asquith, *Memories and Reflections* (2 vols.), Cassell, London, 1928.

Lord Oxford and Asquith, *Fifty Years of Parliament,* Cassell, London, 1926.

Lord Parmoor, *A Retrospect,* Heinemann, London, 1936.

Lord Pethick-Lawrence, *Fate Has Been Kind,* Hutchinson, London, 1942.

Sir C. Petrie, *Life and Letters of Sir Austen Chamberlain* (2 vols.), Collins, London, 1940.

Sir C. Petrie, *The Chamberlain Tradition,* Dickson, London, 1938.

Sir C. Petrie, *Walter Long and His Times*, Hutchinson, London, 1936.

R. Postgate, *The Life of George Lansbury*, Longmans, London, 1951.

Lord Reading, *Rufus Isaacs, First Marquess of Reading* (2 vols.), Hutchinson, London, 1943–45.

R. Rhodes James, *Chips: The Diaries of Sir Henry Channon*, Weidenfeld & Nicolson, London, 1967.

W. T. Rodgers (ed.), *Hugh Gaitskell 1906–63*, Thames & Hudson, London, 1964.

Lord Ronaldshay, *Life of Lord Curzon* (3 vols.), Benn, London, 1928.

K. Rose, *Superior Person: The Young Curzon*, Weybright and Talley, New York, 1970.

Lord Salter, *Memoirs of a Public Servant*, Faber, London, 1961.

Lord Salter, *Slave of the Lamp*, Weidenfeld & Nicolson, London, 1968.

S. Salvidge, *Salvidge of Liverpool: Behind the Political Scenes, 1890–1928*, Hodder & Stoughton, London, 1934.

A. Sampson, *Macmillan, A Study in Ambiguity*, Allen Lane, London, 1969.

Lord Samuel, *Memoirs*, Cresset, London, 1945.

R. Sencourt, *The Reign of Edward VIII*, Gibbs & Phillip, London, 1962.

E. Shinwell, *Conflict Without Malice*, Odhams, London, 1955.

Lord Simon, *Retrospect*, Heinemann, London, 1952.

Philip Snowden, *Autobiography* (2 vols.), Nicholson & Watson, London, 1934.

D. C. Somervell, *Stanley Baldwin: An Examination of Some Features of Mr. G. M. Young's Biography*, Faber, London, 1953.

D. Sommer, *Haldane of Cloan: His Life and Times, 1856–1928*, Allen & Unwin, London, 1960.

J. A. Spender, *The Life of the Rt. Hon. Sir Henry Campbell-Bannerman*, Kraus Reprint, New York, 1969.

J. A. Spender and C. Asquith, *Life of Lord Oxford and Asquith* (2 vols.), Hutchinson, London, 1932.

Wickham Steed, *The Real Stanley Baldwin*, Nisbet, London, 1930.

Mary D. Stocks, *Ernest Simon of Manchester*, Manchester University Press, 1963.

Mary D. Stocks, *Eleanor Rathbone: A Biography*, Gollancz, London, 1954.

Lord Strang, *At Home and Abroad*, Deutsch, London, 1956.

Lord Strang, *The Diplomatic Career*, Deutsch, London, 1962.

Lord Swinton, *I Remember*, Hutchinson, London, 1949.

A. J. P. Taylor, *Lloyd George: Rise and Fall,* CUP, London, 1961.

A. J. P. Taylor, *Churchill: Four Faces and the Man,* Penguin, London, 1969.

Lord Templewood, *Nine Troubled Years,* Collins, London, 1954.

M. Thomson, *David Lloyd George,* Hutchinson, London, 1948.

G. M. Trevelyan, *Grey of Falladon,* Humanities Press, New York, 1948.

Lord Ullswater, *A Speaker's Commentaries* (2 vols.), Arnold, London, 1925.

T. E. Utley, *Enoch Powell: The Man and His Thinking,* Kimber, London, 1968.

Lord Vansittart, *The Mist Procession: Autobiography,* Hutchinson, London, 1958.

Beatrice Webb, *Our Partnership,* Longmans, London, 1948.

Beatrice Webb, *Diaries 1912–32* (2 vols.), Longmans, London, 1952–6.

Sir J. Wheeler-Bennett, *John Anderson, Viscount Waverley,* Macmillan, London, 1962.

Sir J. Wheeler-Bennett, *King George VI: His Life and Reign,* Papermac Books, New York, 1958.

F. Williams, *Ernest Bevin,* Hutchinson, London, 1952.

F. Williams, *A Prime Minister Remembers,* Heinemann, London, 1960.

T. Wilson (ed.), *The Political Diaries of C. P. Scott 1911–28,* Cornell U.P., Ithaca, N.Y., 1970.

Duke of Windsor, *A King's Story,* Cassell, London, 1952.

Earl Winterton, *Orders of the Day,* Cassell, London, 1953.

Earl Winterton, *Fifty Tumultuous Years,* Hutchinson, London, 1955.

Lord Woolton, *Memoirs,* Cassell, London, 1959.

J. E. Wrench, *Geoffrey Dawson and Our Times,* Hutchinson, London, 1955.

J. E. Wrench, *Alfred Lord Milner: The Man of No Illusions, 1854–1925,* Eyre & Spottiswoode, London, 1958.

G. M. Young, *Stanley Baldwin,* Hart-Davis, London, 1952.

K. Young, *Arthur James Balfour,* Dufour Editions, Chester Springs, Pa., 1963.

K. Young, *Sir Alec Douglas-Home,* Dent, London, 1970.

Index